P9-AQS-190

347.4201
S794

128,672

LIBRARY
College of St. Francis
JOLIET, ILL.

DEMCO

The English Court: from the Wars of the Roses to the Civil War

DAVID STARKEY,
D. A. L. Morgan, John Murphy, Pam Wright, Neil Cuddy and Kevin Sharpe

Longman
London and New York

LIBRARY
College of St. Francis
JOLIET, ILL.

Longman Group UK Limited,
Longman House, Burnt Mill, Harlow,
Essex CM20 2JE, England
and Associated Companies throughout the world.

Published in the United States of America
by Longman Inc., New York

© Longman Group UK Limited 1987

All rights reserved; no part of this publication
may be reproduced, stored in a retrieval system,
or transmitted in any form or by any means, electronic,
mechanical, photocopying, recording, or otherwise,
without the prior written permission of the Publishers.

First published 1987

British Library Cataloguing in Publication Data
The English court: from the Wars of the
Roses to the Civil War.
1. Great Britain – Court and Courtiers
2. Great Britain – History – Tudors,
1485–1603 3. Great Britain – History
–Early Stuarts, 1603–1649
I. Starkey, David
942   DA315
ISBN 0-582-49281-5 PPR
ISBN 0-582-01359-3 CSD

Library of Congress Cataloging-in-Publication Data
The English court: from the Wars of the Roses to the
Civil War.

Includes index.
1. Courts – Great Britain – History. I. Starkey,
David.
KD6855.E54 1987   347.42′01′09   86–C33736
ISBN 0-582-01359-3   344.207109
ISBN 0-582-49281-5 (pbk.)

Set in Linotron 202 10/12pt Bembo

Produced by Longman Singapore Publishers (Pte) Ltd
Printed in Singapore

347, 4201
S794

Contents

Cancel 4 Taylor # 33.07

128, 672

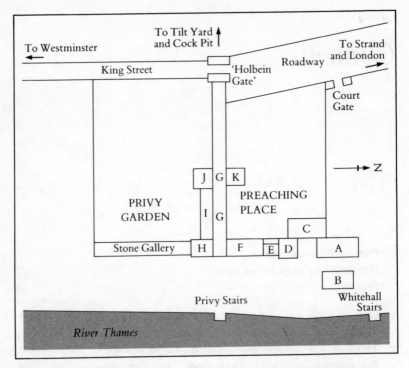

WHITEHALL: Block-plan of the king's apartments, *c*.1540–1640

A Hall
B Chapel
C Guard Chamber   Yeomen of the Guard
D Presence Chamber   Gentlemen Pensioners, Knights and
                         Esquires of the Body, Carvers,
                         Cupbearers, Sewers, Gentlemen
                         Ushers, Grooms

E Closet (i.e. private chapel)
F Privy Chamber   Gentlemen, Gentlemen Ushers, Grooms
G Privy Gallery
H Withdrawing Room
I Lesser Withdrawing Room, closets
J Bedchamber
K Council Chamber   Privy Councillors

A and the service courts formed the Lord Steward's department or
HOUSEHOLD; B–D formed the Lord Chamberlain's department or CHAMBER
until 1603, and E, F and G–J (the Privy Lodgings) were under the Groom of the
Stool as head of the PRIVY CHAMBER. In 1603 the jurisdiction of the Lord
Chamberlain was extended to F, while the Groom of the Stool, now head of the
BEDCHAMBER, with its own Gentlemen and Grooms, was in charge of G–J. After
1540 members of the PRIVY COUNCIL were also part of the inner court, enjoying
access to G, as well as K.
(The plan is based on G.P.V. Akrigg, *Jacobean Pageant* (Cambridge, Mass. 1962),
p. 397 and H.M. Colvin, ed., *The History of the King's Works* (1951–82) IV, p. 309.)

Abbreviations and note on sources

All manuscripts cited are in the Public Record Office, London, unless otherwise stated. All manuscripts in the PRO are referred to by the call number there in use. All printed books in English are published in London and all in French in Paris, unless otherwise stated.

APC	*Acts of the Privy Council of England,* ed. J. R. Dasent *et al.* (46 vols, 1890–1964).
BL	British Library
CPR	*Calendar of Patent Rolls*
CSP Dom.	*Calendar of State Papers, Domestic*
CSP For.	*Calendar of State Papers, Foreign*
CSP Sp.	*Calendar of State Papers, Spanish*
CSP Ven.	*Calendar of State Papers, Venetian*
DNB	*Dictionary of National Biography*
EHR	*English Historical Review*
Foedera	*Foedera, Conventiones, Litterae,* ed. T. Rymer (15 vols, 1704–35).
HMC	Historical Manuscripts Commission
HO	*A Collection of Ordinances and Regulations for the Government of the Royal Household* (Society of Antiquaries of London) 1790.
LP	*Letters and Papers, Foreign and Domestic, of the Reign of Henry VIII, 1509–47,* ed. J. S. Brewer *et al.* (21 vols and addenda, 1862–1932).
PPC	*Proceedings and Ordinances of the Privy Council of England, 1386–1542,* ed. N. H. Nicolas (7 vols, 1834–37).

RO   Record Office
RP   *Rotuli Parliamentorum, 1278–1504* ed. J. Strachey *et al.*
            (6 vols, 1767–77).

Capitalization

Initial capitals are used for the names of all officers and departments
of the royal household, and for the names of all rooms in the royal
palaces. Particularly important is the distinction between 'household'
and 'Household'. The household is the whole royal establishment;
the Household one of its main departments, the Lord Steward's
Department or Household-below-stairs.

Preface

Books change in the making; so do their writers. Both tend to put on weight. This book was conceived as a brief, brisk guide for the undergraduate to the newly developing field of court history. Instead it has become a rather substantial volume. The loss of brevity I regret, but there has been gain in detail and above all in coherence. For in writing the book the several authors discovered – to their own surprise – how far they shared a common vocabulary and a common pattern of concepts. This common ground I have surveyed in the Introduction: Court history in perspective. As the audacious echoes of the title suggest, this is the most ambitious section of the book, in aim if not achievement. It both stakes out a claim for the court as the central political and governmental institution of that first great inter-war period, 1450–1640, and offers a developed framework of analysis. The ideas deployed are often new, though the 'revised' parliamentary history (which is the other side of the coin of court history) has made their general flavour familiar. And even the words themselves may seem a little strange. But they are not barbarous, and they have been taken from contemporary usage and not from the abstractions of the social sciences.

If the changes to the book have been on balance gain, the alterations among the writers have been loss – at least to the historical profession. When I first assembled the team of contributors my aim was to mix established scholars with promising research students. In happier days all the latter would by this time have become colleagues; none has. The loss, as their chapters show, is severe. But at least their contributions here have made their ideas available, albeit in compressed form, to a wider audience.

All is not change and decay, however. Unchanging, nay unremitting, has been the energy and determination of the typist, Mrs Nett Capsey, who worked so hard to reduce a chaos of corrections to an orderly text. I am very grateful to her.

Highbury
London
May 1986

CHAPTER ONE
Introduction:
Court history in perspective

David Starkey

In late February 1643 Henrietta Maria joined the northern Royalist army under the earl of Newcastle. The landing was difficult and her lodgings were bombarded by the Parliamentary fleet. A few days later, Endymion Porter, Groom of the Bedchamber, wrote to Newcastle. He enclosed Charles's letter to his queen; congratulated the earl on the queen's safe arrival, and put in a word for himself and his family. 'I have long wished to place my wife in the queen's Bedchamber. I beseech your lordship to do in it as you shall think best and oblige me according to your accustomed goodness.' It was civil war, but the values and ambitions of the courtier remained unshaken. Nor were they disturbed by exile and poverty. For a few years later in 1647, penniless in France, Porter wrote to a friend lamenting that 'I want clothes for a court'.[1]

It all seems absurd – as absurd as the court itself came to appear after its demise. The obsequies took place in 1837 with the accession of Victoria. The chancellor of the Exchequer announced to the House that the Groomship of the Stool, the chief office in the Bedchamber that had been the target of Porter's family ambition, was to remain unfilled. Mention of the office brought only 'a laugh'.[2] And laughter, sometimes twisted into a sneer (as when A. F. Pollard dismisses George Cavendish's *Life of Wolsey* as 'the classic example of history as it appears to a Gentleman Usher'),[3] has remained the general reaction to the court among 'serious' historians. It will not do. From the late fifteenth century to the early nineteenth,

1. D. Townshend, *Life and Letters of Mr Endymion Porter* (1897), pp. 207–8, 230.
2. D. Starkey, 'Representation through intimacy' in I. Lewis, ed., *Symbols and Sentiments* (1977), p. 219.
3. A. F. Pollard, *Wolsey* (1965), pp. 1–2.

the court was a natural goal for any man of ambition; indeed, for much of the time, it was *the* goal. Faced with this, as Neil Cuddy insists below in his study of one of the least attractive courts in history, that of James I, the historian has a duty to overcome distaste and bewilderment and 'make . . . an effort to understand' (below, p. 174).

This book is a collective 'effort to understand'. In it six historians trace the history of the English court from the middle of the fifteenth century to the middle of the seventeenth. The treatment is predominantly narrative, and is organized round the reigns of kings and queens. Nothing could be more traditional in form – or more subversive in substance. For this is no amble through the court and social pages of history. Instead we have followed the rigorous agenda laid down in Professor G. R. Elton's seminal article on the court of 1975.[4] That is to say, we approach the court as an institution and try to assess its importance politically.

We take, however, a more ecumenical view of these tasks than Professor Elton. He regarded 'reveries on accession tilts and symbolism' as mere diversions from the job in hand.[5] Our experience is different. We have found that tournaments say much about the origins of Henry VIII's Privy Chamber, and the symbolism of masques still more about Charles I's management of his court. Indeed the evidence of material culture is very prominent in several chapters. This is hardly surprising. The court was not only a machine of government; it was also a machinery for conspicuous expenditure. Pictures may tell us more about Charles I's aspirations than any document; palace buildings created a more binding framework for behaviour than any ordinance. This fact was first understood by the late Hugh Murray Baillie. He pointed out that in every major European monarchy a distinctive pattern of palace layout corresponded to a distinctive national court etiquette and organization.[6] This proved to be the Newtonian principle of court history and we deploy it repeatedly: to explain the transformation in household organization under the early Tudors; to unravel the lesser reorganization of 1603 when two clashing national court styles were forced into an uneasy union by the accession of James VI of Scotland to the throne of England; and, more speculatively, to determine

4. G. R. Elton, 'Tudor Government: the Points of Contact; III: the Court', *Transactions of the Royal Historical Society* (1976), pp. 211 ff.
5. Ibid. p. 225.
6. H. M. Baillie, 'Etiquette and the Planning of the State Apartments in Baroque Palaces', *Archaeologia* 101 (1967).

whether the Privy Council did or did not belong to the court.

And our first chapter is scarcely institutional at all. But its concern is not with things but with words. Documents, like history, are written in words. Yet it is surprising how little historians reflect on language. Thanks to David Morgan we do not fall into this trap and his essay explores the origins of the word 'court' itself. These lie in the fifteenth century: at the beginning of that century a member of the royal entourage was known as a 'household man'; at the end, as a 'courtier'. The former was a fighter; the latter a politician. The key to the transformation was the change in the character of the monarchy itself. An early Lancastrian king presided, as a first amongst equals, over the 'joint-stock enterprise' of war with France; the Yorkists and still more the early Tudors elevated themselves unapproachably above even the greatest of their lords. As they did so, serving the king became (what it had not been before) different *in kind* from serving any other master. So different in fact that a new vocabulary was needed. The king's household became the court, and the continental literature of the court was borrowed, adapted or translated to describe it.

The history of the court, therefore, confirms the emerging status of the fifteenth century as a period of major, even revolutionary, change. In sharp contrast to the household, which had been characterized by 'a lack of any sense of questioning of established assumptions' (below, p. 27), the new literature of the court was both aware and critical. And, since it tended to be written by courtiers themselves, it was *self*-aware and *self*-critical. Actors on the political stage became their own critics and playwrights – not to mention their own poets and philosophers. They described political activity with a degree of insight, detail and sheer excited flair unknown before; more soberly they reflected on what they did and sought to categorize the principles underlying their actions. The result is to present the historian not only with a political record of unprecedented fullness, but also – if he will use it – with a contemporary interpretation, developed, rounded and subtle, of these politics. And in general we have chosen to use it. But the fifteenth century did not only usher in a crucial change of consciousness and discourse; it also began a period of institutional change. The household had been notable for its 'absence of organizational innovation' (below, p. 27). This now altered and the next fifty years were a time of flux and reconstruction. The half century, which corresponds to the reigns of the first two Tudors, is the subject of my own essay. And with it our institutional history of the court gets properly under way.

Traditionally the royal house, or rather houses, for there were many of them, were divided into two main areas: the service side of the Hall and Kitchens and so on, under the Lord Steward; and the king's apartment or Chamber, under the Lord Chamberlain. The Lord Steward's 'side' handled accounting and household management; while the Chamberlain and his department both staged public ceremony and provided the king's private service. The developments of the fifteenth century put a strain on these arrangements. There was a general seeking for privacy amongst the upper classes, in which the king fully shared. He built smaller, more comfortable chambers, and he seems to have spent more of both his working and his leisure hours in them. At the same time, the elevation of monarchy, which was the key feature of the last decades of the century, made the closer regulation of access to the royal person politically as well as socially desirable.

The result was that in probably 1495 Henry VII divided the ceremonial and personal aspects of the Chamber. The most private of his new apartments, the Privy Chamber, was cut off from the rest; closed to all but a handful and given a small and humble staff of its own. Henry VIII kept broadly to this outline, but transformed the Privy Chamber's personnel. He filled the apartment with high-born favourites and boon companions, and gave it an elaborate and largely French structure of office. These changes were more or less complete by 1518, and eight years later they were embodied into a new corpus of household regulations, the Eltham Ordinances. These contrast in every way with the last major set of household ordinances, the Black Book of Edward IV. Instead of being traditionalist and discursive they were bold and innovatory; and instead of dividing the household into two departments, the Household and Chamber, they divided it into three, Household, Chamber, and Privy Chamber.

The effect was to put a frontier within the palace and to establish an equally clear line of demarcation between those royal servants who could cross it and those who could not. The frontier lay at the door of the Privy Chamber. Behind lay the world of the Privy Lodgings. These got steadily larger with Henry VIII's relentless multiplication of galleries, closets and chambers, and they provided for more and more of his needs: he walked in the Privy Gallery or the Privy Garden; read in his Library, and slept in his Bedchamber. Yet the whole area was out of bounds to all but a handful of his servants – largely, though not entirely, the staff of the Privy Chamber. Or, to put it the other way round, out of the hundreds of servants of the royal household only a score or so – and once again chiefly the Privy Chamber – came into any but the most formal contact with the king.

But that contact, and with it 'the sight of the royal face',[7] was the goal of the courtier and his *raison d'être*. This leads to a bold and crucial simplification. What mattered was not so much the right of coming within 'his grace's house'.[8] That general access to the court was the mere *pons asinorum* for the courtier. What mattered instead was the particular access to the Privy Chamber and beyond. The history of the court is the history of those who enjoyed that access. It is thus, substantially, the history of the Privy Chamber, and so I have written it.

And so do the other contributors to this volume. For in the century that followed Henry's death the organization of the household changed comparatively little. This stability is remarkable since the monarchy itself endured the vicissitudes of minority, female succession and a change of dynasty. None made much impact. Previous minorities, like Henry VI's, as John Murphy observes in his study of the mid-Tudor court, 'had emptied the court' (below, p. 146). Not so Edward VI's. For after the initial eclipse of the Privy Chamber under Somerset came a 'revival' under Northumberland so strong as to make the years 1549–53 the Indian summer of the department (below, p. 146). Rather more substantial were the changes brought about by Mary's accession. A female monarch meant a female Privy Chamber: 'all the Privy Chamber offices that had been the most coveted in the household now fell into the hands of women' (below, p. 140). This is of course remained the case under Elizabeth I and for very much longer. Yet even then there was no structural change, as Pam Wright shows. 'Despite the unsuitability of the Henrician regulations for female staff no new household ordinances were drawn up at the beginning of the reign.' (below, p. 148) Nor were any subsequently. The result was a 'patchwork establishment' indeed, but one 'tailor-made to [Elizabeth's] needs' (below, pp. 148–9).

The coming of James I, a man and a Scot, at last brought about institutional change. The Privy Chamber, long the centre of the monarch's personal life, was shorn of its intimate functions and re-attached, together with its staff, to the Lord Chamberlain's side. Instead the king's body service was transferred to a new department,

7. Elton, 'Court', p. 218.
8. Ibid. p. 217.

the Bedchamber, which was moreover for the first two-thirds of the reign staffed almost exclusively by Scots. The political consequences, as Neil Cuddy shows, were immense; institutionally though the effects were comparatively small beer: the Bedchamber's 'pattern of offices was wholly English and followed closely the precedent of the Henrician Privy Chamber'; again and even more importantly 'the rules of the *entrée* [to the Bedchamber] were entirely English and preserved jealously the traditional limitations of access' (below, pp. 185, 192).

So despite everything, the broad outlines of the early Tudor household and court survived: there were still three departments, and there was still a rigid separation between public and private, ceremonial and personal. 'No king ... in Christendom', Bishop Goodman noted, 'did observe such state and carried such distance from the subjects as the kings and queens of England' (below, p. 178). Not even James altered that; while, as Kevin Sharpe shows, Charles I, with his love of formality and ceremony, breathed new life into the old principles. This continuity is important. It gave a broad shape and unity to the period; it also gives a coherence to our several narratives.

Thus far, Elton's emphasis on institutional history appears fully justified. But institutions, the institutional historian too easily forgets, are not self-sufficient entities. They are only one side of the story; the other is personality. This fact affected everything at court and our next concern – politics – most of all.

'The government of seventeenth-century England was personal monarchy', Kevin Sharpe reminds us. 'The continuity of institutions and offices, even of personnel, should not lead us to underestimate the power of the king's person.' (below, p. 226). This meant that 'the succession of a new monarch was still the fundamental change' (below, p. 226). At Elizabeth's death, as Robert Carey knew, he would 'begin a new world', in which he determined to make a place for himself by being the first to bring news of his accession to James I.[9] At the next change of monarch, Lucy Hutchinson commented, 'the face of the court was much changed in the king'. The reason, she continued, was that Charles was 'temperate and chaste and serious' – whereas his father had been none of those things.[10]

So cutting across 'the continuity of institutions and offices' of the

9. Robert Cary, *Memoirs*, ed. John Boyle, earl of Cork and Orrery (1759), p. 155 and see below, p. 173.
10. L. Hutchinson, *Memoirs of the Life of Colonel Hutchinson*, ed. C. H. Firth (1906), p. 69 and see below, p. 242.

household was the change of royal personality. Each new reign brought a new sovereign and with him (or her) a new style of court: Henry VII's was the court of the Winter king; Henry VIII's of the Summer prince; Edward VI's, as John Murphy pointed out in an earlier draft of his chapter, had 'the boisterous atmosphere of the household of a young king on the verge of his majority'; for Mary's, on the other hand, the rather 'staid' tone was set by the 'thirty-seven year old spinster' at its head; while Neil Cuddy is able to cite James I himself on the difference between 'a feminine court in the old fashion' and his own (below, p. 196).

These differences of royal personality are, of course, utterly random. This is probably why most historians, who feel safe only with 'rational' explanations, have underplayed their implications so grossly. Contemporaries, at the mercy of the ebbing or flowing tide, could not afford such luxurious detachment. Instead, like practised sailors, they had to keep a weather-eye. 'Have a vigilant and reverent respect and eye to his Grace', the Eltham Ordinances of 1526 commanded the Gentlemen of the Privy Chamber, 'so that by his look or countenance [you] may know what lacketh or is his pleasure to be had or done'.[11] Under Charles I, as Kevin Sharpe notes, such 'a vigilant . . . eye' enabled three of his Bedchamber servants to compile memoirs with notably precise and detailed pictures of the king (below, pp. 245–6). Councillors needed to be just as observant as courtiers: it was Wolsey who drafted the 1526 injunction to the Privy Chamber and a century later another lord chancellor, Francis Bacon, paraphrased it in his *Essays*. 'It is a point of cunning', he stated, 'to wait upon him with whom you speak with your eye, . . . for there be many wise men that hath secret hearts and transparent countenances'.[12] Wolsey, as I illustrate, certainly practised what he preached; so did Cromwell; so too, no doubt, did Bacon.

More importantly from our point of view, however, Bacon, the great proponent of the inductive method, who also taught that 'histories make men wise',[13] incorporated his own observations of kings into his *History of the Reign of Henry VII*. Written in 1621, immediately after his fall, and presented in manuscript to James I, the text translates his particular and painfully acquired knowledge into something like an analytical vocabulary for monarchy. The key to Henry, he writes, was the 'keeping of distance, which indeed he did towards all' (below, p. 73). Some twenty-five years earlier in

11. *HO*, 156.
12. F. Bacon, *Essays*, ed. H. Newbolt (n.d.), p. 115.
13. Ibid. 237.

1597, the year Bacon published the first edition of his *Essays*, there appeared another notable study of monarchy, Shakespeare's *Henry IV*, Part I. In his confrontation with his erring son, Prince Hal, Henry IV employs a range of concepts which anticipate and amplify Bacon. His kingship, he says, had been a kingship of 'distance' (though he does not use the actual word); his son, on the other hand, was following the primrose path of Richard II and indulging in 'vile participation' (below, p. 77). I use these models of 'distance' and 'participation' or 'intimacy' to explore the contrast between another father and son: Henry VII and Henry VIII. And thereafter the concepts, even the words, are resorted to time and again by other contributors to describe other monarchs: Elizabeth ruled as a 'distant, . . . semi-deified Gloriana'; whereas James enjoyed 'populous intimacy' with his courtiers, and Charles, 'stiff, proud and prudish', went out of his way once again to impose 'reverence and distance' (below, pp. 173, 187, 227, 233).

So alongside the mere randomness of the royal personality, we discern a certain pattern. No doubt Henry VII, Elizabeth I and Charles I, on the one side, and Henry VIII and James I, on the other, were all very different people. But the members of each group did have important things in common: the first were 'distant' monarchs; the second 'participatory'. From this flowed two broadly distinct patterns of kingship. Monarchs of the one type or the other would deploy the royal person and the symbolism of monarchy differently; manage relations with their consorts differently; and, above all perhaps, use their Privy Chambers differently. The two styles of kingship can be reduced to contrasting ways of handling the relationship between sovereign and subject. In the front line of this relationship was the Privy Chamber; indeed it *was* the front line. Physically, it marked the frontier between the public and private lives of the monarch; institutionally its staff alone served both of the monarch's two bodies: the actual 'body natural' and 'the majesty of the body politic', which was made corporeal in the king's person.[14] Suspended between public and private, the Privy Chamber, like all frontiers, was sensitive: minor adjustments could bend it to different, indeed opposite, purposes with no need for formal institutional change.

'Distant' monarchs wanted a Privy Chamber to hold their courtiers off. The first step was to enforce the rules of *entrée* strictly. Henry VII invented them; Elizabeth I granted access sparingly and

14. cf. Starkey, 'Representation', pp. 188, 212.

capriciously and jealously protected the servants who enforced her wishes; Charles I reissued the rules and cut down sharply on the distribution of keys to his private lodgings. More significant, however, was the choice and disciplining of personnel. Henry VII's Privy Chamber were of low birth; Elizabeth's were women. This erected a barrier, of status in the former case and of sex in the latter, between the Privy Chamber and influence in public affairs. And Elizabeth reinforced the barrier by a ferocious discipline. Dabbling in patronage was allowed to her Ladies, but involvement in politics was not. Charles relied solely on discipline, for his Bedchamber were of course men and were well born as well. But, probably as 'deliberate policy', he made sure that his personal liking conferred no political power – much to the disgust of the earl of Holland and even of his own queen, whose treatment was, Kevin Sharpe argues, the prime instance of 'the separation of favour from influence which . . . characterized the style of his court' (below, p. 257). In all these ways the public and private persons of the monarch were kept separate; under a 'participatory' king, in contrast, they were confused. Such a king would fill his private apartments with men who, whatever their social status, would be both favoured and favourites. They would be allowed a flamboyant intimacy with the king that occasionally overstepped the bounds of decency under Henry VIII and often and notoriously under James I. And they would also be allowed to translate personal favour into public influence. Indeed royal policy would sometimes require it. Manifestly, then, we are dealing not only with different kinds of Privy Chamber, but different sorts of politics as well.

'A change of personal style', Kevin Sharpe reminds us again, 'could re-arrange the pattern of court politics' (below, p. 227). In the perspective of the whole book we can now classify the political patterns on the same lines as the royal personalities. The politics of 'distance' were characterized by long ministerial tenures, stability, and the quiescence, even the elimination, of faction. The politics of 'participation', in contrast, were marked by the rapid rise and fall of councillors and favourites, repeated crises and more or less open faction war. The final cause of this was the royal personality; the efficient, the differing role of the Privy Chamber. The private apartments of a Henry VIII or a James I were both an alternative power centre to the Council Chamber and a hotbed of factional intrigue. Councillors and courtiers vied for supremacy and insecurity became both a fact of life and an instrument of royal policy. None of this was true under Henry VII, Elizabeth I or Charles I. Then Chamber and Council went their separate ways; while far from being a 'cockpit' of faction the Privy Chamber became a 'barrier' against it. 'Consciously above and beyond the fray', as Pam Wright describes Elizabeth I, the sovereign 'was . . . better able to manipulate the faction struggle itself' (below, p. 159). 'Privacy too enabled the king to work uninterrupted', and Charles I, like Henry VII before him, was sufficiently diligent to formulate policy himself and so preserve his independence against his councillors as well as his courtiers (below, p. 254). Put like that the contrast between 'distant' and 'participatory' politics looks very like a contrast between good government and bad. Neil Cuddy argues powerfully against such an assumption and I think he is right. In reality, 'distance' and 'participation' were simply alternative managerial styles, either of which could work or fail. Charles I may have imposed 'a great calm' at court, but it was followed by civil war in the country (below, p. 255).

This anatomy of court politics seems to me coherent and convincing. It draws strength from the span of time covered by the book, and from the fact that six several authors, writing independently, have perceived the political world in a similar fashion. But it is still incomplete. As well we need to know where this politics stood within the wider polity. What were the connections between court and parliament, or between court and Council? How was the court related to the 'government' (that awkward and probably anachronistic term)? To these sorts of question we offer less certain answers, if only because the other parties in the dialogue – parliament, the Council and government – fall outside our scope. There are important suggestions nonetheless.

About parliament we have the least say. At first sight this seems to endorse the developing agreement among historians that the early modern parliament was more or less apolitical. But Neil Cuddy (again) enters a powerful note of dissent for the reign of James I. He sees James's court, in which both access to the royal person and a prime share of patronage was reserved, as of right, to Scots, as 'a prime sticking point in relations with parliament' (below, p. 203). It was a continuing issue, round which (*pace* the 'revisionists') continuing opposition formed. Others of us find no echoes of such anti-court feeling under the Tudors; on the other hand, as David Morgan shows, the mid fifteenth-century household was controversial also. The issues – patronage, finance and the personnel of the inner entourage – were much the same, as were some of the attempted remedies, like impeachment of ministers and parliamentary assignment of revenue.

Despite these important parallels, however, court–parliament relations were discontinuous. In that, they are rather like the relations of two great powers with widely separate spheres of influence: conflict between them is accordingly rare, but, when it comes, it is perhaps correspondingly nasty. In contrast relations between court and Council, and court and government are close and continuous. These are not foreign affairs, but domestic, not to say familial.

They also represent the most difficult and contentious subject in the book. This is because the historiography of the period, which focuses so largely on 'governmental' questions, was constructed with no thought whatever to the court. Historians either ignored it, or they explicitly denied its importance. The latter, most notably, was the position of Professor Elton in his work on 'government'. His arguments for a 'Tudor Revolution' rest on the elimination of the household from 'government', which passes instead to 'a national bureaucracy under the Privy Council'.[15] For Elton, then, a prime task of his essay on the court was to try to make room for the role of the royal entourage, which he now acknowledged to be great, without trenching on the central ground of his earlier interpretation. The attempt rests on a series of distinctions between 'politics' and 'government', and between 'courtier' and 'councillor'. 'Politics' remains firmly centred on the monarch's person; 'government' does not. The former is the essential domain of the court and courtier; the latter of Council and councillor.[16] This leaves Elton free to paint the picture, sketched in the essay and fully worked up in *Reform and Reformation*, of a politics in which court factions, like Matthew Arnold's 'ignorant armies', 'clash by night'; while, meantime, councillors strive heroically to maintain and even to reform the king's government, which they must do, too often, in the teeth of the indifference, even the hostility, of the actual wearer of the crown.

This attempt at having cake and eating it is ingenious. But it is hard to apply in practice. Indeed the evidence we assemble here proves utterly intractable on two central issues: the personal distinction between courtier and councillor, and the institutional differentiation between court and 'government'. Both are essential for Elton's arguments and neither can be sustained.

15. G. R. Elton, *The Tudor Revolution in Government* (Cambridge 1953), p. 420.
16. Elton, 'Court', espec. p. 218.

Elton clearly wants the distinction between courtier and councillor to be absolute. 'I wish we were able to confine the term courtier . . . to the holders of specifically court offices', he remarks
plaintively. But his historical discernment tells him that that is
impossible. 'There can be', he continues, 'no sense in any interpretation which allocates Lord Treasurer Burghley to a political sphere
separate and distinguishable from that in which the earl of Leicester,
Master of the Horse, had his being.'[17] Despite this admission,
however, he bends all the powers of his pen to arguing that courtier
and councillor *were* different. So different indeed they were like
inhabitants of different countries, who each felt foreign in the other's
territory. Cromwell, we are told, 'no more than Sir Thomas Smith',
'ever fully penetrated [the] essence of the court'.[18] That may very
well be true of a stiff ex-don like Smith, but for Cromwell it is a
travesty. Cromwell, as I show, began his career in the royal service
as collector to the king's Privy Purse and ended as Chief Noble of
the Privy Chamber; while in and between he proved himself a
superb practitioner of the bloody game of court faction. And every
other councillor, who aspired to be more than a cog in the machine
of state, had at least to survive at court, if not to master it. Even
under Charles I, when ministers enjoyed a rare security of tenure,
concern about their standing at court remained a nagging anxiety.
Kevin Sharpe illustrates the point nicely with Laud, who got his men
made both Clerk of the Closet and clerk of the Signet, that he might
have 'the king's ear on one side and the Clerk of the Closet on the
other' (below, p. 252).

On the other hand, every courtier who was fired with the 'ultimate ambition' had to enter the Council. Here Elton is again guilty
of misrepresentation. 'Power in its political guise', he writes,
'continued to depend only in small part on the function and place
of the courtier'.[19] We present a very different picture and show that
of the handful of men who ruled England as minister or favourite
from the reign of Henry VIII to that of Charles I, about half had
served in the Privy or Bedchamber: Cromwell's career we have
already noted; Somerset and Northumberland both started as
Gentlemen of the Privy Chamber, while Northumberland retained
his place there to the end; Hatton followed the same course as
Northumberland; while Carr and Buckingham were entirely creatures of the Bedchamber. There were other routes to the top, of

17. Ibid. pp. 215–16.
18. Ibid. p. 215.
19. Loc. cit.

course, but service in the inner court was arguably one of the most common.

So the differences between courtiers and councillors, which loom so large in Elton's account, shrink in reality. The nature of politics saw to that. Politics, I write, was 'a politics of intimacy'; Kevin Sharpe varies slightly and talks of a 'politics of access and influence' (below p. 248). We are both emphasizing the same point: that all power rested in the king, 'who alone could fulfil or frustrate ambition' (below, p. 249). All aspirants for power had to work with this fact, which means that, far from being foreign or different, courtier and councillor were akin. 'Both . . . were engaged in a struggle for the same goal: "the mind and favour" of the king'; and both necessarily used the same methods: 'the courtier had to have the skills of a politician; the [councillor] the talents of a courtier' (below p. 102). Such a statement is regarded as 'new' and 'revisionist'. It is neither. Instead it is no more than a paraphrase of Gardiner's century-old dictum that Stuart politicians had to 'look to achieve a stateman's ends by the means of a courtier'.[20]

We can go further still. Not only were courtiers and councillors pursuing (and achieving) similar goals and using similar methods, *they were often the same person.* For the overlap in personnel between the Privy Chamber and the Privy Council – save of course in female reigns – was marked and continuous. In Henry VIII's first formally constituted Privy Council of 1540 five or six out of nineteen were also Gentlemen of the Privy Chamber;[21] by January 1547 the proportion had risen to six out of sixteen, with the two Chief Gentlemen sitting *ex officio*;[22] whilst under Northumberland, as John Murphy notes, a similar arrangement obtained, with the six lords attendant on the king in the Privy Chamber being also the most influential councillors. In contemporary listings of the household the connection was recognized by putting the personnel of the two institutions at the head: first the Privy Council, then the Privy Chamber.[23] The suggestion of senior and junior colleagues was systematized by one proposal for governmental reform, which probably dates from Edward VI's reign. In 'an order for redress of the state of the realm', the author wanted the ordinary Privy Council (by which, significantly, he meant that part of the Council 'continually resident in court') to consist only of 'officers of the Household

20. *DNB* sub Bacon, Francis.
21. *PPC* VII, 3–4.
22. *Foedera* XV, 114.
23. For example *LP* XIII i, 1; BL, Additional MS 45, 716A, fo. 4v ff.

and Chamber'. In its turn, the Privy Chamber should be staffed with 'the wisest and honestest sort of gentlemen in the realm, to the intent that as any of the said officers of the Chamber or Household die or decay, they may succeed them in their places.'[24] For this writer, then, the Privy Council was essentially a household one; while the Privy Chamber were cadet councillors.

And the links between court and 'government' prove to be just as close. Instead of the orderly retreat of the household from administration that Elton's arguments require, we find perpetual interaction, or at least the potential for it. I set the scene by showing that under Henry VIII the Privy Chamber became a true inner administration. It had two main responsibilities: the presentation of documents for the king's signature (the sign manual) and storing and administering the cash reserves (the Privy Coffers). These were not, of course, the whole of the machine of government, but they were crucial parts. To pursue the mechanical metaphor, the sign manual was the ignition key; the Privy Coffers, the reserve fuel tank.

And subsequent chapters show that this apparatus remained in full working order. In 1552, as John Murphy documents exhaustively, a revived Privy Coffers was used to carry Edward VI's government through a cash flow crisis that stopped just short of bankruptcy; while under James I a similar, though longer lasting and more entrenched, financial crisis led to similar results. Indeed, Neil Cuddy argues persuasively that there developed 'a two-tier "system" of finance, as an Exchequer in chronic deficit was left to fend off the king's creditors as best it might; while the windfall revenues, from projects, sales of office and titles and the like, which became increasingly important after 1610, were fed directly into the king's Coffers.' (below, p. 201) The secretarial powers of the Bedchamber also flourished in the last two-thirds of James's reign. Once again, as in the last years of Henry VIII, the inner household, represented this time by the Bedchamber favourite Buckingham and Buckingham's own secretary, John Packer were 'almost always more active in procuring the sign manual than either or both of the new Secretaries, Naunton or Calvert'; while under the previous favourite, Carr, the Secretaryship of State was effectively extinguished: the post was resumed into the king's hands, and 'most of the office's important functions were devolved on Carr' (below, pp. 209, 218).

24. Huntington Library, San Marino California, Ellesmere MS 2625. Attention was first called, many years ago, to this important document by Dr Peter Roberts of the University of Kent at Canterbury. I owe my sight of a photocopy of the MS to the kindness of Drs John Guy and Dale Hoak.

Nor did petticoat rule necessarily change things. For even under Mary, as John Murphy shows, the Privy Chamber remained governmentally active. She had a male private secretary in the department; while behind the facade of the restored Exchequer a 'curious hybrid arrangement' preserved the reality of royal control, with more than half the gross revenues passing through the hands of the 'queen's teller' (below, p. 145). The reign of Elizabeth, therefore, stands out as one exception, when there was no trace of any of this. Part of the explanation lay in the queen's special trust in William Cecil, who, as Pam Wright points out in a striking passage, was both 'private secretary and Secretary of State', and private treasurer and lord treasurer (below, p. 153). But the more important reason for the temporary demise of household government lay in the rigorous distinction which, as we have seen already, the queen drew between her public and private capacities. And that explains also the similar quiescence of Bedchamber administration under Charles I – or rather, during the king's peace, for in the king's war it revived with a vengeance and John Ashburnham, Groom of the Bedchamber, became the chief royalist treasurer.[25]

All of which amounts to more than a critique of Elton; it offers the basis for a new synthesis. So far we have identified two centres of government and politics: the inner chambers of the court and the Council. There was also a third: the formal departments of state or administrative courts, which the Tudors inherited but much spruced up and added to. These were administratively important, though probably not of much direct political significance. Everyone agrees that the middle term of this triad, the Council, was the centre of government. The question is where its affiliations lay as between the other two: to the king's court, or to the administrative 'courts'? For the answer to the question determines the whole flavour of government. Elton sees the Council as both the quintessence and the driving force of the bureaucracy. That gives us his revolutionary government by 'a national bureaucracy under the Privy Council'. We, on the other hand, find perpetual intermeshing between the Council and the Privy Chamber or the Bedchamber, which leads us to see government as court government. Elton addresses the issue directly in his essay, and uses the Secretaryship as a test case. It is worth weighing his arguments carefully in the light of our own findings.

The warrant of 1540, which relaunched the office, provided that the Secretaries were to have lodging in the palace and bouche of

25. *DNB*

court; 'yet' Elton remarks, 'that same warrant clearly makes them much more specifically attendants upon the lord privy seal than the king'.[26] The conclusion is that 'they were part of the general machinery of the reformed state, outside the royal household but of necessity often compelled to come to court'.[27] So Elton. Robert Cecil, himself one of the most distinguished holders of the office, saw things rather differently. For him, relations between the Secretary and the monarch were like 'the mutual affection of two lovers, undiscovered to their friends'.[28] If that is not a court, or even a courtier, view of the officer, I do not know what is. And Neil Cuddy in particular shows the disastrous fate of a Secretaryship cut off from its roots at court. Once the all-important procuring of the sign manual had passed to the Bedchamber, the Secretaryship, at various times in James I's reign, was extinguished; reduced 'to a rump of the office', or was caught on the wrong side of a widening gap between 'theory and practice' (below pp. 211, 218).

The same goes for the Council as a whole. A Council that lost the king's confidence became a cipher, unaware even, as in 1624, that a major alliance had been signed. Our conclusions, of course, since we write as court historians, are loaded. But the work of other scholars is moving in the same direction. Whereas Elton writes of 'government through a national bureaucracy under the Privy Council', J. D. Alsop emphasizes the distance between the Council and the largest department of the bureaucracy, the Exchequer. 'The Exchequer was on the very doorstep of the Privy Council', he writes pointedly, 'yet in a sense it was as distant as a midland shire'.[29] John Guy also dissents from the 'bureaucratic' view of the Privy Council. It was not only its administrative functions that characterized it, but the fact that – unlike Wolsey's Council – it was a court Council.[30]

Here I think we have it. For all Professor Elton's loathness, the Privy Council *was* part of the court and, together with the Privy Chamber, formed its inner ring. Elton admits that Burghley and Leicester moved in the same sphere; Penry Williams uses a similar figure and observes that under Elizabeth 'Council, Household and Monarch moved in the same orbit' (cited below). Astrological

26. Elton, 'Court', 215.
27. Loc. cit.
28. J. R. Tanner, *Constitutional Documents of the Reign of James I* (Cambridge 1930), p. 125.
29. J. D. Alsop, 'Government, Finance and the Community of the Exchequer' in C. Haigh, ed., *The Reign of Elizabeth I* (1984), p. 119.
30. J. A. Guy, 'The Privy Council: Revolution or Evolution' in D. Starkey and C. Coleman, eds, *Revolution Reassessed* (1986), pp. 69–72.

metaphors are perhaps inseparable from Astraea, but instead of the Ptolemaic universe it would be better to think in plain terms of the geography of Whitehall. The hub of the palace was the Privy Gallery, which, crossing King Street on the first floor of the Holbein Gate, traversed the sprawling structure from east to west. Opening off its south side were the king's Privy Lodgings, centring on the Bedchamber; while directly opposite the Bedchamber, on the north side, lay the Council Chamber.[31] The doors of the Council Chamber and Bedchamber were thus separated by only the few yards of the width of the Gallery. This proximity explains, almost in itself, the close links of Privy Chamber and Privy Council. They co-habited the same exclusive area of the palace to which, moreover, only they had access. The fate of the Privy Chamber itself after its displacement by the Bedchamber makes the point. Now the Gentlemen no longer had the right 'to pass and repass with your Majesty through the Galleries'; instead they were reduced to 'run[ning] about . . . with all the common people of your court'.[32] Excluded from the Privy Gallery, the original corridor of power, they were naught. On the other hand, those who had the *entrée*, the Privy Council and by now the Bedchamber, had equal shares in a community of privilege: they were specialist but overlapping bodies that both drew their power from their proximity to the monarch. Not for nothing was the Council called 'Privy' as well as the Chamber; not for nothing was it taken for granted that the Privy Chamber were as well able to counsel the monarch as the Privy Council itself; and not for nothing did reform in the Privy Council and reform of the Privy Chamber go hand in hand, as in 1526 with the Eltham Ordinances[33] or in 1549 in the aftermath of Somerset's fall. For in both cases what was being done was the same: Wolsey in 1526, and Northumberland in 1549, were defining which of the king's servants should enjoy the 'nearest access' to the royal person, either as Privy Councillors, or as Privy Chambermen, or in some cases as both.

And the Privy Gallery was a corridor of administrative power as well. Just as the personnel of the Privy Chamber and Privy Council rubbed shoulders in the gallery, so the records of the two bodies – chests of papers and sometimes coffers of money as well – were stored cheek by jowl in the maze of little rooms opening off the

---

31. H. M. Colvin, ed., *The History of the King's Works* (6 vols, 1963–82) IV, p. 309.
32. N. Carlisle, *An Inquiry into the Place and Quality of the Gentlemen of his Majesty's Most Honourable Privy Chamber* (1829), p. 112.
33. Cf. Guy, 'Privy Council', 67 and D. Starkey, *The Reign of Henry VIII: Personalities and Politics* (1985), p. 89.

Gallery's broad and impressive space: the Council's records were housed first in the Study, then in the adjacent Council Chamber, which, as we have seen, lay just across the Gallery from the Bedchamber;[34] Edward VI's special Privy Coffers were kept in the chamber 'where we most accustomably do hear the sermons',[35] which must have been on the north, or Sermon Court, side of the Gallery; while Henry VIII's treasures were coffered up in the Secret Jewel House and in the Chair House, both of which would have been at the east, or river, end of the Gallery.[36]

But if geography united the Privy Council and Privy Chamber, it put asunder the Council and the administrative 'courts'. When Dr Alsop wrote that the Exchequer was 'as distant [from the Council] as a midland shire', he said well; when he observed that this remoteness was in spite of the fact that 'the Exchequer was on the very doorstep of the Privy Council', he fudged. In fact, the Exchequer and the Privy Council were separated by two hundred yards. It seems little enough. But the distance might as well have been two hundred miles, for it separated the two palaces of Westminster and Whitehall. And the two were different worlds.

Westminster was the king's old palace. Already by the fifteenth century it housed much else: the Exchequer was accommodated next to the Great Hall; the Great Hall itself was shared by the three main law courts; while the Lords of parliament usually met in the White Chamber. The palace was badly damaged in the fire of 1512 and thereafter the king abandoned it entirely to his administrators, judges and parliament.[37] They took over what was left of the structure and patched, adapted or rebuilt it to suit their needs. The result must have looked like a country house under war-time requisition. And, like the country house, almost nothing of its previous life as a palace survived. Here, instead, civil servants ran offices and lawyers courts. Rules, precedents and official restrictive practices were the order of the day and, save during parliaments, the dominant colour was black.

Whitehall, on the other hand, was the king's new palace. Henry VIII had seized it from Wolsey in 1529 and rebuilt it at breakneck speed and crippling cost. There, in sprawling splendour, was lodged

34. D. Hoak, *The King's Council in the Reign of Edward VI* (Cambridge 1976), pp. 160–1.
35. W. C. Richardson, *History of the Court of Augmentations, 1536–54* (Baton Rouge 1962), p. 364.
36. E 315/160, fos. 266v, 267; Society of Antiquaries of London, MS 129, fos. 209, 212, 216.
37. Colvin, *King's Works* IV, pp. 286 ff.

the court. And there, at its heart, in the Privy Gallery, lived the king, with his privy servants and councillors.[38] Here men wore not black but gold, and ran not offices but the kingdom. There were rules of course – of etiquette and of formalized business. But, as in all true centres of power, the rules were crossed and overlaid by a camaraderie of power. Just as much business was done, no doubt, when the Council dined together as when they met in proper session, and more and more important affairs were transacted when, late at night and alone, the king and his Secretary were closeted together. When Paget, describing one such occasion, said in an aside, 'as it is well known [Henry VIII] used to open his pleasure to me alone in many things', he is to be believed. But so are Denny and Herbert, the two Chief Gentlemen of the king's Privy Chamber, when they capped Paget by pointing out in their turn that 'his Majesty, God hath his soul, would always when Mr Secretary was gone tell us what had passed between them'.[39] That is what 'government' meant. In a personal monarchy, unless the monarch wished, it could be no other.

This is what Elton failed to grasp. When he asserted that the Secretaries 'were part of the general machinery of the reformed state, outside the royal household but of necessity often compelled to come to court', he was positing both an institutional and a geographical distinction between court and 'government'. Neither existed. The king's court was the government; the king's palace – Whitehall – was the seat of government. Roy Sherwood makes the same point: 'Whitehall had gradually become . . . the principal residence of the monarch and the centre of the national government'.[40] He dates the change to 'the reign of James I'; in fact it had occurred some seventy years earlier under Henry VIII. For not only had Henry VIII acquired and rebuilt the palace; he had remodelled both Council and Chamber. And all at more or less the same time, between 1526 and 1540. This is the true 'Tudor revolution in government'. It did not depersonalize government, as Elton thought. Instead it focused it more directly than before on the king's person and his palace. It was a court government that paralleled a court politics.

Rather, then, than having politics and 'government' or administration go in opposite directions (which is the picture in Elton's later work), we unite them. They develop (or not) similarly, and they

38. Ibid. pp. 300 ff.
39. *APC* II, 16, 19–20.
40. R. Sherwood, *The Court of Oliver Cromwell* (London and New Jersey 1977), p. 21. There are also suggestive remarks in N. Williams, *Henry VIII and his Court* (1971), pp. 25, 115.

display common features. Administration, like politics, clustered closely round the Privy Gallery; administration, like politics, is multi-centred; and administrative, like political, patterns repeat themselves over wide intervals. This of course was understood by contenders for power at the time. The result is a set of ministerial strategies that parallel the alternative royal managerial strategies. The royal strategies created the balance of power within the court between (principally) Chamber and Council; the ministerial exploited it. But they did so with a degree of latitude and inventiveness that made the ministers' contribution almost as important as the king's. Just how far the system could be stretched in different directions, even under the same king, is demonstrated by Henry VIII's two great ministers, Wolsey and Cromwell.

'Wolsey', as I summarize the contrast, 'had ruled over and against the court, as "alter rex" (i.e. "second king") and master of his own great household, which was a mirror image of the court itself; only latterly and reluctantly had he become a faction leader within the court. Cromwell, in contrast, began where Wolsey ended, as a faction leader and court minister. So where Wolsey neutralized the court, Cromwell packed it; and whereas Wolsey played the reform card, Cromwell used more direct and bloody methods.' (below p. 109). Their attitude to the private administration varied similarly: Wolsey inhibited it; Cromwell at first suppressed it entirely (or perhaps, like Cecil under Elizabeth, took it over); once, however, he had got political control of the Privy Chamber in 1536 he tolerated and even encouraged it. These strategies had an immediate re-run in the next reign, when, as John Murphy shows in a fascinating comparison, Somerset modelled himself all too closely on Wolsey, while Northumberland was 'a not unworthy successor to Cromwell' (below, p. 134).

Under the two Tudor queens, things looked different as Council and Chamber necessarily separated. But to very different effect in the two reigns. Gardiner, Mary's first and only chief councillor, was able, thanks to his personal connections and inclinations in policy, to go into alliance with the queen's household. After his death, however, the two centres of power – Council and household – went their own ways: 'the Council itself', as John Murphy notes, 'was run by Paget and the great lords'; while Archbishop Pole 'worked directly with Mary on religion, in which the Council played little part' (below, p. 145). The separation caused much heart burning among members of the Council, which was appeased by Mary's successor. For Elizabeth 'chose to concentrate all power in the hands of her Council' (below, p. 144). Why she made this choice, and whether it was even hers, we do not know. Nor is this the place to speculate. However, the decision offered her councillors the chance to take an unprecedented hold over both the power and the patronage of the crown, which her longevity only entrenched further. So far, indeed, that this 'eccentric arrangement' endured beyond her death until 1610 (below, p. 144) when Robert Cecil, son of Elizabeth's great minister, fell from grace though not from office. Thereafter the revived power of the royal Bedchamber made itself felt and led to a return to the strategies characteristic of the power politics of the reigns of Henry VIII and Edward VI. Northampton engineered an alliance, on equal terms, between his own conciliar power and Carr as Bedchamber favourite; while under Buckingham the whole basis of power tilted into the Bedchamber, and great officers were sent to their destruction as the favourite's policy and inclination turned this way and that.

'Certain it is, that matter is in a perpetual flux, and never at a stay', wrote Bacon, Buckingham's most distinguished victim. Bacon saw not development but 'returns and vicissitudes'.[41] Everything here bears him out. There was no 'revolution in government', nor even an evolution in politics. Instead, at the throw of the dice of royal personality or ministerial calculation a 'new world' began. But it was an old 'new world' that had been tried before – just as the pattern that had been discarded would be tried again. Historians' various perceptions of development are therefore false. Some are based on straightforward misunderstandings, of which John Murphy, in his pointedly titled chapter (Ch. 3) 'The Illusion of Decline', explodes a whole magazine (including some of my own juvenilia). And some, and the more insidious, are based on false perspective. Stop the clock with Elizabeth's death, as Tudor historians are all too inclined to do, and it is possible (just) to argue that government *by* the monarch was developing into government *under* the monarch by the Council. But let the clock move forward, as of course it did, into the reign of James, and the argument for long-term change collapses.

Or at least it does if we focus, as we have largely done, on the gilded chambers of Whitehall. Our first and last essays, however, take a wider perspective and look at the court's standing in the country as a whole. Under the Tudors the question barely arises. In the fifteenth and again in the early seventeenth century, in

---

41. Bacon, *Essays*, pp. 265, 271.

contrast, the country lost patience with the court and the court tried to take a grip on the country. Both were periods of crisis that saw serious attempts at reform: in the fifteenth century Fortescue called for 'a new foundation of the crown';[42] while under Charles I, it was reported there was 'a general reformation in hand for court and country' (below, p. 258). And in both periods the court was seen at once as a prime cause of the crisis and as the key to its resolution.

But there the similarity ends. In the fifteenth century the household was used as an administrative machine at the centre and as a political machine in the localities. Administratively, household surveyors and auditors tightened up the running of the enlarged crown lands, while the fruits of their labours were received, in cash, by the Treasurer of the king's Chamber; politically, the king's household men acted as royal retainers in the counties, so that 'no attempt whatever could be made in any part of the kingdom by any person . . . but what he was immediately charged with the same to his face'.[43] Under Charles, instead (as Kevin Sharpe shows), the king relied on the force of example and exhortation. The example was set by the reform of his household in which he confidently hoped 'to establish [such] government and order . , . [as] thence may spread with more order through all parts of our kingdoms' (below, p. 258). While the exhortation was supplied principally by court masques. The most overtly political of these, *Coelum Britannicum*, gave an idealized picture of the new court and proclaimed its example to be irresistible: 'there is no doubt of a universal obedience where the law-giver himself in his own person observes his decrees so punctually (below p. 259). It was a neo-platonic age; even so, to trust so simply to the 'image of virtue' to bring about political change was pushing things a bit.

Royal taste and intellectual fashion played a part in these contrasting invocations of the royal household. But essentially they depended on very different social and political realities. The late fifteenth-century court was built on rock. The crisis of Lancastrian kingship, brought about by Henry VI's massive inadequacy, had led to an 'incoherent generation of bastard feudal politics' (below, p. 55 note 85), of which the crown was the principal victim. After 1471 it emerged as the principal beneficiary. Edward IV pushed through, as David Morgan has argued more than once, 'a territorial policy which

---

42. Sir J. Fortescue, *The Governance of England*, ed. C. Plummer (Oxford 1885), p. 154 and cf. D. Starkey, 'Which Age of Reform?' in Coleman and Starkey, *Revolution Reassessed*, pp. 12–27.

43. H. T. Riley, trans., *Ingulph's Chronicle of the Abbey of Croyland* (1854), p. 480.

would assimilate the local pattern of land-based lordship to the now more emphatic ascendancy of the Yorkist dynasty' (below p. 64). In the south-east the king himself emerged as the greatest retainer; elsewhere he ruled through a network of great lords who were, or became, members of his family or household. This structure of politics collapsed under its own internal feuding in 1483; Henry VII rebuilt it more firmly than ever and made sure that this time it focused solely on the king's person. Henry was successful, therefore, not because he 'rooted out bastard feudalism', as an older generation of scholars supposed, but because he monopolized it. And from this monopoly of power, as David Morgan suggests and Professor Elton forcibly asserts, the court was born.[44]

'A court is a magical combination of power, visual splendour, outward deference, and a personal household staffed by members of the elite.'[45] All this, and that utterly king-centred government and politics of the years from Bosworth to the Long Parliament, was a product of the sordid, confused machinations of fifteenth-century power politicians that David Morgan describes so well. And, as I argue, the household as affinity continued to underpin the showy splendours of the court until well into Henry VIII's reign. The early Gentlemen of his Privy Chamber were 'the leading members of a royal bastard-feudal affinity; while their semi-fortified houses, scattered throughout the southern counties, were key links in the chain that bound the localities to the centre' (below, p. 91). The military role of both the Privy Council and the Privy Chamber was mightily extended in the last warlike years of Henry VIII and in the faction-torn reign of Edward VI. But there is a certain sense of artificial respiration. Earlier it had been enough to let the king's servants get on with retaining (indeed it had been rather hard to stop them). Now they had to be subsidized in cash at a flat rate for each horseman recruited. And thereafter the courtier as retainer quickly fades. There are a few reminders of the old pattern, like the guard of Privy and Bedchamber men who accompanied Charles I on his progress to Scotland in 1633. But they are isolated instances.

The result of this, I would argue, is that Charles I sought to rule by an 'image of virtue' because he had few more solid instruments to hand. Habit and obedience bound men to him and proved surprisingly durable. But not durable enough to stand the strain of policies strikingly similar to those which Henry VII had pursued

44. Elton, 'Court', p. 212.
45. P. Mansel, *The Eagle in Splendour: Napoleon I and his Court* (forthcoming).

with impunity 150 years earlier. The differences in circumstance were of course great. But one, I think, stands out: Henry VII had a bastard-feudal power base; Charles I did not. And the fate of his court, 'the most regular and splendid . . . in Christendom' (below, p. 230), shows what that meant. For in 1640 the mirror to the kingdom itself broke in pieces at the first shock: the Council collapsed; the household split; and his own Lord Chamberlain fought against the king. Even a Henry VI or a Richard III had been able to do better than that.

'Except during sessions of parliament, the history of this [James I's] reign may be more properly called the history of the court than that of the nation.'[46] David Hume's judgment, derided or disregarded in the nineteenth century, is again coming into its own. As it does so, so there has been need to get the history of parliament into perspective – not to say, down to size. In this process of revision several things have played their part: a proper understanding of parliament as an institution; a due attention to contemporary judgment and description; a rejection of broad based developmental or teleological interpretation, and emphasis instead on circumstance and personality; a return to narrative and a willingness to take the long view.[47]

The plight of court history in one sense has been the opposite: it has suffered from too little attention, not too much; it has needed writing, not re-writing. But in writing it, we have found ourselves echoing most of what parliamentary revisionists have to say. And most of all perhaps to agree on the importance of the long view. Or what amounts to the same thing: periodization. For, as I trust will now be clear, Hume's dictum about the centrality of the court applies not just to the reign of James I but to the whole period covered by this book. And only to this period. David Morgan deals with the beginning of the court, in fact and in language; Kevin Sharpe describes an end: after the Restoration, as he puts it, 'the court lived on as an important focus of politics. Under Charles I it had been *the* focus of politics, the centre of personal monarchy'(below, p. 260). Before 1471 there was a military/aristocratic politics; after 1660, and more definitely after 1688, a parliamentary/aristocratic politics. In between came the court politics of personal monarchy that we began by 'making an effort to understand' and have ended by getting into perspective.

46. D. Hume, *The History of Great Britain* (10 vols. 1810–11) VI, p. 2.
47. Cf. in particular J. S. Roskell, 'Perspectives in English Parliamentary History' in E. B. Fryde and Edward Miller eds, *Historical Studies of the English Parliament: II, 1399–1603* (Cambridge 1970), pp. 296–323.

CHAPTER TWO

The house of policy: the political role of the late Plantagenet household, 1422–1485

D. A. L. Morgan

When in the fifteenth century the king's household prompted attention, it did so for very present reasons; but in doing so, it prompted also a sense of the past. The writer of the *Liber Niger Domus Regis Angliae* composed in the 1470s, having flexed his writing muscles by jotting down on its opening leaves half a dozen edifying household aphorisms from the Bible, Seneca, Aristotle and St Bernard, proceeded to evoke the exemplary domestic regimes of Kings Solomon, Lud, Cassibellanus, Hardeknout, Henry I and Edward III, before venturing on his exposition of the fifteenth-century present. 'The new house of houses principal of England' was presented as no speculative creation thrown up in the hasty construction of a new dynasty's rule: it was to be seen as a conservationist enterprise of refurbishing in all its former magnificence 'the house of very policy and flower of England' as it had stood in the days of those glorious forebears whose legitimate heir was now entering into his own. And if there was not much worthwhile history to the writer's train of thought, his sense of the past has its point for the would-be historian of what he was concerned with.[1]

1. The text of the *Liber Niger* is printed most satisfactorily in A. R. Myers, *The Household of Edward IV: the Black Book and the Ordinance of 1478* (Manchester 1959), pp. 76–197. It became the primary text in subsequent compilations of household regulations and in the works of 'household antiquities. From Sir Simonds D'Ewes's *Basilica Oeconomica* (BL, Harley MS 642, an assemblage of texts ranging from the Black Book to the 1610 'Booke of Howsehold' of Prince Henry) to *A Collection of Ordinances and Regulations for the Government of the Royal Household*, published in 1790 by the Society of Antiquaries (*HO*).

128, 672 College of St. Francis Library
Joliet, Illinois

The household: attitudes and organization

For to begin appraisal of the household in the fifteenth century, is to begin very late: our project may indeed be a case of the owl of Minerva spreading her wings only at the dusk. Conceivably (but in the historical nature of things, hypothetically) the age of the royal *familia*'s greatest force was the span of Anglo-Saxon generations preceding the development of other agencies of governing authority and of their forms of written record: then, kingship was straightforwardly the realization of the group life of warrior drinking companions, fighting as the royal war-band, celebrating and consuming in the familiarity of the hall the spoils of victory. Even within the later era of that evolving pattern of a post-Conquest land settlement and an institutionalizing of society's political and governmental life, the three centuries which follow the first written description of the household's internal articulation – the *Constitutio Domus Regis* of the 1130s[2] – may be as worthy (and as much in need) of the historian's attention as the three centuries which are the concern of this present work[3]

Whatever the relativities of such backward-glancing comparison, however, we may well begin our appraisal with the point that the household was by the mid-fifteenth century a very long-standing thing, at the nub of political enterprise. Over that long preceding span it had shown propensities for developing new forms of expertise – administratively and culturally – but much of the way it

2. Printed in *Dialogus de Scaccario and Constitutio Domus Regis*, ed. and trans. C. Johnson (Edinburgh 1950; reissued with corrections by F. E. L. Carter and D. E. Greenway, Oxford 1983), pp. 128–35.
3. Although the household from the twelfth century until 1399 is fragmentarily illuminated as an administrative mechanism in T. F. Tout, *Chapters in the Administrative History of Medieval England* (6 vols, Manchester 1920–33), it is only in recent years that its functioning as a political institution has begun to be effectively explored, notably by J. E. A. Jolliffe, *Angevin Kingship* (1955; revised ed. 1963) and J. O. Prestwich, 'The Military Household of the Norman Kings', *EHR* 96 (1981), 1–35. For the period of the Hundred Years War there are several valuable unpublished university theses: C. J. Given-Wilson, 'The Court and Household of Edward III, 1360–1377' (St Andrews Ph.D. 1976); A. Rogers, 'The Royal Household of Henry IV' (Nottingham Ph.D. 1966); W. R. M. Griffiths, 'The Military Career and Affinity of Henry prince of Wales, 1399–1413' (Oxford M. Litt. 1981); E. de L. Fagan, 'Some Aspects of the King's Household in the Reign of Henry V' (London M.A. 1935); G. L. Harriss, 'The Finance of the Royal Household 1437–1460'. (Oxford D. Phil. 1952). I am grateful to Dr Given-Wilson for allowing me to read his unpublished paper 'The Royal Household in English Politics 1360–1413'; his book *The Royal Household and the King's Affinity: service, politics and finance in England 1360–1413* (1986), which appeared after the writing of the present essay, is a notable addition to the literature.

retained an age-old style of the companionage and war-band of its lord. 'After the deeds and exploits of war, which are claims to glory', wrote Georges Chastellain, 'the household is the first thing that strikes the eye, and that which it is therefore most necessary to conduct and arrange well'.[4] And in the century immediately preceding the mid-fifteenth, this traditional style was in many ways strengthened rather than weakened, both by the parallel, distinct articulation of other 'out of court' institutions of civil government, and by the heightening of the active role of the household as the king's retinue in that enterprise of the Hundred Years War which so markedly stressed the atavistic personal style of the king as war lord and fused the two concerns of Chastellain's prescription into a single cynosure of political life.

During the years which formed the still more immediate prelude to the writing of the Black Book of the 1470s, that traditional style had undergone an exceptionally testing sequence of political discontinuities. And it may be thought that it was this context which makes the middle decades of the fifteenth century stand out, in the longer perspective of the household's history, as a time of particular self-consciousness. In general, neither the promulgation of regulations re-ordering the personnel of the household nor the publication of treatises descriptive of household procedure were at all frequent occurrences in medieval England: although the 1279 and 1318 ordinances may be only chance survivals from a perhaps larger corpus of occasional regulations,[5] the absence of any complementary corpus of descriptive treatises on the management of great households other than the mid thirteenth-century text ascribed to Bishop Grosseteste,[6] suggests both an absence of organizational innovation and a lack of any sense of questioning of established assumptions. In the fifteenth century this changed. From the 1440s to the 1470s

---

4. Georges Chastellain, *Oeuvres*, ed. Kervyn de Lettenhove (8 vols, Brussels 1863–66) V, p. 364.
5. The 1279 text is printed in Tout, *Chapters* II, pp. 158–63; the 1318 text is printed in T. F. Tout, *The Place of the Reign of Edward II in English History* (revised ed. Manchester 1936), pp. 267–318. There appears to have been an abortive household ordinance drawn up by the reform commission appointed in the parliament of November 1381: 'the Commons asked the king to require the household officers to swear to uphold it, but no text has survived nor is there any other evidence of any reform in the organization of the household' (A. Tuck, *Richard II and the English Nobility* (1973), p. 57, referring to *RP* III, 101, 115).
6. Printed in D. Oschinsky, *Walter of Henley and Other Treatises on Estate Management and Accounting* (Oxford 1971), pp. 388–407. A mid fifteenth-century English version of this French text is printed in *Early English Meals and Manners*, ed. F. J. Furnivall (Early English Text Society, original series 32) 1868, pp. 215–18.

there was produced a sequence of ordinances and treatises seeking to define the household's structure, functions and membership. In 1442 the 'reformation' of the household became a talking-point, the king being asked by the Commons

to ordain and assign by the authority of this your said present parliament such and as many of your lords as it pleaseth your Highness to have sufficient power and authority to see, establish, appoint and ordain that good and sad rule be had in and of your said household, and that ready payment in hand be had for the dispenses of the same household.[7]

Perhaps as a result, in 1445 a set of 'Provisions which be necessary for the king's household' was issued, itemizing the number and rank of servants in the various household offices, with particular attention to the regulation of their enjoyment of the customary perquisites of 'bouche of court' and the procedures designed to secure satisfactory accounting in household economy.[8] In 1449 the Dean of the household Chapel set down in the *Liber Regie Capelle* a description of one of the component parts of the household, starting with its composition and departmental structure, but dwelling more on its ceremonial and liturgical functions; written for presentation to the king's cousin, Alfonso V of Portugal, the treatise serves to remind us of the cosmopolitan ethos which was always one of the distinctive features of courtly society.[9]

Thereafter, however, the mid fifteenth-century sequence of household literature unfolded as a commentary on the more inward compulsions of court politics. In 1454, having waited in vain for more than a year for any sign that the mentally afflicted king might emerge from his stupor, the Great Council promulgated a much-reduced household establishment in the form of a list of the names of those holders of particular household offices who were to be allowed 'bouche of court'.[10] Different again, both in political context and in textual genre, was the set of 'Orders and attendances for the king's Chamber' issued in 1471 immediately after the final demise of Lancastrian kingship and the definitive arrival and recovery of Edward of York: a nominal roster of those designated to serve as the king's immediate entourage for an eight-week period, with twelve injunctions as to how these two dozen servants should func-

---

7. *RP* V, 63.
8. Printed in Myers, *Household*, pp. 63–75.
9. *Liber Regie Capelle: a manuscript in the Biblioteca Publica, Evora*, ed. W. Ullmann (Henry Bradshaw Society, 92) 1961.
10. *PPC* VI, 220–33.

tion as the personnel controlling access to the king's own quarters of inner, middle and outer Chamber.[11] The 1478 Ordinance provided more extended 'directions' for the general administration of both the Chamber and the other components of the Household, without the 1454 and 1471 particulars of names, but appending a schedule resembling that of 1445 of the categories and numbers of servants with their perquisites.[12] The much lengthier discursive, descriptive text of the Black Book no doubt represents much of that process of inquiry and appraisal referred to in the preamble of the 1478 Ordinance: an exceptional undertaking, consciously historicist in its awareness of past as well as present household practice, and self-consciously and rhetorically philosophical in its aphoristic presentation of how the 'domus regis edificabitur sapientia' before getting to grips with how the show of *domus magnificencie* is grounded in the economy of *domus providencie*.[13]

Beside this sequence of texts which are concerned with the household of the king himself, there stand the further regulations issued for the households of other members of the house of York – the 1468 'Stablishments and Ordinances made for the rule and guiding of the household of Edward IV's brother George, duke of Clarence;[14] the 1473 Statutes and Ordinances (revised in 1483) for 'the politic, sad and good rule' of the household of Prince Edward, the king's eldest son;[15] the 1484 Ordinance 'for such number of persons as shalbe in the north as the king's household' at Sandal castle;[16] and finally, by way of epilogue, the 'compendious recitation compiled of the order, rules and construction of the house' of the Duchess Cecily, the king's mother, written in her last years after the brief period of Yorkist rule

11. Printed in Myers, *Household*, pp. 198–202.
12. Printed in Myers, *Household*, pp. 203–28.
13. Besides the text printed by Myers, see Kate Mertes, 'The Liber Niger of Edward IV: a new version', *Bulletin of the Institute of Historical Research* 54 (1981), 20–39. Ancillary to the household investigations of these years was the description of that Burgundian household to which Edward IV had (eventually) received an invitation in 1471 towards the end of his enforced visit to his brother-in-law's territories; the description was provided in 1474 by Olivier de la Marche, *maitre d'hôtel* to the duke, in response to an English request seemingly transmitted by the king's Chamberlain from Calais: 'Estat de la maison du duc Charles de Bourgogne', printed in *Mémoires d'Olivier de la Marche*, ed. H. Beaune and J. d'Arbaumont (Société de l'Histoire de France, 4 vols) 1883–88, IV, pp. 1–94.
14. Printed in *HO* 87–105.
15. Printed in N. Orme, 'The Education of Edward V', *Bulletin of the Institute of Historical Research* 57 (1984), 119–30.
16. Printed in *British Library Harleian Manuscript 433*, ed. R. Horrox and P. W. Hammond (4 vols, Upminster and London 1979–83) III, p. 114.

had ended.[17] Brief though it was, it was that final generation of Plantagenet kingship which thus produced the bulk of medieval writing of this sort. And proliferating in that same mid fifteenth-century span, as a necessary accompaniment to the codes of domestic regulation, is the large further quantity of instructional manuals of household service and etiquette aimed at instilling the manners of correct behaviour into those who embodied and exemplified the sense of courtliness. Such manuals range from the 'Book of Nurture' written *c.*1440 by John Russell (described as Usher of the Chamber and Marshal of the Hall to 'a prince full royal', Humfrey, duke of Gloucester) to expound 'the courtesy of court',[18] through a plethora of others both in verse (such as that of perhaps the 1470s addressed to 'young babies whom blood royal/With grace, feature and high ability hath enformed'[19]) and in prose (such as 'The order how a Gentleman Usher shall serve his great master', owned by Richard, duke of Gloucester,[20] or 'The Book of Service and Carving and Sewing and all maner of office in his kind unto a Prince or any other Estate'[21] put into print by Wynkyn de Worde). These texts must have been closely akin to that 'book of urbanity' which the Black Book mentions as the textbook from which the Master of the Henchmen should school those being brought up within the king's household,[22] and to the 'Royal Book' of those things 'which be necessary to be had in remembrance of the king's Chamberlain and to his Ushers of the Chamber and appertain unto the offices'.[23]

Such is the prescriptive and descriptive literature which, together with the books of accounts[24] recording yearly expenditure on the fees, wages, provisioning and general running costs of those

17. Printed in *HO* *35–*39. Cf. C. A. J. Armstrong, 'The Piety of Cecily, duchess of York: a study in late mediaeval culture', in *For Hilaire Belloc*, ed. D. Woodruff (1942), pp. 73–94.
18. Printed in Furnivall, *Meals and Manners*, pp. 1–83.
19. Ibid. pp. 250–8.
20. Longleat MS 257, fo. 109. The MS was written *c.* 1450.
21. First printed 1508; reprinted from the 1513 edition in Furnivall, *Meals and Manners*, pp. 149–72. The courtesy-book genre demands further attention.
22. Myers, *Household*, p. 127.
23. Printed in E. Jeffrey, ed., *The Antiquarian Repertory* (4 vols, 1807–09) I, pp. 296–341. This text of the time of Henry VII ends with the oath 'that the Chamberlain shall give to them of the Chamber when they shall be charged'; it adds the further reminiscence that 'the Book which all these things been enacted in was wont all way to be in the household. Of the last man that I understand that had it was Hampton Squire for the Body in all these offices and matters' – this being John Hampton (b. *c.* 1391, d. 1472), Usher of the Chamber and Squire of the Body to Henry VI.
24. The books of particulars of account of the Treasurer and the Controller of the Household (only 16 of them now extant, in varying degrees of completeness,

in receipt of 'bouche of court', forms the primary source-material for the household as an institution. It is writing which conveys a sense of complex articulation, with two structural features repeatedly brought out. The first is the structure of the component 'offices' or departments of household administration. Overall, the household complex falls into three clusters, corresponding to the general setting of aristocratic life in which kings like all lords belonged. The first of the three was the out-of-doors sphere of the Stable, presided over by the Master of the Horse; accounting separately, and tending in consequence to figure only tangentially in the general household regulations and descriptions, with the only surviving separate 'appointment' for the Stable belonging to that untypical situation of the 1454 'abridgment' of the household in the special circumstances of Henry VI's incapacity (and immobility), the office looms less large in the historical record than it must have done in the actuality of the life of a court still markedly itinerant and addicted to the alfresco existence of the hunt – catered for by the separately-maintained establishments of the king's Falcons, Harriers, Harthounds, Buck-hounds and Otterhunt.[25] Although both financially and in quantity of personnel the Stable seems not to bulk large, the Mastership of the Horse in both Lancastrian and Yorkist reigns was held consist-

for the period 1422–85: one for 1425–26, nine for 1437–52, three for 1463–67, three for 1477–80), together with summaries of account and subsidiary and associated documents, are in the Public Record Office among the Exchequer Accounts Various (for the period 1422–85, E101/407/13-E101/412/15); the enrol-ments of account are E361/7, rot.15–39. They can be supplemented from other Exchequer materials, especially the Warrants for Issue (E404), the Council and Privy Seal files (E28), and the King's Remembrancer Memoranda rolls (E159). There are no surviving Chamber records for this period. Some further material exists in the records of the Great Wardrobe – an out-of-court 'standing office', accounting separately at the Exchequer, but whose Keeper (deemed by the Black Book an 'officer of Chamber outward') acted on the instructions of the Cham-berlain and the Master of the Horse and was largely occupied in the court's clothing and furnishing; its records have survived in some quantity, mainly in the E101 and E361 categories, and two partially printed Great Wardrobe account books (for 1480 and 1483–84) are accessible in N. H. Nicolas, ed., *Privy Purse Expenses of Elizabeth of York; Wardrobe Accounts of Edward the Fourth* (1830), pp. 115–70, and *The Coronation of Richard III: the extant documents*, ed. A. F. Sutton and P. W. Hammond (Gloucester 1983), pp. 102–89.

25. The 1454 'appointment' is printed in *PPC* VI, 209–14. The only extant book of particulars of account by a Master of the Horse for this period (1481–82) is E101/107/15; E101/106/29-E101/107/12 are summaries of account and subsidiary documents for 1429–57. Sections on the mews occur in the books of particulars of account of the Treasurers of the Household, and there are periodic warrants from the Countinghouse listing the personnel and costs of the offices of the hounds (e.g. E28/91/55, 58, 63).

ently by members of the innermost group of the king's Chamber servants.[26]

Indoors, deriving from the architectural structuring which allocated the domestic commissariat of kitchen and storage to one extremity of the central hall, and the accommodation of the lord – at once more private and more stately – to the opposite extremity, the symbiosis of a *domus providencie* and a *domus magnificencie* was translated into the twofold grouping of agencies headed respectively by the Steward and the Chamberlain. What in later administrative parlance was labelled the 'Lord Steward's Department' consisted first of the domestic offices: Bakehouse, Pantry, Cellar, Buttery, Pitcherhouse, Spicery, Confectionery, Wafery, Chandlery, Ewery, Laundry, Kitchen, Larder, Scaldinghouse, Poultry, Accatery, Scullery, Saucery. Each of these had its own staff, of differing size, smaller units being grouped with larger so that for accounting purposes they formed seven 'charges' each answered for by a Clerk or Serjeant. As the focus of them all was the Counting House staffed by some six Clerks headed by the Cofferer, concerned with disbursing and accounting on a day-by-day basis, and acting as the regulating mechanism at the centre of the domestic economy; the repository of the vital 'checker roll' listing the Household's personnel, and of the periodic inventories listing its plate and other *matériel*; and the producer of the routine documentary record of bills, debentures, day-books, and quarterly and yearly consolidated statements of total receipts and expenses.[27] Above the Cofferer ranked the Treasurer and the Comptroller, who with the Steward – to whom 'the secondary estate and rule under the king of all the excellent household is wholly committed' – and the Cofferer and his Clerks sat as 'the board of doom . . . at the Green Cloth in the Counting House as recorders and witnesses to the truth'; the Steward also exercising the jurisdiction (extending for twelve miles around

26. Sir Walter Beauchamp 1429–30; Sir John Steward 1430–1439/40; Sir John Beauchamp 1439/40–57; John Wykes esq. 1461–62/65; Sir Thomas Burgh 1462/65–69; Sir John Parr 1469–75; John Cheyne esq. 1475–83; Sir James Tyrell 1483–85. Both Cheyne and Tyrell combined the Mastership of the Horse with the Mastership of the Henchmen. Cf. in general (though not always in particular) M. M. Reese, *The Royal Office of Master of the Horse* (1976).

27. The process of household accounting continued much of the way along the traditional lines described by J. H. Johnson, 'The King's Wardrobe and Household', in *The English Government at Work 1327–1336*, ed. J. F. Willard and W. A. Morris (3 vols, Cambridge, Mass. 1940–50) I, pp. 206–49. The most revealing sources for the mechanism of the household economy in this period are the two books covering John Elrington's operations first as Cofferer, then as Treasurer, in 1471–77: E101/412/3 and 5.

the king's place of residence) of the Court of the Verge[28] 'in which he is judge of life and limb', and ceremonially presiding in the Hall when the body of the household assembled under the supervision of the Marshals.

Keyed into this structure of the *domus providencie* for purposes of provisioning and domestic accounting and jurisdiction, but otherwise forming a distinct nexus, was the structurally and functionally very different complex over which the Chamberlain presided. In part this comprised specialist agencies each with its own organization: the Chapel under its Dean, the Signet Office under the king's Secretary, the Jewel House under the Treasurer of the Chamber and Keeper of the Jewels, the Wardrobes of Robes and Beds, the Office of Arms of the Heralds, the Minstrels (incorporated in 1469) and Trumpeters under their respective Marshals, the medical corps headed by the king's Physician and Surgeon. But its central component was the personnel of Knights and Esquires of the Body, Carvers, Cupbearers and Sewers, Gentlemen and Yeomen Ushers, and Yeomen, Grooms and Pages of the Chamber – a staff for whom the demarcations of departmental 'offices' do not signify.

For with this world of the Chamber we move towards the second of the two structural features highlighted in the contemporary literature of household treatises and records: the discrimination of the personnel of the various parts of the household by a vocabulary of social rank, which acts as the woof to the web of the vocabulary of functional office. Broadly speaking (and aside from the 'chief officers' of 'the board of doom'), the social nomenclature of the staff of the *domus providencie* predominantly belongs to the lower ranks of yeomen and below, only the Serjeants of the domestic offices (and the Master Cooks and Marshals) being on occasion styled gentleman or esquire. In the *domus magnificencie* it is the higher ranks of gentleman and above which predominate: even the king's Barber, says the Black Book, is 'to be taken in the court after that he standith in degree, gentleman, yeoman or groom'; and in practice the same held true of Yeomen of the Crown and Chamber, despite those traditional designations of their household rank, which reached much further back in time than the shift in general social vocabulary occurring in the first half of the fifteenth century with the advent of the new

28. Cf. W. R. Jones, 'The Court of the Verge: the Jurisdiction of the Steward and Marshal of the Household in Later Medieval England', *Journal of British Studies* 10 (1970), 1–29. Fragments of the *placita aule* and proceedings of the coroner of the Marshalsea are in E101/259; a few more are recorded in E159 and C262/1/4.

designation 'gentleman'. By the time the 1449 description of the Chapel was written, the king's Chaplains were asserting their 'status as gentlemen'.[29] Essentially, that sector of the household which more immediately formed the king's entourage belonged – by social origin or social destination – to that world of gentility which was also the world of politics. The role of the Chamber staff lay partly in the enactment of the show of ceremonial 'magnificence', partly also in those group activities which fostered a sense of courtly culture with its distinctive mores:

these Esquires of Household of old be accustumed winter and summer, in afternoons and in evenings, to draw to lords' chambers within court, there to keep honest company after their cunning (i.e. knowledge), in talking of chronicles of kings and of other policies, or in piping or harping, singing, other acts martial, to help occupy the court and accompany strangers.

But equally, such Esquires were 'to be chosen of their possession, worship and wisdom, also to be of sundry shires, by whom it may be know[n] the disposition of the countries'; more particularly if they were Esquires of the Body, their 'business is many secrets'.[30] From their individual point of view, their role was no doubt a means towards realizing careerist hopes: as one of the contemporary courtesy poems spelt out the point, 'Keep these precepts if ye list yourself to advance/ Among them that been of the country of fame'.[31] But in aiming at their individual advancement, they had equally to seek to advance the interests of their masters. Their role as a group was to realize kingly style in its various manifestations, and to embody the king's sense of his own role in the conduct of affairs. Accordingly, it is necessary to explore the ways in which these men of the court related to that wider context of political society, and thereby served as a means to political action.

Politics: the household of Henry VI

The specific context for that spate of mid fifteenth-century household writing, which is both descriptive and prescriptive in character and intention, was a process of political unsettlement. Over those

29. Cf. D. A. L. Morgan, 'The Individual Style of the English Gentleman', in *Gentry and Lesser Nobility in Late Medieval Europe*, ed. M. C. E. Jones (Gloucester 1986), p. 33 note 58.
30. Myers, *Household*, pp. 111 and 129.
31. J. Nicholls, 'A Courtesy Poem from Magdalene College Cambridge Pepys MS 1236', *Notes and Queries* 227 (1982), 3–11. The poem occurs in a MS compiled *c.* 1460–80, which also includes 135 musical compositions, some by Gilbert Banaster, one of the 'Gentlemen Clerks' and from 1478 to 1487 'Master of Song assigned to teach' the Children of the king's household Chapel.

decades, there came into play the short-term pressures and changes of a political breakdown degenerating into civil war, and as a political institution the household was inevitably affected by this process. The size and membership of the household became contentious issues, caught up in factional rivalries; and in step with this, there developed changing attitudes and ideas as to the household's role in government. But at the start of the process, there was a shift away from the style of the household as a war-band; and paradoxical though the argument may seem, the upshot of the ensuing onset of civil war – however much the waging of that war may have accentuated the fighting character of the king's entourage in the short term – was to confirm rather than to reverse that change.

In the long-term perspective, this shift (which made itself felt in the 1430s and 1440s) is the underlying justification for singling out the mid-fifteenth century as a significant watershed in the history of the household. Not that the shift occurred either abruptly or with conscious deliberation; it was the result of the practicalities of policy rather than the cause of any reappraisal of purpose or overt renunciation of an age-old outlook. Castiglione, at the outset of his *Book of the Courtier* which in many ways epitomizes the change of style, could still formulate that outlook into the doctrine that 'the principal and true profession of a courtier ought to be in feats of arms',[32] and we need not think that in this respect his sixteenth-century English readers were heretical dissenters. But from the mid-fifteenth century the course of English policy ran obliquely to the continued affirmation of such doctrine. Although thereafter there were certain moments when the household figures in its old role as the active nucleus of war enterprise, and sufficiently often for there to be no complete and tidy discontinuance of the household's functions as a warfare institution, by and large the household came to play instead the changed political role which the language of 'the court' is used to emphasize – used both by modern historians and by contemporary commentators.

The link between this long-term shift from retinue to court (on the one hand), and the short-term stresses of political breakdown (on the other), is to be found in the unlooked-for circumstances of English kingship in the 1430s and 1440s. At the outset of that

---

32. Baldassare Castiglione, *The Book of the Courtier, translated by Sir Thomas Hoby* (1974), p. 35. For Castiglione's personal ambivalence to the doctrine and his lack of genuine engagement with the soldier's way of life, see J. R. Hale, 'Castiglione's Military Career', in *Castiglione: the ideal and the real in Renaissance culture,* ed. R. W. Hanning and D. Rosand (New Haven 1983), pp. 143–64.

generation, the old style of the household as war-band was emphatic. The minority regime of the 1420s was predicated on political and governmental enterprise continuing to be the realization of Henry V's war-lord form of kingship. This fundamental premise was solemnly and elaborately reiterated at what was deliberately staged as the moment of the royal advent of Henry V's son and successor – the double-coronation of 1429-31, whose staging required that the ceremonial at Westminster be followed by the military expedition of the king's voyage to France in 1430–32. The 1430 expedition was fully in the tradition of earlier things, the household (both in its 'below stairs' elements as a commissariat, and in its 'above stairs' elements as a retinue) being the nucleus of a larger gathering of similar aristocratic followings.[33] As such, the expedition was a fuller and more active rendering of the interplay of kingship and aristocratic community which in 1425 had led the minority Council to issue an instruction that all heirs of tenants-in-chief down to the grade of baron who were in the king's wardship as minors, should be about the king's person in his household, each with a *magister* maintained at the king's expense, in the traditional manner which Sir John Fortescue commemorated in his laudation of the household as 'the supreme academy of the nobles of the realm'.[34] In 1428 (when the king, in his seventh year, graduated from the female world of the nursery and the male entourage of his Chamber began to be formed, with the earl of Warwick as the king's *magister*), the Council followed up its general instruction with a more specific directive that, among others, the young Richard of York (knighted at Whit-suntide 1426 by the king, immediately after his own dubbing, in the first of the group ceremonies of the reign of such inductions to the chivalrous fraternity) be brought to reside in the king's household. Richard of York duly took part in the 1430–32 'voyage'.[35]

In the intention of the guardians of both the person of Henry V's heir and the legacy of his political strategy, the episode reaffirmed the household's role as that of the focus of the aristocratic community, in whose ethos of group endeavour the personal 'feat

---

33. There is a large quantity of documentation which illustrates the markedly household character of the 1430–32 expedition in both organization and personnel: e.g. the material concerning the Treasurer of the Household's activity as 'tresorier de nos guerres' in E361/7, rot.20–25, E101/52/6, 33–35, 39, E101/408/9, 11, 13.

34. *PPC* III, 170; Sir John Fortescue, *De Laudibus Legum Anglie*, ed. and trans. S. B. Chrimes (Cambridge 1949), p. 110.

35. *PPC* III, 292–5. Still a minor, and only given livery of his lands on return from the expedition, York served as a member of the king's retinue (*Foedera* X, 446; E361/7, rot. 22).

of arms' of the king himself was the classic set-piece. In the event, the fate of the king's Chamberlain, Lewis Robessart, lord Bourchier (knight of the Garter, formerly standard-bearer to Henry V) – killed in action near Amiens in November 1430, in a manner which elicited contemporary comment on the force of the chivalrous ethic[36] – was both symptomatic of the traditional style and a completely incongruous harbinger of the generation which witnessed the dissolution of the medieval polity. For instead of 1430–32 marking the advent of the next generation of old-style warrior kingship, it turned out to be the false start of a ruler whose reign did indeed remain dominated by the continued enterprise of war in France, but who personally never again set foot in France after his return (still aged only ten) from his coronation expedition and whose later appearances on battlefields were altogether involuntary. In consequence, his entourage (as such) ceased to figure as the power-house of war enterprise: if individual household servants still participated in the French war during the twenty years after 1432, they did so on secondment from the king's personal service in the followings of those noblemen (such as Richard of York) who as the king's lieutenants sought to stand upon the ancient ways.[37]

That expectations at the time when the king came of age were that the house of Lancaster would maintain its own traditions and foster 'feats of arms' and chivalry is signalled by Joanot Martorell of Valencia, whose stay at the English court in 1438–39 was aimed at engaging in a duel of honour under King Henry's auspices, but who had to rest content with turning the visit a generation later into the wish-fulfilment of the early scenes of the exploits of 'William of Warwick' and the eponymous protagonist of his romance *Tirant lo*

---

36. Chastellain, *Oeuvres*, II, pp. 133–5; Ghillebert de Lannoy, *Oeuvres*, ed. C. Potvin (Louvain 1878), 457–9. I am obliged to Margaret Condon for verifying from his inquisition post mortem (C139/51/52) that the date of Robessart's death is indeed 27 November 1430 – not 1431, as given in all works of reference and secondary literature; when correctly dated, his decision to fight to the death can be seen to have not only a chivalrous, ethical motivation but also a political sense in the context of the delicate state of the military situation in Picardy and of Anglo-Burgundian relations.

37. Such participation is signalled at least for the 1443 expedition led by John Beaufort. Council minute of 15 March 1443 (*PPC* V. 146–9). The Articles of Richard of York's appointment as king's lieutenant in France in 1440 include a stipulation concerning those members of the king's household whom he wishes to take with him, asking that they be 'better recommended unto our said sovereign lord's good Grace because of their great labours and goings' (*Letters and Papers of the Wars of the English in France*, ed. J. Stevenson (Rolls Series 22) 1861–64 II, [585]–[591]).

Blanc;[38] or again, by the duels which did take place in the king's presence in November 1440 between the Portuguese knight Pedro Vasques de Saavedra, Chamberlain to Philip of Burgundy, and Sir Richard Woodville, and in January 1442 between the Aragonese knight Felip Boyl and the king's household Esquire and foster-brother John Astley, knighted for his victory and over the next generation a leading exemplar of the chivalrous tradition.[39] But such occasions did not set the tone of Henry VI's court, any more than the French war became the king's paramount concern of policy; for the 1440s proved to be the time when such expectations were cheated.

It is with this negative feature, of the abandonment of the household's pre-eminent role hitherto as the instrument by which the militant purpose of kingship might be achieved, that the characterization of Henry VI's household must start.[40] What more positive character it developed is less easy to suggest – necessarily so, since the household was governed by the individual propensities of kings, and with Henry VI the negative force of the king's antipathies makes itself felt more strongly than any clear sense of positive purpose.

Attempts have been made to offer some positive characterization by resolving the ambiguities of Henry VI's kingship in a more clear-cut way than he himself ever achieved. They have taken the form of an interpretation of the politics of the decade and a half of Henry's adult reign which in 1437 succeeded the decade and a half of his minority, an interpretation which suggests that the household moved to the fore as the nexus of patronage/clientage relationships and in due course (not least because of the inescapable tensions of that matter of policy which was the unresolved issue of the continuing war in France) as an 'interest group' whose failure to reflect the wider spectrum of the interests and attitudes of the aristocratic community induced an alienation of court from country. In this interpretation

38. *Tirant lo Blanc* by J. Martorell and M. J. de Galba, trans. H. Rosenthal (1984). Cf. M. de Riquer, *Cavalleria fra realtá e letteratura nel quattrocento* (Bari 1970).
39. Both duels were widely reported and assiduously written into the contemporary 'books of fame': e.g. on the first, *Paston Letters and Papers of the Fifteenth Century*, ed. N. Davis (2 vols, Oxford 1971–76), II, no. 439, and Georges Chastellain, *Oeuvres*, III, p. 455; on the second, Viscount Dillon, 'On a MS Collection of Ordinances of Chivalry of the Fifteenth Century', *Archaeologia* 57 (1900), 29–70, and G. A. Lester, *Sir John Paston's 'Grete Boke'* (Woodbridge 1984), pp. 92–5. Cf. M. de Riquer, op cit., pp. 180–8, 197–212.
40. In general on Henry VI's household see R. A. Griffiths, *The Reign of King Henry VI* (1981), especially pp. 295–375, and B. P. Wolffe, *Henry VI* (1981), especially pp. 93–116. Wolffe takes the view that the 'rapidly expanding household of Henry VI's majority grew to be the greatest political affinity, or faction, in the kingdom' (p. 99), and Griffiths that 'during the 1440s Henry VI's affinity became very largely Suffolk's too' (p. 33).

the household is viewed as a 'monolithic' institution of which (in default of active personal assertiveness on the part of King Henry himself) William de la Pole earl (in 1444 marquess, in 1448 duke) of Suffolk, first as Steward of the Household from 1433 to 1447 and then as Chamberlain of England from 1447 to 1450, acted as the managing director and accordingly became an exemplar of the *privado* type of court minister.

That Suffolk acquired an understood primacy both as the exponent of high policy (above all in diplomacy, with his leadership of the 1444–45 embassies to France for the negotiation of the king's marriage and the suspension of military enterprise) and as the broker of much royal patronage and largesse, is evident. If the town of Hull set its heart upon a new charter, it had to budget for expenditure on the necessary fees and *douceurs* totalling £238 (well over a year's income); £140 of the total went to the Steward of the Household, though perhaps his family's special connection with the town inflated his profit far beyond the normal going-rate for services rendered by 'good lordship',[41] But to probe a little further into the nature of his ascendancy, it may be worth pausing on a deposition made by a fellow-courtier, Master John Somerset, concerning a partially abortive attempt in 1447 to suborn him to surrender the Wardenship of the Mint and sell the reversion of the Chancellorship of the Exchequer:[42]

First I say that many men were about to have the reversion . . . that I might have no rest for their business, of whom I was greatly vexed for importunity of suit. This knew John Lemanton, and wilily he went to my lord of Suffolk, and prayed him to be mean to me that he should be preferred thereto afore any other. And what he gave my lord I wote well enough, an hundred mark by his own relation. Then soon after when I was come to Westminster, I was sought all about that I should anon forthwith come to my said lord's chamber and speak with him, and so I did when he was set down at his meat, albeit that I stood not greatly in his love and affection. And anon when he saw me he rose up from the board and spake to me at

41. The consequent 1440 charter did involve the exceptionally grandiose endowment of the town with county status. Other payments are noted in *Charters and Letters Patent granted to Kingston upon Hull*, ed. J. R. Boyle (Hull, 1905), pp. 47–69. Cf. R. Horrox, 'Urban Patronage and Patrons in the Fifteenth Century', in *Patronage, the Crown and the Provinces*, ed. R. A. Griffiths (Gloucester, 1981), p. 155.

42. PRO C1/19/65. Cf. *CPR* V (1446–52), 54, 313; VI (1452–61), 43. The theme of office as property and the trade in reversions (noticeably active in the mid 1440s, cf. next note) would repay further exploration: see the interesting indications in R. L. Storey, 'England: Ämterhandel im 15. und 16. Jahrhundert', in *Ämterhandel im Spatmittelalter und im 16. Jahrhundert*, ed. I. Mieck (Berlin, 1984), pp. 196–204.

the cupboard, prayng me with most instance that no man should be preferred afore the said Lemanton if he would agree me as well as any other. The which I granted and durst not say nay. But afterward there were made means enough to bring the bargain about, ever rehearsing of the pleasance or displeasance of my said lord . . . Thus my lord of Suffolk got the bill signed and so forth the patents ensealed, but Lemanton set not by the counsel of wise Cato, 'In morte alterius spem tu tibi ponere noli' . . . . Afterward a good while, Thomas Thorp sued in a Christmastide to the king for a reversion after Lemanton, to have to himself and his heirs male, which was a marvellous bill endorsed of subtlest contents that ever I and my counsel saw . . . And nevertheless, for all that Lemanton had given before time to my lord, yet my lord turned to Thomas Thorp's intent. Then was Lemanton wode [mad] wroth . . . so angry that my lord was Thorp's friend and doer that he had never joy to give him money after. Then when there was great labour in Eastertide to have out letters patents for Thomas Thorp, it was so purveyed for that all was revoked . . . .

In telling his tale Master Somerset is at pains to adorn it with its moral: 'if I had the double payment I would not give these executors [of John Lemanton] one penny, to teach men to buy reversions by maintenance of lords'. For his conscience was clear, notwithstanding his 1,000 marks from Lemanton (which in any case he had devoted to his exhaustively itemized works of piety and charity),

. . . never taking in the king's court bribes for furtherance of men into the king's court nor into office nor for speeding of causes, but ever kept mine hands inpollute from acceptions of gifts and lived on easy livelihood, never man of mine occupations in any king's time of so little lived and unspotted of anything that can or may be notorious proved upon me sith I came into the king's service, for all the false voice and noise that the fiend voicith now on good men unguilty, *quia vox populi* is now *vox diaboli* . . .

That my lord of Suffolk came out of it all somewhat less 'inpollute' and 'unspotted' was clearly implied.[43] But we may think the moral to extend to something more than just a further supererogatory mite of evidence for corruption in high places. In helping us to see how the household could short-circuit the processes of open petitioning so as to subvert the Council's control of the distribution of royal patronage and crown office,[44] the story testifies to a situation of some complexity within the household itself. For this deposition, if in one way a testimony to Suffolk's role as the paramount 'doer' of

43. The bid for the chancellorship of the Exchequer and mastership of the Mint was not John Lemanton's only such venture, and had we any equivalent to Master Somerset's deposition it seems likely, from the skeletal record that exists, that the story of his other transactions would throw further light on Suffolk's *modus operandi*: cf. *CPR* IV (1441–46), 353; V (1446–52), 87, 213; *Calendar of Close Rolls*, V (1447–54), 69).
44. *Select Documents of English Constitutional History 1307–1485*, ed. S B. Chrimes and

the day, may also be thought to argue against the view that the household of the 1440s was merely the consolidated syndicate of Suffolk and his creatures.

The membership of the household was in origin diverse and diffuse; overall, its incoherence is its dominant feature in these years which culminated in a disintegration of royal authority. In numbers, it expanded hugely from the miniature establishment of a child-king, numbers soaring above all in the grades of the household Esquires and the Yeomen of the Crown and Chamber; the 1445 Ordinance, issued at the time when the king's marriage opened the prospect of a further large increment in the shape of the queen's household, strove to check that increase, but not successfully.[45] Such recruitment of course introduced younger men of the king's own generation, but not by displacing earlier arrivals: an important feature is the seniority of the more consequential members of the household, who tended to be closer in age to the generation of the king's father than to the king himself. Just like Suffolk (25 years older than the king), the successive Chamberlains – William Phelip, lord Bardolf (1432–41, born 1383), Ralph Boteler, lord Sudeley (1441–47, born 1390s), James Fiennes, lord Say (1447–50, born 1395), all as old as Suffolk – were men with long careers of Lancastrian service behind them and powerful claims to status and office in their own right. Whatever differential calculus of mutual interest developed between them, if Suffolk was *primus inter pares* his ascendancy was no influx of 'new men'. And it was exercised within a grouping of what, in part at least, remained the king's *familiares*.

The men who were appointed as the initial establishment of Henry's household in 1428–32 (before Suffolk's accession to the Stewardship in 1433) and more particularly as members of the

A. L. Brown (1961), pp. 277–9, for the articles concerning 'the rule and order' to be followed in the handling of petitions, seeking to regularize their transmission through the king's Secretary.

45. In 1438–39 names of household servants listed in the 'Feoda et Robe' and 'Dona' sections of the book of particulars of account totalled 523; in 1448–49 the comparable total (slightly truncated by the loss of a leaf of the account book) was 875. Over that decade the number of Esquires of the Household rose from 128 to 316, and that of Yeomen of the Chamber from 28 to 71. On the additional quantity of the queen's household, see BL, Additional MS 23,938; A. R. Myers, 'The Household of Queen Margaret of Anjou, 1452–3', and 'The Jewels of Queen Margaret of Anjou', *Bulletin of the John Rylands Library* 40 (1957–58), 1–75, and 42 (1959–60), 113–31; *Letters of Queen Margaret of Anjou*, ed. C. Munro (Camden Society, 1st series 86) 1863. The 1449 *Liber Regie Capelle* (above, note 9) states that those servants of the king and queen named 'in rotulo scaccarii hospicii' totalled 1200 (p. 56).

Chamber (to which Suffolk did not belong)[46] retained a special closeness to the king – first and foremost the cadet members of that Beauchamp family in which Henry grew up,[47] but also others, including
Master John Somerset who in 1427–29 was translated from his
schoolmaster's life at Bury St Edmunds to become the king's Physician and tutor in grammar.[48] On occasion, Henry acted forthrightly
enough as 'good lord' of those close to him. In 1447, immediately
he had news of the death of Cardinal Beaufort, he saw to it that his
signet letters were dispatched post haste and with peremptory crisp-
ness of language to secure the bishopric of Winchester for that other
schoolmaster, his chaplain William Wayneflete, whose sole claim to
favour was his part in the king's personal enterprise of the foundation of Eton College.[49] It was that enterprise alone – 'the primer
notable work purposed by me after that I . . . took unto myself the
rule of my said realms', extended between its inception in 1439–40
and 1449 both in itself so far as the scale of Eton went, and into the
parallel scheme of what became King's College, Cambridge – which
elicited the king's positive, committed personal concern.[50]

Revealingly enough, it is in connection with Eton that we are
offered a glimpse of the personal factor which lay at the heart of this
regime's incoherence; for in composing his portrait of the king as
educator, Henry's chaplain John Blacman chose to highlight his
master's sense of the disjunction between the juxtaposed milieux of
his school and his court: if the king discovered Etonians straying
across the river to Windsor, 'he sometimes restrained them with a

46. In his earlier years as Steward, Suffolk had shown himself less than confident
that his position at court was secure: cf. *CPR* II (1429–36), 590, 514. Clearly he
did come to command constant access to the king; but conceivably his assumption of the Chamberlainship of England in 1447 (in succession to Humfrey of
Gloucester), in place of the Stewardship of the Household, was designed to
tighten his hold. The Chamberlain of England was listed in the Household
accounts at the head of those receiving fees and robes, though the household
descriptions do not characterize the office as part of the ordinary mechanism of
the Chamber's activity.
47. The prominence of the Beauchamps in Henry VI's household brings to a fitting
culmination the history of a family whose household service in both the senior
and cadet lines was incessant from the time of Edward I.
48. N. Orme, 'Schoolmasters 1307–1509', in *Profession, Vocation and Culture in Later
Medieval England*, ed. C. H. Clough (Liverpool 1982), p. 228. As a literary
memorial, besides the vigorous vernacular prose of his 1450–52 Chancery
deposition, he left the *Querimonia* in Latin hexameters reproaching for its ingrati-
tude the king's foundation at Cambridge, in whose planning he had played a part.
49. R. Chandler, *The Life of William Wayneflete* (1811), 299–303 and 38.
50. J. Nichols, *A collection of All the Wills now known to be extant of the Kings and
Queens of England* (1780), pp. 291–319. Cf. J Saltmarsh, *King Henry VI and the
Royal Foundations* (Cambridge, 1972); B. P. Wolffe, *Henry VI*, pp. 135–45.

rebuke, bidding them not to do so again, lest his young lambs should come to relish the corrupt deeds and habits of his courtiers'. If Henry himself felt less than fully at home in his own household – and sufficiently exercised about its moral condition to take his suspicions to the length of keeping 'careful watch through hidden windows of his chamber, lest any foolish impertinence of women coming into the house should grow to a head, and cause the fall of any of his household' – his Eton and Cambridge foundations may have expressed his own strategy of 'inner emigration' and dissociation from at least some of the constituent elements of a household which was not in its membership properly of his own making.[51]

If so, it is in the 1440s and in the context of the incoherence of his own household that the disjunction between the king and the world of politics first made itself felt. The years starting with the suspension of war enterprise in 1444 saw a move towards the privatization of policy, into a semi-secret process of family correspondence and court diplomacy so far as the matter of France was concerned, emphasized by the protestation at the conclusion of the 1445–46 parliament of the king's sole responsibility for the negotiations.[52] But even before these methods reaped the whirlwind of public reaction first to the surrender of Maine in 1447–48 and then to the collapse of Normandy in 1449–50, the household was attracting public attention and critical comment. In the successive parliaments of 1439–40, 1442 and 1445–46 the twin issues of household finance and purveyance were reactivated as a result of the large increase in the household's size;[53] despite the ensuing 1445 Ordinance, they proved recalcitrant, the Council by November 1447

51. *Henry the Sixth: a reprint of John Blacman's memoir*, ed. and trans. M. R. James (Cambridge 1919), 12, 34; 8, 30. Cf. R. Lovatt, 'John Blacman: biographer of Henry VI', in *The Writing of History in the Middle Ages: essays presented to R. W. Southern*, ed. R. H. C. Davis and J. M. Wallace-Hadrill (Oxford 1981), pp. 415–44, and 'A Collector of Apocryphal Anecdotes: John Blacman revisited', in *Property and Politics: essays in later medieval English history*, ed. A. J. Pollard (Gloucester, 1984), pp. 172–97. Despite the founder's views, it was precisely behaviour fitting for courtiers that was urged on the scholars of Eton in the fifteenth-century courtesy-poem *Castrianus*: 'O magnum filii, nostri commensales,/In vestris operibus sitis curiales . . .' (printed in S. Gieben, 'Robert Grosseteste and Medieval Courtesy-Books', *Vivarium* 5 (1967), 71–4).

52. *RP* V, 102–03. For the ambassadors' audience in the king's Chamber in July 1445, and the exchange of personal correspondence between Henry VI, Margaret of Anjou and Charles VII in 1445–46, see *Letters and Papers of the Wars of the English in France*, ed. J. Stevenson (Rolls Series 22) 1861–64, I, 87–159, 164–7, 183–6; II, 368, [639].

53. *RP* V, 7–9, 32, 62–3, 103–04. For the earlier development and political sensitivities of purveyance, see C. J. Given-Wilson. 'Purveyance for the Royal

(when agreeing that the household should have absolute priority over all other claims on the 'ordinary' revenues of the crown) betraying its sense of dilemma as to how the circle might be squared, 'the king willing as well the estate and honour of his household to be performed and kept in all thing as it ought as the good and sure contentation of his debts to his people', and its bleak awareness that what would subvert its efforts was the 'importune labour and pursuit made unto the king' by which the Exchequer would be 'overruled'.[54]

By then, in Norfolk at least, the household was becoming a topic of more general concern to the king's people. When in February 1453 Lord Cromwell presented before the Council a set of charges against an 'untrue, unclean, unhonest' and generally tiresome product of the schools of Cambridge, he recalled 'what slanderous language the same priest uttered of the king's house in his open predication at Norwich the 26th year [September 1447] . . . the Lady Morley and the most part of the city of Norwich could remember, if they were required, it is supposed'.[55] In July 1447 Edmund Paston reported to his brother John a conversation with a local constable:

He enquired me of the rule of my master Daniel and my lord of Suffolk, and asked which I thought should rule in this shire; and I said both, as I troth, and he that survivith to hold by the virtue of the survivor, and he to thank his friends and to acquit his enemies. So I feel by him he would forsake his master and get him a new if he wist he should rule, and so ween I much of all the country is so disposed.[56]

Although the bizarre prospect of the 'rule' of Norfolk by an obscure Cheshire *arriviste* soon faded, Thomas Daniel – one of the younger household servants, king's Henchman in 1440, Usher of the Chamber by 1446 – proved to have greater powers of survival than the duke of Suffolk when the time of reckoning came for this ubiquitous yet far from monolithic royal affinity which, having lost its group identity as the retinue the king led to war, had found no

Household, 1362–1413', *Bulletin of the Institute of Historical Research* 56 (1983), 145–63, and A. Compton Reeves, *Purveyors and Purveyance* (Notre Dame, Indiana 1983).

54. C49/26/18: memorandum of 28 November 1447, with the king's sign-manual. The underlying and incorrigible problem was that personal propensity of which the Council was aware as early as 12 November 1434, when it admonished the king for his susceptibility to 'stirrings or motions màde to him apart in things of great weight and substance' (*PPC* IV, 289).

55. *CPR* VI (1452–61), 100.

56. *Paston Letters*, ed. Davis, no. 79. Cf. nos. 128 and 449 – in which last Lord Scales cuts the menace of Thomas Daniel down to size; William Worcester, *Itineraries*, ed. J. H. Harvey (Oxford 1969), pp. 252–3.

satisfactory substitute as the exchange and mart of royal patronage, let alone as the instrument of a royal educational maecenate aimed at fostering the virtues of *devotio moderna*.

Politics: the household and political strife, 1450–1464

The reckoning was presented in 1450, under the pressure of the military debacle in France. Focused first on the parliamentary proceedings against Suffolk – and like them progressing from charges of misconduct of outward policy to allegations of inward malfeasance – the search for 'guilty men' rapidly widened; in the surge of popular justice the king's Chamberlain and the king's Confessor, as well as Suffolk, went to their deaths, and the violence penetrated well below the top level of the household. In the verse lampoons, in the manifestos which accompanied Jack Cade's rising, and in the indictments presented to judges and commissioners, men of the household individually and collectively were singled out for retribution.[57] When after the turbulence of the summer the course of politics returned in the autumn to the more normal procedures of lordly and parliamentary action, the household remained under threat, for as Justice Yelverton's clerk reported to John Paston (when recounting the king's personal rebuff when he asked Sir William Oldhall, the duke's Chamberlain, 'that he should speak to his cousin York, that he would be good lord to John Penycock', the king's long-serving Yeoman of the Robes and Esquire of the Body),

my lord [of York] was with the king and he visaged so the matter there that all the king's houshold was and is afeared right sore; and my said lord hath put a bill to the king and desired much thing which is much after the Commons' desire, and all is upon justice and to put all those that be indicted under arrest without surety or mainprise, and to be tried by law as law will.[58]

---

57. E.g. *Historical Poems of the XIVth and XVth Centuries*, ed. R. H. Robbins (New York, 1959), nos. 76, 84, 85, 86; C. L. Kingsford, *English Historical Literature in the Fifteenth Century* (Oxford 1913), pp. 364–5 (names of 32 indicted at Rochester in August 1450, all of the Household) and 366 (names of those killed in 1450, including Thomas Est and [John] Wodehouse, Yeomen of the Crown). On the indictments, cf. R. Virgoe, 'Some Ancient Indictments in the King's Bench referring to Kent, 1450–1452', *Kent Records* (Kent Archaeological Society) 18 (1964), 216 n. 2, 220–43, and *CPR* V (1446–52), 443–5, 532.

58. *Paston Letters*, ed. Davis, no. 460. York's zeal for justice cannot have been blunted by the efforts of the king's household men in north Wales to impede his return from Ireland (cf. R. A. Griffiths, 'Richard duke of York and the royal Household in Wales, 1449–50', *Welsh History Review* 8 (1976), 14–25).

When parliament met, with Oldhall as Speaker of the Commons, it proceeded to demand both an effective resumption of royal grants (aimed simultaneously at stripping their dubiously-acquired assets from those who had engrossed the king's favour, and thereby facilitating the endowment of the crown with an income sufficient for household provision) and the removal of those who 'hath been of misbehaving about your royal person and in other places, by whose undue means your possessions have been greatly amenused [i.e. diminished], your laws not executed, and the peace of this your realm not observed'.[59] The twenty-nine such delinquents named, for the most part household servants, covered a wide spectrum: Suffolk's widow, John Penycock, Thomas Daniel, John Somerset . . . But by accepting the resumption with only slight qualification, while limiting his consent to the demand for the removal of his servants to a twelve-month rustication (unless during that time good cause could be shown why their removal should be made permanent), and by further reserving his right to waive even this penalty for those 'which have been accustomed continually to wait upon his person, and know how and in what wise they shall [or] may best serve him to his pleasure', Henry signalled the limit beyond which 'reformation' should not pass.

Perhaps more by good judgment than by luck, this proved a politically viable package, for it could be thought to converge with the discriminations which made the crisis of 1450 a less than absolute court/country confrontation and one lacking some of the makings of a revolutionary situation. As Cade and his fellows said, 'we will that all men know we blame not all the lords, nor all those that is about the king's person . . .': their target was 'the false progeny and affinity of the duke of Suffolk'.[60] In the parliament of 1449–50, while the proceedings were launched against Suffolk, and his satellite the household Esquire William Tailboys was 'noised for a common murderer' in the scandal of his attempt to mug Lord Cromwell within the palace of Westminster,[61] a Petition was urged in favour of the defence of the Isle of Wight being entrusted to Henry Bruyn, for he 'is the king's houshold man and born to great reputation and well inherited, and at no time corrupt, but equally rulith the said

---

59. *RP* V, 216–20. Of these 29 misbehavers, 20 had been among the 32 indicted at Rochester the previous August (above, note 57).
60. *Three Fifteenth-century Chronicles*, ed. J. Gairdner (Camden Society, new series 28) 1880, p. 96; Kingsford, *English Historical Literature*, p. 360.
61. R. Virgoe, 'William Tailboys and Lord Cromwell: crime and politics in Lancastrian England', *Bulletin of the John Rylands Library* 55 (1972–73), 459–82.

island after justice without complaint, and enriched the country with his great stuff if need of the war required'.[62]

Some of the household went unscathed – notably, several of those servants who had never been Suffolk's creatures and who were able and willing to co-operate with his enemies. The new king's Chamberlain was Ralph, lord Cromwell, Suffolk's bitterest enemy among the lords and the promoter of his impeachment; but 'new' has to be given a historical gloss, for Cromwell had already served as Chamberlain in 1430–32 and was now resuming a post whose loss he had resented.[63] John, lord Stourton continued in office as Treasurer of the Household, as did Ralph Boteler, lord Sudeley (Chamberlain 1441–47, and Cromwell's successor as treasurer of England in 1443–46) as Steward of the Household, alongside his cousins John, lord Beauchamp of Powick (king's Carver in 1430, Master of the Horse from 1439–40, in June 1450 appointed treasurer of England) and William Beauchamp, lord St Amand (king's Carver since 1430). When in 1452 Sir John Fastolf proposed as arbitrators in one of his property disputes lords Cromwell, Sudeley, Beauchamp, St Amand and Stourton,[64] he showed a shrewd appreciation for the men of real use and lasting influence – the hardy perennials who had served the house of Lancaster over the decades and whose continued centrality kept the unsettlement of 1450 from reaching the inner sanctum. Whether their rally held out a genuine prospect of achieving a 'firm endowing of the crown' and a reformation along the lines spelt out in that tract for the times written by another royal servant of the same generation, Chief Justice Fortescue's *Governance of England*, still awaits appraisal. Fortescue's remark of twenty years later that the king should 'not be counseled by men of his Chamber, of his Household, nor other which cannot counsel him' may or may not be pertinent to them.[65]

---

62. *RP* V, 204–5.
63. In 1432 Cromwell had made a formal protest over his deprivaton of the Chamberlainship after the king's return from his coronation expedition to France (*RP* IV, 392). Partial mollification was provided by his appointment as *Grand Chambrier* of France on 11 July 1434 (Anselme, *Histoire Généalogique de la Maison royale de France* (9 vols, 3rd edn, 1726–33) VIII, p. 428), and his appointment to succeed the duke of Bedford as Keeper of the king's Falcons restored him to the English household establishment.
64. A. Smith, 'Litigation and Politics: Sir John Fastolf's defence of his English property', in *Property and Politics*, ed. Pollard, p. 73, quoting Magdalen College MS Southwark 201. I am obliged to Dr Smith for his advice as to the date of this MS.
65. Fortescue's remark occurs in his 1470–71 'Articles' addressed to Henry VI's son (printed in *The Governance of England*, ed. C. Plummer (Oxford 1885), p. 350).

Whatever his talents, Lord Cromwell at least was no paragon of selfless endeavour; and lurking behind these 'front men' were distinctly shady characters seeking to evade the reckoning of their demerits. But until 1453, such renewed confidence and stability as Lancastrian government (headed now by that other old servant of Henry V, John Kemp, as Chancellor and with the seventy-year-old war-horse John Talbot back in militant action in France) could muster – together with the prospect held out to parliament in the spring of 1453 that besides labouring within the realm to put down disorder, the king (still aged only 31) might at last be minded to 'labour in his royal person' in his wars in France, just as he had recently become alive to his family duties (as the queen's pregnancy bore witness) – all need to be seen in relation to the determination of these men of the older generation to maintain the traditional order of the world they had not yet lost.

For the household, as for the world of politics at large, the change which had been averted in 1450–53 was precipitated when the king in the summer of 1453 went absent without leave from any further performance of an activist role. With no unseemly haste, the lords who as the Great Council had assumed governing authority in November 1453 proceeded a year later on 13 November 1454 to ordain 'a sad and a substantial rule in the king's household . . . saying that so great a number of people can nor might easily be kept in the said household as hath now a certain season be therein, but of very necessity must be abridged and reduced to a reasonable and competent fellowship'.[66] In so reducing the household establishment they were studiously careful to leave in place the servants particularly intimate with the king: the designated lords, Carvers, Esquires of the Body, Ushers of the Chamber belonged to the core of the royal *familiaritas*. Both in this conciliar ordinance and again in the preamble to the further Act of Resumption in the parliament of 1455–56,[67] the touchstone invoked was the 'worshipful, noble and honorable' household kept 'in the days of the most victorious prince of blessed

The relation of this text to Fortescue's longer treatise, and the possibility that that may have been written *c.* 1450 (B. P. Wolffe, *The Royal Demesne in English History* (1971), pp. 120, 227–8), are overdue for further investigation.

66. *PPC* VI, 220–33. The abridgment prescribed 428 servants for the king (roughly half the previous establishment), plus 120 for the queen and 38 for the prince. The seemliness of this measure was in keeping with the designation of Lords Beauchamp and St Amand to have the immediate superintendence of the king (*RP* V, 248). Unfortunately, the implementation of the Council act of 23 July 1454, empowering the duke of York as Protector to distribute 80 collars of the king's livery (*PPC* VI, 209), seems untraceable.

67. *RP* V, 300.

memory', the king's father. When household reform was written into those heads of business which were presented at the start of that parliament in July 1455 as the prescription for sound policy and government (the household figuring as the first of the eight points), the desideratum of securing 'an ordinate and a substantial rule' in its conduct might reasonably be thought a politically uncontentious matter.[68]

But political contention had already reached so far as the physical wounding of the king at the 'male journey' of St Albans, and the changing situation of the man who was elected Speaker of the Commons in the 1455 parliament, Sir John Wenlock, showed well enough the way in which the household was affected by the intensifying feuds from which such violence stemmed. Wenlock had made his mark as a soldier of Henry V and later as a diplomat before entering the king's household in 1442, in 1445 being seconded to the newly-formed household of the queen as Usher of her Chamber and then in 1447–48 her Chamberlain. He too was wounded at St Albans, in the king's entourage; but whether he was still the queen's Chamberlain seems doubtful, for he seems likely in the summer of 1453 to have been the recipient of the following letter under the king's signet and sign-manual:[69]

Welbeloved, we greet you well. And forasmuch as afore this time ye have let us weet that ye were disposed with our licence to go certain pilgrimages beyond the sea, and in the time of summer as we suppose is most convenient to do it, we licence you therefore now in this season for to do it. And for that cause and other that moven us, we have you excused and discharged as for the office of Chamberlain with the queen. Letting you weet that if your demeaning be in alwise from henceforth as may and ought to be to the pleasure of us and of the queen after your said pilgrimage done and ye comith again, we in some other thing will show you our favourable lordship. Furthermore we let you weet that one the greatest causes wherefore we discharge you is because that in the untrue troublous time ye favoured the duke of Y. and such as [be]longed to him as O. and other.

The concluding allusion is presumably to the activities of York and his retainers (in particular, his chamberlain Sir William Oldhall) in 1451–52; but whatever the circumstances, the political message is

68. *RP* V, 279.
69. BL, Additional MS 48,031, fo. 70. The year in which this letter was issued would seem, from the king's itinerary, to have been 1453; the only alternative might be 1452. Wenlock was the queen's chamberlain on 25 January 1452, and had ceased to be so by 17 July 1454 (Windsor: The Aerary, xv.21.78 and 83). By 1454–55 he was in receipt of an annuity of £20 from the Duke of York (SC6/870/5). Cf. J. S. Roskell, 'John lord Wenlock of Someries', in his *Parliament and Politics in Late Medieval England* (1982–84), III, pp. 229–65.

clearly conveyed: Lancastrian allegiance now had to be understood to be exclusive. The same point had been made more forcibly to Wenlock's fellow M.P. in 1455, Walter Blount, until very recently an Esquire of the king's household with generations of family service to Lancaster behind him, not least in the administration of the Duchy of Lancaster honors of Tutbury and High Peak. In 1453–54 he became a retainer of Richard of York, and as a result in May 1454 his house at Elvaston was sacked by a vengeful posse of the neighbouring gentry of Staffordshire and Derbyshire, with banners flying and trumpets blowing, 'for the said Walter Blount was gone to serve traitors'.[70]

In fact, the years after the king's collapse into nullity saw not only the move to 'abridge' the household into an 'unpolitical' fellowship of purely domestic character, but also its restyling into a coherent Lancastrian affinity. In a sense, this was an old-style, atavistic move, in that it went hand-in-hand with the dynasty's retreat to the patrimonial lands of its *Hausmacht*: falling back on the 'demesne interest' of private lordship, the crown would seek security in the personal loyalism of its own 'bastard feudal' following. But equally, such a shift amounted to a new departure, a move away from the pattern of the previous generations in which the distinctness of royal and aristocratic service had been consciously blurred and assimilated into a 'joint stock enterprise' of public life.[71] Contemporary narratives draw our attention to a sign of the times which seems to have made a vivid impact on observers of the political scene: heralded in comment on the *événements* of 1450 and 1452, more strongly in evidence from 1454–55, comes a stream of comment on the outward marks of the politics of affinity. To the assembly of parliament in November 1450 came 'every lord with his retinue well harnessed [i.e. armoured] and well be-seen; and every lord had his badge upon his harness, and their men also, that they might be known by their badge and liveries'; next month 'the king come from Westminister, riding thorough London, and with [him] the duke of York and the most deal in substance of all the lords in this land, with their retinues of fensible men; which was a gay and glorious sight if it had been in France, but not in England . . .'.[72] Scarcely more than a year

70. R. L. Storey, 'The Sack of Elvaston', in his *The End of the House of Lancaster* (1966), pp. 150–58. Blount is listed as an esquire of the Household from 1441, and was still so in 1451–52 (E101/409/9, 410/9).
71. The metaphor is K. B. McFarlane's: *England in the Fifteenth Century: collected essays* (1981), p. 20.
72. *The Historical Collections of a Citizen of London in the Fifteenth Century*, ed. J. Gairdner (Camden Society, new series 17) 1876, pp. 195–6.

later, the aristocratic community was converging not in a single cavalcade but in divided companies, with the king reacting to York's deployment of his own and allied retinues for a *coup de main* by gathering other lords around him whose appearance demonstrated Lancastrian allegiance: 'they had liveries white and blue, writhen [twisted] like rope on baldricwise'.[73]

In 1455 the clash which had then been avoided came about in the fight in which the wounding of the non-combatant king, and the failure of his household to do more than contribute to the casualties of the losing side, symbolized clearly enough the nullity of Lancastrian rule. When a pungent if partisan chronicler looked back on these years in which 'the realm of England was out of all good governance' as the point of departure for his story of the onset of a civil war, he found a succinct and aptly negative formula with which to sum up what had gone amiss: the king 'held no household nor maintained no wars'.[74] But as the same perceptive writer went on to stress, the house of Lancaster did in the event go down fighting, and in that fighting the household enacted an adaptation of its role as the royal war-band.

Its adaptation was put in hand in the spring of 1456 when the queen decamped from Westminster with her two-year-old son, newly created prince of Wales at the conclusion of that parliament which had convened the previous summer in the aftermath of the violence at St Albans, and which had in the end proved unable to convert its 'heads of business' into a restored political consensus and equilibrium. With the king following in her footsteps some three months later, Queen Margaret made for the north-west midlands, for her own dower-lands of the Duchy of Lancaster honors of Tutbury, High Peak, Leicester and Kenilworth, and also the apanage of her son as prince and earl of Chester. And it was on the basis of those territorial resources that both financially and politically – and in due course, militarily – she proceeded to act. She 'allied unto her all the knights and squires of Chestershire for to have their benevolence, and held open household among them; and made her son called the prince give a livery of swans to all the gentlemen of the country, and to many other throughout the land; trusting through their strength to make her son king'.[75]

73. John Piggot's memoranda, printed in Kingsford, *English Historical Literature*, p. 373. In the political verse of these years, the public scene becomes a *tableau vivant* of the heraldic signs and portents of the politics of affinity (e.g. *Historical Poems*, ed. R. H. Robbins, nos. 84, 87).
74. *An English Chronicle*, ed. J. S. Davies (Camden Society, 1st series, 64) 1856, p. 79.
75. Ibid. pp. 79–80. The order of 12 April 1457 to the sheriffs against the giving

As the immediate organizing focus of this 'bastard feudal' complex, the prince's household and council were constituted, the personnel of which meshed together this local connection and the Lancastrian affinity as a whole. Viscount Beaumont, Chamberlain of England since 1450, chief steward of the queen's lands since 1445, was appointed chief steward of the prince's lands also; Lord Stanley, the leading man of substance in the counties palatine of Chester and Lancaster, who had served as Controller of the king's Household 1439–51 and had been made king's Chamberlain in 1455, became one of the prince's 'tutors'; Sir Richard Tunstall, a Lancashire man, Esquire of the King's Body and Carver since 1452 and Stanley's successor as king's Chamberlain in 1459, became chamberlain of Chester; Sir Edmund Hampden, Marshal of the Hall by 1439, Usher of the queen's Chamber and her Carver from 1445, became Chamberlain of the prince's household.[76] In the country at large, the members of this affinity were drawn upon more heavily than usual in the years after 1456 to act as sheriffs and to provide some reality in what was otherwise becoming a tenuous network of governmental authority.[77] Otherwise they formed a court which in 1458 amused itself with 'jousts of peace',[78] but which in 1459 at Blore Heath and Ludford moved in earnest into warlike action.

Some of the salient questions which suggest themselves as to the restyling of the household into a Lancastrian party are easier to ask than to answer: was the size of the household significantly increased, or was the thrust towards making it a more compact and cohesive grouping, attuned to a policy of 'rigour',[79] and becoming more exclusive in the way adumbrated by Wenlock's demission from the queen's Chamberlainship? The unhelpful condition of the records

of liveries of badges and cloth contrary to the statutes, specifically excluded the king's and prince's liveries (*Calendar of Close Rolls*, VI (1454–61), 205.

76. The prince himself remained in the care of Alice, lady Lovel until his seventh year, when on 23 March 1460 she was discharged 'because he is now so grown as to be committed to the rules and teachings of men' (*CPR* VI (1452–61), 567). The fragmentary letter of Jasper Tudor (SC1/51/86, dated 26 March, perhaps 1460) which refers to Hampden as the prince's Chamberlain, may imply that Lord Scales (whose wife ranked as the chief Lady of the queen's household) was acting as the prince's *magister*.

77. R. Jeffs, 'The Later Mediaeval Sheriff and the Royal Household: a study in administrative change and political control, 1437–1547' (unpublished Oxford D.Phil. dissertation, 1960), pp. 146–7.

78. *The Great Chronicle of London*, ed. A. H. Thomas and I. D. Thornley (1938), p. 190, for the jousts before the king and queen in Whitsunweek 1458; E404/71/2/71 for the jousts of peace to be performed in the king's presence on 21 August 1458.

79. The word occurs, with key-note resonance, in the 1459 tract 'Somnium Vigilantis' (*EHR* 26 (1911), 512–25).

makes it impossible to be sure. Even impressionistically, the events of 1459 when the political issue was put to the military test, suggest a situation more uncertain than clear-cut. At Bloreheath, Lords Audley and Dudley commanding 'the queen's gallants', those 'notable knights and squires of Cheshire that had received the livery of the swans', were worsted by the retinue of Richard Neville, earl of Salisbury; at the subsequent Coventry parliament, Lord Stanley (the son of the king's Chamberlain who had died six months earlier) was threatened with impeachment for his failure to fight, and since his brother William fought for the Nevilles and Lord Stanley himself had recently married Salisbury's daughter, his failure might well seem deliberate subversion of the drive for local Lancastrian solidarity. At Ludford a fortnight later, by contrast, the Yorkist lords were stampeded into flight by the refusal to fight against the king of Andrew Trollope, master porter of Calais under Richard Neville, earl of Warwick's captaincy, but an Esquire of the king's household since the 1440s,[80] who unlike his confrere Walter Blount (seconded by York to serve under Warwick as marshal of Calais)[81] had not as it proved severed his Lancastrian connection.

Whatever its size and composition, the household did not succeed in reasserting mastery: in 1460–61 the change of dynasty was determined by the wider field of force which was the political community at large and not least the strength of aristocratic retinues in relation to local factors. After the defeat at Northampton, the Lancastrian cause became dependent not on the heartland of Lancaster's own patrimony, but on the partisan resistance of the Welsh and northern periphery; and those household loyalists who refused to give up even after the king's capture, had to fight as an adjunct to the local leadership. If at the second battle of St Albans 'the substance that got that field were household men and feed men', they were the members of a plurality of households, though still maintaining the show of an overall Lancastrian affinity: 'the queen's men and every lord's men bare the lord's livery, that every man might know his own fellowship by his livery. And beside all that, every man and lord bare the prince's livery, that was a bende of crimson and black

---

80. E101/410/1. Like others of the Calais establishment, Trollope's appointment as master-porter predated Warwick's appointment as captain in 1455–56.

81. BL, Cotton MS Vespasian F XIII, fo. 35. This letter from York to Warwick is dated 15 October, and must belong to 1456–58. Another of York's retainers, Sir Edmund Mulso, was similarly seconded to serve with Warwick in Calais in 1456 (*Reports of the Deputy Keeper of the Public Records* 48 (1887), 412); his interesting will was made there on 1 May 1458 and proved on 27 January 1459 (PROB11/4 (Register Stokton), fo. 189–91), and it may be that Blount replaced him as marshal.

with ostrich feathers'.[82] And their success in regaining the person of Henry VI promptly brought his reign to an end.

In March 1461, to the accompaniment of a literary celebration of the blossoming new style of white roses and suns-in-splendour badges and blue and murrey livery colours,[83] Edward of York rode north at the head of the retinue with which at Mortimer's Cross he had substantially won the struggle for mastery in Wales, and without which he could not have assumed the crown. As was already becoming his unfailing habit, he made a point of adding to his battle honours by winning the toughest of the civil war encounters at Towton. But that victory notwithstanding, civil war continued for three more years, and the need to fight it maintained the need for the household to function as the king's war retinue.

It had to do so in a local context in which royal dominance was particularly difficult to achieve, for the house of York was no more at home in the north than the house of Lancaster had been, and in the proper connotation of the phrase 'the problem of the north' – in no sense other than that of Anglo-Scottish warfare a real political characteristic of later medieval England (despite the premonition of the start of the Lancastrian period) – emerged in the 1450s and 60s. The cause of Lancaster by 1461 had become dependent on the fighting power of the northern lords; the cause of York had equally to be grounded in a more effective realization of its northern supporters' hopes of local ascendancy. Neither at Wakefield nor at St Albans had the Nevilles shown themselves to much effect; in the northern war of 1461–64 it was their political survival in the first instance which was at stake. But necessarily it was on them that the conduct of the war predominantly fell.

The king himself went five times to the north between March 1461 and June 1464; both during his stays and when he was elsewhere, his household men formed part of the armies waging the siege and field warfare of the border. William Neville, earl of Kent, Steward of the Household until his death in January 1463, may have commanded some of the household contingents; others were led by the king's Chamberlain, William, lord Hastings (married to Katherine Neville by February 1462); a further household troop was sent to hold Newcastle in the winter of 1463–64.[84] Although, had measles

---

82. *The Historical Collections of a Citizen of London*, p. 212.
83. E.g. *Historical Poems*, ed. Robbins, nos. 90,92. For assessments of the northern war see J. Gillingham, *The Wars of the Roses* (1981), 136–55 and A. E. Goodman, *The Wars of the Roses* (1981), 55–65.
84. E404/72/4/78, 79 lists 62 of 'our servaunts of household such as were of late by our commandment at our town of Newcastle-upon-Tyne for the surety and safeguard of the same'. The list is headed by 'Thomas Fauconbrigge', the bastard

not supervened, the king's expedition of November 1462 might have had a more pronouncedly personal style of war leadership, it was an entirely convincing rendering of the traditional form of military enterprise, with thirty-nine lords demonstrating by their presence their acceptance of the Yorkist regime. That in 1464 it was John Neville whose victories at Hedgeley Moor and Hexham brought the Lancastrian resistance to an end in what was as much a settling of the scores of Neville–Percy and Neville–Beaufort and Neville–Neville feud as the quietus of Lancastrian loyalism, was perfectly in keeping with the whole political process from which the change of dynasty derived.[85] For family quarrel though the Wars of the Roses was, it was a multiple one within the extended family of the Plantagenet kindred and connections; and if in the causation of civil war local factors were secondary, in the waging and outcome of the conflict their importance was primary.

Politics: the Yorkist household

Twenty years after Henry VI's third and final re-entry into London in June 1465 in the wake of defeat and capture (this time, no longer as king), the house of York was in its turn about to go to the wall. It may therefore be thought to have failed to solve the problem of how to turn military victory into political stability.

Central to that problem was the political role of its household, for that was inextricable from the crucial issues of policy, both internal and external: how to achieve that reformation of the firm endowing of the crown whereby the king might live of his own and (in the words which Edward IV himself addressed to the parliamentary Commons in 1467) not 'charge my subjects but in great and urgent causes concerning more the weal of themself, and also the defence of them and of this my realm, rather than mine own pleasure'; how nonetheless to relaunch that outward enterprise of war whose collapse was the primary failure of the previous generation; how above all 'to set a perfect love and rest among the lords of this land, to the entent that they may draw directly together in one union and accord in that may be sown to the honour, prosperity

son of William Neville earl of Kent, who was to cut a more prominent military figure in 1471.

85. In the late 1450s John of all the Nevilles stood closest to the house of York, being Duke Richard's retainer (*CPR* VI (1452–61), 552–3; *Ancient Deeds* IV, 26–7). His subsequent career, sketched in G. E. Cokayne, *The Complete Peerage* (revised edn, 13 vols, 1910 49) *sub* Montagu, epitomizes the court/country dilemmas of this incoherent generation of bastard feudal politics.

and welfare of the king our sovereign lord and the politic and restful rule and governance of this his land and people'.[86]

The difficulty of reconciling those aims was formidable. But before we conclude that the house of York fell victim to the inexorable play of structural incompatibilities, we might heed a different diagnosis of the civil war and its outcome: 'In talking of causes it is necessary to avoid the temptations of profundity. It was after all, as Henry VII's reign bears witness, at a superficial level that all cures were found'.[87] If Yorkist rule failed to take root it may be for reasons as superficial, and compelling, as the play of personal sympathies and antipathies, and the personal accident of the sudden and premature death of a ruler who, whatever his success or failure in matters of policy, had shown himself repeatedly able while he lived to master the course of politics.

Whether with the deliberate aim of achieving household economy, or whether from personal preference, the Yorkist household began as a comparatively small establishment; and from the start, in the particularities of its composition, personal preference rather than just an acceptance of inherited relationships was formative of its political style. Certainly many of Edward IV's servants had previously served his father; but then the Yorkist affinity even before 1460 was a distinctly eclectic fellowship, and a singularly recalcitrant fit in terms of the suggested model of a 'bastard feudalism' in which connections of lords and followers were of an essentially local derivation.[88] Undeniably the main centres of family landholding and residence – Clare in East Anglia, Fotheringhay in the east midlands, Conisburgh and Sandal in Yorkshire, Ludlow, Montgomery, Denbigh and Usk in the march of Wales, Trim in Meath – did act as recruitment centres for some of Richard of York's servants, alongside the *palais royal* in Rouen and Baynard's Castle in London; but no pre-existing ties of territorial lordship and neighbourhood will account for his links with other of his leading retainers even in his earlier years, let alone his later attraction for

86. *RP* V, 572, 279 (the second passage coming from the 1455 'heads of business' which enunciated the Yorkist programme). On Edward IV's household see in general C. Ross, *Edward IV* (1974), especially pp. 257–77, 308–32. I have tried to suggest some points of interpretation in 'The King's Affinity in the Polity of Yorkist England', *Transactions of the Royal Historical Society*, 5th series 23 (1973), 1–25.

87. K. B. McFarlane, 'The Wars of the Roses', *Proceedings of the British Academy* 50 (1965), 98.

88. This 'localist' interpretation is advanced, for example, by C. Carpenter, 'The Beauchamp Affinity: a study in the working of bastard feudalism', *EHR* 95 (1980), 517.

those Mamluks (to borrow the contemporary term for those 'infidel' servants of their natural lord generated by Franco-Burgundian politics) such as Walter Blount. As for his son and heir, he was prepared to take his 'friends and lovers' as and where he found them; some of them, like his wife, he found in quite unlikely ways.

The one steady impulse dictating the king's choices seems to have been the determination to prove them upon his own pulses, and whether or not a deliberate gambit of policy, it was perfectly well attuned to putting the partisan past quickly behind him. But his household service did not become an open-access affair: to get into it proved too daunting an undertaking for the young John Paston. As his uncle Clement reported to his father, the boy was too shy:

I feel by W. Peacock that my nephew is not yet verily acquainted in the king's house, nor with the officers of the king's house. He is not taken as none of that house, for the cooks be not charged to serve him nor the Sewer to give him no dish, for the Sewer will not take no men no dishes till they be commanded by the Controller . . . Wherefore it were best for him to take his leave and come home till ye had spoke with somebody to help him forth, for he is not bold enough to put forth himself.

Shyness was further handicapped by parental niggardliness – though John Paston the elder had no excuse for his self-defeating reluctance to 'spend somewhat of your good now and get you lordship and friendship there, *quia ibi pendet tota lex et prophetae*' (good advice given him a dozen years before), for when even younger than his son now was he had himself put in time as a Yeoman of the king's Stable.[89] In later life the son (who never lost the hankering to be about the court) had to console himself as best he could with the thought that he 'was never yet lord's sworn man'; but his younger brother and namesake, less fond of sour grapes, was claiming in 1462 (a few months after his brother's abortive attempt) to be 'well acquainted' with leading luminaries of the household while serving alongside them in the northern war as a member of the duke of Norfolk's retinue, and in 1479 when he succeeded to the headship of the family he spelt out his strategy for dealing with a family dispute: he intended to 'come to London to speak with my lord Chamberlain and to win by his means my lord of Ely if I can; and if I may by any of their means cause the king to take my service and my quarrel together, I will, and I think that Sir George Browne, Sir James Radcliffe and other of mine acquaintance which wait most

---

89. *Paston Letters*, ed. Davis, nos. 116, 463; E101/408/25 for John Paston as Yeoman of the Stable in 1438–39 (he had ceased to be so by 1441, when we next have an equivalent list).

upon the king and lie nightly in his Chamber will put to their good wills. This is my way as yet . . .'.[90] In the longer term, and via further service to the de Veres, he did become an Esquire of the king's Body – to Henry VII.

Others fared better than the Pastons. Edward's household did increase somewhat in size from its modest beginnings: selectively, he was prepared to recruit somewhat in excess of the natural wastage rate. But such additions as there were, were incidental to the durability of the men around him from an early, formative stage. The tone was set by William, lord Hastings, in Edward's service before 1461 and holding office as king's Chamberlain throughout the reign. Because they were so personally, and lastingly, the king's men, it was those 'which wait most upon the king and lie nightly in his Chamber' who could represent their master and implement his will across the range of his concerns. If their recruitment was competitive, their performance was expected to be omnicompetent, though special expertise might be exploited as it developed. Thus Sir Thomas Montgomery – nephew of that long-lasting luminary of Henry VI's household, Ralph Boteler, lord Sudeley; son of an Esquire of Henry V's household and of Edward IV's godmother; and Knight of the Body from the start of Edward's reign – was made sheriff of Norfolk and Suffolk in November 1461 specifically because he was (as an Essex man) an outsider to that disturbed local scene, sent 'to set a rule in the country' by bringing the Norfolk gentry to an awareness of the new king's determination to assert himself, and letting it be known that 'he would neither spare for good nor love nor fear, but that he would let the king have knowledge of the truth'. When they proceeded to hold the sessions in Norwich, his colleague Justice Yelverton left the locals in no doubt that 'as for a knight there was none in the king's house that might worse a-be forborne than the sheriff might at that time';[91] and indeed Montgomery (whose involvement in central affairs brought him in due course the designation of king's councillor) became one of the leading exemplars of 'the house of policy's' role in the high politics of the king's outward causes, ranging across Europe as envoy to Burgundy, France, the Empire and Hungary. When in 1489 this much-travelled man (who understandably bequeathed £100 for the remedying of the roads) made his will, he envisaged an extension of his vocational journeyings beyond the grave, for he not only arranged for thirty days-worth of commemorative prayer for the

90. *Paston Letters*, ed. Davis, nos. 271, 320, 383.
91. Ibid. no. 67.

souls of his two patrons, Lord Sudeley and King Edward, in his chantry chapel on Tower Hill, but also directed that two honest priests should go to Rome to sing for King Edward and for him at Scala Celi and to perform the pilgrimage of the stations of the Cross.[92]

Such servants might win through to a thankful sense of virtue rewarded. But they certainly earned their passage. The indications are that Edward's household was a buyer's rather than a seller's market in terms of the calculus of payment for services rendered. Although in 1469 the mounting debts of the household could serve their (minor) turn as a propaganda issue in the politics of faction, after 1471 the accountants and auditors of the *domus providencie* saw to it that the household operated within cash limits on an approximately pay-as-you-go basis.[93] Not that the *domus magnificencie* failed to live up to its name. The court was showy, impressing the king of Bohemia's brother-in-law in 1466 with its ceremonial protocol[94] and staging a strong chivalric revival; with the king himself, and the Lord Chamberlain, as occasional participants and frequent spectators at the feats of arms, the Chamber personnel was on its mettle to uphold the prestige of its horsemanship and martial artistry. That star prize-fighter of the previous generation, Sir John Astley, one of the early recruits from Lancastrian service, was appointed the king's Standard-bearer in 1461. John Tiptoft, earl of Worcester, Steward of the Household 1463–67 and simultaneously constable of England, promulgated the 'ordinances for jousts and triumphs' of 29 May 1466 and supervised the particularly elaborate Smithfield jousts of 1467. His successor as constable was that other famous chivalric performer of the 1440s, Richard Woodville, now earl Rivers and the king's father-in-law, and the Woodvilles (conscious as they were of their Luxemburg ancestry) assumed the role of protagonists of Burgundian 'magnanimity'.[95]

92. PROB 11/10/22 (Register Vox). The bulk of the will is printed in *Transactions of the Essex Archaeological Society*, 1st series, 3 (1865), 169–75. He had been prone to put his diplomatic travel to pious use, in 1468 for instance combining a mission to the Burgundian court with a pilgrimage to Our Lady of Aire (Lille: Archives du Nord, B.2068, fo. 212v).

93. A. R. Myers, *Household*, 35–47. For the king's settling of his household debts in 1475, see E370/143/5, and E407/6/136.

94. *The Travels of Leo of Rozmital*, trans. M. Letts (Hakluyt Society) 1957, pp. 45–8. A further description of the court in 1471–72 is 'The Record of Bluemantle Pursuivant', printed in Kingsford, *English Historical Literature*, pp. 379–88.

95. S. Anglo, 'Anglo-Burgundian Feats of Arms: Smithfield, June 1467', *Guildhall Miscellany* 2 (1965), 271–83; G. Kipling, *The Triumph of Honour: Burgundian origins of the Elizabethan Renaissance* (Leiden 1977). Cf. the narrative of the 1478 jousts celebrating the marriage of the king's son Richard in *Illustrations of Ancient*

In all of this there was a good deal of political purpose: the 'feats of arms' of 1465–68 were integral to the formation of the Anglo-Burgundian alliance and the king's personal declaration of his intent to resume a policy of outward war in France. Militarily and diplomatically, his household men were much employed in the prosecution of that policy, both before Edward's 1470–71 Burgundian exile and after. It was in these years, which saw men of the Chamber in frequent diplomatic transit, that the office of the king's Secretary became an agency significantly involved in the conduct of diplomacy: in 1472, while Master Secretary Hatteclyff was away on continental missions, his secondary and ultimate successor Oliver King devilled away for sixteen days in the diplomatic documents deposited in the Treasury of Receipt.[96] From 1471 under Lord Hastings's captaincy that hitherto dangerously volatile quantity the Calais garrison – mutiny-prone and politically seducible – became tied into the household network of the king's own authority; thereafter both Hastings and those other Chamber men who served as his staff officers were much involved both in military administration and in diplomatic missions to France and Burgundy.[97]

It was diplomacy rather than warfare which made more frequent calls on the household's skills and energies during this generation which in the event did not see the sustained relaunching of military enterprise. That was in keeping with the course of policy; when policy so demanded, the household could still supply the needs of the king as war lord. In 1481–82, household men such as Sir John Elrington (Treasurer of the Household and of the Wars) and John Sturgeon (Esquire of the Body and master of the Ordnance) provided the administrative corps and *matériel* in the Scottish campaigns which the king waged vicariously, the network of his wider affinity contributing the fighting personnel. In 1475, it was

State and Chivalry, ed. W. H. Black (Roxburghe Club, 1840), pp. viii–xi, 27–40. In 1467 Edward himself took part in a *pas d'armes* at Eltham (*Paston Letters*, ed. Davis, no. 236).

96. E405/55, m. 2. For William Hatteclyff, who served as king's Physician to both Henry VI and Edward IV before becoming king's Secretary in 1464, see G. E. Burtt, 'The Activities of Household Officials in the Fifteenth Century as illustrated by the Hatteclyff family' (London M.A. thesis, 1955), who on pp. 165–7 tabulates Hatteclyff's 30 diplomatic commissions between 1464 and 1476, when Oliver King was appointed French Secretary and took over much of the 'foreign office' business. Cf. A. J. Otway-Ruthven, *The King's Secretary and the Signet Office in the Fifteenth Century* (Cambridge, 1939), a pioneering study which now needs a successor.

97. Cf. L. Stark, 'Anglo-Burgundian Diplomacy, 1467–1485' (London M.Phil. dissertation, 1976). The neglected theme of the Calais garrison is now being investigated for the period 1436–77 by Mr John Rainey of Rutgers University.

those same household administrators along with their Calais colleagues and the whole roster of the king's *familia* – Knights of the Body each indenting to provide over a hundred troops, others in due proportion – who formed the central mechanism of the king's own expedition to France.[98]

At the conclusion of that expedition the king's household servants had the satisfaction of being rewarded for their efforts by the king's enemies: starting with the Lord Chamberlain, Louis XI of France thought fit to award pensions to key English courtiers for their goodwill in securing a settlement.[99] That Edward IV was aware of and undisturbed by this arrangement seems entirely probable: after all, not only did he himself become the best-paid of Louis's pensioners, but the arrangement reflected his general expectation that it was from others than himself that his servants should benefit. On occasion, he indicated that things had to be kept within limits: his minstrels were adjured not to be 'too presumptuous nor too familiar to ask rewards of the lords of his land'.[100] But their social betters scarcely needed to ask: the rewards flowed in as an understood part of the system of the king's government.

The men of the household were the necessary go-betweens in that process of petitioning from which most royal action stemmed. William Hatteclyff was styled Master of Requests as well as king's Secretary, and apart from his diplomatic engagements was responsible for the processing of the bills and petitions which came to the king[101]; hardly surprising, therefore, that on the same day that the king's signet-letter was issued in furtherance of a suit of Sir William

---

98. J. R. Lander, 'The Hundred Years War and Edward IV's 1475 Campaign in France', in his *Crown and Nobility 1450–1509* (1976), 220–41 and 321, ventures a quantification of the household's contribution. But the wealth of documentation for the expedition deserves further attention – preferably in the comparative perspective of the preceding and succeeding royal expeditions of 1430 and 1492.

99. Philippe de Commynes, *Mémoires*, ed. J. Calmette and G. Durville (3 vols, 1924–25) II, pp. 52–3, 241–5; C. L. Scofield, *The Life and Reign of Edward the Fourth* (2 vols, 1923) II, pp. 146–7, 170, 173; J. Calmette and G. Périnelle, *Louis XI et l'Angleterre* (1930), 214–16. These French pensions had been preceded by Burgundian, though Hastings's refusal to provide Louis with a signed receipt may indicate some perception of difference in view of his willingness to sign for his 1000 *écus* from Duke Charles in 1474 (Lille: Archives du Nord, B.2103, no. 67580).

100. Myers, *Household of Edward IV*, p. 132. In fact, rewards to the king's minstrels (who spent much of their time on tour, not always in the king's company) are ubiquitous in town and private records. It is unlikely that they had to emulate the clamorousness of the heralds to obtain largesse.

101. For his style 'magister requestarum' in 1471 see C71/103, m. 23. In 1464 James Goldwell (king's Secretary 1460–61) was also so styled (C76/148, m. 15), having

61

Stonor's, Stonor granted Hatteclyff an annuity.[102] In 1483 the town of Bristol granted Oliver King an annual fee and pension 'whilst he is in the office of Secretaryship'.[103] Early in the reign Christopher Furneys (a low-ranking household servant) alleged he had spent £20 in procuring a signet-licence for the bishop of Chichester to absent himself from parliament; the resulting complaint to the chancellor over the bishop's non-payment showed that these procedures might provoke irritation,[104] but the fragmentary evidence seems to suggest that by and large all this was on a financially very modest level, and did not give rise to the outraged feelings of the 1440s about court profiteering. When the town of Lynn set about securing a royal charter in 1474, the mayor spent a good deal of time in London, wining and dining gentlemen of the household such as Sir Robert Wingfield and Brian Talbot, Esquire of the Body (and his wife), bestowing 40 shillings on the king's Secretary, 10 shillings on the king's Confessor, and 20 shillings on William Wade the king's Esquire and Sewer of the Chamber 'for his attendance in speaking to the king', besides the secretarial costs of writing the bill of supplication to the king, the standard fees of privy seal and chancery, and the inevitable lawyers' charges; but the whole matter quite lacks the brazen racketeering evoked by the town of Hull's experience in 1440.[105] Lord Hastings (who adopted his royal master's principle that it was not for him to pay for what other men were prepared to buy, and accordingly did not fee his retainers) accumulated a plethora of fees and annuities from lay and ecclesiastical lords, abbeys, town corporations and gentry; neither the 27 such grants noted so far, nor the occasional 'regards' which came his way, suggest any exorbitant

in 1462 been termed Master of the king's Recognizances ('magister recognicionum', E361/6, m. 54v).

102. *The Stonor Letters and Papers 1290–1483*, ed. C. L. Kingsford (Camden 3rd series 30) 1919, nos. 238, 239.

103. *The Great Red Book of Bristol*, ed. E. W. W. Veale (Bristol Record Society) 1931–53, Text part ii, pp. 152–3.

104. C1/47/3. The bishop had 'desired him to make means and ways to our said sovereign lord', whereupon Furneys had 'sued and laboured by the means of divers his masters and friends'. He was a yeoman of the household offices (E101/411/13). The annotations to petitions for exemption from Acts of Resumption bring out the household's intercessory role: e.g. the 1465 provisos for the prior and convent of Sixhill (Lincs.) 'ad instanciam Thome Burgh militis', and for the late mayor of Chester 'per manus W. Stanley militis . . . in camera Regis' (C.49/55, 44; 56/37), Burgh and Stanley being Knights of the Body.

105. King's Lynn: Borough archives, Chamberlain's account 1473–74, C.39/61. The town's charter was issued on 16 July 1474. A similar impression is conveyed by the record of the 1471 appointment of a new abbot, and of the payments made when the king visited the abbey, in Peterborough: Dean and Chapter muniments, Register Bird, fo. 67–8.

exploitation of his opportunities.[106] But he would no doubt have agreed with the general postulate of the Devon parson who (with his eye on securing the office of crier of the shire for a kinsman) encouraged his local patron (who happened to be a Knight of the Body) to labour to be made sheriff, 'for it will get you acquaintance and it is better to govern than to be governed'.[107]

Internally, much household service was invested in the king's enterprise of real estate management, which developed as the more positive and acquisitive corollary of the bid for domestic economy, and the realization of the policy of enabling the king 'to live upon mine own'. Here, as in other respects, the sense of a purposive intention to put things in order strengthens after the short-lived but far-reaching unsettlement resulting from the dissolution in 1469–71 of the political syndicate which had established the Yorkist regime in 1460–61. Thereafter, the administrative structure of a household network of the stewards, constables, parkers and receivers of the king's own lands, channelling their revenues to the Treasurer of the Chamber and the king's own Coffers, solidified; it was from the fees and wages accruing from appointment to such local offices that the king's servants gained their chief remuneration, but in return they were required to provide their master with a landed income which grew to equal the yield from the customs on overseas trade (granted to Edward for life in 1465) as the king's 'ordinary' revenue.[108] It was from the proceeds of such estate management that the king financed his building works at Windsor, Eltham and Nottingham, and his extension of the hunting park at Leeds in Kent, and it was from those household men who acted as his local managers that the implementation of such improvements came.[109]

At the same time, this system of estate administration, besides

---

106. The general style of the fees he received is conveyed by Bishop Wayneflete's grant to him of £10 a year for life 'pro suis assistencia, auxilio et favore nobis impensis et imposterum impendendis' (Winchester: Hampshire Record Office, Register Wayneflete ii, fo. 33v). That grant was dated 20 December 1461, at the end of the week in which the king and lords in parliament had found for the bishop in his dispute with his tenants at East Meon (Chandler, *Life of Wayneflete* pp. 111–13, 348–52).

107. *Stonor Letters* no. 300.

108. Wolffe, *Royal Demesne*, pp. 143–80.

109. An excellent example of the intermixture of local and central resources in the working of this system, together with the directness of the king's personal oversight, is provided by the accounts of Gervase Clifton, Esquire of the Body and receiver of lands in Nottinghamshire and Derbyshire, as master of the king's works at Nottingham: E101/478/15–17; E159/257, Recorda, Hilary m. 32; E159/258, Recorda, Easter m. 11; E404/76/4/116, 119.

achieving the firm endowing of the crown and its financial self-sufficiency (so long as the active policy of the prince eschewed outward war), took on an extra political dimension as the king sought to create an overall structure of territorial lordship which might solve those problems of bastard feudal localism arising from the process of civil war. Especially in 1472–74 the king showed himself intent on pushing through a territorial policy which would assimilate the local pattern of land-based lordship to the now more emphatic ascendancy of the Yorkist dynasty. In Wales and the marches a household and council were set up for his son and heir, based at Ludlow, to act as the directing focus for the region; in the north, the Neville interest was transmuted into the rule of the king's brother Richard; and besides these two main blocs, three further local groupings were constructed – in the south-west, in Lancashire and Cheshire, and in the north-central midlands, where primacy was accorded respectively to the king's stepson Thomas Grey, to the Stanleys, and to Lord Hastings. Involving a further, definitive Act of Resumption, the scheme bears the marks of a deliberate tidy-mindedness and a force of will-power which, while responsive to the reality of local situations and relationships, was prepared to redesign such particularities in order to achieve the overall sense of the scheme.

Necessarily, such a territorial policy had both a localist and a centralist aspect. In some respects, the localist aspect obtrudes more immediately. As separate spheres of interest and influence, the regional blocs were clearly demarcated. Soon after the 1473–74 arrangement for the rule of the north had been achieved – the king acting as 'stifler' between his own brothers in their competition for the Neville inheritance, and also overseeing the treaty in which the crucial working-partnership between Richard of Gloucester and Henry Percy, earl of Northumberland, was formulated[110] – Sir William Plumpton was read a lesson by his London agent in the current way of the governmental world:

Sir, now of late I have received from you diverse letters, of the which the tenor and effect is this; one, that I should labour to Sir John Pilkington to labour to my lord of Gloucester or to the king, they to move my lord of Northumberland that ye might occupy still at Knaresborough. Sir, as to

110. E.B. de Fonblanque, *Annals of the House of Percy* (2 vols, 1887), I, 549, for the 1473–74 'appointment' and indenture between Gloucester and Northumberland; *Paston Letters*, ed. Davis, nos. 267 and 281 for the king as 'stifler'. Cf. A.J. Pollard, *The Middleham Connection: Richard III and Richmondshire 1471–1485* (Middleham 1983).

that, it is thought here by such as loves you that that labour should rather hurt in that behalf than avail; for, certain it is, as long as my lord of Northumberland's patent thereof stands good, as long will he have no deputy but such as shall please him and can him thank for the gift thereof, and no man else, and also do him service next the king: so the labour shall be fair answered, and turn to none effect but hurt . . . And as for the message to my Lord Chamberlain, what time I laboured to him that I might be justice of the peace, he answered thus, that it seemed by your labour and mine that we would make a jealousy betwixt my lord of Northumberland and him, in that he should labour for any of his men, he being present. Sir, I took that for a watch word for meddling betwixt lords.[111]

So far as Duchy of Lancaster deputy stewardships and appointments to the commission of the peace in the West Riding of Yorkshire were concerned, there was to be no trenching by outsiders on the agreed local balance of power. But the scheme of government to which such discriminations of patronage belonged did not amount to a policy of simple devolution: each local bloc was linked to the court and did not form a totally self-contained grouping, although some had a more localist political character than others.

In the south-west, both Thomas Grey and his younger brother Richard and such others as Thomas St Leger (married to the widowed duchess of Exeter, the king's sister), Thomas Bourchier the younger (the king's cousin), and John Sapcote (steward to Fulk Bourchier, lord Fitzwarin, and then marrying his widow Elizabeth Dinham), all Esquires of the Body, were outsiders endowed with confiscated local estates or positions within the administration of such estates as the king retained and in the Duchy of Cornwall. In Wales, local interests such as the Herberts were more the victims than the beneficiaries of the Woodville-dominated establishment at Ludlow.[112] In the north west, the pre-eminence of Thomas, lord Stanley in Lancashire was locally rooted, but his appointment in 1471–72 as Steward of the king's Household drew him within the court – to his local advantage, as the king demonstrated by arbitrating Stanley's quarrels with such Knights of the Body as Sir James Harrington and Sir John Pilkington;[113] the further extension of

111. *Plumpton Correspondence*, ed. T. Stapleton (Camden Society, old series, 4) 1839, 31–33. Cf. K. R. Dockray, 'The Troubles of the Yorkshire Plumptons', *History Today* 17 (1977), 459–66.

112. D. E. Lowe, 'The Council of the Prince of Wales and the Decline of the Herbert Family during the Second Reign of Edward IV (1471–1483)', *Bulletin of the Board of Celtic Studies* 27 (1977), 278–97.

113. C49/53/4 (Harrington), and PS01/36/1893A (Pilkington). Cf. M. J. Bennett, ' "Good Lords" and "King-Makers": the Stanleys of Lathom in English politics, 1385–1485', *History Today* 31 (1981), 12–17.

Stanley ascendance in Cheshire and north-east Wales was more especially the concern of Thomas's younger brother Sir William, Knight of the Body throughout Edward IV's reign, and with an interesting career in central politics still before him. In the north midlands, the pattern was one of the installation as local manager of the established gentry community of one of themselves – William Hastings, whose designation for the role came not from inherited pre-eminence but from his special closeness to the king.[114]

The interlocking pattern of such situations, from the point of view of one of those many individual interested parties out of whom the pattern was composed – by a king endowed with 'such a wide memory that the names and circumstances of almost all men, scattered over the counties of the kingdom, were known to him just as if they were daily within his sight even if, in the districts where they operated, they were reckoned of somewhat inferior status'[115] – can be glimpsed in the will made in the summer of 1478 in the castle of Skipton (acquired by Richard of Gloucester in 1475 thanks to a royally-superintended arrangement with Sir William Stanley) by Sir John Pilkington. As a Yorkshireman who was also Knight of the Body he appointed as his executors his two immediate 'good lords', Gloucester and Hastings; and it was in relation to their good offices that he expressed his hopes for his son and heir (who was presumably the king's godson):

I will that my son Edward be forthwith after my death be had to my lords of Gloucester and my Lord Chamberlain, heartly beseeching them as they will in my name beseech the king's good Grace that mine executors may have the wardship and marriage of my said son and my land, paying to the king 500 marks, which shall be delivered to them in money; and then I will beseech my lord of Gloucester that my said son Edward may be in the house of my Lord Chamberlain to he be of the age of 16 year, and then to be put at the king's pleasure . . . Item, it is my will that all the revenues growing of my lands, over the finding of my said son, shall be kept with my Lord Chamberlain, to buy for my said son a marriage with land.[116]

114. W. H. Dunham, 'Lord Hastings' Indentured Retainers, 1461–83', *Transactions of the Connecticut Academy of Art and Science* 39 (1955), 1–175; I. Rowney, 'The Hastings Affinity in Staffordshire and the Honour of Tutbury', *Bulletin of the Institute of Historical Research* 57 (1984), 35–45, and 'Resources and Retaining in Yorkist England: William Lord Hastings and the Honour of Tutbury', *Property and Politics*, ed. Pollard, pp. 139–55.
115. *The Crowland Chronicle Continuations: 1459–1486*, ed. and trans. N. Pronay and J. Cox (1986), p. 153.
116. *Testamenta Eboracensia*, iii (Surtees Society, 45) 1864, 238–41. Gloucester granted the boy's wardship and marriage, with £40 for his upkeep, to his retainer and the boy's uncle Charles Pilkington, the farm of the estates going to the boy's mother and her new husband Sir Thomas Wortley, Knight of the Body

At the end of the day, the point of view from which this proprietorial scheme of land and lordship made sense was that of the king himself. And on 9 April 1483 Edward IV unexpectedly died. Then, indeed, the absence of 'perfect love and rest among the lords of this land' entered into play – and precipitated the collapse of this court-country regime. On 13 June 1483 it was Sir John Pilkington's brother Charles (Usher of the Chamber to Edward IV) and his brother-in-law Sir Robert Harrington who carried out the putsch in which Richard of Gloucester put Lord Hastings to death and put Lord Stanley's fate in question.[117] That opened the way to the accomplishment of a power play which rapidly sent the house of York the way of the house of Usher.

Whether Richard might, in time, have succeeded in replacing his brother's scheme of rule by some variant of his own, we cannot tell, though no doubt that will not prevent us from trying. When in fact his time ran out in the summer of 1485, his regime was still essentially that localist, northern affinity which was his *damnosa hereditas* from his brother.[118] Yet 1483 is a centripetal political process. The rival locally-based interest groups literally converged on the capital for the crucial show-down in the spring; the so-called 'Buckingham's rebellion' which aborted in the autumn, despite its implication of that Stafford magnate never assimilated into Edward IV's scheme of things, was the backlash of 'court' rather than 'country' political forces whose association arose from their common identity as men of Edward IV's household. And 1485, when Richard's failure to fight down the heterogeneous coalition of his challengers perhaps resulted from the disintegration of even his own northern following, was in its turn a struggle for overall mastery. As such, it created for the Tudor court its *raison d'être*.

Retrospect: court and household

If politically the house of York contrived to immolate itself amidst

(E159/261, Brevia Directa, Michaelmas m. 11). Cf. J. Hunter, *South Yorkshire: the history and topography of the deanery of Doncaster* (2 vols 1828–31) II, pp. 311–14, 329.

117. D. Hay, *Polydore Vergil: Renaissance historian and man of letters* (Oxford, 1952), pp. 204–5.
118. On Richard III and his household, see in general C. Ross, *Richard III* (1981) and A. J. Polland, 'The Tyranny of Richard III', *Journal of Medieval History* 3 (1977), 147–65. We await the further enlightenment which will follow from the publication of R. Horrox, 'The Patronage of Richard III' (unpublished Cambridge Ph. D. dissertation, 1975).

the tensions of a pattern of court/country interplay which in 1483–85 collapsed into the internal haemorrhage of dynastic suicide, it bequeathed something more than just the *disiecta membra* of its household servants to be recycled into the regime of its Tudor successor. Its legacy comprised a complex of ideas and attitudes, as well as social habits and institutional forms, which had given 'the court' a new or at least an acutely intensified self-consciousness. The language of 'the court' is indeed already there at the outset of that sequence of descriptive and prescriptive writing which stretches from the 1440s through the period of civil war and is marked by the adoption of English as the public idiom. In the first of the household ordinances of those years, the regulations of 1445, the word 'court' does occur, but only glancingly; significantly, in the earliest English-Latin dictionary, the *Promptorium Parvulorum* of *c.*1440, 'court' figures only as the term equivalent to the much less specific 'curia'. But in the 1483 dictionary, the *Catholicon Anglicum*, there is added the term 'courtier' to convey the sense of 'curialis', and between whiles the new usage seems to catch on. By the time we reach the Black Book in the 1470s, its increasing currency is noticeable; and we may note its occurrence in other sorts of writing, such as John Somerset's deposition of 1450–2 or the letter of 1468 in which John Paston, attending the festivities in Bruges at the time of Charles of Burgundy's marriage to Margaret of York, and wishing in his letter back home to his mother to say something more than that it was all a cut above the home-life of the Norfolk gentry, ventured the thought that 'As for the duke's court, as of lords, ladies and gentlewomen, knights, squires and gentlemen, I heard never of none like it save King Arthur's court'.[119] In different vein is the phrase – perhaps proverbial, but perhaps more recently coined; at all events, now given wider vogue – included in the listing of collective terms which, at the start of the new enterprise of English printing, Caxton appended to his two editions of Lydgate's *The Horse, Sheep and Goose* in 1475–76, alongside such usages as 'a state of princes', 'a dignity of canons', '[a] boast of soldiers': '[a] threat of courtiers'.[120]

119. *Paston Letters*, ed. Davis, no. 330.
120. L. Hellinga, *Caxton in Focus: the beginning of printing in England* (1982), pp. 63–8 and 83 for the dating. Such lists are not infrequent and occur with many variants in several mid fifteenth-century commonplace books. This particular phrase is not in the list headed 'A little book of doctrine for young gentlemen' in Bodley, Rawlinson MS D.328, fo. 171–72, dated before 1445; but it does occur ('a threatening of courtiers') in the section headed 'Note the properties that longeth to a young gentleman to have knowing of . . ' in BL, Egerton MS 1995, fo.57v, written after 1470.

It is as we come to the end of the final, fraught generations of Plantagenet kingship that we find the word developing a particular connotation as a term of peculiar art, both in its ordinary usage and in literary typology. In 1479 the London Mercers admitted a young man to their company as shopholder only on condition 'that he sadly dispose him and mannerly both in his array and also in cutting of his hair, and not to go like a gallant or a man of court'.[121] In the 1480s – besides the incidental felicity of phrasing in one of his most lastingly popular works: 'Reynard the fox is now a squire and a courtier and right great and mighty in the court'[122] – Caxton put into circulation two works whose titles drew attention to the word as a vehicle of cultural expression. The first was the poem *The Court of Sapience*, printed 1480–83: a high-didactic exposition of science and received wisdom, written during the middle third of the fifteenth century and ascribed (not very convincingly) to a member of Edward IV's household.[123] The second, printed in the second half of 1483, was the prose epistle *The Curial*: Caxton's translation of the French version of Alain Chartier's treatise, written at the Valois court probably in the 1420s and becoming one of the two most influential fifteenth-century treatments of the distinctive and distasteful character of the courtier's way of life. In the political situation of the 1480s it is scarcely surprising that it was the critical and disabused note of *The Curial* rather than the conventional platitudes of *The Court of Sapience* which found a resonance as a *pièce d'occasion*:

The court, to the end that thou understand it, is a convent of people that under fantasy of common weal, assemble them together for to deceive each other . . . For among us of the court we be mechant and newfangle that we buy the other people. And sometime for their money we sell to them our humanity precious. We buy other, and other buy us. . . .[124]

121. *Acts of Court of the Mercers' Company, 1453–1527*, ed. L. Lyell (Cambridge 1936), p. 121.
122. *The History of Reynard the Fox*, ed. N. F. Blake (Early English Text Society, old series, 263) 1970, deemed by its editor 'our first printer's best-loved work'.
123. *The Court of Sapience*, ed. E. R. Harvey (Toronto 1984), who comments that the 'suggestion that the author of the *Court* was the author of the *Babees Book*, who might also have been the 'Master of the Henxmen' (well-born pages) of Edward IV, can be neither proved nor disproved' (p. xxiv).
124. *The Curial made by maystere Alain Charretier*, ed. F. J. Furnivall (Early English Text Society, extra series, 54) 1888. For the dating on typographical grounds to July–December 1483, see G. D. Painter, *William Caxton* (1976), pp. 130–1. Bodley, Rawlinson MS A.338 comprises fifteenth-century English translations of Chartier's *Quadrilogue* and *Curial*; appropriately, it was owned by Robert Dudley, earl of Leicester. Cf. P. M. Smith, *The Anti-Courtier Trend in Sixteenth-century French Literature* (Geneva 1966), pp. 13–54; C. Uhlig, *Hofkritik in England des Mittelalters und der Renaissance: Studien zu einem Gemeinplatz der europaischen*

A generation later, Alexander Barclay in his *Eclogues of the Miseries of Courtiers* put into English the other chief fifteenth-century contribution to this genre – Aeneas Sylvius's *De Curialium miseriis epistola* of 1444 – and by adding in further material from Mantuan's *Adolescentia seu Bucolica* (written largely before 1463) heightened the invidious 'topos' of court/country comparison in the pastoral mode already evoked in *The Curial*.[125] It proved (along with Skelton's *Bouge of Court* of *c*. 1498–99) to be the start of a literary disquisition on the court as an arena of the conflicts of morality which lasted as long as the court continued to enact its role as a political institution. Ironically, it would seem that the readers and writers of the anti-courtier literature were more often than not the courtiers themselves expressing their self-consciousness. And it is therefore fitting that, when both the politics and the culture of courtly life had run their course, it was Jane Austen who composed their epitaph: 'In my opinion, the service of a court can hardly be too well paid, for immense must be the sacrifice of time and feeling required by it.'[126]

Moralistik (Berlin 1973). Much of the content of these fifteenth-century works was far from new: see, for example, E. Třk, *Nugae Curialium: le règne d'Henri II Plantegenet (1145–89) et l'éthique politique* (Geneva, 1977).

Cf. P. M. Smith, *The Anti-Courtier Trend in Sixteenth-century French Literature* (Geneva 1966), pp. 13–54; C. Uhlig, *Hofkritik in England des Mittelalters und der Renaissance: Studien zu einem Gemeinplatz der europaischen Moralistik* (Berlin 1973). Much of the content of these fifteenth-century works was far from new: see, for example, E. Türk, *Nugae Curialium: le règne d'Henri II Plantegenet (1145–89) et l'éthique politique* (Geneva, 1977).

125. *The Eclogues of Alexander Barclay*, ed. B. White (Early English Text Society, old series 175) 1928.

126. *Jane Austen's Letters*, ed. R. W. Chapman (Oxford, 1932), no. 126: letter of 1 April 1816, to the Rev. James Clarke, librarian to the Prince Regent and chaplain to the Prince of Cobourg.

CHAPTER THREE

Intimacy and innovation: the rise of the Privy Chamber, 1485–1547

David Starkey

'Consider', Sir Thomas Cheyney was warned at an awkward stage of some marriage negotiations with Sir Anthony Denny in the 1540s, 'the man to be near about the king and so unmeet to be trifled or mocked with in any cause'.[1] Cheyney, privy councillor and lord warden of the Cinque Ports, was one of the great men of the kingdom,[2] but Denny was stronger still. As Groom of the Stool he was Henry VIII's most personal servant; as Chief Gentleman of the Privy Chamber he was head of the inmost department of the royal household. This made him 'near about', indeed nearest, the king, which in a personal monarchy was what mattered.

So nearness – intimacy – was the key to the Privy Chamber's importance. Almost as crucial though was its newness – innovation. By the 1540s Denny's main office, the Chief Gentlemanship, was only ten years old; the department itself had existed in its mature form for only twenty, and even its remotest origins only went back to the previous reign. Nevertheless, in this short time, the rise of the new department had transformed the organization of the royal household; refashioned the instruments of household government, and given birth to a centre of political power and initiative second only to the Council and above all to the principal councillor, Wolsey or Cromwell, himself.

1. SP1/245, fo. 160 (*LP* Addenda I ii, 1794).
2. *DNB*.

From distance to participation: the origins of the Privy Chamber,
1485–1518

'We will unite the white rose and the red', proclaims the triumphant
Richmond at the end of *Richard III*.[3] And that Henry VII's government was heir to the Yorkists has become almost a commonplace.
In his management of the household, however, the contrasts were
as strong as the continuities. Edward IV's own handling of the
household had been two-edged. His use of the household, both
politically and administratively, had been bold and innovatory, if
erratic; in terms of the household's internal organization, in contrast,
he had been conservative. The doubleness showed clearly in the
Black Book.[4] The packaging was dramatic, with rhetoric, excursuses
and antiquarianism all trumpeting the importance of the 'house of
houses principal of England in times of peace' in the king's scheme
of government.[5] On the other hand – and as the perpetual antiquarian appeals to the 'statutes of noble Edward III' themselves
suggest[6] – far from reforming, much less Burgundianizing, the
machinery of his domestic service, Edward had striven only to
restore and systematize it. He had succeeded, with the result that the
Black Book is an end not a beginning: the high-water mark of the
late medieval household and its two characteristic departments of the
Household and Chamber.

Of the two the Chamber, moralized by the Black Book as the
'Household of Magnificence',[7] was the more important. It was so
symbolically, as the most direct expression of the king's style and
personality; it was so in terms of power as well. Close always to the
source of power, the king himself, the Chamber had a major influence over patronage and an independent voice in politics; administratively too it was to the Chamber, not to the Household (despite
the latter's much more elaborate bureaucratic structure), that the
king usually turned for auxiliaries in those areas of government he
chose to undertake himself. In all these respects the Chamber, like
the household as a whole, had reached an apogee under the Yorkists.
Under Henry VII it retained its administrative importance: the
Treasurer of the Chamber advanced still further to become
paymaster of the whole royal finances; while the Secretary, who was

---

3. Shakespeare, *Richard III*, act V, scene 5.
4. A. R. Myers, *The Household of Edward IV* (Manchester 1959) and above p. 25.
5. Myers, *Household*, p. 86.
6. Ibid. pp. 136, 146, 148, etc.
7. Ibid. p. 86 and plate I.

also a member of the Chamber, remained a linchpin of government. Politically, though, the record is more uneven. The Chamber continued to play a major part in the management of the localities,[8] but its influence over central politics and the distribution of patronage diminished sharply. The explanation was intimacy, or rather the loss of intimacy, which Henry VII's style of kingship entailed.

The essence of this style, the most idiosyncratic of any king of England, was best understood by Francis Bacon, whose perceptions were sharpened by the problems of counselling James I, Henry's antithesis. 'It was', Bacon wrote, 'but keeping of distance, which indeed he did towards all'.[9] This attitude coloured the whole of Henry's government, but at court it led specifically to reform.

The background to the reforms was the slowly increasing comfort of the palace. At first the king's private apartment, the Chamber, had been just that: one room in which the king slept; ate most of his meals, and conducted most of his public business and all of his private. It was vast: at Westminster it was 80 feet long, 26 wide and more than 30 high and became the Parliament Chamber.[10] But for all its size it was still only a bedsit that struggled to contain too many conflicting functions. In the course of the fourteenth and fifteenth centuries, however, the one-room Chamber was replaced by a suite of three more-or-less specialized apartments. These were called, in the early-Tudor nomenclature, the Great or Guard Chamber, where the Guard stood (this is the only one of the Tudor sequence to survive at Hampton Court); the Presence Chamber, dominated by the throne and canopy, where the king dined in state, received important visitors, and met his Council; and finally the Privy Chamber, which was both the king's bedroom and his private dayroom. But despite the multiplication of rooms, there was no organizational change: the staff of the Chamber continued to serve the whole suite.

Then, in about 1495, as we know from a household ordinance whose text survives only in a reissue of 1526,[11] Henry VII took

8. Cf. Margaret Condon, 'Ruling elites in the Reign of Henry VII' in Charles Ross, ed., *Patronage, Pedigree and Power in Later Medieval England* (Gloucester 1979), p. 127.
9. Francis Bacon, *History of the Reign of King Henry VII*, ed. J. R. Lumby (Cambridge 1902), pp. 214–15.
10. J. Enoch Powell and Keith Wallis, *The House of Lords in the Middle Ages* (1968), p. 275.
11. College of Arms, Arundel MS XVII², dated by David Starkey, 'The King's Privy Chamber, 1485–1547 (unpublished Cambridge Ph. D. dissertation, 1973), 18 ff. and printed from an inferior MS in E. Jeffrey, ed., *The Antiquarian Repertory* (4 vols, 1807–09) II, p. 184 ff.

action: the Secret or Privy Chamber was separated from the other two Chambers and given its own staff. To them was transferred the entire responsibility for the king's private service; while the old Chamber was left only with the public ceremonial of the two outer Chambers. The contrast between the old and the new departments was great. The staff of the Chamber numbered hundreds and, at its upper levels, was socially distinguished, with knights and esquires, and a peer, the Lord Chamberlain, at its head. The Privy Chamber, on the other hand, was tiny, consisting of half a dozen Grooms under the Groom of the Stool, and it was humble: the Groom of the Stool was a mere gentleman and some of his subordinates were hardly even that.

Formally the change only brought England into line with France and Burgundy; it may indeed have been modelled on the former. In both the prince's closest personal attendants consisted of a group very like the English Privy Chamber: a handful of *valets* headed in France by the *premier valet*,[12] and in Burgundy by the *sommelier de corps*.[13] But England differed in two important respects. Unlike their continental equivalents, the Groom of the Stool and his subordinates were attached, exclusively, to one room which was forbidden to all others; moreover they were of distinctly lower status. The result was to cut England off not only from her own past but from other west-European monarchies as well. Instead Henry VII's private service resembled, by similarity of circumstance rather than imitation, the household of an Italian princeling. For many of the latter chose, as Castiglione puts it in his defence of the practice, to keep in their private chambers 'persons of little worth except in the matter of knowing how to give good personal service'[14] – just like Henry VII. This guaranteed them privacy; it was also, and this surely is what attracted Henry VII, an extremely effective way of 'keeping distance'.

Bacon had gone on to define the 'keeping of distance' as 'not admitting any near or full approach, either to his power or to his secrets'. And 'not admitting' was the *raison d'être* of the Privy Chamber with its strictly limited and jealously guarded right of *entrée* or access. The firmly closed door of the apartment protected the king physically from the court nobility and so morally from the

---

12. Olivier de la Marche, *Mémoires*, ed. H. Beaune and J. d'Arbaumont (4 vols, 1888) IV, p. 157 and cf. Pierre Champion, *Louis XI* (2 vols, 1928) I, p. 218.
13. de la Marche, op. cit. IV, pp. 15–16.
14. B. Castiglione, *The Book of the Courtier*, trans. George Bull (Harmondsworth 1967), p. 127.

constant, insidious pressure they could ordinarily bring to bear. That denied 'near or full approach . . . to his power'. Approach to 'his secrets' was similarly guarded against. In the narrow sense, since the new arrangements made it far easier to keep the unauthorized out of the Privy Chamber – the *arcana imperii*, where most private conversations took place and most confidential papers were kept (it was no accident that under Henry VII the more usual name for the room was the 'Secret Chamber'). And in the broader sense too, since, freed from the time-consuming ceremonial which the service of the socially distinguished inevitably entailed, Henry was able to devote himself to the long, lonely hours of toil over accounts and dispatches which gave him a more detailed knowledge of the operations of his government than any English king before or since. Armed with such knowledge, Henry needed councillors only as the agents of his will, not as advisers: the 'secrets' of his high policy were his alone, to be shared with none.[15]

Most historians of Henry's reign have described how the king's household ruled the kingdom; here on the other hand I have tried to suggest how the king ruled his household. The resulting tightness of royal control came at a crucial moment. Edward IV had built up the royal affinity, centred as always on his household, to new heights; the blood-letting of Richard III's reign had eliminated any noble rivals. Circumstances had ensured that Henry VII benefited from both achievements with the result that his court was, for the first time in generations, the sole centre of power. The most dangerous potential threats to the king, therefore, came not from without – from the rebellions and pretenders about which both Henry and his historians have worried too much – but from within – from divisions within his household and affinity. An act of 1487 addressed the problem directly. A jury of members of the royal household was empowered to enquire whether any household man, below the rank of peer, had conspired to murder the king, or any councillor, or the Steward, Treasurer or Controller of the Household. The act also made any such conspiracy a felony.[16]

The events of 1495 show that such precautions were necessary; they also help fit the Privy Chamber into the picture. The exact year that the Privy Chamber was established cannot be determined. But everything points to one year: 1495. In January, Sir William Stanley, the king's step-uncle, had been arraigned for treasonable communi-

15. Condon, 'Ruling Elites', p. 128.
16. A. Luders *et al.*, eds. *Statutes of the Realm* (11 vols, 1810–28) II, pp. 521–2; and cf. S. B. Chrimes, *Henry VII* (1972), p. 78.

cation with the pretender Perkin Warbeck. Stanley had played a decisive part in the victory at Bosworth; he was also Lord Chamberlain. At the same time, John, lord Fitzwalter, the Lord Steward and head of the Household-below-stairs, was also implicated in the affair.[17] So Henry had been betrayed by both head officers of his household: what more natural than to set up the new department of the Privy Chamber; staff it with nonentities who could not play politics even if they would, and retreat there to live and rule alone?

Henry's mother, Lady Margaret Beaufort, showed a similar determination to rule her household. Bishop Fisher praised her for drawing up 'reasonable statutes and ordinances' for her household, and having them read quarterly; for going out of her way 'lovingly [to en] courage' her officers to do well; and above all, for the 'great discretion' with which she put right 'any strife or controversy' among her servants. 'If any factions or bands were made secretly among her head officers', Fisher noted approvingly, 'she with great policy did bolt it out'.[18] 'Bolt' in this sense means 'sift'. But Margaret's son Henry went further and by setting up the Privy Chamber bolted out faction in the more ordinary meaning of the word. Normally the door of the room in which the king was present was kept by a Gentleman Usher, 'so it be not in his Council or in his Secret Chamber'. When Henry was in Council the Usher was 'to deliver the keeping of the said door to one of the lowest of his Council'; when he was in his Secret Chamber the Usher gave place 'to such one as he thinketh by his discretion should best content the king's mind and is accustomed thereto'.[19] That specially guarded door protected Henry not only from the pressure of individual courtiers; it was also a supremely effective barrier against the larger, more dangerous forces of faction.

But few institutional barriers are strong enough to resist the pressures of personality and circumstance. And these were soon brought dramatically to bear by a new reign. In April 1509 Henry VII died and the young Henry VIII came to the throne. He dismissed and executed two of his father's principal ministers; repudiated and reversed his fiscal policies and stood his style of kingship on its head.

The change showed most strikingly in court entertainments (the principal shop-window of monarchy). Henry VII had put on, when

---

17. Ibid. pp. 55, 58, 85, 138.
18. J. E. B. Mayer, ed., *The English Works of John Fisher* (Early English Text Society, extra series, 27) 1876, p. 296.
19. Jeffrey, *Antiquarian Repertory* II, p. 188.

necessary, splendid spectacles.[20] But, as part of his keeping of distance, he had never taken part in them. Instead, as Bacon again noticed, he was no more than 'a princely and gentle spectator'.[21] and, it could be added, a remote one.[22] This was not good enough for the young Henry. He chafed at the bit for the first eight months of the reign; then broke free. In January 1510 a tournament was held at Richmond, to which two knights turned up *incognito* and won great praise by their prowess. One, however, was 'hurt sore and like to die'. Whereupon 'one person there was, that knew the king, and cried "God save the king"'. And indeed the uninjured stranger-knight turned out to be Henry VIII.[23] The taboo on royal participation thus broken, even at some cost, Henry was unstoppable and became the star of a dazzling sequence of tournaments and revels that made England the Hollywood of Europe and Henry the *jeune premier* of Christendom.

Contemporaries were dazzled by the splendour of these spectacles;[24] modern historians have discussed their significance as propaganda.[25] But their real importance is simpler: they were social events, which in personal monarchy meant that they were political too. A king, like Henry VIII, who gave and received hard blows in the lists and took part in the public and only lightly ritualized love-making of the revel, had a quite different kind of relationship with his court and nobility from one like Henry VII. The father's was a kingship of distance; the son's was, in the word Henry IV flings at Prince Hal, a kingship of 'participation', which, like his namesake, led him to 'stand the push of every beardless vain comparative' and grow 'a companion to the common streets'.[26] So two languages for two types of kingship: Henry VII's 'distance' created splendid isolation; Henry VIII's 'participation', good fellowship, boon companions, friends and favourites.

The power of intimacy thus revived, the question was how would it be manifested. The first straw in the wind of change came in the Richmond tournament itself. Then Henry had chosen as his sole

20. Sydney Anglo, *Spectacle, Pageantry and Early Tudor Policy* (Oxford 1969), pp. 1–107 *passim*.
21. Bacon, *Henry VII*, p. 210.
22. Cf. Richard Marks and Anne Payne, *British Heraldry, from its origins to c. 1800* (catalogue of an exhibition at the British Museum, 1978), no. 62 and plate.
23. E. Hall, *The Union of the Two Noble and Illustre Families of Lancaster and York* [The Chronicle] (1809), p. 513.
24. Cf. ibid. pp. 513–14.
25. Anglo, *Spectacle*, *passim*.
26. Shakespeare, *Henry IV: Part 1*, act III, scene 2.

companion and confidant in the escapade William Compton. Compton was a leading *privado* or favourite,[27] who was important both politically (receiving large foreign pensions)[28] and personally (managing Henry's various love affairs);[29] he was also Groom of the Stool and head of the Privy Chamber.[30]

The contrast between Compton and Hugh Denys, his colourless, hard-working predecessor under Henry VII, is striking. Compton's appointment becomes even more surprising when the origins of the Groomship are traced. These go back beyond the Privy Chamber's own. In the middle ages the normal form of sanitation was an open shaft cut into the thickness of the wall and venting directly into the moat. It usual name was the 'draught', which well conveys one of its drawbacks. In the fifteenth century a more comfortable device became general: the close-stool, which the *Oxford English Dictionary* defines as 'a chamber utensil enclosed in a stool or box'. The vessel was made of pewter; while the stool could be elaborately upholstered and trimmed (a handsome seventeenth-century specimen stands in William III's State Bedchamber at Hampton Court). The habit was for every major item of royal equipment – the king's books, his bows, his 'beast' – to be given a keeper.[31] At first the close-stool was entrusted to a Yeoman and William Grimsby, Yeoman of the Stool to Henry VI, was an important figure in the extreme Lancastrian court party of the 1450s.[32] Sometime later its custody was transferred to the Groom. But the Groom was not simply in charge of the close-stool; he also waited on the king while he relieved himself on it – like Thomas Heneage in the 1520s who had to be available 'to give attendance upon the king's Highness when he goeth to make water in his Bedchamber'.[33] And with the setting up of the Privy Chamber the Groom's responsibilities multiplied. He became the principal royal body servant, who waited on the king when he ate, when he got up and went to bed, and at all other times both within the palace and (usually) without. He was in charge of the staff of the Privy Chamber and its equipment – the royal linen and the king's everyday clothes, jewels and plate. Finally, as we shall see, he acquired important administrative responsibilities.

27. *LP* I i, 474.
28. *LP* I i, 734; ii, 3502; III i, 1321/iii.
29. *LP* I i, 474.
30. *LP* I i, 94/27.
31. Myers, *Household*, p. 116.
32. J. C. Wedgewood and A. D. Holt, *Biographies of the Members of the House of Commons, 1439–1509* (2 vols, 1936–8) II, pp. 400–1.
33. SP1/47, fos. 56–7 (*LP* IV ii, 4005).

So clearly, despite its origins and previous occupant, the Groom-ship of the Stool was an office that could be made big enough to take a man even of Compton's pretensions. The same was not true, however, of any other office in the department. The result was that Compton was the only court favourite of the first years of the reign to enter the Privy Chamber. The rest held a miscellany of posts and in any case did not survive long: some were killed in the French war and the others were elbowed aside first by the ascendant Wolsey and later by the rise of a new group of favourites.

The new favourites, like the old, were creations of the joust. Their first appearance came in April 1515, when Henry, 'delighting to set forth young gentlemen', sponsored a tournament in which the two most important and founder members of the group – the brothers-in-law Nicholas Carew and Francis Bryan – were the stars.[34] And their final hold over the king was proclaimed in the great jousts of July 1517, in which Carew again was the principal attraction as the 'Blue Knight', while he and his friends made up the bulk of the king's team or 'band'.[35] Even twenty years on, at the height of his power, Carew had himself painted by Holbein in the pose and armour of the jouster he had been when he first made a mark at court.[36]

But the picture necessarily omits the other and decisive quality which had captured the king: his youth. In 1515 Carew was still under twenty and the rest were of an age.[37] Their youthfulness is emphasized in Hall's account of the *début* joust of 1515; it even gave them their name. They were universally known as the king's 'minions', which is most politely to be translated as 'pretty boys'.[38] It is of course difficult to imagine that the hard and shifty men who appear in Holbein's great sequence of drawings of Henry VIII's cour-

34. Hall, *Chronicle*, p. 581.
35. R. L. Brown, ed., *Four Years at the Court of Henry VIII* (2 vols, 1854) II, p. 101; *LP* II ii, p. 1510.
36. John Rowlands, *Holbein: The Paintings of Hans Holbein the Younger* (Oxford 1985), no. R. 25, where the authenticity of the painting, though not the prep-aratory drawing (also in armour), is rejected.
37. S. T. Bindoff, ed., *The History of Parliament: The House of Commons, 1509–1558* (3 vols, 1982) I, p. 578, would put Carew at 19. Wolsey, however, wrote in 1517 that Carew was of Henry VIII's 'own bringing up', which would suggest that he was considerably younger. Similarly, Bryan's own *Dispraise of the Life of a Courtier* (1548) assumed that the courtier had come to court 'very young' (sig. n i(v), or elsewhere at the 'first time of knowledge, which is 15 years' (sig. i iii(v)–iv).
38. Hall, *Chronicle*, p. 598; BL, Cotton MS Caligula D VII, fos. 121–2 (*LP* III i, 246).

tiers were ever young, still less pretty. But the recently discovered portrait of one of the minions, William Carey, does convey with its fresh flesh tints, half smile and jaunty quarter profile the fine insouciant youthfulness of this court generation.[39]

Why this so attracted the king is easily guessed. By 1515 Henry, the erstwhile *jeune premier* of Christendom, was approaching the threshold of Tudor middle age. Naturally he did not like it. Neither his minister Wolsey, at forty, nor his first group of court favourites, most of whom were in their forties also, could offer much consolation.[40] So he turned elsewhere, to the minions, who could. Together the king and his new favourites formed a recognizable youth sub-culture at court. It was characterized, as most are, by an addiction to sport; mild delinquency like snowball throwing;[41] and occasional gestures of cosmic defiance at the inevitable, like the masque of 1519 whose decorations boasted in an execrable visual pun 'that the flower of youth could not be oppressed'.[42]

Within this sub-culture hierarchy was brushed aside. The minions, 'not regarding [Henry's] estate or degree, were so familiar and homely with him and played such light touches with him that they forgot themselves'. Which the king in his turn 'suffered and not rebuked nor reproved'.[43] Distance was lost totally. Instead there was an intimacy that took the minions into the king's bosom – they were 'his very soul'[44] – and into the Privy Chamber as well. There a change came over their position. No longer did they merely divert the king's leisure hours; they also began to act as his body servants. Carew, in particular, behaved almost as a regular member of the inner royal household: he bought goods for the king; kept part of the royal plate, and appeared on official lists of the royal establishment.[45] Indeed in 1511 at the very beginning of his court career he had actually been made a Groom of the Privy Chamber. But in the list of Grooms another hand has inserted the word 'Gentleman' after his name by a scribbled interlineation and a caret – clearly to distinguish the young favourite from his workaday colleagues.[46]

---

39. *The Renaissance at Sutton Place* [ed. Ben Shephard] (exhibition catalogue) Guildford 1983, no. 22.
40. Cf. G. R. Elton, *Reform and Reformation* (1977), p. 47.
41. E36/218, fo. 10v (*LP* III i, 152).
42. Hall, *Chronicle*, p. 597.
43. Ibid. p. 598.
44. Brown, *Court of Henry VIII* II, pp. 269 ff. (*LP* III i, 235).
45. *LP* II ii, p. 1477; BL Royal MS 7 C XVI, fo. 68; HMC, *Duke of Rutland MSS* I, 21–2.
46. BL, Additional MS 18, 826, fo. 21 (*LP* I i, 771).

Office and occupant were ill-matched (it was only Carew's extreme youth which had made the appointment at all feasible) and within a year he had abandoned the post. With the other minions, of whom all like Carew had been born with silver spoons in their mouths, the experiment was not even tried. A peer (Devon)[47], or the son of a peer (Edward Neville)[48] or the offspring of knightly families with a tradition of royal service (Carew himself, Bryan, Henry Guildford or William Carey, who had more than a dash of Beaufort blood in his veins)[49] could not be made Grooms, whose duties still included, in theory, the cleaning of the apartment; the putting up and taking down of trestle tables and the bearing of torches.[50]

This problem, which had earlier prevented the entry of the first group of royal favourites into the Privy Chamber, had also affected the court of France. There the title of the king's body servants, *valet de chambre*, had begun as a respectable rank, but already it was on its way down to its modern meaning. Against this background Francis I had come to the throne in 1515. Even younger than Henry VIII and just as dashing, he had quickly built up a similar circle of high-born favourites and boon companions. They too were called minions. But, unlike England, the structure of the royal household was promptly altered to accommodate them. The king's body service was transferred from the valets to the holders of the new post of *gentilhomme de la chambre*. The title was high-flown enough to satisfy the proudest and, as had been the intention all along, Francis's minions were appointed to it *en masse*.[51]

At first, despite the appositeness of the precedent, none of this mattered much as relations between England and France were strained to the point of war. Then in 1518 overtures for peace were made and in September a great French embassy came to London. Prominent in its train were Francis I's leading *gentilshommes de la chambre*. Their arrival presented the English government with a nice problem of precedence. Obviously the *gentilshommes* should be paired off in processions and the like with Henry's own minions. The latter, however, held no formal office and so could not claim equality of status with their French counterparts. The problem was solved at

47. G. E. C[okayne], *The Complete Peerage*, new edition revised by V. Gibbs and later H. A. Doubleday (13 vols, 1910–49), *sub. tit.*
48. *DNB*.
49. Bindoff, *House of Commons*; 'Cary: Viscounts Falkland', *Herald and Genealogist* 3 (1868), 39.
50. Jeffrey, *Antiquarian Repertory* II, p. 202 ff.
51. R. J. Knecht, *Francis I* (Cambridge 1982), pp. 89–90.

a stroke by borrowing the French post of *gentilhomme de la chambre* for the English household and appointing the English minions to it in a body. Again, like the rise of the minions itself, the fact was announced in court ceremonial. For on 23 September, at the first *entrée* of the French embassy into London, the six freshly created English *gentilshommes de la chambre* rode under their new title two-by-two with their French namesakes.[52] At first the name of the new post remained as French as its origins, which in a still partly bilingual court presented few difficulties. But, in the course of the next few years and after a few false starts, the definitive English form of 'Gentleman of the Privy Chamber' entered the language.[53]

With even its name uncertain to begin with, the establishment of the new post was as unplanned and contingent as could be. Nevertheless it was crucial, fulfilling what Compton's appointment as Groom of the Stool had promised and bringing the organization of the king's personal service fully into line with his life style. In so doing it completed, almost a decade after his death, the erosion of Henry VII's kingship. The innovations of *c.* 1495 had created a Secret Chamber which institutionalized distance; those of 1518 reshaped the Privy Chamber into an institutionalization of intimacy.

And this intimacy is the key to the Privy Chamber's importance in government, administration and politics.

Representation through intimacy: the privy chamber and government

Governments are like the dinosaur: they have difficulty in communicating between their head and their extremities. The problem is universal, but it was made worse for late medieval English government by two facts. First, there was no local bureaucracy whatever and local government instead was in the hands of unpaid gentry commissioners, whose prime loyalties were to their own neighbourhoods and their own class. And second, there was a very undeveloped notion of delegation. Or, as Hugh Latimer put it, too many would say, '"When the king's Majesty himself commandeth me to do so, then I will do it, not afore"'.[54] This Latimer condemned flatly as 'a wicked saying', and indeed the preaching of

---

52. BL, Harley MS 433, fos. 294v–5 (*LP* II ii, 4409); Hall, *Chronicle*, pp. 593–4.
53. SP1/17, fo. 145 (*LP* II ii, 4512); SP1/25, fo. 286 (*LP* III ii, 2374).
54. Cited in D. Loades, *The Oxford Martyrs* (1970), pp. 68–9.

political obedience under the threat of eternal damnation was one way of coping with the problem. But there were more direct methods as well. Edward IV, faced with acute domestic crisis, used his own person and went on judicial tours of particularly badly affected areas.[55] Or other members of the royal family could be used to head regional councils, like the Princess Mary in the Marches of Wales in the late 1520s or Henry VIII's bastard son, the duke of Richmond, in the North at the same time.[56] More and more, however, Henrician government applied a common solution to the whole range of difficulties: the sending of a Gentleman of the Privy Chamber.

This had a double aspect. From the king's point of view it was largely a question of confidence: if he could not rely absolutely on his most intimate servants, whom could he trust? From the point of view of the king's subjects the matter was more complex, even mystical, and is best understood by the doctrine of 'representation through intimacy'.[57] The foundation of this was that the Privy Chamber, uniquely, served both of the 'two bodies' that contemporary lawyers and theorists distinguished as making up the entity of 'king'. As the royal domestics, they attended on the king's personal, physical body; but as men of high birth and distinction they were also servants of the king in his other, public capacity as the embodiment of the 'body politic' or the state itself. The first, intimate attendance, meant that they were both feared and respected. Feared, as men 'near about the king', who could exercise profound influence over him; and respected, as men on whom, through perpetual intimate contact with the king's person, something of the magic and majesty of kingship had rubbed off. While the second, public standing, meant that they could deploy the power of intimacy on the stage of events.

Put thus in the abstract the idea is perhaps elusive. It will become clearer in the practice. The most direct use of the Gentlemen was as special messengers to embody the king's absolute will that would not brook nay: their mere word and presence were enough, without any form of written authority, to set the machinery of patronage in motion;[58] to command a queen, Catherine of Aragon, to surrender

---

55. J. R. Lander, *Conflict and Stability in Fifteenth-Century England* (1969), p. 102.
56. G. R. Elton, *The Tudor Constitution* (Cambridge 1962), pp. 197–8.
57. This is fully discussed in David Starkey, 'Representation through Intimacy' in Ioan Lewis, ed., *Symbols and Sentiments* (1977).
58. *LP* XV, 436/40 and 942/121.

her jewels to the king's mistress, Anne Boleyn;[59] or, as Wolsey was to discover to his cost, to arrest the greatest subject of the realm.[60]

More interesting and more important than their use as simple vehicles of the royal will was their employment as agents of royal policy : in diplomacy, military affairs and local government. In the early sixteenth century the preferred form of diplomacy was the summit conference, like the Field of Cloth of Gold. By their very nature, though, such events were too infrequent to act as the normal channel of foreign relations. The alternative, and a very effective one, was 'Chamber diplomacy'. This had for its foundation the remarkable structural similarity of Renaissance courts. As we have seen, England had imitated Francis I's reform of his household in 1518, and Charles V followed suit at about the same time. The result was that by 1520 the monarch's private service was organized in the same way in the three great courts of western Europe: it was performed by men of similar background, functions and status and all called by some variation of the name 'gentleman'. They were not kings but they were, literally, the nearest things.

The diplomatic consequences were realized immediately. In August 1520, less than two years after the Privy Chamber reforms of 1518 and in the immediate aftermath of the Field of Cloth of Gold, Henry VIII dispatched a new ambassador to France. His instructions ordered him to thank Francis for 'his comfortable words and pleasant messages', sent 'as well by letters of his own hand as by sundry of his familiar servitors of his Privy Chamber'. Then he was to explain that 'for *réciproque* his Highness hath sent [himself], Sir Richard Jerningham, being of his Secret and Privy Chamber'. And, to underscore the novelty and importance of this exchange of Gentlemen of the Privy Chamber, the references to the French and English Privy Chambers were inserted at a late stage of drafting, to correct the vagueness of the original text.[61] Jerningham in fact was only the second of such Privy Chamber ambassadors, though the first whose position was spelled out so clearly. His predecessor was Sir Richard Wingfield, also of the Privy Chamber, as were most of his successors.[62] And even when they were not, like Sir William Fitzwilliam, Francis I showed an embarrassing tendency to treat them as though they were.[63] The result was that within about five

59. PRO 31/18/2/1 (*LP* V, 1377).
60. R. S. Sylvester and D. P. Harding, eds, *Two Early Tudor Lives* (1962), p. 160.
61. SP1/21, fos. 20–7 (*LP* III i, 936).
62. Cf. Starkey, 'Representation', p. 202.
63. BL, Cotton MS Caligula D VIII, fos. 24–5 (*LP* III i, 1202).

years diplomatic service was seen as as much a part of a Gentleman's job as the monarch's domestic service, of which, as I have argued, it was a symbolic extension. The point was spelled out in the Eltham Ordinances of January 1526, which noted that of the six Gentlemen of the Privy Chamber, 'divers be well-languaged, expert in outward parts, and meet and able to be sent on familiar messages, or otherwise, to outward princes, when the case shall require'.[64]

Which is not to say that Chamber diplomacy simply took over. Instead, characteristically, there were double embassies, in which a Gentleman would be paired with more traditional types of envoy, like ecclesiastics or canon lawyers. The actual balance of diplomatic skills on such joint embassies depended on the accident of both personalities and circumstances. Some Gentlemen were just about capable of bearing a present and cutting a fine figure; others developed an impressive expertise. The different types of ambassador could also be directed at different targets. Lawyers and churchmen could wheel and deal in latin with ministers; while Gentlemen could strike up direct rapport in the vernacular with the no less influential royal favourites. On balance, however, it is clear that the symbolic role of Chamber ambassadors was uppermost. But then symbolism, as a glance at any modern embassy building will show, has always been crucial in diplomacy.

On the other hand, whether symbols or negotiators, their importance was more than diplomatic. Chamber ambassadors were treated differently from other diplomats. When an English Gentlemen of the Privy Chamber went to France, or vice versa, he would be welcomed into the host king's Privy Chamber. There he would perform the same intimate tasks of body service as he did to his own master and mix on the same close terms with its servants as he did with his colleagues of his own king's Privy Chamber. The upshot was a kind of exchange of nationalities, so that Charles de Solier, who had first come to England as a young minion in 1518,[65] actually looked 1ike an Englishman when he was painted by Holbein on another embassy here in 1534;[66] while, on the other hand, boyish Anthony Browne, painted on or soon after an extended stay in France in 1518–19, is the very image of a Frenchman *à la Clouet*.[67] Browne's relations with his second country turned sour,[68] but most

---

64. *HO*, 155.
65. BL, Harley MS 433, fos. 294v–5 (*LP* II ii, 4409).
66. Rowlands, *Holbein*, no. 53.
67. *LP* III i, 111, 246; *English Portrait: Tudor to Georgian*, (catalogue of an exhibition in the Sabin Gallery, 1976), no. l.
68. *LP* XIII ii, 641.

others seem to have preserved close and affectionate ties even across the gulf of war.[69] These ties were important culturally as well as politically and in England acted as vehicles for the importation of both the Renaissance and Reformation.[70] For even Browne, despite his eventual Francophobia, is buried in a tomb which is a product of French Renaissance taste at its most opulent.[71]

The other area of government which concerned a king most directly was the continuation of diplomacy by other means: war. Henry VIII in fact led his armies into battle in person no more frequently than he held summit conferences with his fellow kings. Instead his role was divided between two groups of men. His place as overall commander went to great nobles, like the dukes of Norfolk and Suffolk; his task as cheer-leader and morale-booster was impersonated by Gentlemen of the Privy Chamber, who, though only in the second rank militarily, were nevertheless of crucial importance. This is shown clearly by the earl of Surrey's appeal in October 1523. Almost overwhelmed by the Scots and the weather, he begged for the dispatch of 'some noblemen and gentlemen of the king's house . . . though they bring no great numbers with them'.[72] So it was not a question of material reinforcement, but of the exemplary, even symbolic, effect which the presence of the Privy Chamber had on the army, for generals and private soldiers alike. Hence the fact that the department was strongly represented on every major expedition, by sea as well as on land. 'Many . . . of the king's Privy Chamber' were involved in the amphibious attack on Morlaix in 1522;[73] three of the most important of the Privy Chamber (including Compton, the Groom of the Stool) had originally accompanied Surrey north in spring 1523,[74] and in response to his later call for help the two Gentlemen who were closest to Henry of all, Carew and Bryan, were sent to join him.[75] The Privy Chamber was equally active later in the reign: against the Pilgrimage of Grace

69. *LP* IV i, 335.
70. Cf. Anthony Blunt, 'L'influence française sur l'architecture et la sculpture decorative en Angleterre pendant la première moitié du XVIᵉ siècle', *Revue de l'Art* 4 (1964), 17 ff; Knecht, *Francis I*, p. 263; John Rowlands and David Starkey, 'An old tradition reasserted: Holbein's portrait of Queen Anne Boleyn', *The Burlington Magazine* (1983), 88–92.
71. I. Nairn and N. Pevsner, *The Buildings of England: Sussex* (Harmondsworth 1965), p. 408.
72. H. Ellis, ed., *Original Letters Illustrative of English History* (11 vols, 1824–46) I, pp. 223–7 (*LP* III ii, 3405).
73. Hall, *Chronicle*, p. 641.
74. *LP* III ii, 3360.
75. *LP* III ii, 3434.

of 1536 and on the Boulogne expedition of 1544.[76]

Furthermore, despite Surrey's emphasis on the symbolic rather than the practical role of the Privy Chamber, their actual military strength was substantial. Not a few were great landowners, by inheritance or royal grant; more held stewardships of royal or ecclesiastical lands. And in the early sixteenth century the ownership or stewardship of land conferred the right to lead the men who lived on the land into battle. Indeed with stewardships this right, the 'manrede', was often the most valuable perquisite: as in the case of the stewardship of Winchcomb Abbey, where the fee of only £5 p.a. was far outweighed by the 'pretty manrede' of two or three hundred men.[77] Some of the Privy Chamber built up great concentrations of such stewardships: like Compton, who obtained about twenty in the first four years of the reign,[78] or Henry Norris, his successor as Groom of the Stool.[79] Their aim was military power: Norris valued 'the stipend' of a stewardship in the gift of the bishop of Salisbury 'not. . . at all . . . but the sovereignty and leading of the men'.[80] And the rights thus acquired were defended jealously: in May 1513 Compton procured royal letters patent addressed to the tenants of all manors where he was steward commanding any who had been retained to other men 'to desist and leave off the same'.[81] The result was that he was able to muster 578 men for Henry VIII's invasion of France later that year (only one less than all the rest of the Chamber put together) and to go on to win glory and his knighthood in the Battle of the Spurs.[82] Nor was Compton alone. Carew and Cheyney could each muster two hundred men against the Pilgrims in 1536;[83] while Anthony Denny, Henry VIII's last Groom of the Stool, was just as anxious as Compton would have been to slap down the J.P.'s of Middlesex when they ventured to encroach on his right as steward of Westminster to muster the inhabitants.[84]

James Rufforth, the man who handled Denny's side of the dispute, was his servant and deputy as Keeper of the Palace of West-

---

76. *LP* XI, 580; XIX i, 275.
77. *LP* XIII i, 505.
78. Listed in G. W. Bernard, 'The rise of Sir William Compton, early Tudor courtier', *EHR* 96 (1981), 759–61.
79. *LP* X, 878/ii.
80. SP1/104, fo. 67 (*LP* X, 986), and see the useful discussion in Felicity Heal, *Of Prelates and Princes* (Cambridge 1980), p. 37.
81. *LP* I ii, 1948/73.
82. *LP* I ii, 2053/2, 2301.
83. *LP* XI, 580.
84. *LP* XX ii, appendix 34, 35 and cf. *LP* XXI i, 108.

minster.[85] The office was scarcely a martial one and his involvement is symptomatic of the militarization of the whole Privy Chamber establishment in the prolonged warfare of the 1540s. Between 1541 and 1545 at least eight licences to retain were given to members of the Privy Chamber. The grantees were empowered to retain between ten and forty men, above and beyond their household servants, and give them 'livery and cognizance'.[86] Those involved were hardly a representative sample of the department. Three were Seymour adherents; another three were the key figures in the Denny faction; while Sir Ralph Sadler was Cromwell's most distinguished court appointment and William Herbert was Catherine Parr's brother-in-law. All in short were to be members of the alliance of the 'new' that swept to power in Henry VIII's last months (below, p. 116); of the still powerful conservative grouping in the Privy Chamber there was not a single representative.

Too much perhaps should not be read into this. The 'new' were new men indeed. They needed the prestige retainers could give while the surviving Gentlemen of an earlier generation were established enough not to bother. Maybe. On the other hand, the evident zest with which the 'new' men took to their military role is noteworthy. Sir Edward Neville, a Gentleman of the old school (and old family) had sneered at his new colleagues as 'a sort of knaves' that made life in the Privy Chamber unbearable.[87] Yet within a few years Sir Philip Hoby (of an obscure Welsh family) had emerged as the most effective commander of the foreign mercenaries on which the government increasingly relied to stiffen its own forces;[88] while Sir Peter Mewtis (grandson of Henry VII's French Secretary) had become the acknowledged expert in hand guns.[89] Mewtis in fact was the authentic man of action: he was 'quite tall and strongly built, and wears his beard somewhat long, well-trimmed and blond'.[90] In 1537 he 'was sent oversea to slay the Cardinal Pole with handgun';[91] while

---

85. *LP* XX i, 1244.
86. *LP* XVI, 1135/14; XVII, 714/21, 1012/9; XIX i, 80/51; XX i, 282/32, 418/48; XX ii, 910/51, 1068/47.
87. SP1/138, fos. 219–20 (*LP* XIII ii, 804/7).
88. The genealogy's claim that the Hobys were 'one of the three families that in times past hath been of greatest fame and authority in Radnorland' really amounts to very little. 'Hoby Pedigree', *Miscellanea Genealogica et Heraldica* 1 (1868), 143; *LP* XX i, 59, 106 *et seq.*
89. W. B. Bannerman, ed., *The Visitations of the County of Surrey* (Harleian Society, 43) 1899, p. 76 ff.; *LP* XII ii, 617/10; XVIII i, 630 *et seq.*
90. G. Lefèvre-Pontalis, *Correspondance Politique d'Odet de Selve* (1888) no. 43 (*LP* XXI ii, 259).
91. SP1/138, fo. 224 (*LP* XIII ii, 804/III).

in 1546 he spent a month as a spy in Normandy, undetected since his perfect French enabled him to pass himself off as a native.[92] Cromwell, in our historiography, is the bureaucrat minister, and his appointees, in the earl of Surrey's phrase, 'catchpoles' and 'civilians'.[93] It is worth remembering, however, that Cromwell started his career as a soldier of fortune; that in politics he ever preferred the bold stroke and in personal relations the bold, even rash, man. And certainly his Privy Chamber appointments would bear this out.

But the militarization of the Privy Chamber was institutional as well. Once again it starts with Cromwell and the setting up of the band of Gentlemen Pensioners as part of the household reforms of 1539–40. The Band, an extravagantly equipped bodyguard of fifty spears, is the subject of dismissive remarks by Professor Elton. It 'existed largely for display'; it 'offered splendid chances of promotion to young men of good family'; otherwise 'it was altogether a surprisingly useless and spendthrift arrangement for which the king may have been largely responsible'.[94] In fact the setting up of the Band was the first of a series of measures which in the next few years made the Privy Chamber one of the military powerhouses of the kingdom.

The Pensioners, resplendent in their gold chains and gilt pole axes, stood outside the Privy Chamber in the Presence Chamber, but their Captain, Sir Anthony Browne, was one of the senior Gentleman.[95] Four years later, as a preliminary to the Boulogne campaign, another and still larger guard of two hundred gentlemen-at-arms was raised.[96] Once again the commanders were drawn from the Privy Chamber. The Lieutenant, or second-in-command, was Sir Thomas Darcy, a Seymour cousin and more distant connection of Denny and John Gates;[97] while the Captain was William, brother of Catherine Parr and earl of Essex, who sat to Holbein in what may have been his ceremonial dress.[98] The gentlemen-at-arms were

92. See note 91.
93. M. A. S. Hume, trans., *Chronicle of King Henry VIII of England* (1889), p. 147.
94. G. R. Elton, *The Tudor Revolution in Government* (Cambridge 1953), pp. 387–8.
95. Cf. W. J. Tighe, 'The Gentlemen Pensioners in Elizabethan Politics and Government' (unpublished Cambridge Ph. D. dissertation, 1984), pp. 15–18.
96. Ibid. p. 18.
97. *LP* XIX ii, 524/I i (13). The link in both cases was through the Wentworths of Nettlestead: W. C. Metcalfe, ed., *The Visitations of Essex by Hawley, 1552 . . .* (2 vols, Harleian Society, 13–14) 1878–79, I, pp. 44–5, 225; II, p. 574.
98. *LP* XIX ii, 524/IV ii (1); K. T. Parker, *The Drawings of Hans Holbein* (1945), no. 57; J. Nevinson, 'Portraits of Gentlemen Pensioners before 1625', *Walpole Society* 34 (1958), 1–13 confuses Parr's office.

quickly reduced from their wartime level, but still numbered forty-four at Henry VIII's funeral.[99] Darcy, the Lieutenant, was a military pluralist, and succeeded John Dudley, lord Lisle (and also a Gentleman of the Privy Chamber) as Master of the Armoury in June 1544 at the start of the Boulogne campaign;[100] while the head of the other main munitions department, the Ordnance, was yet another Gentleman, Sir Thomas Seymour, who was appointed a few months earlier in autumn 1543 as the preparations for the campaign hotted up.[101] And it was of course in the Boulogne campaign itself that the Privy Chamber's military strength was most forcibly displayed. Many of its most important members were also councillors and mustered with the Council; even so the department formed a small army-within-an-army on the Boulogne expedition of 450 horse and 2,500 foot.[102]

It is important to get these figures in perspective. The musters taken for the Boulogne campaign show that the earl of Arundel, for instance, could raise at least 1,272 'able men', including 106 household servants. But some leading figures in the Privy Chamber could rival or even exceed these numbers *on their own*: John, lord Russell mustered 100 horse and 1,200 foot; William Parr, earl of Essex, 400 men and even knights like Sir Thomas Cheyney and Sir Anthony Browne, 300 horse and 500 foot. Collectively, therefore, even the magnate of the most ancient and distinguished lineage was dwarfed by the Privy Chamber; moreover, it is striking that whereas Arundel was required to field only 60 of his horse, Browne captained 300.[103] 'The Tudor king himself was the lord who had by far the largest number of retainers and who set the pace for the peerage'.[104] The military record of the later Henrician Privy Chamber amply confirms W. H. Dunham's dictum; it also shows that it was the Gentlemen who took over from the moribund king's knights as the key members of the royal entourage.

So the Privy Chamber were crucial to the Tudors' military power; they were also the shock troops of local government. Almost all held the key county office of J. P., and many of the more prestigious regional posts went their way as well. The lord wardenship of the Cinque Ports was held successively by two Gentlemen of the Privy

99. Tighe, 'Gentlemen Pensioners', p. 18.
100. *LP* XIX i, 812/30.
101. *LP* XIX i, 442.
102. *LP* XIX i, 275/I i, 4.
103. Loc. cit. *passim.*
104. W. H. Dunham, 'Lord Hastings' Indentured Retainers, 1461–1483' *Transactions of the Connecticut Academy of Arts and Sciences* 39 (1955), 107.

Chamber, George, viscount Rochford and Sir Thomas Cheyney;[105] The lord presidency of the Council of the West by another, John, lord Russell;[106] the chamberlainships of North Wales and Chester respectively by two more, Henry Norris and William Brereton;[107] while Compton was succeeded in his life sheriffwick of Worcestershire, as in his wife, by his colleague Sir Walter Walsh.[108] At least four of the resulting spheres of influence have been studied: Russell, appointed in the wake of the attainder of the West's greatest magnate, the marquess of Exeter who was also of the Privy Chamber, set himself to win hearts and minds;[109] on the other hand, Compton was oppressive and greedy;[110] while Brereton and Sir Richard Clement, a former Groom of Henry VII's Secret Chamber who eventually retired to Kent, too often behaved as mere gangsters.[111] But though their conduct differed their loyalty to the dynasty did not: they wore the king's livery chain, as Compton's battered tomb-effigy still does;[112] and they decorated their houses with the royal badges which still appear everywhere at Compton Wynyates or Clement's Ightham Mote.[113] They were in short, just as much as Edward IV's Knights and Esquires of the Body, the leading members of a royal bastard-feudal affinity; while their semi-fortified houses, scattered throughout the southern counties, were key links in the chain that bound the localities to the centre.

Already, then, we can see how misleading it is to draw clear-cut distinctions between 'court' and 'government' or 'court' and 'country'. Instead the early Tudor courtier had his feet firmly in the country, where he normally spent the summer months when the full court of the winter 'season' broke up for the progress-time.[114] Nor was he a palace popinjay,[115] leaving the rough-and-tumble of

105. *LP* VII, 922/16; X, 1015/16.
106. *LP* XIV i, 743.
107. *LP* V, 506/25; IV iii, 6490/11.
108. *LP* II i, 2684; IX, 914/13.
109. Diane Willen, *John Russell, First Earl of Bedford: one of the King's Men* (Royal Historical Society) 1981, usefully summarized in her 'Lord Russell and the Western Counties, 1539–1555', *Journal of British Studies* 15 (1975), 26–46.
110. Bernard. 'The rise of Sir William Compton', 754–77.
111. E. W. Ives, *Letters and Accounts of William Brereton of Malpas* (Record Society of Lancashire and Cheshire, 116) 1976, espec. pp. 28–41; David Starkey, 'Ightham Mote: politics and architecture in early Tudor England', *Archaeologia* 107 (1981), 153–63.
112. W. B. Compton, *History of the Comptons* (1940), p. 20.
113. Ibid. p. 26; Starkey, 'Ightham Mote'. And for a full discussion, see M. Howard, *The Early Tudor Country House* (forthcoming).
114. Cf. *LP* II ii, 4276; XVII, 290; XII ii, 661.
115. Cf. J. A. Murphy, 'Popinjays or professionals: officers and ministers of the mid-Tudor Household', *Exeter Studies in History*, 1981.

government to others. Instead he was to be found acting as the king's eyes, ears and hands in the army, in diplomacy, in the localities: everywhere in fact that royal power was most stretched and vulnerable. In all this he acted in two capacities: he was both the king's representative and a royal retainer. The elevation of Renaissance monarchy had strengthened the former; change in court and society had not yet weakened the latter. It was a unique and fragile conjunction of old and new that accounts for much of the effectiveness of the rule of Henry VIII.

Privy Purse and Dry Stamp: the Privy Chamber and administration

The same goes for administration as well. Here we step into one of the great historiographical minefields of the sixteenth century. The facts themselves are not much in dispute. Under Henry VIII the Chamber wholly lost the administrative pre-eminence it had enjoyed under Henry VII: the Treasurer of the Chamber shrank into a mere household paymaster; while the Secretary, though he rose to ever greater things, severed his links with his old department. What is disputed, however, is the explanation of these changes. Professor Elton, in *The Tudor Revolution in Government*, argued that they were deliberate and planned; that they were the work of one man, Cromwell; and that they embodied Cromwell's conscious determination to reduce the royal and personal element in government and increase the national and bureaucratic. Such notions seem to me both anachronistic and improbable. That must sound like *lèse majesté*. But try to translate 'bureaucratic' into sixteenth-century English, or to imagine the scene in which Cromwell explained his intentions to the king. I do not, however, propose to debate the 'Tudor Revolution' in detail; instead I shall put forward an alternative pattern of explanation for administrative change.

That, once again, is intimacy. To begin with – that is, in the mid-fifteenth century – the Treasurer of the Chamber himself had been a sort of keeper of the privy purse and handled the king's personal day-to-day expenditure. This made him the financial officer closest to the king's person. It was this closeness in turn which led Edward IV and Henry VII to use the Treasurer as the receiver – and paymaster – general of the new, cash-based system of finance they set up haphazard and *ad hoc* alongside the Exchequer. By the later part of Henry VII's reign the Treasurer's hold over the crown finances was almost complete. But the greater his responsibilities the less time he had for his original tasks as keeper of the privy purse and the more imperative was it that he settled down at Westminster instead of accompanying the still peripatetic king.[116]

The king, however, still needed a privy purse. And the obvious keeper for it was the Groom of the Stool: he was always in attendance and already handled most of the arrangements for the king's everyday life. Even William Grimsby, holder of the ancestral office of Yeoman of the Stool under Henry VI, had, we may guess, heavy financial responsibilities since he went on to become Treasurer of the Chamber and undertreasurer of England.[117] And certainly, from the very beginning of the Groomship under Henry VII in about 1495, the Groom, Hugh Denys, handled certain categories of expenditure: he paid out the king's alms and his innumerable 'rewards' (or tips, more or less); covered his trifling gambling debts and made minor purchases. None of this represented much of a challenge to the Chamber: the Treasurer was already handling £100,000 a year; the Groom's account in contrast was mere petty cash at £200–500 a year. Moreover the Groom had no independent financial existence; instead he was merely an account of first instance to the Chamber, from which all his monies came. At first he was reimbursed item by item; then, as his expenditure grew, he submitted consolidated bills or was given substantial cash floats.[118]

Nevertheless, despite the smallness of scale, a crucial change had taken place. The foundation of the Treasurer's eminence had been his place as the financial officer most intimate with the king. With the setting up of the separate privy purse account however, that place was lost to the Groom of the Stool. Just then as the Treasurer had risen at the expense of the Exchequer, so could the Groom rise at the expense of the Treasurer. And before the end of the reign there were clear signs that this was happening. As part of his policy of screwing his financial exactions ever tighter, in September 1508 Henry VII had made Sir Edward Belknap surveyor of the king's Prerogative. Within the next four months Belknap had received £450 as the 'down-payments' on 'fines . . . assessed by the king's Highness'. Almost all was paid over directly to Denys.[119] The privy purse had now bypassed the Chamber and was receiving revenue inde-

116. Cf. B. P. Wolffe, *The Crown Lands, 1461–1536* (1970), *passim*.
117. *HO*, 18; Wedgewood, *Biographies* II, pp. 400–1.
118. For all this see Starkey, 'Privy Chamber', pp. 357–61.
119. E101/517/15.

pendently of it; it had ceased to be a subordinate account and had become an autonomous and perhaps rival treasury.

The rivalry became much clearer in the next reign and with the next Groom of the Stool, William Compton. A great royal favourite, as we have seen, he expanded the financial – like every other – aspect of his post to accommodate his pretensions. New revenues were seized from the Chamber, including the whole surplus of the Hanaper, which collected the king's profits from Chancery, as well as large sums from the General Surveyors, the main accountants for the royal lands whose revenues had been the mainstay of the Chamber. And new areas of expenditure were staked out: in particular, buildings, loans and jewels, which largely disappear from the Treasurer's account at the beginning of the reign.[120]

Probably, in fact, the Chamber was saved from speedy dismemberment only by the rise of Wolsey. Compton he hated as a rival in the king's favour; on the other hand Sir John Heron, the Treasurer of the Chamber, was a mere bureaucrat and amenable to all his purposes. So the privy purse was cut down to size in two stages. First the revenues it had stolen were restored to the Chamber, which made the privy purse once more a subordinate account.[121] Then, as part of what we shall see was the highly politicized reform programme of 1519–20, the Groom's expenditure was reduced and regularized to £10,000 a year.[122] This was something of a triumph for Wolsey; at the same time it shows how hugely the scale of the privy purse had increased since Henry VII's parsimonious days.

Such was the rather betwixt and between state of the privy purse in January 1526 when Compton resigned; was pardoned (as was usual for outgoing office-holders) as among other things 'keeper of our everyday monies'; and handed over the keepership, along with the other varied responsibilities of the Groomship of the Stool, to Henry Norris.[123] Clearly the Groom's account was fully formalized, and, though it was not actually described as the 'Privy Purse' till Edward VI's reign, we can henceforward safely use the term as a title rather than, as hitherto, as a convenient nickname.[124] Indeed, within three years, in the *interministerium* between the fall of Wolsey in November 1529 and the rise of Cromwell, the Privy Purse

---

120. See the account abstracted in Wolffe, *Crown Lands*, pp. 179–82, and Starkey, 'Privy Chamber', pp. 366–9.
121. Ibid. pp. 370–2.
122. BL, Cotton MS Titus B I, fos. 188 ff; Starkey, 'Privy Chamber', pp. 372–5.
123. C66/646, mm. 41–2 (*LP* IV i, 2002/22).
124. Cf. E101/625/4; E101/426/8.

reached its peak. This happily is fully documentable, thanks to the unique survival of the Privy Purse account book for the crucial three years 1529–32.[125] In these three years £53,000 was spent, in three main categories: £4,700 (15%) on the personnel of the private household (fools, falconers, bargees, *etc.*); £30,500 (57%) on the king's personal expenditure, ranging from building (£5,000) and jewels (£15,000) to gambling (£3,200) and the king's linen; and £17,000 (30%) on affairs of state, including the final disastrous embassy to Rome, the costs of Wolsey's own arrest and the ministerial expenses of his would-be successors Norfolk, Gardiner and Cromwell.[126] What all this meant becomes clear from a comparison with the Treasurer of the Chamber's own accounts for this same period. In effect the old, global Chamber account of Henry VII's reign had been split into two: the larger, but routine, part, like wages, remained with the Treasurer; the smaller, but much more important, 'extraordinary' part, like the king's personal expenses and political expenditure, had been transferred to the Privy Purse.[127]

So, weighing importance against size, the Privy Purse was now a co-equal treasury with the Chamber in terms of monies handled; even more striking is the change in the source of such monies. Hitherto the Privy Purse had continued to be financed, more or less as Wolsey had prescribed in 1519, by large lump sums from the Chamber. These however cease in June 1529[128] and instead the Privy Purse was financed in part from another private royal treasury, or rather series of treasuries, the Privy Coffers. In most of the major palaces, like Greenwich or Windsor, the king kept substantial cash hoards. These consisted partly of accumulated reserves, which were clearly far larger than historians have so far reckoned, and partly of windfalls like the French pension, which the diplomacy of Wolsey's last years had contrived to hoist to £20,000–50,000 clear a year.[129] The most spectacular windfall of all, however, was Wolsey's own spoils, and these, combined with the political revolution that followed his death, transformed the Privy Coffers. Henry took over Wolsey's palace of Whitehall; one of his leading agents, Thomas Alvard, and his treasures. Whitehall was made the site of the central

---

125. BL, Additional MS 20,030, printed as N. H. Nicolas, ed., *The Privy Purse Expenses of King Henry VIII* (1827).
126. See the full analysis in Starkey, 'Privy Chamber', pp. 384–5.
127. This is fully worked out in David Starkey, 'Court and Government' in C. Coleman and D. Starkey, eds, *Revolution Reassessed* (Oxford 1986).
128. *LP* V, p. 312.
129. F. C. Dietz, *English Government Finance, 1485–1558* (2 vols, 1964) I, p. 101; *LP* IV iii, 6701/2; V, 222/2 & 3, 1065/2–5, 1504.

treasury of the Privy Coffers and Alvard appointed its keeper. He then acted rather as the deposit account to Norris's current account: when the Privy Purse was low Alvard would transfer money to Norris; on the other hand, when Norris was flush, say after the twice-yearly receipt of the French pension which seems to have been sent to him directly from Calais, he would place large sums 'on deposit' with Alvard, as well as making substantial block-payments to other spending departments like the Cofferer of the Household or even to the Chamber itself.[130]

There is a certain symmetry about all this: just as the Privy Chamber had displaced the Chamber as the centre of the king's private life, so had the financial agency of the Privy Chamber, the Privy Purse, displaced the Chamber as the king's principal, though not largest, treasury. But the symmetry is purely formal: Henry VII's Chamber finance rested on the careful husbanding and exploitation of the royal lands; Henry VIII's Privy Purse, in contrast, was bonanza finance, depending on windfalls and the liquidation of capital to meet current expenditure.

And, bonanza-like again, it was temporary. It was created only by the king's assumption of the reins of day-to-day government and it ended with his relinquishing of them to Cromwell. The new minister moved swiftly, like Wolsey with Compton, to bring the Privy Purse under control. First he took over the supervision of the Privy Coffers, which is what, essentially, his great accumulation of petty financial offices was about.[131] Second, and in the face of Norris's blank incomprehension, he fought to deny the Groom all independent initiative in finance and patronage.[132] And finally, with the dissolution of the monasteries, he did away with the dependence on hand-to-mouth finance which had characterized 1529–32 – though it can be plausibly argued that the dissolution was simply the biggest windfall of them all.

The impact of this assault on the private finances varied. The Privy Purse was finally reduced to a specialized spending department and never recovered its national pretensions; the Privy Coffers, though, took on a new lease of life. Thanks to the dissolution, there was now money to spare. Part Cromwell used directly to fund his government. These monies were channelled through John Gostwick, treasurer of First Fruits and Tenths, whom the minister employed

130. Starkey, 'Privy Chamber', pp. 389–90, 399–401.
131. Elton, *Tudor Revolution*, pp. 139 ff.
132. See for example Cromwell's attitude to Lord Lisle's suit, made through Norris, for his predecessor, Lord Berners's plate: *LP* VII, 461, 614, 627.

in effect as his personal treasurer.[133] But the rest went to the king's hands and the Privy Coffers. First the surplus of Augmentations; then the proceeds of heavy direct taxation; and finally the renewed French pension – all were creamed off.[134] Some was kept by the king himself in his 'own' or 'Secret Jewel House', 'in the old gallery' at Whitehall, which was later 'in the only custody' of Henry's virtual successor in the sovereignty, Protector Somerset;[135] while some was in charge of Sir Anthony Denny, Chief Gentleman of the Privy Chamber (i.e. deputy Groom of the Stool) in his capacity of 'Keeper of the Palace of Westminster', which in practice meant Whitehall.[136] The two hoards were distinct, in that money was regularly handed over by Henry to Denny 'out of his Highness own 'Secret Jewel House' at his Palace at Westminster by his own hands'.[137] But in practice the two treasuries, as well as other temporary hoards like the 'removing coffers'[138] which accompanied the king on his progresses, can be regarded collectively as the 'Privy Coffers'. Denny alone received £241,000 between 1542 and 1546, including £122,000 in the single year 1543–44; Henry himself handled even greater sums.[139] Financially at least, therefore, Cromwell's labours produced not reformed government but the largest private royal cash hoard since the Conquest.[140]

Nor, moreover, was this merely the result of the accident of Cromwell's fall and the king's return, like a dog to its vomit, to the large-scale European war of his first years. Rather it had been intended all along. This is made clear by the important 'memoranda concerning the financial administration' of 1537.[141] Each revenue-raising body, both the new (Augmentations and First Fruits and Tenths) and the old (the Chamber, the Exchequer and the

---

133. Elton, *Tudor Revolution*, pp. 157, 191 ff.
134. For Augmentations see *LP* XIII ii, 457/13; XIV ii, 236/11; XVIII ii, 231/12; XIX ii, 328/12; XXI ii, 775, all tabulated in Starkey, 'Privy Chamber', p. 406. For the subsidy, see E 405, tabulated in Starkey, 'Privy Chamber' p. 407. For the French pension see *LP* XXI ii, 770/3.
135. *Three Inventories . . . of Pictures*, ed. W. A. Shaw (n. d.), pp. 16, 19.
136. E315/160, fo. 264 ff.
137. Ibid. fo. 266v.
138. Ibid. fos. 266v, 267v.
139. Ibid. fos. 264–9v, tabulated in Starkey, 'Privy Chamber', p. 409, and see note 134 above.
140. Full details of Denny's expenditure, in which war and building bulk largest, are in BL, Lansdowne Roll 14. This document, noted in W. C. Richardson, *History of the Court of Augmentations, 1536–54* (Baton Rouge 1962), 356 n. 94, will be subject to fresh analysis by Dr D. Hoak in a forthcoming article.
141. Printed in G. R. Elton, *The Tudor Constitution* (Cambridge 1960), pp. 142–3.

Duchy of Lancaster) was listed and each was required to draw up a 'declaration' of income and expenditure, and then to strike a balance showing 'what the whole remainder to the king's use will yearly amount unto'. The aim, the last clause stated, was twofold: first, to enable 'the king's Highness [to] know his estate, and by means thereof [to] establish all his affairs'; and second 'to put an order how certain treasure yearly may be laid up for all necessities'. Where the treasure was to be laid up is not made clear, but it is hard to think of what repository, other than the Privy Coffers, could have been envisaged.

And in any event, the Privy Coffers is what was used. Filling them, on the other hand, was hardly the orderly process laid down by the 'memoranda'. Instead of waiting for a yearly transfer, the king tended to launch a series of *ad hoc* raids on each treasury. Sometimes he seems to have struck without rhyme or reason, as in 1539 when Sir Brian Tuke, the Treasurer of the Chamber, who was always strapped for money, 'with much ado . . . made for the king's Majesty to his own Privy Coffers at Easter last 5,000 marks' (i.e. £3,333 6s. 8d.).[142] More usually his demands came when he had got wind that some treasurer had received a large injection of cash – like the instalment of a subsidy, or a payment of the revived French pension. Then a warrant would be issued ordering immediate payment of the bulk of the sum 'to your Majesty's own hands'.[143] But casual though the Privy Coffers might be, they were also effective. They formed an important buffer against emergencies; they also introduced an element of centralization into an otherwise intolerably diffuse and fragmented financial system. Thanks to the Coffers the king knew more or less how much cash-in-hand he had, and he knew exactly where to put his hands on it.

The story of the secretariat is parallel. And it too rests on a certain insight into coarse material reality. The Privy Coffers were important because Tudor money was *real*: that is, lumps of gold and silver that were eminently stealable. So keeping money – not collecting or spending it, as financial historians have always assumed – was the key task. Similarly, the Secretary's importance had depended on physical fact: his control of the smallest royal seal, the Signet. But in the late fifteenth century that physical reality was undermined by another: the king's signature, or Sign Manual, more and more replaced the Signet as the principal form of authoriz-

142. SP1/153, fos. 9–10 (*LP* XIV ii, 13).
143. E.g. *LP* XXI i, 1382/13.

ation.[144] And whereas a seal could easily be alienated to a keeper a signature could not be. The result was an extraordinary diffusion of secretarial responsibility in the early part of Henry VIII's reign, with the Secretary himself, favoured household officers or councillors, like More,[145] and the Privy Chamber all being involved.

But underlying the diversity a clear basic pattern was emerging: responsibility for drafting state papers rested with the minister and his personal secretariat; responsibility for getting the king's signature increasingly belonged to the Privy Chamber.[146] And it was no mean task, since, as is well known Henry, loathed writing even his name and would put it off on any excuse, including a cold in the head.[147] At first Cromwell's ministry sharply interrupted the development. He mistrusted Norris, the Groom of the Stool, too much to give him such a delicate task, and instead used his own servants, in particular, Ralph Sadler, to 'promote' (in the contemporary jargon) ministerial papers to be signed by the king.[148] But the setback was only temporary. Once he had got absolute political control of the Privy Chamber in May 1536 and once, above all, his own client, Heneage, had been appointed Groom of the Stool and Chief Gentleman (below, p. 114), Cromwell reversed his policy. The promotion of documents to the Sign Manual was now concentrated in the hands of the Groom; a regular procedure was developed; and a proper record, 'the king's book', was kept for one vital part of the business at least – the distribution of royal patronage.[149]

The real threat to the Groom's position came not from Cromwell's tenure of the Secretaryship but from his resignation. In his hands the Secretaryship had been swallowed up in the chief councillorship; when he passed the divided office over to his servants Wriothesley and Sadler its independent potential was revealed. Wriothesley was seconded to the minister as his *chef de bureau*; Sadler was attached to the king as a member of the Privy Chamber.[150] This meant that he was able, for the first time in many a long year, to reunite the two main secretarial tasks: he both drafted letters, often

---

144. Cf. J. Otway-Ruthven, *The King's Secretary and the Signet Office in the Fifteenth Century* (Cambridge 1939), pp. 25–6, 39, and the fuller discussion in Starkey, 'Court and Government', pp. 46 ff.
145. Elton, *Tudor Revolution*, pp. 56–9.
146. For Heneage: *LP* IV ii, 4005, 4144, 4299; for Russell: ibid. 4799.
147. *LP* III ii, 1399.
148. *LP* IX, 905, and see Starkey, 'Privy Chamber', pp. 321–3.
149. *LP* XIII i, 332; XIV ii, 201; BL, Cotton MS Titus B I, fo. 457 (*LP* XII i, 1315) and *LP* XI, 227. And see the fuller discussion in Starkey, 'Court and Government', pp. 53–4.
150. Elton, *Tudor Revolution*, pp. 313–15; Starkey, 'Privy Chamber', p. 334.

to the king's dictation, and got them signed as well. The results were recorded in the docket book he kept of instruments sealed with his signet between 1540 and 1542.[151] This is the first such register to survive since the docket book of an even more important holder of the office, John Kendal, Secretary to Richard III.[152] But Sadler lost the Secretaryship in the factional feuding of the 1540s and none of his successors was appointed to the Privy Chamber. Into the vacuum stepped once more the Chief Gentleman.

His position was consolidated mightily by the peculiar circumstances of the king's declining years. Increasing ill-health and tetchiness turned Henry's aversion to signing into a phobia. To spare him a Dry Stamp was made. This left a faint impression of a facsimile signature in the paper which was then filled in in ink by a skilled clerk. From September 1545 all papers, whosoever had drafted them, were signed only with the Dry Stamp, oversight of which was entrusted to Denny; while his brother-in-law, fellow Gentleman of the Privy Chamber and factotum, John Gates had the actual custody of the stamp. Their assistant, who did all the work, was a certain William Clerk, who had begun as Heneage's servant; been appointed a clerk of the Privy Seal, and now, in effect, became office manager of a new Sign Manual office.[153]

So the early sixteenth century saw not only the decline of Chamber administration, but the rise of Privy Chamber administration as well. This means that the changes do not herald the replacement of household by bureaucratic government; still less were they one of the birth pangs of the modern state. Instead they were merely another turn in the ancient cycle of 'going out of court': that is, the process, first identified by T. F. Tout,[154] by which the inner servants of the royal household became involved in the business of national government and were absorbed by it; meanwhile their neglected household duties were taken over by others, who subsequently displaced them in their governmental activities as well – and so on. If there was a 'Tudor Revolution in Government', it was a revolution in their sense of the word, not ours: a turning, not a turning point.

151. BL, Additional MS 33, 818 and A. J. Slavin, *Politics and Profit: A Study of Sir Ralph Sadler, 1507–1547* (Cambridge 1966), p. 55 ff.
152. BL, Harleian MS 433, ed. by Rosemary Horrox and P. W. Hammond (4 vols, Upminster and London 1979–85).
153. *LP* Addenda I ii, 1705; XVII, 1154/59; Starkey, 'Court and Government', p. 56.
154. T. F. Tout, *Chapters in the Administrative History of Medieval England* (6 vols, Manchester 1920–33).

Purge and packing: the Privy Chamber and politics, 1518–1547.

Finally and most importantly there was a politics of intimacy. Power, that is came from influence over the king, which was fought for among a small group and with manipulation as the key weapon. Such a politics was as old as monarchy. But at the beginning of the sixteenth century circumstances made it visibly more important and stimulated a European literature.[155] Most systematic – indeed amounting to a 'philosophy of the courtier' – was Baldassare Castiglione's *Book of the Courtier*, which was eventually printed in 1528. Castiglione based himself on the central corpus of an earlier tradition of manipulative politics: Cicero's discussions of the place of the orator and oratory in the Classical city-state. First the qualifications of the courtier-manipulator were listed. Here Castiglione added the high birth and the social and athletic acquirements, from jousting to the art of love, of the late medieval gentleman to the essentially intellectual achievements of Cicero's orator. Then came the techniques of manipulation – 'how to win friends and influence people'; and finally the justification of manipulation and the manipulator:

> The end of the perfect courtier . . . is, by means of the accomplishments attributed to him by these gentlemen, so to win for himself the mind and favour of the prince he serves that he can and always will tell him the truth about all he needs to know, without fear or risk of displeasing him.[156]

So Castiglione both had his cake and ate it. Partly *The Courtier* was smooth moralization, heightened by delicate nostalgia; partly it was a highly practical manual to the no-holds-barred game of manipulation. The ambiguity was the key to its success, which was instant and universal, even in remote England.

The England of Henry VIII, in fact, experienced the politics of manipulation in an acute form. This was due, on the one hand, to the king's character, and, on the other, to the reconstructed Privy Chamber of 1518. For Henry VIII, behind Holbein's image of the archetypal strong king, was profoundly open to influence. His imitation of France, exemplified in the blind copying of the post of *gentilhomme de la chambre*, was slavish; his submission to political pressures at once so complete and so erratic that Foxe could state baldly that 'King Henry, according as his counsel was about him,

---

155. See above pp. 68–70, and David Starkey 'The Court: Castiglione's Ideal and Tudor Reality', *Journal of the Warburg and Courtauld Institutes* 45 (1982), 232 ff.
156. Castiglione, *Courtier*, p. 284.

so was he led'.[157] And around this royal target, the creation of the post of Gentleman of the Privy Chamber set as his servants and companions men who fulfilled to the letter Castiglione's recipe for masters in the art of manipulation. Their high birth, charm and athleticism we have already seen, but they also had the more solid Ciceronian qualities as well. Wolsey, who was hardly partial, offered Carew a ringing testimonial: he was 'well mannered, having the French tongue [and] of your [i.e. Henry VIII's] own bringing-up'.[158] Carew's brother-in-law Bryan had a truly professional command of language, both on paper, where he was a published author and a poet highly regarded by contemporaries, and in speech. Added to this was a larger-than-life character that earned him the nickname of the 'Vicar of Hell'. The result was a unique relationship with Henry: 'the said Sir Francis dare boldly speak to the king's Grace the plainness of his mind and that his Grace doth well accept the same'.[159] The words are curiously familiar, for reaching across a wide gap of culture and language they are a faithful paraphrase of Castiglione's 'end of the perfect courtier'. In this case the echo was accidental; but Sir Thomas Wyatt makes the point explicitly in his 'Third Satire', by portraying Bryan as the embodiment of Castiglione's ideal.[160]

So the institution of the office of Gentleman of the Privy Chamber and the appointment to it of superbly qualified courtier-orators like the minions made the Privy Chamber a major centre of political influence. In fact it came second only to the Council and above all to the principal councillor or minister, Wolsey or Cromwell himself. And henceforth, it is the struggle between courtiers and councillors that gives the politics of the reign one of their characteristic rhythms. We tend to think of the two as different; in fact they were akin. The courtier had to have the skills of a politician; the minister, the talents of a courtier: during business, for example, Wolsey diverted Henry with curios; while Cromwell amused him with sixteenth-century executive toys.[161] For both councillors and courtiers were engaged in a struggle for the same goal: 'the mind and favour' of the king.

157. J. Foxe, *Acts and Monuments*, ed. J. Pratt (8 vols, 1874) V, p. 606.
158. *LP* Addenda I i, 196.
159. Starkey, 'The Court: Castiglione's Ideal', and SP1/132, fos. 96 ff. (*LP* XIII i, 981).
160. Starkey, 'The Court: Castiglione's Ideal'.
161. Polydore Vergil, *Historia Anglicana*, ed. and trans. by D. Hay (Camden Society, 3rd series, 74) 1950, p. 247; *LP* X, 76, and for a fuller and more balanced assessment of the politics of influence, see Starkey, *Reign of Henry VIII: personalities and politics* (1985).

The first episode in the struggle came quickly. Its grounds were the control of patronage and foreign policy. Already in 1517, even before the minions' position in the Privy Chamber was regularized, Mrs Vernon, a wealthy widow whom Wolsey had intended as the bride of one of his own servants, was snatched from under his nose by one of the minions, William Coffin, aided and abetted by another, Nicholas Carew. The means by which they won their victory are charted in the newly unearthed few pages of a 'Privy Chamber letter book', which shows how at every stage they, and not Wolsey, were able to wheel the king out in support.[162] The result was a defeat for the minister that reverberated from the court to Derbyshire – at which, as Compton smugly reported, 'my lord Cardinal is not content withal'.[163] And what the minions had achieved in patronage they threatened in foreign policy. To follow up the Treaty of London a return embassy was sent to France in which the minions (headed by Carew and Bryan) were prominent.[164] Once there, they behaved rather like a visiting rugby team, riding with 'the French king . . . daily disguised through Paris, throwing eggs, stones and other foolish trifles at the people'.[165] This outrageous royal indulgence, which went far beyond even what they were used to at home, swept them off their feet, and they returned victims of a bad dose of French fever. They were rude about English fashion, cooking and beer and began, more seriously it was suspected, to exercise a strongly pro-French influence on foreign policy.[166] But both patronage and foreign policy were only symptoms of what from Wolsey's point of view was the real disease. This was well understood by the Venetian envoy Giustiniani, who reported that the minister's greatest fear was that the minions had become 'so intimate with the king, that in the course of time they might have ousted him from the government'.[167] Faced by this ultimate threat, Wolsey struck first.

He did so by reversing his whole style of management of the king. Hitherto the minister had encouraged him in his pleasures.[168]

162. Bodley, Ashmole MS 1148/XI and see the fuller account in Starkey, *Reign of Henry VIII*.

163. Edmund Lodge, ed., *Illustrations of British History* (3 vols, 1791) I, p. 28 ff. (*LP* II ii, 3807).

164. *LP* II ii, 4512 ('Chamberlain' is Pace's Latinized English for *gentilhomme de la chambre*); Hall, *Chronicle*, p. 597.

165. Hall, *Chronicle*, p. 597.

166. Loc. cit.; *LP* III i, 235.

167. Loc. cit.

168. Sylvester, *Early Tudor Lives*, p. 13.

Now he plunged Henry into business. From the beginning of 1519, even though things were only consolidated into a firm package in the autumn, the air was thick with proposals for reform. These included improved auditing, Exchequer reorganization, job-creation, frontier security, the settling of the Irish question, and the better protection of the royal person.[169] The schemes were glossy enough to attract the king's attention, which the ordinary business of domestic government could never do; they also imposed enough detailed administration to keep him busy at his desk. With Henry in this rare mood of self-sacrificing, and no doubt self-righteous, devotion to the public weal, it was easy to blackguard the minions as worthless young wastrels. The ploy worked and in May 1519 almost the whole group was packed off to Calais, the early Tudor India, which they found 'sore displeasant'.[170] In their wake was hurled a got-up stream of abuse which included *Magnificence*, a verse-play by the poet laureate, John Skelton. Traditionally seen as a satire against Wolsey, its victims were almost certainly in fact the minions, who appear either as the Frenchified, double-dealing and manipulative Court Vices, or, in the case of the youthful brothers-in-law Carew and Bryan, as the brother Fools, Fancy and Folly.[171]

The first battle for royal favour thus won and the minions dismissed and defamed, Wolsey filled their posts with men of his own choosing: elderly, distinguished and amenable.[172] At the same time, they, and the rest of the Privy Chamber, were given proper wages.[173] The result was ironically to reinforce the changes of September 1518. The status of the new appointees, who included a knight of the Garter, elevated still further the importance of Privy Chamber office; while the granting of salaries, as we shall see, entrenched it in law. Moreover Wolsey's victory was short-lived as well as double-edged. For by October 1519 Henry had summoned the minions – so temptingly near in Calais – back to court. There, by way of pendant to *Magnificence*, they celebrated their return to favour in a masque in which the minister's appointees to the Privy Chamber appeared as the ridiculous old buffers of the antemasque; while the king and the minions inhabited the gracious world of eternal youth of the masque proper.[174]

169. BL, Cotton MS Titus B I, fos. 188–92.
170. Hall, *Chronicle*, p. 598.
171. Maria Dowling, 'Scholarship, Politics and the Court of Henry VIII' (unpublished London Ph. D. dissertation, 1981), pp. 104–8.
172. *LP* III i, 235; Hall, *Chronicle*, p. 598.
173. Starkey, 'Privy Chamber', pp. 115–18.
174. Hall, *Chronicle*, p. 599.

But fate promptly put a new instrument of control in Wolsey's hands in the tortuous foreign policy of the early 1520s. This led first to frenetic diplomacy, then to war. And in both the Privy Chamber were heavily involved.[175] As we have already seen, this was as it should be. But contemporaries accused Wolsey of perverting evident necessity to his own ends. Polydore Vergil, the humanist historian of the reign, claimed that Compton's dispatch on the Scottish campaign of 1523, which was indeed the only time in the whole period that the Groom of the Stool was sent on such a mission, was 'at Wolsey's instigation, so that the latter might gradually cause him to be hateful to Henry' during his absence.[176] And John Palsgrave laid the general charge that the Cardinal had 'undone all the young gentlemen of England that served [the king] and sent some beyond sea on embassies and devised means to linger them there still . . . because he would have them out of the way'.[177] Both men were Wolsey's enemies and neither report is checkable; yet they have the ring of truth. And in any case the minister cannot have been sorry to see his enemies away from court.

In 1525, however, came peace and with it the return of the Privy Chamber to court. Once again Wolsey played the reform card, but with a difference. In 1519 Wolsey had used a general reform programme as a cover for a purge of the Privy Chamber. He had abandoned the programme quickly: partly under the pressure of war; partly because it had served its political purpose. In 1525–26, however, he purged the department directly by the household reforms of the Eltham Ordinances. There was in fact a genuine need for reform, since the wars had led to a great increase in the size of the household, still of course the centre of the royal war-machine, and a general dislocation of its structure. As usual Wolsey got to work quickly – anticipating the actual signing of the Treaty of the More by a fortnight.[178] And, as far as the Household and Chamber were concerned, he produced quick results. Separate reforming orders for these two departments were prepared and published in the last months of 1525;[179] a third set covering the Privy Chamber were also drawn up. These, however, survive only in draft and it is most unlikely that they were ever formally issued.[180]

175. See notes 61–2, 73–5.
176. Vergil, *Historia*, p. 309.
177. SP1/54, fos. 244–52 (*LP* IV iii, 5750).
178. *LP* IV i, 1572.
179. LS13/278, pp. 146 ff, 158–62; Starkey, 'Privy Chamber', pp. 71–3.
180. BL, Cotton MS Vespasian C XIV, fos. 257–94v.

For the Privy Chamber presented a special problem. The reduction in size of the two outer departments of the household was a merely administrative matter, and was so treated in the final text of the Ordinances; on the other hand the cutbacks in the Privy Chamber were a major political question that made heavy demands on the minister's own energy and time. It would have been so anyway. But the minister's difficulties were made worse by the fact that the wage grants of 1519 had been made by letters patent. These gave the full protection of the law, so members of the Privy Chamber could not simply be dismissed, as in 1518; instead they had to be bought out. And to accumulate the purchase price took a six-month moratorium on patronage.[181] But by Christmas all was ready and Wolsey drew up in his own hand, such was the importance and secrecy of the task, the list of quid pro quos that were to be offered to those marked down for dismissal.[182] The Privy Chamber thus settled, the way was open to the general reform of the household. Henry had spent Christmas in the comparatively small palace of Eltham with, as a taste of things to come, a much reduced household. There in the first weeks of January he was joined by the Cardinal and, with characteristic triumphalism, the Eltham Ordinances were promulgated.

Essentially their text was a fusion of the three separate departmental orders of the previous autumn, together with interpolated sections dealing with the reduction, accomplished or intended, of each departmental establishment. In terms of regulation there were few surprises, since the Ordinances only reflected the developments of the last thirty years. So for the Household-below-stairs, save for the tightening up of accounting, there was no change; the Chamber on the other hand was demoted to the semi-public reception area it had become; while the Privy Chamber stepped into the limelight, since in its 'good order . . . consisteth a great part of the king's quiet, rest, comfort and preservation of his health, the same above all other things before mentioned is principally and most highly to be regarded'.[183] Much more striking was the reduction in establishment: whether of the Guard, which attracted all the contemporary comment,[184] or of the Privy Chamber. The latter Wolsey reduced from getting on for thirty to fifteen. In so doing he got rid of both his ineffective supporters, who were the survivors of the appointees

---

181. Starkey, 'Privy Chamber', pp. 142–9.
182. SP1/37, fo. 102 (*LP* IV i, 1939/14).
183. *HO*, 154.
184. Hall, *Chronicle*, p. 703.

of 1519, and his anything but ineffective enemies, who included Carew, Bryan, George Boleyn, Anne's brother and the king's Page, and Compton himself. The last had been bought off only with Sir Thomas More's office of undertreasurer of England, which was one of the most valuable in the king's gift. More's compensation, the chancellorship of the Duchy of Lancaster, was inadequate, but Wolsey was not one to let the deserts of a loyal servant get in the way of his own self-interest.[185]

On only one point had the minister met defeat. The king had insisted on retaining his cousin, Henry Courtenay, marquess of Exeter, whom Wolsey regarded as an enemy, in the department.[186] So to counterbalance him the Cardinal had added in his own hand to the list of Gentlemen the name of Sir John Russell, later earl of Bedford, the most courtly and distinguished of his own adherents.[187] Otherwise, the survivors in the Privy Chamber were cautious neutrals, like Henry Norris, the new Groom of the Stool. And the Ordinances commanded them to persevere in this neutrality by 'not pressing his Grace, nor advancing themselves . . ., or also in suits, or inter-meddle of any causes or matters whatsoever they be'.[188]

Wolsey managed to hold this line for about two years; then it was broken, like so much else, by the advent of that remarkable woman, Anne Boleyn, who even her worst enemy had to admit had 'sense, wit and courage'.[189] For just as Lady Margaret Beaufort had repressed faction, so Anne bred it. Right from the beginning she had her own faction in the king's Privy Chamber, of which she was the much more than nominal leader; while her brother, now as Viscount Rochford one of the two Noblemen in the Privy Chamber, acted as her lieutenant. Her rise also, by unlocking Wolsey's grasp on power, allowed the ex-minions, expelled for the second time in 1526, to return to the Privy Chamber, where ungratefully most of them lined up behind Queen Catherine and the Princess Mary as the second, 'Aragonese' faction. And, most important, Anne finally forced a change of style on Wolsey himself. Hitherto rightly confident in his own direct relationship with Henry on the one hand, and deeply distrustful even of his own appointees at court on the other,[190] he had, as we have repeatedly seen, not packed the court

185. J. A. Guy, *The Public Career of Sir Thomas More* (Brighton 1980), p. 27.
186. *HO*, 154.
187. SP1/37, fo. 65 (*LP* IV i, 1939/4).
188. *HO*, 155–6.
189. PRO 31/18, 2/2 (*LP* X, 1069).
190. Cf. Elton, *Tudor Revolution*, p. 57.

but neutralized it. But now, his special relationship with the king ruptured by the rise of Anne, he was reduced to one faction leader among others, who had to insinuate his own men into the Privy Chamber and rely on them, as the third faction there, to shore up his position.[191]

So only in 1528, with the rise of Anne Boleyn, does faction, the key structural element in the politics of intimacy, become a constant and continuing factor. This was a symptom of Wolsey's decline; its first effect was to complete his ruin. This was brought about by a general alliance of opposites. Boleyns joined with Aragonese and both linked with the dominant aristocratic party in the Council, which had also factionalized in the twilight of Wolsey's power but on rather different lines from the Privy Chamber.[192] The Cardinal was first driven from office; then harried out of the south-east, and finally arrested by the earl of Northumberland and Walter Walsh, Groom of the Privy Chamber. It was to the latter he surrendered, in words that are a striking illustration of the doctrine of 'representation through intimacy'. '"You"', he said to Walsh, '"are a sufficient commission yourself . . . in as much as ye be one of the king's Privy Chamber, for the worst person there is a sufficient warrant to arrest the greatest peer of the realm, by the king's only commandment without any commission." '[193] The department he had fought so long to bridle had bridled him.

The Cardinal gone, the alliance which had destroyed him had no further grounds for unity and split particularly on both the issue and the handling of the Divorce. The time was ripe for a fresh alignment. This was triggered by the rise of Thomas Cromwell. Of all the would-be successors to Wolsey, like Norfolk and Gardiner, Cromwell was the outsider. But he had three advantages. First, as Wolsey's former man-of-affairs, he inherited the support of Wolsey's faction in the Privy Chamber and later its leadership (for the faction, as was not uncommon, had survived its patron's fall with nothing worse than a few blows from the rough edge of Anne Boleyn's tongue).[194] Second, his early royal employment as collector-general for the Privy Purse took him into the inmost recesses of government – far more effectively, for example, than his rival Gardiner's

191. *LP* IV ii, 3213/18 (Sir Richard Page); *LP* IV ii, 3964 (Thomas Heneage). And see generally, Starkey, 'From Feud to Faction', *History Today* 32 (1982).
192. Loc. cit, and Guy, *Public Career*, pp. 30–1.
193. Sylvester, *Early Tudor Lives*, p. 160.
194. E.g. *LP* IV iii, 6199.

Secretaryship.[195] Finally, and above all, there were his ideological
and political strengths. He alone shared Anne's passionate commitment to evangelical Christianity; and he alone proffered a policy that
cut the Gordian knot of the Divorce. The result was a new ministry
and a new grouping of factions. The Boleyns and the ex-Wolseyians
came together under the joint leadership of Anne and Cromwell as
the 'ins'; leaving the Aragonese and aristocrats on the Council as the
'outs'.[196]

The origins of Cromwell's power coloured deeply his exercise of
it. Wolsey had ruled over and against the court, as 'alter rex' (i.e.
'second king') and master of his own great household, which was
a mirror image of the court itself;[197] only latterly and reluctantly had
he become a faction leader within the court. Cromwell, in contrast,
began where Wolsey ended, as a faction leader and court minister.
So where Wolsey neutralized the court, Cromwell packed it; and
whereas Wolsey played the reform card, Cromwell used more direct
and bloody methods.

In fact, for all his fame as a reformer, Cromwell's record with the
Privy Chamber was meagre. The Orders of 1532 were trifling and
in any case were probably not his at all (it is better for his reputation
that they were not). Rather, they look like an attempt by the
accounts department of the Household-below-stairs to cope with the
problem of the sudden increase in the size of the Privy Chamber that
had resulted from its repoliticization in the late 1520s.[198] The financial worries which had underlain the Orders were swept aside by the
dissolution, and indeed the effect on the Privy Chamber of Cromwell's main attempt at household reform, the Ordinances of
1539–40, was merely a post-dissolution binge. Everybody without
wages was given them; while everybody who had them already was
given a substantial increase, which for the first and last time in the
sixteenth century brought salaries into line with inflation.[199]

Partly the absence of reform reflects the lack of need for it. Under
Wolsey the Privy Chamber was experiencing the growing pains of
adolescence; under Cromwell it had entered into plump maturity.

195. Starkey, 'Court and Government'.
196. Starkey, 'Feud to Faction'.
197. Sylvester, *Early Tudor Lives*, pp. 19–22.
198. BL, Additional MS 9835, fos. 24 and 26, and see Starkey, 'Privy Chamber',
    pp. 185–200 and contrast with Elton, *Tudor Revolution*, pp. 379–80.
199. BL, Additional MS 45, 716A, fos. 13–15; Royal MS 7 C XVI, fo. 129 and see
    Starkey, 'Privy Chamber', pp. 211–16 and contrast with Elton, *Tudor Revolution*,
    p. 405.

But there was also the question of character. Cromwell, though no mean orator,[200] was a much less rhetorical politician than Wolsey. So he accepted the Privy Chamber's influence as a fact of life that was unlikely, as Wolsey seems to have hoped in the Eltham Ordinances, to be conjured away by words. This acceptance led to no passivity though. Instead, as the 'master-Machiavel' of contemporary judgment, he was determined to fight, by frankly political means, for control of an institution that was one of the two principal keys to power.

As it happened, his first battle, the Boleyn affair of May 1536, was not on ground of his choosing, though, like the great political tactician he was, he turned even his opponents' strength to his own advantage. Rather the attack on Anne was initiated by the Aragonese faction in the Privy Chamber, led by Sir Nicholas Carew and the marquess of Exeter. Carew was now Master of the Horse, that is, the equivalent of the Groom of the Stool when the king was outside the precincts of the palace, and Privy Councillor, while Exeter was also a leading councillor. This sudden going on to the offensive of conservatism was possible because the Aragonese, despite the repudiation of Catherine and the bastardization of Mary, had clung on to both office and favour in the Privy Chamber. There, always mindful that as Anne had risen so could she fall, they had spied their time. It came in the winter of 1535–36. Catherine of Aragon died; Anne miscarried and mishandled the king; and chance put the chosen instrument into their hands: Jane Seymour. Anne was strident and abrasive; Jane calm and soothing. Her motto, which she chose after she became queen, says all: it was 'Bound to obey and serve'.[201] The Aragonese and their ladies groomed her and introduced her to the king. Jane, though not of the brightest, had enough wit to live up to her type-casting and Henry was caught.[202] On St George's Day 1536 he made his preference known. There were two candidates for election to the Garter: George Boleyn, viscount Rochford, Anne's brother, and Sir Nicholas Carew, the leader of the Aragonese. Carew was chosen.[203]

All this presented Cromwell with an appalling dilemma. True there had been tensions, inevitable in coalition rule, between the minister and the queen. There were clashes over foreign policy with

200. J. Anstis, ed., *The Register of the Most Noble Order of the Garter* (2 vols, 1724) II, p. 408.
201. Starkey, *Reign of Henry VIII*; SP3/7, fo. 28 (*LP* X, 1047); Lord Howard de Walden, ed., *De Walden Library* (3 vols, 1904) I ii, frontispiece, pp. 17–19.
202. *LP* X, 601.
203. Anstis, *Register* II, 398 (*LP* X, 715).

Anne and her brother[204]; with Norris, the Groom of the Stool, who was personally, though I suspect not politically, identified with the queen, there was the long war of attrition over Cromwell's claims to an exclusive control of finance and patronage (above, pp. 96, 99); and finally there are signs that the immense local, and hence military, strength of both Norris himself and the otherwise fairly obscure Groom of the Privy Chamber, William Brereton, was worrying the always security-conscious Cromwell, if not the king.[205] But the other pan of the scale weighed far more heavily. The Aragonese, religiously 'Catholic', and politically conservative, stood for everything Cromwell most detested and hated him in return. In the natural course of events, therefore, the minister's fall would follow the queen's. Cromwell escaped by a characteristically bold change of front. He offered his support and expertise to the Aragonese and their allies, the Imperial ambassador, Chapuys, and Mary herself, and, thanks to their naiveté and his skill (Mary was the only one to display proper caution), persuaded them of his sincerity. He then took over the plot against Anne, as he later boasted to Chapuys.[206] The Aragonese had intended to get rid of her by charging her in effect with bigamy;[207] Cromwell instead substituted an accusation of treason on grounds of multiple adultery, with her followers, including her brother, as the co-respondents.[208] The former would have left Anne divorced and disgraced but alive and with her court party intact. The latter involved both Anne and her supporters in a common and terrible death. After some problems with the evidence, which in the event was properly dismissed by one of the judges in his notes as mere 'bawdy and lechery',[209] the trials were fixed and Anne, her brother, Henry Norris, the Groom of the Stool, and three other members of the Privy Chamber were executed.[210] Cromwell's master-stroke followed. He turned on his erstwhile allies the Aragonese, who found themselves accused, correctly, of having sought to restore Mary to the succession.[211] They were saved from the block only by Mary doing what she had hitherto steadfastly

204. *LP* X, 699, 1069.
205. Ives, *Brereton*, pp. 38–41.
206. *LP* X, 1069.
207. *LP* X, 752, 782.
208. Charles Wriothesley, *A Chronicle of England*, ed. W. D. Hamilton (Camden Society, new series, 11) 2 vols, 1875–77, I, pp. 191 ff (*LP* X, 876).
209. Printed as an Appendix to E. W. Ives, 'Faction at the Court of Henry VIII', *History* 57 (1972), 169–88.
210. Ives, op. cit., and G. R. Elton, *Reform and Reformation*, pp. 250 ff. (the latter incorporating many of my own views) offer useful complementary accounts.
211. *LP* X, 1134, 1150.

refused to do and recognizing her own bastardy.[212] But though alive, and indeed still in office, the Aragonese were politically neutered.

These extraordinary events echoed far outside the narrow circle of the court. In fact, it has been argued,[213] they offer the key to the Pilgrimage of Grace, the great rebellion of 1536, which has hitherto been seen as a 'spontaneous, authentic condemnation' of Henry VIII and his Reformation.[214] Far from being spontaneous, however, the rebellion had long been planned. Lord Darcy, an ex-courtier and administrator in restless retirement in Yorkshire (which hardly makes him a 'Northern Marcher lord')[215] had joined with the conservatives at court to plot a general attack on the king's religious policies. But in early 1536, when their triumph over Anne seemed assured, the courtiers, always most reluctant rebels, understandably backed off. By autumn of course their triumph had turned to ashes and the rebellion went ahead, but at half-cock and without the palace revolution that would probably have guaranteed its success.

The arguments for all this are thinly documented, though it would have been surprising if the conspirators had kept careful records. But they are plausible and supported by the government's own actions. For clearly suspecting their complicity, the king sent Exeter, the leader of the Aragonese, together with Francis Bryan and Anthony Browne, who had found themselves hauled over the coals for their partiality to Mary, into action as commanders against the rebels.[216] As known sympathizers to the Pilgrims,[217] they were deliberately placed in the van (the marchioness of Exeter lamented that 'my lord is gone to battle and he will be one of the foremost';[218] while behind them and watching their every move rode Richard Cromwell, the minister's nephew, who was himself to be put in the Privy Chamber in 1539.[219] This was a hideous humiliation, at least for the marquess. But worse was to come and in the course of 1538–39 Exeter, Carew and Sir Edward Neville, their fellow conservative and Gentleman of the Privy Chamber, were condemned and executed for treason.[220]

---

212. *LP* VII, 1172 (dated to 18 June 1536); XI, 7.
213. G. R. Elton, 'Politics and the Pilgrimage of Grace' in B. Malament, ed., *After the Reformation* (Philadelphia 1980), pp. 25–56.
214. J. J. Scarisbrick, *Henry VIII* (1968), p. 341.
215. Ibid. p. 340.
216. *LP* XI, 615, 715, 751.
217. *LP* XI, 1196, 1210.
218. *LP* XIII ii, 765, 804/5.
219. *LP* XI, 656 and especially 756; *LP* XIV ii, 572/3/vii.
220. Elton, *Reform and Reformation*, pp. 279–81.

Cromwell's double purge, of the Boleyns in 1536 and the Aragonese two years later, more than half emptied the Privy Chamber. In the vacant posts he put his own men, who thus became by far the largest and strongest court faction. This absolute ministerial victory over the Privy Chamber was crucial for both religion and politics. Anne Boleyn herself had been religiously committed. If not Lutheran, she was certainly an evangelical: an importer of suspect continental religious texts, like her magnificent Psalter, and a *dévote* who gave her ladies-in-waiting vernacular translations of the Bible which she encouraged them to read.[221] This personal commitment was translated into action through her patronage. She had a direct hand in the appointment of at least three of the leading reforming bishops, Cranmer, Latimer and Shaxton (whom she proprietorially described as 'my bishops');[222] while indirectly, through the king's radical physician, William Butts (also a member of the Privy Chamber), her influence was used to pick out promising young reformers at Cambridge, like John Cheke; protect them and promote them into the royal service.[223] And, for all the importance of indigenous protestantism in the universities and the City, it was this penetration of reform into the inmost circles of the court – into the king's Privy Chamber and his very bed – that gave the 'new' its crucial break in England.

All this was imperilled by Anne's fall and 'her' bishops reacted accordingly. Cranmer begged Henry VIII to remain steadfast 'forasmuch as your Grace's favour to the Gospel was not led by affection unto [Anne] but by zeal unto the truth';[224] while Shaxton beseeched Cromwell 'in the bowels of Christ' to be no less ardent for God's 'holy word than when the late queen was alive and often incited you thereto'.[225] Their panic proved unnecessary, for, however doubtful Henry's convictions, Cromwell's were real enough. So though he destroyed Anne, he preserved and extended her achievement. Butts's patronage network survived, merely looking to Cromwell instead of Anne;[226] while Cromwell's own appointees to the Privy Chamber – Denny, Mewtis, Hoby,

221. Maria Dowling, 'Anne Boleyn and Reform', *Journal of Ecclesiastical History* 35 (1984), 30 ff; *Catalogue of Western Manuscripts and Miniatures*, Sotheby's, 7 December 1982, pp. 71–5.
222. Dowling, 'Anne Boleyn', pp. 37–8; BL, Cotton MS Otho C X, fo. 228v (*LP* X, 797).
223. Dowling, 'Anne Boleyn', pp. 38, 40–1.
224. BL, Cotton MS Otho C X, fo. 230 (*LP* X, 792).
225. Ibid. fo. 269v (*LP* X, 942).
226. Dowling, 'Scholarship, Politics', pp. 139 etc.

Thomas Cawarden, Sadler – were, since they were a generation younger, more assured, more extreme, and above all better-educated 'protestants' than the men they replaced.[227]

Religiously, then, 1536 secured the continuity of the Reformation; politically, it laid bare the foundations of Cromwell's ministry. His first act, once Anne's destruction was accomplished, was to wrest control of the Groomship of the Stool from his Aragonese allies. They had put their own candidate, Sir Francis Bryan, into the post. For Bryan, the 'Vicar of Hell', had swung wildly from being an enthusiastic supporter of Anne during her ascendancy to a deter- mined opponent during her decline.[228] Such a man in such a place was intolerable. So Cromwell first froze the appointment; then in a fortnight of frantic manoeuvring, during which it was even rumoured that the office would be suppressed, secured an ingenious victory. Bryan was left as Chief Gentleman of the Privy Chamber. This office, again borrowed from France, had been given to Norris, the then Groom of the Stool, in 1532. The intention was partly to give him parity with his French colleague at the meeting of Henry VIII and Francis I at Boulogne in October of that year; and partly to restore to him the overall headship of the department which the Groom had lost with the appointment after 1518 of so many Gentlemen of the Privy Chamber of higher social standing than he was. But alongside Bryan was appointed another Chief Gentleman, Thomas Heneage. He was originally Wolsey's appointee; now he was Cromwell's ally and client. And Heneage, not Bryan, was given the Groomship of the Stool with its crucial administrative respon- sibilities. So the Aragonese was left with prestige; the Cromwellian with power.[229] His political control thus secured, Cromwell, as we have seen, threw his attitude to Privy Chamber administration into reverse: hitherto he had impeded it; now he developed it.

And he developed his political control too with the ensuing stream – broadening into a flood – of Cromwellian appointees to the Privy Chamber. Henry seems to have objected to only one of these, the rebarbative propagandist Richard Moryson, and even then Cromwell eventually had his way.[230] The result was that by late 1539 the minister's dominance was complete. Not only had he eliminated

---

227. Cf. Starkey, *Reign of Henry VIII.*
228. *LP* IV iii, 5519; VII, 1554.
229. Starkey, 'Privy Chamber', pp. 234–6; *LP* X, 865, 994.
230. *LP* XIII i, 1296; XIV i, 733.

the core of the Aragonese party; he had also contrived to bring into acute disfavour both Bryan and Sir Anthony Browne, the only two surviving Gentlemen of independent political stature.[231] Browne quickly regained his feet, but Bryan never fully recovered.[232] The Cromwellianization of the court was then made manifest. By late January 1539 Denny, Cromwell's man, had replaced Bryan.[233] That, since the senior Chief Gentleman was Heneage, also the minister's client, apparently sewed up the Privy Chamber. But not tightly enough for Cromwell who, that same month, himself joined the department by stepping into the dead Exeter's shoes as chief Noble of the Privy Chamber; then a year later he was made Lord Great Chamberlain as well.[234] Hitherto the Great Chamberlainship had been merely hereditary and ceremonial; now it was Cromwell's intention to turn it into the real working headship of the whole household–above-stairs: Chamber and Privy Chamber alike. The minister's fall prevented the full realization of the scheme, but enough survived the wreckage to show that the Great Chamberlainship was not a stately irrelevancy, acquired merely for prestige, as has hitherto been assumed, but the crown of his career as a court minister.[235]

Yet control of the court was not everything. Cromwell had it but he fell all the same. For there was also the council and parliament, where his control was more open to challenge. And it was through the Council and parliament, using his patronage of extreme reformers as the excuse, that he was destroyed.[236] But as with Wolsey a decade earlier, the minister's court party survived the minister (except, that is, for the king's *bête-noire* Moryson).[237] This meant that when ordinary political life resumed after the turmoil of 1540 it took the form of a struggle between the Privy Council, dominated by Cromwell's conservative enemies, and the Privy Chamber, dominated by his radical appointees. The latter found a

231. *LP* XIII ii, 1120, 1163; XIV i, 144.
232. *LP* XIV i, 37, 144.
233. Loc. cit.
234. *LP* XIV i, 2; XV, 611/38.
235. Here I argue against myself (Starkey, 'Privy Chamber', p. 289) on the grounds that subsequent Lord Great Chamberlains take over the effective headship of the household: e.g. *LP* XVI, 1465; XVII, 741.
236. Susan Brigden, ' Popular Disturbance and the Fall of Thomas Cromwell and the Reformers', *Historical Journal* 24 (1981), 257 ff; Muriel St. Clare Byrne, ed., *The Lisle Letters* (6 vols, Chicago and London 1981) VI, pp. 211 ff.
237. *LP* XVI, 394/6.

leader drawn from their own ranks, Sir Anthony Denny, who, as we have seen, had replaced the disgraced Bryan as second Chief Gentleman of the Privy Chamber in January 1539. The two sides were evenly balanced. So though attacks aplenty were launched on both conservatives, like Sir John Wallop, and Privy Chamber radicals, like Cawarden, Mewtis, Hoby and George Blage (who was nicknamed the king's 'pig', and avoided being turned, as he put it, into roast pork by a hair's breadth), in the event neither faction was strong enough to press things to a conclusion and the intended victims escaped.[238]

It was only the peculiar circumstances of the last months of the reign that produced a decisive swing in the balance of power. Then the radical minority party in the Privy Council, which was led by Edward Seymour, earl of Hertford and Prince Edward's uncle, and John Dudley, viscount Lisle and a member of the Privy Chamber since 1542 or 1543,[239] and advised and abetted by Sir William Paget, the Secretary, went into firm alliance with the Denny grouping in the Privy Chamber.[240] The councillors had the claim on power, but the Privy Chamber alone could supply the means. As a necessary preliminary, the Denny faction had to establish a stranglehold on the Privy Chamber itself. In October 1546 Heneage, the long-serving Groom of the Stool and first Chief Gentleman, was dismissed and Denny promoted into his place; while Sir William Herbert, Queen Catherine Parr's brother-in-law and another evangelical, was brought in as second Chief Gentleman.[241] Then, in the following months as the king's health went into constant if uneven decline, this control was brought devastatingly to bear. First, Denny and Herbert used their power over access to exclude their rivals from court. There, and literally behind closed doors, Henry's mind was poisoned against the conservatives: Gardiner was disgraced; Surrey executed and Norfolk himself only escaped because the king died first. At the same time the text of the king's will was doctored: on the one hand, to give the radicals and their leader Seymour a clear working majority on the Privy Council, and, on the other, through the 'unfulfilled gifts clause', which stated simply but astonishingly that what the king had intended but failed to grant in life the Privy

---

238. *LP* XVI, 541, 678/41; XVIII ii, 241/6; Foxe, *Acts and Monuments* V, pp. 464, 473, 494, 564; *LP* XXI i, 1382/43.
239. *LP* XVII, 418; XVIII i, 701 and see Starkey, 'Privy Chamber', p. 226.
240. *LP* XIX i, 293; XXI ii, 555/18.
241. *LP* XXI ii, 331/43; *LP* XXI ii, 634/1, 648/60 and see Starkey, 'Privy Chamber', p. 243.

Council were empowered to grant after his death, to enable the radicals both to reward themselves and also to buy the silence of their surviving opponents. The subtle and minimal forgery used to effect all this points clearly to Paget, the Secretary and 'master of practices', as its author. But the authentication of the will, as indeed of Norfolk's attainder, was carried out by Denny and his brother-in-law and Privy Chamber factotum, John Gates, using the Dry Stamp of the king's signature which they controlled. Henry, that is, signed neither, and moreover was probably dead already when the Stamp was applied.[242]

'We may know historical facts to be true, as we may know facts in common life to be true. Motives are generally unknown. We cannot trust to the characters we find in history.'[243] Dr Johnson could well have been thinking of Henry VIII when he pronounced his dictum. For the evidence I have interpreted in one sense has been presented by other historians in the opposite sense. Instead of a struggle to control Henry, we have Henry's determination to control his ministers.[244] The evidence will bear either interpretation and the truth may well have been a mixture of the two. Until the last, that is. For in the crisis over his will, mortality delivered the king into the hands of his courtiers and councillors.

But if the immediate issue of motive, or at least responsibility, is clear, the broader significance of these events remains highly debatable. In the last weeks of the reign, political power swings visibly from the Council Chamber to the Bedchamber, and administrative power follows a similar course, with everything hanging on the Dry Stamp held by the Privy Chamber. What does this mean? Was it a mere flash in the pan, an aberration resulting from Henry's physical and mental decline? Or was it something more? Following some incautious and frankly ill-informed guesses in my own earlier work, Professor Elton came down strongly in favour of the first position.[245] What follows here proves both of us wrong. Far from being an aberration, the Privy Chamber's part in the events of 1546–47 was the culmination of its role in the rest of the reign. And

242. For all this see Elton, *Reform and Reformation*, pp. 330–3; Helen Miller, 'Henry VIII's Unwritten Will' in E. W. Ives *et al* eds, *Wealth and Power in Tudor England* (1978), and Starkey, *Reign of Henry VIII*.
243. J. Boswell, *Life of Johnson*, ed. R. W. Chapman (Oxford 1953), p. 408.
244. For this interpretation, see L. B. Smith, *The Mask of Royalty* (1971). Dr Glyn Redworth is also about to publish a sensitive reappraisal of the debate in *History Today* (1987).
245. Starkey, 'Privy Chamber', pp. 418–19; Elton, *Reform and Reformation*, p. 220 n. 19.

far from being a flash in the pan, the Privy Chamber's activities offered a precedent that was still alive at the beginning of the following century. Politics under James I, as under Henry VIII, was a politics of intimacy; and his reign, like Henry's, ended with a Chamber favourite 'cutt[ing] off all access' (below p. 223).

CHAPTER FOUR

The illusion of decline: the Privy Chamber, 1547–1558

John Murphy

Imagine, if possible, that Tudor England had been equipped with the trappings of the contemporary political scene, like commentators and heavy-weight journalists. Where better for the historian to begin examination of the reigns of Edward VI and Mary I than with the comments of one of these well-placed political observers? The historian might be in for a few shocks, however. If such an observer were struck not by how much things changed after the death of Henry VIII but rather by how much things remained the same, the historian might rightly be surprised or even sceptical. Were a reporter at the court of Edward VI in 1552 to write neither of the Privy Council as the decisive centre of political power nor of the grip of John Dudley, duke of Northumberland upon the reins of government but rather of the continued importance and activity of the Privy Chamber, his comments might arouse genuine disbelief. Similarly, were the same observer, in his assessment of the impact of the accession of England's first queen regnant upon the political system, to dwell upon the structural changes in the royal household rather than upon the potential divisions in the Privy Council or the deep rivalry between Bishop Gardiner and Baron Paget, his report might be met with a similar sense of incredulity. Of course such an approach, unmodified by a wider context, would be too bald and too simple. However, its emphasis upon the vital importance of the control of the household and the focal point of politics, the Privy Chamber, would in essentials be correct.

For only by taking into account the active role of the royal household in the political developments of the reigns of Edward and Mary can any real sense and cohesion be imposed upon events. Without this central element the whole period is no more than a series of convoluted chapters in a story with no unifying theme, but only a Byzantine plot.

However, it should be said that such an interpretation challenges almost everything that has recently been accepted by historians. The works of Professor Elton, Dr Hoak, Dr Leamasters and Professor Loades,[1] though they tend to vary in their emphasis, look upon these mid-Tudor reigns as the dawn of the conciliar government that was the hall-mark of the golden age of Elizabeth. Everything that was wise, responsible, far-sighted, enlightened and sensible took place in the Privy Council where the heirs of Thomas Cromwell earnestly worked to continue the enterprise of their great mentor.[2] Everything that was foolish, extreme, ill-conceived, rash and dangerous, had its origin in the peculiarities of a royal minority or the stubborn bigotry of a religious fanatic, who had the misfortune to be both stupid, half-foreign and wholly a woman.[3] Though it has been observed that this is hindsight with a vengeance, the very unanimity of the judgment has reinforced its authority.

Moreover, the tendency to tack on the reigns of Edward VI and Mary I as a despairing postscript to the history of Henry VIII or as a grim preface to the age of Gloriana has only confirmed the prejudices of the centuries. In fact, 1547 and 1553 were not echoes or anticipations, but fresh assaults upon the problems of the age by individuals with very different perceptions and priorities. In both cases a common understanding of how the political system worked and could be made to carry through policy was bent to diametrically opposed ends. There were special difficulties, of course, and the accession of a minor and then a female inevitably disturbed the delicate mechanisms which governed political life and had their axis in the private apartments of the royal household. Yet neither this novelty nor the policies pursued destroyed the essential principles of effective government. In short, there was no more than an illusion of decline, later sanctified into myth and hallowed by generations

1. G. R. Elton, *Reform and Reformation* (1977); D. Hoak, *The King's Council in the Reign of Edward VI* (Cambridge 1976); G. A. Leamasters 'The Privy Council in the reign of Queen Mary I' (unpublished Cambridge Ph. D. dissertation, 1971); D. M. Loades, *The Reign of Mary Tudor* (1979). However, in his recently-published article, 'The King's Privy Chamber, 1547–1553' in D. J. Guth *et al.*, eds, *Tudor Rule and Revolution* (Cambridge 1982), Dr Hoak moves much nearer to the position taken in this chapter.
2. Elton, op. cit. pp. 328–75.
3. Ibid. p. 376.

of propaganda into what theologians call the certain truth of tradition.

The history of the Privy Chamber itself has three main phases: first, decline from the centre of the royal establishment to an adjunct of Protector Somerset's household; second, revival after 1549 and gradual re-emergence as a focus for political life; third, remodelling after 1553 to suit the peculiar requirements of a woman whom fate had placed at the head of a society dominated by men.

The Somerset experiment: 'an interregnum'

The fact that the coronation of Edward VI was marked by 'no very memorable show of triumph or magnificence' underlines the novelty of the accession of a minor.[4] Normally a new reign and a new monarch marked some discernible turning point in political history; sometimes measures were changed, and almost always men. A new king brought with him his own friends and favourites, who could expect to be found room in the household establishment and to whom the perquisites and plums, the major fruits of household office, would fall. Edward's accession was to witness no such immediate transformation.[5]

There were of course changes in February 1547. But they were carried through by Protector Somerset on behalf of his young charge, and they were mere tinkerings with personnel – a modest working through, in fact, of the consequences of the successful exclusion of Gardiner and the elimination of the Howard clan in the last weeks of the old reign. Room was found in the new establishment for a handful of officers from Edward's princely retinue. John Ryther replaced Sir Edmund Peckham as Cofferer; Robert Beverley graduated from the princely Counting House to the royal Kitchen; several religious conservatives, like Bishops Thirlby, Heath and Day and Chaplain Oglethorpe lost their court offices and were replaced with reformers like Richard Cox, Hugh Latimer and Nicholas Ridley.[6] The king's tutors were given access to their charge, though in the case of John Cheke no specific household office was given to

---

4. *CSP Sp.* IX (1547–49), 47 ff.
5. LC 2/3, 4(1), 4(2), 4(3). These are the coronation and funeral lists drawn up by the Great Wardrobe. There are also a number of other lists of household officials in e.g. BL, Additional MS 34,010, 34,320 and Stowe MS 571. All these lists should be used with great caution: they are not attendance registers.
6. Ibid.

him.[7] Several Grooms who had long been Edward's companions, like Edward Rogers, were made Grooms in the Privy Chamber.[8] Finally, Somerset placed his brother-in-law, Sir Michael Stanhope, in his own stead as Gentleman of the Privy Chamber.[9] From this it is fairly clear that continuity rather than change was the order of the day. Denny continued to dominate the Privy Chamber, lending appropriate assistance to Somerset's seizure of Henry's private treasure.[10] Major court officers like St John (the Great Master), Arundel (the Lord Chamberlain), all the Gentlemen of the Privy Chamber – even poor old Ralph Sadler – and Sir Anthony Wingfield (the Vice-chamberlain) continued to hold their posts. True, in June Paget ousted Sir John Gage from the Controllership.[11] But few thought this had much significance. Even the royal Barbers remained on the payroll for two quarters, though they now served a beardless boy. The whole court had the appearance of dwelling in the half-light of Henry VIII's shadow.

At first sight this prolonged sense of interregnum is hard to explain. In January 1547 Somerset had secured for himself both the office of Protector and the Governorship of the king's person. All power was his; on the other hand, he seemed to make no direct attempt to assert himself in either office but contented himself with primacy in status. Why ? The reason turns on how Somerset won power in the hours and days after Henry's death. It has long been suspected that J. A. Froude's assertion that all was achieved without a struggle is well wide of the mark.[12] That Henry's will was a product of intense struggle is now almost certain. That strife continued into the new reign is likely too. For though the will had settled one set of questions, it had left open another. In particular, the nature and extent of Somerset's power in the new regime was undetermined. There were two precedents: under Edward V the offices of Protector of the realm and Governor of the king's person had been combined by Richard of Gloucester; in the minority of Henry VI they had been kept separate.[13] Somerset aimed for the first; others preferred the second.

7–9.   Ibid.
10.   SP10/3/7
11.   S. T. Bindoff, ed., *History of Parliament: The House of Commons, 1509–1558* (3 vols, 1982) II, p. 180.
12.   J. A. Froude, *The Reign of Edward VI* (1910), p. 4. And see above, pp. 116–17.
13.   J. S. Roskill, 'The Office and Dignity of Protector of England, *EHR* 58 (1953), 230ff; S. B. Chrimes, 'The Pretensions of the duke of Gloucester in 1422', ibid. 45 (1930), 102 ff.

Traces of the dispute surface fitfully. Even Van der Delft, not the shrewdest observer, noted the incipient rivalry betwen Somerset and John Dudley, created earl of Warwick in February 1547.[14] The same source tells us that there were also tensions between Somerset and his impossible brother, Thomas Seymour. The latter put in a bid for a division of the spoils with the Governorship of the king's person falling to his share. We know that Dudley was involved in settling this dispute, and we know also that Thomas Seymour's admission to the Council and appointment as admiral were direct consequences of the settlement. We know further that practically every councillor received a grant of land and title in the aftermath of Somerset's proclamation as Protector.[15] Subsequent criticisms of Somerset also offer useful clues. No one criticized his policy. Instead Thomas Seymour attacked his treatment of the king – who, he claimed, was brought up like a ward and had a beggarly appearance.[16] While about the same time, Dudley complained to Cecil about Somerset's exercise of patronage wherein, he claimed, the honour of himself and others was little considered.[17]

From these facts it is impossible to provide a detailed account of how and on what terms Somerset won power in January 1547. But it is possible to provide an explanation of why the 'good duke' was so restrained in exercising his notional authority for the first months of 1547. The proposal that Somerset should be made Protector of the realm and Governor of the king's person was made after Henry's demise and Paget was almost certainly the chosen salesman of the scheme (just as he had been the master-surgeon behind the doctoring of Henry's will). The proposal as retailed to the other councillors almost certainly raised immediate doubts, not only among conservatives like Wriothesley and Arundel but also amongst pragmatists like Dudley, Herbert and Russell. But Somerset was prepared to pay a price – the titles and lands bestowed on his fellow councillors early in February 1547. It was naked bribery. At this point, either Thomas Seymour supported by Dudley and others, or Seymour on his own initiative, approached Somerset directly and demanded the Governorship of the king's person for himself.[18] Somerset was then forced

14. *CSP Sp.* IX (1547–49), 49.
15. H. Miller, 'Henry VIII's Unwritten Will: grants of lands and honours in 1547' in E. W. Ives *et al.*, eds, *Wealth and Power in Tudor England* (1978), pp. 87 ff.
16. G. E. Corrie, ed., *Sermons by Hugh Latimer* (Parker Society, Cambridge 1844), p. 184.
17. SP10/4/26.
18. BL, Additional MS 48,126, fos. 6–16.

to make larger concessions than he had originally intended. Thomas Seymour was admitted to the Council and it seems from Dudley's later comments that Somerset agreed to share the spoils of the patronage network which he would control by virtue of his position as the king's Governor. Somerset's power then was so conditionally acquired that he had no choice but to exercise it cautiously. Hence the conservatism and absence of clean-sweep which left the Privy Chamber in particular in limbo: still the Henrician department in personnel, but deprived of its old role and not yet given a new one.

Quite suddenly in August 1547 all this changed. The reason was the Scottish war. As preparations got under way for the campaign, a whole series of *ad hoc* arrangements had to be made. Officers of the household were called upon to help in the victualling of the army, and means of communication between the Protector in Scotland and the Council in London had to be arranged.[19] The chosen agents were officers of Somerset's own household and Sir Michael Stanhope in the Privy Chamber. Stanhope took over the administration of the Privy Purse in August 1547 and by the end of that month had replaced Denny as First Gentleman of the Privy Chamber.[20] From this personally-controlled source of cash, Stanhope paid for various messengers bringing news between Scotland and London. Just as the circumstances of war necessitated changes so the outcome of the war confirmed and enhanced them. Somerset as architect and general of the Scottish war returned to London after the devastating victory at Pinkie a conqueror and national hero. In the light of his new-found prestige the political balance, so carefully maintained since Henry's death, tipped firmly in the duke's favour. By the end of 1547 he had achieved a *translatio imperii* as complete in its kind as Henry's break with Rome. Power moved from Whitehall Palace to Somerset House.

The Somerset experiment: the Privy Chamber in decline

As Somerset, with all his characteristic recklessness, threw aside the political shackles that had held him in check, so a new shape began to form in the household. The Privy Chamber had continued to be a focus for political contact – and the exclusion of Gardiner and

19. *DNB.*
20. *History of Parliament* III, p. 368; E351/2932 contains the Privy Purse accounts of Stanhope during his period as First Gentleman of the Privy Chamber.

Wriothesley from the court was the main reason for their continuing political impotence. Henceforth, however, the Privy Chamber became the domain of Sir Michael Stanhope. He gradually excluded from the court all Somerset's rivals. Arundel, the Chamberlain, retired to the country in disgrace and gave Stanhope the chance to act as Lord Chamberlain as well as First Gentleman. He took direct control of the Revels; organized such court ceremonial as was deemed necessary for the king to partake in;[21] and managed the king's personal money – keeping him so short of funds, indeed, as to encourage the boy to accept illicit gifts.[22] About the private apartments he placed Somerset's cronies like Edward Wolfe. The palace guard was supplemented by a group of paid mercenaries responsible for the security of the court. As offices in the Privy Chamber fell vacant, they were filled by nominees of the duke. Above all, Stanhope curtailed direct access to the king and deliberately distanced him from his subjects.

The king's entourage was rapidly becoming a sub-department of the Protector's household. It is hardly surprising that comparisons with Wolsey were drawn.[23] But so sure was the Protector of his position that he left the whole discharge of the functions of Governor to Stanhope. And Stanhope saw that just as the idiosyncrasies of age and immobility had dictated much of what had happened in Henry VIII's Privy Chamber in the last years of the reign, so the direct imposition of a pattern of life and routine in a minority could effectively exclude undesirable influences from the king.

Effectively, then, Stanhope was Governor: it was said in 1549 that Thomas Seymour wanted to have 'the governance of [Edward] as Mr Stanhope had'. And as such he created a characteristic atmosphere – unwelcoming and austere – in the private apartments. But while Stanhope built this regime, he failed to make it secure. Seymour, embittered and resentful of his brother and jealous of Stanhope's intimacy with the king, which he perceived to be his right, turned his hand to conspiracy.[24] Employing the assistance of a Groom of the Privy Chamber, John Fowler, Seymour began to

21. *Documents relating to the Revels at Court in the time of King Edward VI and Queen Mary*, ed. A. Feuillerat (Louvain and London 1914). The introduction draws attention to Stanhope's role.
22. Cf. *APC* II, 249, 259.
23. BL, Cotton MS Titus F III, fo. 27.
24. *APC* II, 260; SP10/6/10; J. G. Nichols, ed., *The Literary Remains of King Edward VI* (2 vols, Roxburghe Club 1852), I, pp. cxv–cxxi.

conduct a direct correspondence with the king.[25] Money was passed over; notes were exchanged and good wishes extracted from the king. Having thus, as he thought, won a secure place in the king's affections, Seymour set about turning this asset into political capital. In association with Sir William Sharington, another former officer of the Privy Chamber, vast amounts of money were embezzled from the Bristol Mint. With this cash Seymour seems to have intended to buy himself further support. Later in the year he took his campaign a step further and tried to build up a party of supporters among the excluded officers of the court and the disgraced members of the Council. In short, while Somerset busied himself with affairs of state his brother took advantage of his neglect of the court and penetrated the citadel of his power. And that with any Tudor servant – even the servant of a minor – exposed him to the ultimate danger.[26]

However, patience was not the admiral's most striking virtue. He could not wait for his plans to mature and his moment to come. Instead he risked all on a foolhardy attempt to abduct the king from his bedroom. The bizarre scheme failed. Even so it placed Somerset's whole reputation at stake. If as Governor of the king's person he could not ensure the safety of his royal charge, how could he provide as Protector for the security of the realm ? In order to shore up his failing power, the Protector turned to those whom he had deliber-ately excluded.[27] Arundel, Wriothesley, Dudley and others were summoned back to the court and reinstated on the Privy Council. For the trial and execution of Somerset's brother had to look to all the world like a collective act rather than an attempt by the Protector to cover up his own neglect of duty. The pulpit lent its voice too and Latimer, as preacher extraordinary to the court, refuted Seymour's assertion that the king was being brought up in an unsuitable manner. Meanwhile Somerset entrusted the Council with financial responsibility for the household,[28] but could not bring himself to do anything about Stanhope. His failure to re-establish his authority as Governor of the king ruined his remaining political

---

25. SP10/6/1–16 covers the proceedings against the lord admiral. Cf. also *APC* II, espec. 246–56, 258–60.
26. Ibid.
27. W. K. Jordan, *Edward VI, the young king* (1966), pp. 374–82; also see W. K. Jordan, *Edward VI, the threshold of power* (1968). These two volumes are still the most comprehensive history of Edward's reign.
28. SP10/10/7.

credit. For Stanhope's methods were exposed. Instead of controlling the Privy Chamber, he had only created a vacuum which others might fill more successfully than Seymour. The risk was intolerable. But the problem remained of how to detach the king from Somerset. The regrouped alliance of January 1547 – Arundel, Dudley and Wriothesley – saw only too clearly the danger of using force to seize, as Seymour had tried to do, the person of the king. They chose instead to force Somerset to relinquish the king to them. When in the summer of 1549 the domestic crisis at the court combined with the wider political crisis of rebellion in the country their opportunity came.

By October 1549 Somerset faced an opposition which controlled London but which still lacked the one vital element that could legitimize their position: Edward himself.[29] Somerset made his last stand when late one evening he took the king from the comfort of Hampton Court to the grim security of Windsor Castle. Once there, surrounded only by Somerset's creatures and Stanhope, the king bewailed his 'prison' and conveniently developed a severe cold which kept him from his uncle's side. As pressure mounted from London, Somerset was made vividly aware at last of his isolation. When offered his life, if not his liberty, the duke capitulated. An escort of councillors arrived from London; Somerset, Stanhope and the rest were taken to the Tower and the king's health miraculously recovered.[30] The Somerset experiment had ended in failure.

Government by a Protector from his own household had none of the legitimacy of the Privy Chamber politics of Henry VIII's last years. This vital weakness was perceived by Somerset's brother. And though his attempt to build up a court party, dependent on the support of the young king, was badly misplaced in its judgment of Edward VI, it was essentially correct in its perception that the king alone could provide a stable basis for government. With this in mind, the victorious faction turned its immediate attention to the Privy Chamber.

Northumberland's ascendancy: reform and revival

Dudley's *coup d'état* did much more than remove Somerset and his henchmen from the royal establishment. It inaugurated a period of

29. *APC* II, 248–56.
30. W. K. Jordan, ed., *The Chronicle and Political Papers of King Edward VI* (1966), pp. 17–18; *APC* II, 330–44.

reform which culminated in the revival of the Privy Chamber as a focus for government and politics; it also laid the basis for a recreation of the Privy Chamber as an administrative and financial centre. The immediate goals were of course more limited. Dudley and his allies planned only to undo the novelties of Somerset's regime and make proper provision for the continuing education of the king.[31]

But what of the king in all this? The changes would profoundly affect Edward and would have to be carried out in his name. However, none of the faction leaders, Dudley, Wriothesley or Arundel, showed any signs of anticipating problems in getting their young sovereign to agree to this (or anything else). This is hardly surprising as Stanhope's regime had prevented them from developing any sort of intimacy with Edward. But they may have presumed too easily. Edward had already developed a mind of his own, at least about religion, and the signs are that he swiftly brought it to bear.[32]

The first act of the faction was the re-ordering of the Privy Chamber. Two things stand out about this: first that these reforms were carried through with Edward's specific endorsement,[33] and second that, apart from Arundel, all the new appointees were either co-religionists of the king or pragmatic reformers like Dudley himself. No traditionalist was allowed office in the inner chambers of the palace even though, as Professor Elton points out, religious conservatives had technical and numerical superiority on the Council. It would seem from this that the purge of the Council completed by January 1550 was a consequence of the packing of the Privy Chamber and not vice versa. If this be the case, how were the dominant faction out-manoeuvred? The most obvious and satisfactory explanation points to the king: that he was not willing to have men of the 'catholic sort' about him. He had after all told Somerset that he was not surprised that Bishop Thirlby should have voted against the Prayer Book, as a bishop who had spent so long with the Emperor was bound to 'smell of the Interim'. Such royal intervention would explain both the surprising exclusion of traditionalists from the Privy Chamber, and (since it was unexpected) the equally strange talk of making Mary regent, which surfaced only after the battle to control the royal apartments had been lost and won.[34]

31. *APC* II, 344–5. *Chronicle*, 18, 24, 26.
32. H. Robinson, ed., *Original Letters relative to the English Reformation* (2 vols, Parker Society 1856), pp. 645: Burcher to Bullinger.
33. Edward's phrase is 'by my consent', *Chronicle*, p. 18.
34. This interpretation conflicts with those of Professor Elton and Dr Hoak. Elton, *Reform and Reformation*, pp. 351 ff; Hoak, *King's Council*, pp. 248 ff.

Doubtless there will be those who will argue that Edward could not have exercised, either in 1549 or at any time thereafter, such a decisive influence on events. He was the hapless victim of circumstances and the powerless puppet of whichever faction was victorious. But in this case at least the onus of proof must lie on the doubters. Edward had already made his tastes in religion known. And it would have been a foolish, as well as a bold, councillor who would have forced on his sovereign personal servants whom he was bound to dislike. Moreover, it should be remembered, as contemporaries certainly did, that the king was only five years at most from his majority, which he showed every sign of living to enjoy.

Be all that as it may, the facts are clear. The new personnel in the Privy Chamber shared two characteristics: the king's religion and the king's personal favour. Sir Edward Rogers, Sir Henry Sidney, Sir Richard Neville, Sir Robert Dudley and Barnaby Fitzpatrick were all appointed Gentlemen after 1550 and they all basked in Edward's particular regard. Sir Nicholas Throckmorton, another of the group, is even supposed to have bragged of the fact.[35]

As well as the personnel, the structure of the Privy Chamber was altered. The office of First Gentleman was abolished and replaced by the four Principal Gentlemen of the Privy Chamber. Two of these were to be permanently with the king. The four had a salary of £50 each and received an additional £50 for the special care they had to take of their royal charge.[36] The first four appointments were Sir Edward Rogers, Sir Thomas Darcy, Sir Andrew Dudley and Sir Thomas Wroth. After Rogers's disgrace in 1550, the opportunity came for the elevation of Sir Anthony Denny's brother-in-law, Sir John Gates.[37] Further point was given to these reforms in May 1550 when the provisions for the security of the Privy Chamber were overhauled. Two attendants were to be placed outside the king's Bedchamber each night; a special new court guard was created and it was laid down that only the Principal Gentlemen could have access to the royal bedroom. Entrance to the 'inner chamber' was forbidden any other officer of the Privy Chamber.[38]

Just as the office of First Gentleman was abolished, so the Governorship of the king's person was now placed in commission. Six Councillors were appointed to attend on the king in his Privy

35. *History of Parliament* III, p. 459.
36. *APC* II, 344–5.
37. *History of Parliament* II, p. 198; III, pp. 206–7.
38. *Chronicle*, p. 26. These provisions came into force just before the rehabilitation of Somerset. *APC* III, 29–30; Hoak, *King's Council*, pp. 199–201.

Chamber to oversee Edward's education in what were called 'these his tender years'.[39] The six included Dudley, who acquired the title of duke of Northumberland and the offices of Lord Great Master of the Household and lord president of the Council, Arundel, the Lord Chamberlain, who was expelled from the court in January 1550, Northampton, Wentworth, St John and Russell. Again, at least two of these councillors were to be permanently attendant on the king, even when public business was pressing. Though doubtless designed only as a convenient means of linking the king directly with his Privy Council, the Governorship-in-commission had the effect of creating two sorts of councillor: those who had direct access to the king in his Privy Chamber and those who did not. And what may not have seemed in the autumn of 1549 of much importance became in a little time of great moment. For this access to the king was the real means by which Northumberland was to gain control of his colleagues on the Privy Council.

Secretarial changes also played a part in the developing pattern. The appointment of William Thomas as clerk to the Council in 1550 created yet another link between the Privy Chamber and the Privy Council.[40] Thomas, a royal favourite, who had probably been introduced to the king by Throckmorton of the Privy Chamber, kept Edward informed of decisions in the Council; he also supplied him with a series of idiosyncratic position papers on the great issues of the day, some of which were reflected in Edward's own memoranda. Later in 1550 came a parallel, though more significant, development with the appointment of William Cecil as a third Principal Secretary. As such he had two main functions. He acted as Northumberland's private secretary, just as he had once been Somerset's; and he took over as Edward's private secretary as well. Under Henry VIII the private secretaryship had been part of the province of the Chief Gentleman of the Privy Chamber; under Elizabeth the principal Secretaryship of State and the private secretaryship were to be fused in Cecil's own person.[41]

These alterations to the structure of the Privy Chamber had a significant impact on government. By drawing the Council and the Privy Chamber more closely together, they provided the political coherence which Somerset's methods so patently lacked. As well,

39. *APC* II, 344 ff.
40. E. R. Adair, 'William Thomas: a forgotten clerk of the Privy Council' in R. W. Seton Watson, ed., *Tudor Studies* (1924).
41. *Chronicle*, p. 46, and cf. ibid., pp. 39, 47, 90; above, pp. 98–100 below, p. 153.

they bestowed an enhanced status on certain councillors which must have created a natural leadership within the Council. Edward benefited too, since he was better informed and more able to participate in discussions. This gave him both the opportunity to develop his ideas and a practical training in politics and administration. But the change was not only educational. The relative importance of the king's role increased. Better informed and doubtless more confident, he now had ample opportunity to express his views and opinions. Where these views were asserted, it became prudent to take them into account. If they were impractical it was possible to demonstrate them to be so. But the danger was that the king might dig his heels in. If he did, it was no small matter to overrule him.[42] Thus the management of the king ceased to be simply a matter of keeping him in his Chamber. Moreover, each year that passed brought him ever closer to the point at which he might take his own way regardless of the pressures brought to bear upon him. The new role of the king, already great and becoming greater, was the real reason why the struggle between Northumberland and Somerset after 1550 resembled in so many ways earlier battles for the king's confidence in the reign of Henry VIII.

The structural changes in the Privy Chamber, with all their implications for politics, demonstrate how easily the Privy Chamber's machinery could be adapted to the ever-changing circumstances of personal monarchy. But the continuities were just as important. The Gentleman of the Privy Chamber were still, uniquely, servants of both the monarch's bodies: his public as well as his private person. The fact was reflected in their range of extra-curial employment. Among the Gentlemen were still regular ambassadors like Sir Philip Hoby and Sir Richard Moryson; experts on Irish affairs like Sir Anthony St Leger and Sir Edward Bellingham, or on Scottish matters like Sir Ralph Sadler; and military experts like Sir William Herbert, later earl of Pembroke, as well as those like Sir John Gates whose careers were of a more political and administrative character. The Gentlemen continued to hold key offices in the localities as J. P.'s, as well as regional military commands like the captaincy of Hull. They also served in parliament, where they remained a crucial link between court and kingdom. All this had threatened to lose meaning with Somerset's devaluation of the department, but with the revival of the Privy Chamber after 1549 there came a fresh surge of activity. Particularly

42. Cf. below, pp. 139–40, and note 52.

important was the role assigned to the Privy Chamber in the government's military schemes. The events of 1549 had raised two spectres: social revolution on the one hand, and palace coup on the other. The special household guards of May 1550 were designed to deal with the latter; the new provincial levies with the former. And the Privy Chamber held key commands in both.[43]

David Starkey once thought that a royal minority meant the end of the Privy Chamber. It is clear that the requiem was premature. Indeed we can go further. For with 1549 the tendency to enhance the Privy Chamber's standing, both within the household and without, which had been so marked in the later years of Henry VIII, resumed with a vengeance. Not only did the ties between the Privy Council and the Privy Chamber become ever closer, so did the Privy Chamber's hold on the rest of the household. From 1549 the great officers of the household were regularly members of the Privy Chamber. Northumberland, as Great Master and Northampton as Great Chamberlain served in the department; while as the Lord Chamberlainship passed in turn from Arundel to Wentworth to Darcy it too carried automatic membership of the Privy Chamber. The double office of Vice-chamberlain and Captain of the Guard was also held by one of the four Principal Gentlemen from November 1549; indeed, it seems to have been used to designate the senior of the four Principal Gentlemen.[44] And, to complete the continuities with the 1540s, the senior Principal Gentlemen was also re-emerging as a major royal administrator, at least in finance (below, pp. 135–9). Had a Cromwell been around, it would have been tempting to ascribe all this to some grand scheme of rationalization; as it was, it would be safer to think only of adaptation to circumstance, political pressures, and the usual insatiable demand for office and power.

Northumberland's ascendancy: the Privy Chamber and faction politics

So the *coup d'état* of 1549 had resulted in the radical reorganization of the court. That reorganization was consolidated and elaborated

---

43. *History of Parliament* I, pp. 414–15; II, p. 341–3, 366–8, 633–5; III, pp. 249–52; *Chronicle*, pp. 124, 132; D. Hoak, 'The King's Privy Chamber, 1547–1553', pp. 87–108.
44. Thus Sir John Gates combined these offices in succession to Sir Thomas Darcy.

during the remainder of Edward VI's reign. However, the immediate effect of the changes was to move the focus of government and politics away from Somerset House and the Privy Council and back to the court. There the new balance of forces put the anti-Seymour alliance under acute strain. Following Edward's emphatic expression of his religious preferences, Northumberland executed a *volte face*. For much of the previous year he had displayed some indications that he intended to halt, if not reverse, the Reformation; now he allied himself with Cox, Cheke, Sir Anthony Cooke, John Hooper and the other radical reformers who were so close to the king, and had been responsible for much of his education. At the same time as Northumberland swung 'left', his erstwhile allies went overtly 'right'. Piqued by their exclusion from the Privy Chamber, they floated wild schemes like the Marian regency.

The result was that the alliance, which, as the previous record of the parties suggested, was eminently workable, broke up and Northumberland moved into the attack. In January 1550 Arundel was deprived of his Chamberlain's staff, and both he and the other conservative leader, Wriothesley, were rusticated. At the same time, a number of lesser lights in the traditionalist group, including the former Cofferer Peckham, were similarly banished from the Council and the court. Though this must have been pleasing to the king, it posed problems for Northumberland. For with the traditionalist faction pushed aside and the Somerset group disgraced, the duke's political power now rested on a very narrow base. True, he had in the young king a powerful friend and ally, but the king was still perhaps four years from his majority. With these thoughts in mind it was logical to attempt a *rapprochement* with Somerset. Thus, in easy stages the duke was released from the Tower and fined; then he was rehabilitated as a privy councillor; finally in May 1550 he was readmitted to the Privy Chamber as one of the august group of councillors governing the king's person. His table at court was restored and the putative alliance sealed with a marriage between Somerset's son and Dudley's daughter. As Northumberland left the court in June 1550, all seemed set fair for an era of co-operation.[45]

It was not to be. With the death of Wriothesley in May 1550 the conservative party, which had been in disarray since the previous autumn, was without a leader. This was the mantle that Somerset now tried to assume. The means were to be Bishop Gardiner's reconciliation to the regime and restoration to favour. Edward's

45. For all this, see Jordan, *Edward VI, threshold of power*, pp. 28–73.

Chronicle charts each step. First, taking advantage of Northumberland's absence, Somerset arranged for a delegation of his fellow lords-attendant in the Privy Chamber to visit Gardiner to see if he would accept the Prayer Book. Gardiner, clearly primed for this 'surprise' interview, was uncharacteristically all sweetness and reason. He would indeed accept and set forth the new liturgy. Thus having set the stage at the court, Somerset now involved the Council. Meanwhile Northumberland had got wind of the plan and came scurrying back to court. The next delegation to the bishop contained a number of his notable adversaries, including Bishop Ridley. Under their more rigorous questioning Gardiner's moderation evaporated and the plot to secure his release collapsed. Somerset retired from court in a sulk. Within a month another plot – to spirit the Princess Mary away – was uncovered.[46] Although the two events were almost certainly unconnected, to Northumberland and the king they must have appeared to be more than a coincidence. Worse came with Mary's steady resistance to Edward's very personal attempt to force her to renounce the Mass. Perpetually her chief protector, the Imperial Ambassador, trotted out Somerset's promise in June 1549 that Mary would not be troubled in religion until the king came of age. On every issue, it seemed, Somerset was out of step. Blindly he presumed on his blood relationship with Edward. But whatever affection the king might have felt had vanished with the events of October 1549. By the autumn of 1550 Somerset's disgrace was the talk of the court and a year later he was arrested, tried and executed in January 1552.[47]

Somerset, careless for his own safety and casual in his assumptions about Edward, had largely brought his fate on himself. It was he who took issue with Northumberland and he who threatened the political balance of the court. The result had been a period of faction struggle very like the 1530s, with Northumberland as a not unworthy successor to Cromwell. He had displayed a talent for opportunistic organization and a political timing second only to the earlier minister's. He too moved immediately to secure the Privy Chamber, and he showed, above all, a similar sensitivity to the wishes of the king.

But it is perhaps a mistake to focus on this familiar story of high politics. For underpinning and shaping it was the much less familiar revival of the role of king and entourage. One of the most striking

46. *Chronicle*, pp. 34–6, 39–40.
47. Jordan, *Edward VI, threshold of power*, pp. 73–98.

episodes is the career of Sir John Gates. Already Vice-chamberlain, senior Chief Gentleman and Keeper of the Privy Purse, his activities spread out far and wide from the Privy Chamber: it was he who was dispatched into East Anglia when the rumours of Mary's planned escape first surfaced; he was involved in the strengthening of the fortifications of the south coast, in the diplomacy surrounding the French embassy, and in the programme of land sales.[48] But always his activities as a financial administrator were the most important. In 1552 he became chancellor of the Duchy of Lancaster and played a prominent part, along with his predecessor Darcy, in the series of commissions that was busy recasting the structure of royal finance in the last year of the reign. The commissioners' report had two main proposals. The first, for the fusion of the multiplicity of revenue courts into the Exchequer, has received all the attention. Just as important, however, were their actual financial recommendations. These look back directly to the Cromwellian 'memoranda' of 1537. An 'estate', a balance sheet of income and expenditure, was drawn up, with the prime purpose of providing for an annual surplus, that 'there might remain yearly to his Highness's affairs such an overplus in treasure as might suffice honourably his extraordinary occasions'.[49] In other words the Privy Coffers were to be revived.

Edward died before the report could be put fully into effect. But it is clear that many of its most important recommendations – including the revival of the Privy Coffers. – had already been implemented. Here it is important to distinguish between two Privy Chamber accounts. On 10 January 1550 – some three months, that is, after the office of Groom of the Stool had been put in commission among the four newly-appointed Principal Gentlemen – the Privy Purse account (in suspense since Stanhope's dismissal) had been revived and given an initial float of £700. The account was to be administered by the four Principal Gentlemen, who were to handle all payments 'as had been usually paid by Sir Anthony Denny knight deceased, and other late occupying the room or office of the Groom-ship of the Stool'. The declared account of the four knights shows that is just what they did: they paid for the king's linen and close-stools; his private alms and rewards; and for the wages of some private servants and dependents including Will Somers, the royal fool. The categories are those of the Privy Purse as it had established

48. *History of Parliament* II, pp. 198–9; *Chronicle*, p. 40.
49. *Chronicle*, p. 134; W. C. Richardson, ed., *The Report of the Royal Commission of 1552* (Archive of British History and Culture, II, Morganstown 1974), espec. pp. xxiii ff., 227–8, and above, pp. 97–8.

itself between *c.* 1495 and 1530; but the sums, as was natural for a minor with a much reduced establishment, were smaller and totalled just short of £4,000 for the two years from 10 January 1550 to 1 January 1552, when the account ended.[50]

The audit of the Privy Purse in January 1552 had been called for, almost certainly, because the Council had decided to institute a second and much more important Privy Chamber account in parallel to the first. The Council letter ordering the audit was sent out on 10 December 1551; on 30 December a commission was issued to call in royal debts; whilst a second similar commission was directed 'to the earl of Bedford, and to the Mr Vice-chamberlain' on 12 January. The monies so raised, the Council decided on 8 February, should be paid over 'weekly' by the officers of the revenue courts to Peter Osborne, 'indenting with him . . . for . . . such sums as shall be paid to his hands'. The indentures between Osborne, 'clerk to the four knights attending on the king's majesty's person' (i.e. the four Principal Gentlemen of the Privy Chamber), and the Exchequer and Augmentations survive. From the Exchequer he received £580 of 'debts and arrearages' in five more or less weekly instalments scattered between February and July 1552; while from Augmentations came the much larger sum of £16,667 paid in the same months, with almost religious regularity.[51]

The aim, recorded by Edward himself in his so-called 'Memorandum on Ways and Means', was that these 'arrearages' were to 'be left for a treasure, or not dismembered by these payments [of the crown's debts]'. That rather gives the game away. Edward would put pressure on his own debtors; his creditors, however, would as far as possible be put off. It is the technique of any small businessman in a tight corner. And it is the government's financial straits which explain Osborne's sudden prominence. Already treasurer for called-in debts he now became, briefly, both the receiver- and paymaster-general of Edward's government. Any ready cash that was going was siphoned off from the debt-ridden (and possibly corrupt) revenue courts and handed over to Osborne. Once again the chicanery is transparent. Creditors, in particular the king's own servants, were kept waiting; but at least the government got its hands on money to pay for its most pressing needs.[52]

The 'policy' was put into effect with the new financial year

50. E101/426/8.
51. *Chronicle*, pp. 102, 106; *APC* III, 437, 475; E101/625/4; E314/19; Richardson, *Report*, p. xxiv.
52. *Chronicle*, pp. 174–5.

beginning on Lady Day, 25 March 1552. From early April a 'stop' was progressively put on payments: first the Exchequer received the king's 'express commandment' that monies coming in from the 'Relief' voted in the parliamentary session of 1549 were to be 'reserved . . . for certain special service of his Majesty's', and not to be paid out but by special warrant of the Council. Then a similar embargo was put on all payments from Augmentations, and the Duchy of Lancaster; finally the stop was broadened into a general instruction to all the revenue courts on 29 May 1552.[53] The stop was hard to enforce (the treasurer of Augmentations had to be imprisoned for defying it); quickly modified and in any case of doubtful benefit. From the 'Relief' Osborne received largish sums; otherwise it was like applying a tourniquet to an already bloodless corpse: in early May, for example, Augmentations and the Exchequer (from its ordinary revenue) were unable to raise £600 between them.[54]

For a time, then, the government of England depended on the dribs and drabs of taxation voted three years earlier and whatever could be wrung out of royal debtors. Like many an individual in a similar plight, Edward's government shut up shop and retired to the country. In May an unusually extended progress, through Hampshire to the south coast, was decided on, and on 27 June Edward left for Hampton Court on the first leg of the journey. He only returned to Whitehall on 10 October, and in the interim, as the Council told Anne of Cleves, he was 'resolved not to be troubled with payments'. In these three months 'government' reduced itself to the king's household and entourage, both of which were financed by his household treasurer, Osborne. On 9 July Osborne paid £7,000 to the Cofferer of the Household for 'his charges this progress time', and £2,000 to the Treasurer of the Chamber; while in September he paid wages for the gendarmes assigned to the Council and Privy Chamber. A contingent of these accompanied the king through the progress, and their wages and their fellows' totalled a staggering £6,875.[55]

The new financial arrangements were sufficiently striking to come to the attention of the Imperial Ambassador Scheyfve. 'The king's monies', he reported in January 1553,

53. Ibid. p. 122; *APC* IV, 27, 37, 46, 48, 62. J. D. Mackie, *The Earlier Tudors* (Oxford 1952), p. 500.
54. *Chronicle*, p. 128; *APC* IV, 41, 45–6.
55. *Chronicle*, pp. 123, 133, 149; *APC* IV, 94, 109, 111, 132–3.

which used to be under the direct control of the lord high treasurer and the receivers who managed the finances, are now being taken either to the Tower or to the Jewel House at Westminster, and only one or two intimate friends of the duke are given access to them.

The ambassador got rather the wrong end of the stick: he assumed that the procedure was unprecedented; he also hinted very strongly that Northumberland was keeping Edward in the dark or even cheating him. Neither was true. The use of the private finances in 1552 followed the clear precedents of 1529–32 and 1542–7. In terms of circumstances (financial crisis), the parallel was with the former; in terms of procedure, with the latter. In 1529 the Privy Purse account itself had been inflated to deal with the task of government; on the other hand, in 1552, as in 1542–47, the Privy Purse remained a small-scale personal treasury, while new, and much larger, payments were directed through a separate Privy Coffer or 'special affairs' treasury. The explanation lay in the changed character of the Privy Purse. In 1529 the account was half-formed and therefore easily expandable; by 1542 it was not. In the decade following Cromwell's assault on the personal finances at the beginning of his ministry, the Privy Purse had settled down into a well-defined treasury, paying out small, fixed sums. It was thus singularly unfitted to deal with the large, irregular payments that characterized any expansions of the private finances. So when such expansion took place, either in the 1540s, or again in 1552, a separate treasury was needed. Hence Henry VIII's directly administered Privy Coffers in the former period, and the 'special affairs' treasury in the latter.[56]

But not only was Scheyfve ignorant of the precedents for the new arrangements for the king's monies; he also badly misjudged the king's role. First, as his own papers show, Edward was fully, even minutely briefed: he knew all about the 'arrearages', and the '£50,000 of treasury money for all events' – that is, the target for the Privy Coffers. Second, and this has not hitherto even been guessed, he was on the point of taking the whole thing over. Osborne's file of warrants has survived. Almost all are Council warrants; then at the end of the file come half a dozen signet warrants, bearing Edward's own sign manual. The first is dated 19 February 1553; the last 14 May. This final warrant marked the closing down of Osborne's special account and the setting up of a more conventional Privy Coffer account in the custody of Sir Andrew Dudley, 'one of the chief Gentlemen of our Privy Chamber'. The warrant directed

56. *CSP Sp.* XI (1553), 4, and see above, pp. 92–8.

Osborne to hand over £216 11s, being 'the remain of tharrearage of our debts remaining in your hands', and another £1,431 that had come from various other sources. The money was to be kept by Dudley 'in our Privy Coffers'. Osborne then submitted his own accounts and received a formal quittance. The latter shows that between the opening of his account in January 1552 and its closing in May 1553 he had accounted for just under £40,000.[57] All this puts his activities into perspective. His account was a one-off; designed to cope with a particular crisis, and wound up as soon as the immediate emergency was passed. In its place went a new Privy Coffer account, under the direct supervision of the king. And under Edward's ruthless oversight, no doubt, the Privy Coffers would indeed have turned into the central organ of the reformed finances, as the 1552 commission envisaged.

That is a might have been but it is a guess firmly grounded on the fact of Edward's informed involvement in finance. The same went for other areas of government. And a prime source of information, as of course it was for finance, was his Privy Chamber, with whom he did much more than pass the time of day. Wearing their other hats, or rather putting their hats on as they left the royal presence, they became, as we have seen, leading men of affairs: ambassadors, military experts, administrators. Edward talked to them and questioned them and wrote it all down in his *Chronicle*, which becomes from 1549 the fullest and best informed political narrative of the day, fuller often and more reliable even than the Council registers. But, again as in finance, Edward was not simply a reporter; he was an actor, who thanks in large measure to his Privy Chamber network, already knew his part as well as any king ever had. The pressure he brought to bear on his sister Mary was ruthless and insistent and only the very real threat of war from Charles V saved her.[58] Where such defences did not apply his will was ungainsayable. Rich, the lord chancellor, was the best-known victim. He had refused to forward for sealing a royal commission because not enough councillors had countersigned it. Outraged, Edward riposted that such a refusal was to put him 'in bondage'.[59] Rich capitulated; fell ill and was eased out of the chancellorship. The letter in dispute was one that Edward 'had willed some[one] about me to write' – in other words, it had been produced by the private sec-

57. *Chronicle*, pp. 174–8; E101/549/19 (unfd.); *CPR* V (1553), 85, 185.
58. *Chronicle*, pp. 41, 55–6.
59. *Ibid.* p. 84.

retariat of the Privy Chamber. That showed very clearly which way the wind was blowing.

It was Northumberland's great skill to trim his sails to that wind. Almost too well in fact. With the king he was everything; without him he was nothing. It may have been his understanding of this which drove him to follow the king down the path that led to his final destruction. Yet equally it could be said that the attempt to place Jane Grey on the throne was precisely the sort of calculated risk which had paid such dividends at earlier stages of Northumberland's career. This time though the gamble failed, and with its failure the way was open for Mary's victory and triumphant entry into London. It must have seemed that history had reached a turning point. It was inevitable that much of the recent past would be swept aside; would the Privy Chamber vanish with the rest?

The reign of Mary I: survival and adaptation

It is ironic that Mary had more impact on the development of the Privy Chamber than those self-conscious reformers Wolsey and Cromwell. For her accession in 1553 brought crashing down the whole impressive edifice built up over the previous forty years. Of course this collapse was accidental and due not to planning but to the queen's sex. The private apartments of the queen were not and could not be the sort of place where men could freely associate with their sovereign; nor could a queen be served by male body servants. Thus all the Privy Chamber offices that had been the most coveted in the household now fell into the hands of women. And this effectively neutralized them. For the women chosen by the queen to fill her private apartments were not only of irreproachable character, like Cecily Barnes, Frideswide Strelly and Susan Clarencieux, but they had no ambitions either to attempt a 'petticoat government' in the style of Sarah Churchill and Abigail Masham in the reign of Queen Anne. Mary did supplement her Privy Chamber favourites, drawn as they were from her own princely entourage, with a number of Ladies and Gentlewomen of the Privy Chamber who were the wives or other female relations of her leading councillors. But as the queen was neither a particularly withdrawn figure nor particularly susceptible to pressure from her female servants, these women did not play much part in procuring either patronage or favour for their menfolk. Indeed, the most these women could really hope for was to make a good marriage for their family. Here, of course, Mary had a decisive voice – though like Elizabeth later she seemed to have had an aversion to her closest servants attaining the same blessed state that she herself aspired to.[60]

The demise of the Privy Chamber did not mean the demise of a second centre in politics and administration, however. Mary's own formidable character saw to that. From the outset, over appointments, her marriage negotiations, in the establishment of the religious settlement, in the settling of financial policy and in the reform of the revenue courts, Mary showed a determination to be far more deeply and routinely involved in business than her father had ever been. The Venetian ambassador, surprised, made particular note at the length of time Mary spent on state business and in giving audiences.[61] Her conscientiousness in fact resembled Henry VII's and it expressed itself in a similar way in the confidence she reposed in a small group of household officers.

Almost all, like the Ladies of her Privy Chamber, were taken from her old princely household. From this source came Sir Robert Rochester her Controller, Sir Henry Jerningham her Vice-chamberlain and Captain of the Guard, and the courtly Sir Edward Hastings, the Master of the Horse.[62] Between them they governed access to her apartments and her person. They guarded her security and were in every way the chief figures of her court. Above all they alone, because of their place and personal favour, saw the queen regularly. To these she added a handful of others: Sir John Norris, the Principal Gentleman in her Privy Chamber; James Basset, Gardiner's secretary and servant, her private secretary and Chief Gentleman of her consort's Privy Chamber, and Bishop Day, who also straddled the two royal households as Almoner to both king and queen.[63] These men were in themselves not a Privy Chamber. But they fulfilled much of the role of one. They were the chief channel of access to the queen; her eyes and ears in court and country, and a necessary stiffening to the whole machinery of government. They did not aspire to be the formulators of policy; on the other hand, those who did

60. Henry Clifford, *The Life of Jane Dormer, Duchess of Feria*, ed. J. Stevenson (1887). Mary felt unable to allow Dormer to marry the duke of Feria till 1558.
61. *CSP Ven.* V (1534–54), 533
62. LC4(2), 4(3); *APC* IV, 419 ff.
63. For Norris, see *History of Parliament* III, pp. 19–20; for Basset see M. St Clare Byrne, *The Lisle Letters* (6 vols, London and Chicago 1981) V, pp. 468–525; VI, pp. 262–75.

could not hope to work without them, or, still more, without their mistress.

The two principal contenders for power, Paget and Gardiner, took very different attitudes to all this. Paget sought to base his power on his relationship with the Habsburg ambassador Renard (who overrated himself and has been overrated by all but the most recent generation of historians), and later on Mary's Habsburg consort, King Philip. Neither technique was very successful. Gardiner, in contrast, allied himself with Mary's household men. The alliance was a natural one, being based on shared religious inclinations and a shared hostility to the policies and personnel of Edward VI's government. It was also effective. As it was being forged, Rochester, the Controller, who had been entrusted with the task of 'restraining' the household, 'by the queen's own command-ment' published his new set of ordinances.[64] In the main they were a reissue of Cromwell's of 1539–40, but tagged on were the final clauses of Wolsey's Eltham Ordinances of 1526. And these bestowed the ultimate oversight of the whole household on the lord chancellor, which post Mary had given Gardiner in the first days of the reign. The same team of Gardiner and Rochester worked together to settle Philip's establishment as king.[65] The Council was excluded entirely and it was a servant of Gardiner's, James Basset, who was appointed as Philip's Chief Gentleman. Since he was also (as we have seen) Mary's private secretary, he became the principal go-between of the two sovereigns and was sent in 1558 to tell Philip 'sure advice of her being pregnant'.[66] Others too came from Gardiner's stable, with the result that the royal household – lay and ecclesiastical – became a fusion of Mary's princely affinity with the bishop of Winchester's following. The double affinity survived the deaths of both its chief founders, Gardiner and later Rochester, and preserved its distinc-tiveness throughout. It never became close to Paget or to the great lords of the Council; instead it was the queen's own. Mary recog-nized this too, and after Gardiner's death went to extraordinary lengths to get control of his private correspondence.[67] He, and his, had become hers.

64. *APC* IV, 421; LS13/279, fos. 5 ff.
65. Edward Arber, ed., *An English Garner* (1903), p. 191.
66. J. A. Muller, *Stephen Gardiner and the Tudor Reaction* (1926), pp. 69, 170, 183, 196, 291; *CSP Ven.* VI (1555–56), 1432.
67. *CSP Ven.* VI (1555–56), 558, 571, 578–79. See C. Erickson, *Bloody Mary* (1978), pp. 430–4. Details of Mary's interest in Gardiner's papers are to be found in Muller, *Gardiner and the Tudor Reaction*.

This intimacy of queen and chief minister was not built overnight. Their growing trust in one another had to overcome a history of suspicion: Gardiner, after all, had betrayed the queen's mother in the 1530s; he also put himself, apparently, badly out of step at the beginning of the reign on one of the two great issues of policy, the queen's marriage. It was Paget who supported the queen's increasingly obvious determination to marry Philip; Gardiner and her household who backed the rival candidature of Edward Courtenay, earl of Devon. Both bishop and household were then brought sharply into line by Mary herself, and subsequently supported her policy as warmly as they had opposed it. Rochester and his colleagues worked hard to persuade the court and through the court the country.[68] Gardiner even managed to turn his opposition to the marriage into a crucial negotiating counter and it was in large part to win him over that Charles V and his advisers conceded such extraordinarily generous terms to the English in the marriage treaty.[69] On the other hand, Paget gained much less than he had hoped for, and in any case threw everything away by the stance he adopted on the second great question of policy: religion. Here there was no confusion about where sympathies lay. Mary and Gardiner were set on a complete Catholic restoration; Paget was against, or at any rate only conditionally for. The dispute became acute in the spring of 1554 with the preparations for the second parliament of the reign. Gardiner was pressing for the summoning of parliament to Oxford and a sweeping programme of religious legislation, including the revival of the heresy laws.[70] Gardiner was eventually defeated over the summons to Oxford; on the other hand his religious programme – somewhat camouflaged – got through the Council's legislative committee, though it stuck at the full board. Both Paget and Gardiner therefore had grounds for dissatisfaction with the Council as it stood and they co-operated in a short-lived scheme for a reduced Council. When parliament met, however, their dispute flared into the open. Gardiner introduced his heresy bill and got it through the Commons; but Paget led successful opposition in the Lords on the grounds that it had not been approved by the Council. That ditched him. Mary told the Council as a whole to

68. *CSP Sp.* XI (1553) deals in detail with the marriage negotiations. See especially 153–4, 236, 337–45, 416; ibid. 444.
69. Ibid. 372.
70. For this and what follows see S. R. Gammon, *Statesman and Schemer: William, first Lord Paget* (1973), pp. 200–9, and cf. A. Weikel, 'The Marian Council Revisited' in J. Loach and R. Tittler, eds, *The Mid-Tudor Polity* (1980), pp. 66–7.

leave her chancellor alone to get on with his job, while for Paget personally she reserved a special venom that sent him to his knees in tearful apology.

This was not the first time that Paget had accused Gardiner of acting without the Council, nor was it to be the last. Earlier in 1553, in the aftermath of Wyatt's rebellion, he had complained to Renard that the chancellor despised his colleagues; that he acted without their consent; took private measures over religion; proceeded faster than was wise and planted suspicions in the queen's mind about the loyalty of his fellow councillors. And eighteen months later, in an audience with Renard's master Charles V, he returned to the same themes, accusing Gardiner of a 'self-sufficiency and asperity' that were incompatible with the corporate enterprise of conciliar government.[71] Even those who have defended Mary's Council against Renard's charges of faction-ridden incompetence have by and large accepted the thrust of Paget's criticisms. Yet they are equally insubstantial. For the monarch to make religious policy in consultation with only a handful of the Council or even outside it altogether was entirely normal. Henry VIII did it; Elizabeth did it; even Edward VI did it in his interventions, for example, over the Black Rubric. So why not Mary? Equally Gardiner, as chief councillor, was exercising only the same sort of independence and discretion as Cromwell, Paget's supposed mentor, had done. Such autonomy, so long as it was backed by the will of the sovereign and supported by the royal entourage, was legitimate – if often irksome. In fact, Paget's grouses have gained respectability only retrospectively and by accident – by the accident that Elizabeth chose to concentrate all power in the hands of her Council, and by the even stranger accident that twentieth-century historians have chosen to see that eccentric arrangement as 'the authentic Tudor Privy Council'.

That Paget suffered from fewer delusions is suggested by his subsequent behaviour. After the debacle of spring 1554 and his ensuing lengthy banishment from court he returned to the Council and accepted, if not always graciously, a lesser role. Rumblings of discontent there were, and he continued to see in Philip, for no very good reason, a hope for better things. But the reality was revealed by the events of 1555. As far back as early 1554 Paget had been pushing for some sort of restricted Council. The schemes had been formally agreed to then and were revived in rather different form once Philip was installed in England as king-consort. On both occasions, however, Gardiner and his allies in the household had

71. *CSP Sp*, XII (1554), 166–8; XIII (1554–8), 87–90.

used their place in the queen's confidence to circumvent them. What gave the schemes a sudden significance was the termination of Mary's false pregnancy in May 1555 and her consequent hysterical collapse which lasted for several months. In these circumstances the 'Council of State' took on fresh life: in May it was given its own seal and in the same month the parallel sets of Council minute books, one kept by Secretary Bourne, a household man, and the other by Secretary Petre, Paget's ally, ended and Petre instead kept one master record. All that this reflected, however, was the usual response to the incapacity or withdrawal of the sovereign. Once that ended so did the dominance of the Council of State.[72]

Mary's mourning for the child that never was ceased with Gardiner's own death in November 1555. Paget's hopes rose again but were dashed when the great seal went to Archbishop Heath, with only the privy seal as a consolation prize to him.[73] Thereafter it was, rather surprisingly, business as before. Pole, by this time archbishop of Canterbury, worked directly with Mary on religion, in which the Council played little part save for the public persecution of 'Protestant martyrs'.[74] The Council itself was run by Paget and the great lords; Rochester and Hastings, who was now the rising star at court, acted as the crucial link with the household;[75] while the machinery of household government actually strengthened as the queen's health declined. Basset, the private secretary, acted as intermediary between the queen and ministers like Paget; he had also taken over the promotion of state papers to the royal sign manual.[76] Even finance was not wholly lost to the household; instead it was subject to a curious hybrid arrangement. Formally the Exchequer had resumed its sway in the reforms of 1553–54; in practice one of the tellers, Nicholas Brigham, handled the great bulk of revenue (between half and two-thirds in the last three years of the reign) as the 'queen's teller'.[77]

72. See D. Hoak, 'Two Revolutions in Tudor Government' in C. Coleman and D. Starkey, eds, *Revolution Reassessed* (Oxford 1986), pp. 107–11. The emphasis on the decisive role of the queen's state of mind is mine, however.
73. See Gammon, *Statesman and Schemer*, pp. 223–6.
74. See Erickson, *Bloody Mary*, p. 403 ff, which summarizes the traditional view of the persecutions; *APC* V, 120.
75. For Hastings, see *History of Parliament* II, pp. 315–7.
76. B. L. Beer and S. M. Jack, 'The Letters of William, Lord Paget of Beaudesert, 1547–63' in *Camden Miscellany*, XXV (Camden Soc. 4th series, 13) 1974, pp. 117–20, 139–41.
77. J. D. Alsop, 'Nicholas Brigham (d. 1558): scholar, antiquary and crown servant', *Sixteenth-Century Journal* 12 (1981), 49–67 and C. Coleman, 'Artifice or Accident? The reorganization of the Exchequer of Receipt, c. 1554–1572' in Coleman and Starkey, *Revolution Reassessed*, pp. 176–7.

But though the machine ticked over, its sense of direction, so strong until the queen's collapse in 1555, had gone. In default of a Catholic heir Elizabeth would succeed. Mary could not bear to contemplate the thought; her subjects had to. Thus, as the spring of 1558 turned into a summer marred by an epidemic of influenza, so the courtiers and councillors melted away to gather round the rising sun at Hatfield House. All the issues of 1547, 1549 and 1553 were once again on the political agenda. But whatever else the mid-Tudor years left unsettled, one thing is clear. The household had withstood a threat far worse than the chimera of Cromwell's supposed antipathy. Previous minorities, like Henry VI's, had emptied the court and dismantled the machinery of household government. In this regard Somerset was doing no more than follow precedent. But so ingrained had the practices of Henry VIII's reign become, that the revival of the Privy Chamber in 1549 was greeted with an almost audible sigh of relief. Similarly a female succession changed much. But a would-be chief councillor determined to work through the household on the one hand, and a queen who kept the machinery of the private secretariat and treasury at work on the other, meant that more remained the same. Historians' insistent obituaries for the household have proved to be somewhat premature.

CHAPTER FIVE

A change in direction: the ramifications of a female household, 1558–1603

Pam Wright

The accession of Elizabeth I in 1558 initiated a new period in the history of the sixteenth-century household. In it the development of the Privy Chamber as an administrative force was halted while the domestic functions of the department became once more prominent. And the change was not planned but merely contingent on the fact of having a long-standing queen regnant on the throne. Two areas in particular were affected: administration and politics.

The institutional consequences of Elizabeth's accession were clear-cut and immediate. The coronation list of 1559 is the first establishment list for the new Privy Chamber and is the basis upon which the department was constructed throughout the reign.[1] Automatically ladies were substituted for gentlemen and provision was made for a three-tiered structure of feed posts occupied by women, namely Ladies of the Bedchamber, Gentlewomen of the Privy Chamber ('maids') and Chamberers. Furthermore, staff numbers were augmented by the appointment of a group of unsalaried women and an additional skeleton staff of men. The effective elimination of the post of Groom of the Stool from the Privy Chamber was evident from its omission from the coronation list and, as will emerge, this was significant for the administrative development of the department.

On coming to the throne in 1558, Elizabeth understandably moved close friends and relations into positions of service on her person and, therefore, into the Privy Chamber. But there was no attempt to remodel the structure of the department, established in her father's reign, to meet her needs as a female sovereign. Despite

1. LC2/4(3); BL, Lansdowne MS 3, fo. 88.

the unsuitability of the Henrician regulations for a female staff, no new household ordinances were drawn up at the beginning of the reign. Henry VIII had provided for a paid staff of eighteen Gentlemen of the Privy Chamber and six Grooms (including two Groom-Barbers).[2] Thereafter the number of Gentlemen held steady but by 1552 there were twelve Grooms in wages.[3] Elizabeth, however, threw all this into reverse. During the whole of her reign she appointed only two Gentlemen and at no time had more than eight paid Grooms in her service.[4] This apparent understaffing was compensated for by the appointment of women to equivalent posts.

There are several plausible explanations why Elizabeth and her ministers did not attempt a revision of the household ordinances in 1559. First the new queen was well able to staff the department according to her own needs without bothering about the formal structure of the Privy Chamber. Second, although there is no reason to believe that the Privy Chamber created in 1558–59 was in any way intended to be temporary, it is perfectly possible that the queen's expected marriage made any plans to remodel the household a very low priority – something that could wait until a new king's establishment had to be provided for. Third, the principal impetus behind the construction of the Henrician ordinances had been political. No parallel situation existed in 1559. Indeed, the absence of any attempt to remodel the household during the reign is indicative of the domestic, uncontentious nature of the Privy Chamber. Efforts were made to cut expenses and to restrict the number of servants kept by those holding office,[5] but there is never any indication that the great politicians on the Council felt the need for Privy Chamber reform to bolster their hold on power.

So the Privy Chamber created in 1558–59 turned out to be very much a patchwork establishment. The old structure of the King's and Queen's Sides of the household was simply adapted to function without a male sovereign. Elizabeth enlarged the Queen's Side of

2. E36/231, pp. 68–9 (*HO*, 169; *LP* XX ii, Appendix 2/2/vi).

3. BL, Stowe MS 571, fos. 30–30v.

4. For Asteley's appointment see LC2/4(3), fo. 104; BL, Lansdowne MS 3, fo. 88; for Hatton's E351/1795, fo. 31. No further Gentlemen of the Privy Chamber are noted as receiving a wage either in the Cofferer's accounts (E351/1795) or in the extant fee lists (BL, Lansdowne MS 3, fo. 88; 104, fo. 18; 29, fo. 68; 34, fo. 30; 59, fo. 22). For the Grooms, see fee lists and LC5/31–7, which list the liveries received by the Grooms, but do not distinguish between feed and unfeed.

5. BL, Lansdowne MS 34, fo. 24 (June 1582); 103, fo. 76 (October 1592); 21, art. 67 fo. 141 (undated). But attention was already being given to expenditure by 1572 when the expenses of the 16th year were compared to those of the 8th (ibid. 21, art. 67, fo. 143).

the household to provide for her own establishment and reduced the King's Side to a ceremonial Lord's Side presided over by whichever leading nobleman happened to be at court at the time. Much of the Queen's Side was made up by the Privy Chamber staff. Although never given official formalization the resulting structure meant that Elizabeth had managed to create a household tailor-made to her needs.[6]

The household of Catherine Parr (of which Elizabeth had personal experience) appears to have provided the main model for the structure of the new Privy Chamber.[7] The main difference between the two households was that Elizabeth formally assigned a handful of the Privy Chamber to service in the Bedchamber, thereby creating a definite hierarchy based on nearness of access.[8] It is likely that the Bedchamber women also divided most of the domestic duties of the office of Groom of the Stool among themselves, as Elizabeth never formally appointed anyone to the post. The precedent for this arrangement came from Northumberland's reforms in Edward VI's Privy Chamber. These had similarly suppressed the Groomship of the Stool, instead putting its responsibilities into commission, as it were, among the four Principal Gentlemen, who alone were to have access to the Bedchamber (above, p. 129).

Elizabeth followed the precedent fairly faithfully. Four Ladies of the Bedchamber, Catherine (*née* Carey), lady Knollys, Blanche Parry, Catherine Asteley and Elizabeth Norwich, were appointed in 1558 and were the women closest to the queen.[9] But only one, Catherine Asteley, seems to have been called Chief Gentlewoman of the Privy Chamber and it was she who performed the traditional lavatorial task of the Henrician office – to receive and be the keeper of the queen's close-stools.[10] The only specific reference made to a Groom of the Stool under Elizabeth is later and comes from the officers of James I's Jewel House. They referred to Catherine (*née* Carey), lady Howard, and later countess of Nottingham, as having occupied the post when chasing her recently widowed husband about some cutlery that had gone missing during her term of office.[11] This should not be taken too literally but rather as a further indication that the everyday duties of the Groom of the Stool were being

6. Ibid. 102, fo. 2 (undated); 111, fo. 6 (1569).
7. E179/69(47).
8. LC2/4(3), fo. 104; BL, Lansdowne MS 3, fo. 88.
9. See note 8 above.
10. C47/3(38); E351/541, fo. 38; LC5/33, fo. 128.
11. E351/1956, fo. 15.

carried out by the female head of the Privy Chamber without the addition of the formal title.

The office of Chief Gentlewoman of the Privy Chamber is, in itself, a difficult one to document. Catherine Asteley and Blanche Parry are the only women definitely known to have held the position,[12] although their probable successors were Lady Howard and Mary Radcliffe.[13] It is clear, hovever, that the status of the office was very different from that of its Henrician ancestor. Both the Keepership of the Privy Purse and of the Dry Stamp of the sign manual were removed from the list of duties of the Chief Gentlewoman. The post was thus stripped of its political significance, becoming primarily a domestic one with the holder responsible for the queen's personal jewellery and some of the furnishings and equipment of the private apartments, in particular the royal close-stools. The other office of prominence held by the women in the Privy Chamber was that of Mistress of the Robes. From the extant documentation it seems clear that the post was separate from the office of Chief Gentlewoman. As with the former post it is difficult to list with certainty all the occupants, but women who held the post include Frances, lady Cobham, Dorothy, lady Stafford and Mary, lady Scudamore. The holder took responsibility for the receiving of large deliveries of fabric and completed garments, and would sometimes oversee the delivery of items of clothing to other members of the Privy Chamber. Other members of the department were also involved in the receipt of fabric. For example, Elizabeth, lady Carew was for many years in charge of the production of the queen's hoods and the Chamberers were often in receipt of holland cloth to make sheets. Probably the Mistress of the Robes can be seen as the supervisor of this hive of activity.[14]

And – it almost goes without saying – the rest of the department shared the fate of its two most senior posts and retreated into mere domesticity. In addition to the four Ladies of the Bedchamber, there were on average between seven and eight Gentlewomen of the Privy Chamber paid at the same rate, £33 6s. 8d., as well as four Cham-

12. Blanche Parry's tomb in St Margaret's Westminster bears an inscription which describes her as 'Chief Gentlewoman of Queen Elizabeth's Most Honourable Privy Chamber and Keeper of Her Majesty's Jewels'.
13. BL, Sloane MS 814, fo. 35 shows the succession of Blanche Parry, Lady Howard and Mary Radcliffe as 'Keeper of the Jewels'; E351/1954, fo. 11 shows Lady Howard presiding over the table for the Ladies of the Privy Chamber.
14. C115/L2/6697; LC33–37; C47/3(88).

berers who were given £20.[15] Unpaid members of the Privy
Chamber at the beginning of the reign included six Ladies of high
social rank and an 'extraordinary' group to serve 'when the queen's
Majesty calleth for them'.[16] The Maids of Honour, although never
listed as Privy Chamber staff, gave service too in the department and
usually numbered six.[17] The Privy Chamber was, therefore, staffed
by a maximum of sixteen waged female servants, with a small
unsalaried group of women in attendance and a further reserve list
'on call'.[18]

Although the unfeed Privy Chamber staff did not receive financial
recompense for their services, it cannot be assumed that their
positions were merely honorific. Those appointed at the beginning
of the reign were Margaret, duchess of Norfolk (wife of Thomas
Howard, duke of Norfolk), Margaret, lady Howard of Effingham
(wife of William Howard, lord Howard of Effingham and Lord
Chamberlain), Elizabeth, lady Clinton (wife of Edward, lord Clinton
and lord admiral), Mary, lady Sidney (wife of Sir Henry Sidney
and sister of Lord Robert Dudley), Anne, lady Parry (wife of Sir
Thomas Parry, Controller of the Household) and Anne, lady Carey
(soon to be Lady Hunsdon after the elevation of her husband, Sir
Henry Carey the queen's cousin, to the peerage).[19] Certainly Lady
Clinton and Lady Hunsdon were both engaged in practical service.
The former was responsible for paying the annuity given to Lady
Mary Grey,[20] and the latter is specifically mentioned as late as 1585
as a Lady of the Privy Chamber when a forfeit of £160 was made
over to her for her 'faithful service'.[21] It is probable that these
members of the Privy Chamber without wages constituted an elite
backdrop to the department, on hand to provide a prestigious show
on ceremonial occasions.

Duties performed by feed members of the Privy Chamber were

15. E351/1795; BL, Lansdowne MS 3, fo. 88; 104, fo. 18; 29, fo. 68; 34, fo. 30; 59,
    fo. 22. The number of feed women in the Privy Chamber dropped towards the
    end of the reign as the queen ceased to replace her old servants on their deaths.
16. LC2/4(3), fos. 104–5.
17. See the New Year's Gift lists for the reign: e.g. C47/3(38) (1563); BL, Additional
    MS 9772 (1568); Eton College, MS 192 (1581); C47/3(41), and the Subsidy Lists:
    E179/69(82); 69(93); 266(13); 70(107); 70(115).
18. LC2/4(3), fos. 104–5; BL, Harley MS 6265.
19. LC2/4(3), fos. 104–5.
20. E404/113, fo. 122. Lady Clinton seems to have acted as guardian of the Carey
    sisters and advised Lady Catherine on her marriage: BL, Harley HS 6286,
    fos. 78–83.
21. S03/1, fo. 34.

of a straightforwardly domestic nature. The Chamberers, for example, are mentioned frequently in the records of the Wardrobe as being responsible for the queen's linen – primarily bed-linen.[22] Indeed, the main responsibility for the everyday running of the Privy Chamber seems to have devolved on the Chamberers. They were, for instance, in receipt of an assortment of coffers, some to store plate, others to store linen, as well as a collection of water-bowls, locks, keys and a variety of other materials.[23] On the other hand, there is no indication that the feed upper servants of the Privy Chamber – the Ladies and Gentlewomen – had specific duties to perform, unless they were given additional posts such as Mistress of the Robes, Keeper of the Jewels and Plate or Keeper of the queen's Books.[24] How these women were valued by ambassadors, agents and suitors alike at court because of their ease of access to the queen will be described later. But their role as intermediaries, however important, was in no sense a part of their official duties.

So, from the top to the bottom of the department, the picture is of a Privy Chamber pared to its essentials. Elizabeth, as a woman, needed a corps of female attendants to wait upon her in a private capacity; as a queen she needed an intimate entourage to accompany her on state occasions. Her regular, salaried staff could fulfil both these tasks, helped out when necessary by the extraordinary women in service and by the extra prestige afforded by the unfeed Ladies of the Privy Chamber. The chief casualty of this emphatic domesticity was the sudden administrative prominence of the Henrician Privy Chamber. Its newly developed secretarial and financial responsibilities faded into oblivion – or, more accurately, passed into the hands of the queen's Secretary, Sir William Cecil.

Cecil, in fact, restored to the Secretaryship the powers over the royal signature usurped by the Henrician Grooms of the Stool; he also added to the Secretaryship (as Cromwell had showed signs of doing) the most important aspects of the Groom's financial tasks as well. These had had a double aspect. As Keeper of the Privy Purse, the Chief Gentleman was in charge of an important and sometimes dominant spending department; he was also, as Keeper of the Privy Coffers, the principal deposit treasurer of the kingdom (above, pp. 92–8). Both tasks were lost under Elizabeth. The Privy Purse survived as a household department, but it returned to being only

---

22. LC5/33–37.
23. E.g. LC5/33, fos. 15, 145.
24. See notes 12 and 13, and for Blanche Parry's receiving books: C47/3(38) (1562–63).

the personal petty cash of the sovereign. And it was in the charge, not of the Chief Gentlewoman, but of one of the Grooms of the Privy Chamber. The only surviving Privy Purse account was drawn up on the death of the Keeper, John Tamworth, in 1569. It details the minor domestic expenditure of the Privy Chamber: paying for the queen's jewels, horses and perfumes, and casual expenses such as riding charges, fabric costs and small rewards. One interesting entry shows also what had happened to the Privy Coffers. Tamworth notes that a substantial loan was made to the earl of Murray in 1568, but that the £500 handed over was 'received out of her Highess's Privy Treasure by the delivery of the Right Honorable Sir William Cecil' and given to Tamworth to dispatch to Scotland. So the machinery of the Privy Purse was in use, but it was Cecil who had control of the purse-strings by managing the queen's Coffers.[25]

The same went for the obtaining of the queen's signature – the prime motor of government. Here the informal free-for-almost-anyone-who-mattered of Henry VIII's reign was replaced, as both practice and Robert Beale's classic account make plain, by increased formalization and bureaucracy. And in control of the new procedure was the Secretary, not the Chief Gentlewoman. Ladies of the Privy Chamber still had a part to play, even in Beale's scenario, but they were only barometers of the queen's mood, to be tapped by the Secretary to make sure whether the weather were foul or fair. The explanation for the change was partly the accident of a female-dominated Privy Chamber; partly that Elizabeth had, unlike Mary, no male private secretary in the department – or rather she had, but it was Cecil who was both private secretary and Secretary of State.[26]

But the decline of the Privy Chamber was not only *vis-à-vis* government; it was also demoted within the household as well. Here it is the post of Lord Chamberlain which is the crucial indicator. Having a predominantly female Privy Chamber with no male head of department created a sort of administrative vacuum. Once more following Edwardian precedents, the office of Lord Chamberlain continued its mid-century revival. Rescued from its Henrician obscurity, even obsolescence, the post was dusted down and given new responsibilities as working administrative head of the Privy

25. BL, Harley Roll, AA23. See also the 'short table' of Cecil's disbursements 'at the Queen's command', May–August 1561, HMC, *Hatfield MSS* I, p. 261.
26. C. Read, *Mr. Secretary Walsingham and the Policy of Queen Elizabeth* (3 vols, Oxford 1925) I, p. 437, and above pp. 98–100, 141, 145 and below p. 187. Cecil also kept a stamp of the sign manual: HMC, *Hatfield MSS* I, p. 465.

Chamber as well as of the whole household 'above stairs'. While the financial and secretarial powers of the department had passed to Cecil, along with responsibility for piecemeal adjustments to the household regulations (usually for reasons of economy),[27] the Lord Chamberlain regained his influence over the organization of the royal progresses and, more importantly, over the allocation of lodgings at court. It is evident that he was no longer just the ceremonial head of the household, but someone who could effectively veto the residence at court of anyone he considered unwelcome – a useful weapon in the faction struggles of the reign. To give an example, Thomas Radcliffe, earl of Sussex, as Lord Chamberlain used his position to try and keep Mary, lady Sidney, away from court at a time when she was a potiential ally of her brother, Lord Robert Dudley. By offering Lady Sidney unsuitable lodgings, her return to the Privy Chamber was delayed, and it was only when she threatened to inform the queen that her absence was due to the intransigence of the Lord Chamberlain that Sussex's opposition ceased.[28] There is no evidence, however, that the Lord Chamberlain exercised any role in the day-to-day running of the Privy Chamber or that he had direct control over its staff. Nor have any letters survived that indicate that he was approached by suitors to secure them a place in the Privy Chamber. But he certainly was involved in helping members of the department in patronage suits and he was considered to be a person of influence whose assistance was invaluable to anyone seeking the queen's favour.[29] Deputy to the Lord Chamberlain and head of the household above stairs when the Chamberlainship itself was vacant was the Vice-chamberlain. This office too rose in importance as the Privy Chamber declined.

Two of Elizabeth's Vice-chamberlains, Thomas Heneage and John Stanhope, were promoted from the Privy Chamber, where they were unfeed Gentlemen, via the Treasurership of the Chamber.[30] This brings us to the male members of the Privy Chamber. Though they formed only a tiny fragment of its personnel, they could – given the passive role accorded to women in the sixteenth-century scheme

27. See note 4 and BL, Lansdowne MS 105, fo. 2. Ibid. 43, fo. 57 shows Cecil working in conjunction with the Lord Chamberlain.
28. BL, Cotton MS Titus B II, fo. 302. In ibid. fo. 346, Helena, marchioness of Northampton requests the intervention of the Lord Chamberlain to secure her access to court. The day-to-day allocation of lodgings was normally done by a Gentleman Usher, like Simon Bowyer: John Nichols, *The Progresses and Public Processions of Queen Elizabeth* (3 vols, 1823) I, pp. 385–6, n. 3.
29. Lambeth Palace Library, Bacon MS 652, fo. 312 (211).
30. Heneage was Vice-chamberlain 1589–95; Stanhope, 1601–16.

of things – be expected to enjoy an importance out of all proportion to their numbers. Hence, if the Privy Chamber retained any of its former administrative power it would be natural to expect that it would be executed by the Gentlemen and Grooms of the department.

Only two men were paid as Gentlemen of the Privy Chamber during the reign: John Asteley, from the beginning of the reign until his death in 1595,[31] and Christopher Hatton from 1572 until his death in 1591.[32] Asteley was paid at the lower rate of £33 6s.8d. and also held the position of Master of the Jewel House. There is no evidence to indicate that Asteley's post of Gentleman was anything other than an honorary title – a reward for past services and in line with his wife's appointment to the Privy Chamber. If he did perform practical duties, no record of their nature has survived. Probably he was more occupied with his duties in the Jewel House.[33] Nor can the appointment of the much more important and obviously courtier-like Hatton be linked with practical service. There were contacts between members of the Privy Chamber and Hatton and his name appears constantly in lists of lodgings at court or on progress.[34] But this only denotes a requirement to attend on the queen and need not be a function of his Privy Chamber office. Thus, while his career was in the making, his Gentlemanship was not the means of his ascent so much as a useful springboard, which gave an honorific title, a small income and guaranteed access to the queen. Thereafter it became only a drop in the ocean of his greatness as he rose successively to the Captainship of the Guard, knighthood and the lord chancellorship itself. But it was a drop he retained to the end.

This absence of definable duties notwithstanding, there is no doubt that it was convenient for the queen to have at least one Gentleman 'on call'. The two feed Gentlemen could not possibly provide sufficient cover, and so the queen revived the Henrician precedent of unfeed supernumeraries (as she had also done with her extraordinary Ladies). This ensured a constant supply of male servants when needed without the expense or risk of gossip attached to having a regular paid group of Gentlemen at court. Among the unfeed Gentlemen ready to attend the queen when called were

31. E351/1795, fos. 12–56.
32. Ibid., fos. 31–51.
33. He was appointed Master of the Jewel House at the Coronation (LC2/4(3), fo. 104) and held the position till his death.
34. For Hatton as court contact see SP46/34, fo. 144; for lodgings at court, SP12/108, fo. 74; BL, Harley MS 609.

Thomas Heneage, Henry Killigrew, John Stanhope and Fulke Greville. The posts carried prestige for their holders and gave them a position from which they could promote their talents (as the elevation to Chamber office of both Heneage and Stanhope shows). For the queen they provided both a prestigious group of attendants and an available team of men of significant rank ready to act as her envoys, mediators abroad or representatives in the localities. Killigrew, for example, was particularly active as the queen's personal messenger.[35]

The Grooms of the Privy Chamber were significantly more numerous. Six appear in the coronation list,[36] although one of them, Thomas Litchfield, also held the position of supervisor of the Queen's Music. Here again Henrician precedents were being followed. But unlike Mark Smeaton or Philip Van Wilder, Litchfield drew a larger salary than his fellows.[37] Only three of the remaining posts were feed and this combination of salaried and non-salaried posts continued throughout the reign. The Grooms in receipt of a wage rose to a peak of eight during the 1580s, although once more real numbers were greater at about twelve, with the difference being made up by four Grooms Extraordinary. These received livery but no fee and often had to wait for dead men's shoes before obtaining an established Groomship with the fee.[38] The office was staffed at the beginning of the reign by the trusted servants of Elizabeth's previous households,[39] and subsequent appointments were men of respectable backgrounds with bright futures such as Edward Carey, Thomas Knyvet and Edward Denny, who could all well have held the higher post of Gentleman.[40]

The duties of the Grooms varied. Some were concerned with the traditional responsibilities associated with the office under Henry

35. Hatfield House, Salisbury MS 32, fo. 50; HMC, *Cowper MSS* I, pp. 30–1.
36. LC2/4(3), fo. 107; LC5/31, fo. 171.
37. E351/1795, fos. 12–34; BL, Harley Roll AA23; LC5/49, fo. 157.
38. LC5/31–7; and cf. BL, Harley MS 6265. The Cofferer's Accounts (E351/1795) record the entry of Grooms into feed service. Edward Darcy, for example, who replaces his father-in-law Thomas Asteley as a feed Groom in October 1595, on the latter's death, had been liveried as a Groom Extraordinary since 1581 (LC5/35, fo. 274).
39. For example, John Baptist Castellion was listed among Elizabeth's household at the funeral of her father (LC2/2); while Henry Sackford was a servant of Sir Henry Bedingfield's when Elizabeth was in his custody under Mary (BL, Additional MS 34,563, fo. 74).
40. Carey (E351/1795, fo. 14: 24 February 1562); Knyvet (ibid., fo. 29: 17 January 1570); Denny is recorded as receiving livery for two years past in 1584 (LC5/35, fo. 404). He remained a Groom Extraordinary.

VIII – that is keeping the actual apartment in order. They are noted as receiving brushes, wood and general items for the department.[41] Others were given specific tasks, like John Baptist, a Groom from the beginning of the reign, who had the job of overseeing the mending of the queen's clocks.[42] And others again, while remaining Grooms, held, like their superiors the Gentlemen, offices elsewhere in court. The posts involved included the Master of the Toils, the Keeper of Westminster Palace and the Treasurer of the Chamber.[43] Such offices benefited the holder through additional fees and perquisites; they also helped co-ordinate the otherwise intolerably diffuse and fragmented administration of the household – which is why no doubt the practice had become so ingrained in the Henrician Privy Chamber as well. Away from court Grooms were sometimes used by the queen as her personal messengers at home and abroad and were often in receipt of riding charges.[44]

The remaining Privy Chamber office held by men was that of Gentleman Usher. It is likely that the occupant of the post was a working deputy to the Lord Chamberlain and kept a close watch on the etiquette of the Privy Chamber as well as the *entrée*. The post was feed at £30 per annum and was occupied by only three men during the reign: Drue Drury, John Norris and Sir George Howard.[45] Drue Drury's problems with Robert Dudley will be detailed later, but, despite that upset, the long tenure of the Ushers indicates the secure and stable nature of the Elizabethan Privy Chamber.

Predictably then the activities of the men of Elizabeth's Privy Chamber were more wide-ranging than the narrow round of the Ladies. But even among the Gentlemen and Grooms there is not a trace of the weighty administrative responsibilities that had gone far to making the Henrician Privy Chamber the second power in the kingdom. The institutional and administrative regression of the department went hand in hand with the almost complete stagnation of the personnel of the Privy Chamber. The Elizabethan Privy Chamber was a conservative, almost static department, with an incredibly low turnover of staff. The women and men held office for decades and it was death rather than resignation or dismissal that

41. LC5/33, fos. 110, 131; E351/1945, fos. 6, 13.
42. E404/114 (15 July 1561).
43. E403/2362, pt 4, fo. 22; E351/543, fo. 21; Eton College MS 192; C47/3(41);
     Maidstone RO, U1475 (Sidney MSS), C12, fo. 39.
44. E351/541, fo. 151.
45. E351/1795, fos. 12, 32, 36.

usually terminated their appointment.[46] The queen's own longevity determined that only Dorothy Edmunds, Gentlewomen of the Privy Chamber, and Henry Sackford, one of the Grooms, held office from the beginning of the reign to the end.[47] But women such as Frances (*née* Newton), lady Cobham, Elizabeth (*née* Norwich), lady Carew and the countess of Nottingham died with an average of forty years' service to their credit. Indeed, during the whole reign only twenty-eight women occupied paid posts in the Privy Chamber.[48] Among the unfeed the changeover appears to have been higher. But as the stable, salaried corps, who numbered fourteen to sixteen at any one time, made up the majority of the department, this does not affect the overall position very much.[49] The stability also extended to the families of the Ladies. Indeed, recruitment to the Privy Chamber was virtually a closed shop, with members of the Howard, Carey, Radcliffe, Stafford, Brooke and Knollys families being omnipresent in the department. This means that the Privy Chamber was very much the queen's *familia* in both senses of the word. The Howards, Careys, Radcliffes and Knollys were, as it were, members of the Tudor affinity with a tradition of Privy Chamber service going back at least to early in Henry VIII's reign. And the tradition continued under Elizabeth herself, with daughters following in the mothers' footsteps.[50] These same clans were also part of the queen's family in the modern meaning of the word: her maternal grandmother was a Howard, while the Knollys and Careys were spliced to the Boleyns through Mary, Anne's sister. As members twice over of the queen's family the Ladies had to endure attentions that were sometimes suffocating – as Elizabeth's well-known hatred of her Ladies'

46. E351/1795; BL, Lansdowne MS 3, fo. 88; 104, fo. 18; 29, fo. 69; 34, fo. 30; 59, fo. 72.
47. Dorothy, lady Edmunds, entered the Privy Chamber as an 'extraordinary' member at the beginning of the reign (LC2/4(3), fo. 105); became a feed Gentlewoman on 15 November 1570 (E351/1795, fo. 30), and is still listed among the Privy Chamber at the queen's funeral (LC2/4(4), fo. 46). Henry Sackford was appointed a Groom of the Privy Chamber in 1558/9 (LC2/4(3), fo. 107) and remained a feed Groom for the rest of the reign (E351/1795). In 1569 he succeeded John Tamworth as Keeper of the Privy Purse.
48. E351/1795, fos. 12–63; ibid. 1796 and cf. BL, Lansdowne MS 3, fo. 88; 29, fo. 68; 34, fo. 30; 59, fo. 72; 104, fo. 18.
49. Compare LC2/4(3), fo. 105 with BL, Harley MS 6265: only Lady Cheke remained from the original list. In 1592 the unpaid members of the Privy Chamber numbered about thirteen.
50. For example, Lady Dorothy Stafford was joined by her daughter Elizabeth Stafford; Lady Catherine Knollys by her daughters Lettice and Elizabeth; while Catherine Carey, lady Howard, was niece to Lady Knollys, and her own mother, Anne, lady Hunsdon was also an unfeed member of the Privy Chamber.

marrying shows. But in fact the storm was usually weathered and the Ladies continued in service after marriage. And in any case the advantages far outweighed the occasional problems: as the queen's women, long in service and high in favour, the Ladies were standard figures at court, virtually immovable and hard even to persuade.

The result was a quite different sort of Privy Chamber from Henry VIII's. Then the Privy Chamber had been the cockpit of faction. Faction leaders, or at least their high lieutenants, were members of it, and the heat of a battle at the very centre of his own private life inevitably involved the king (above, pp. 101–18). Elizabeth knew none of this. As women, her Ladies could not be faction leaders; while as members of her *familia* they were not even faction followers either: their first loyalties were to the queen, not to one of her great men. In short, Elizabeth's Privy Chamber (as it had originally been under Henry VII) was a barrier or a cocoon. Behind and within the monarch could strictly control access; also the queen, consciously above and beyond the fray was better able to manipulate the faction struggle itself. The most striking illustration of all this is the way in which the great crises of the reign washed around the Privy Chamber, leaving it quite untouched. Whereas under Henry VIII each revolution in politics tended to be accompanied with an upheaval in the Privy Chamber, under Elizabeth politics and the Privy Chamber went separate ways. Neither the Northern Rebellion nor Norfolk's treason early in the reign affected the members of the department – and even the arrest of Lord Cobham during the Norfolk episode had no repercussions on his wife's position in the Privy Chamber or on her close relationship with the queen.[51] Similarly, the clashes in court between Cecil, Sussex and Leicester in the first two decades of the reign and even the turbulence of the Essex revolt at the end had no direct connection with or effect on the Privy Chamber staff. For although the women in the Privy Chamber were often kin to the men involved, the domestic nature of the department together with the fact that the majority of the staff were women effectively distanced them from the controversy.

Nevertheless, despite the neutralization of the Privy Chamber, the key to political power at court remained – as it always had been – access to the sovereign. Once factions had secured this directly through Privy Chamber office; under Elizabeth office and access became separated, with the right of *entrée* to the Privy Chamber

---

51. Cf. E351/1795, fos. 12–52; BL, Lansdowne MS 34, fo. 30; 59, fo. 22; SP12/200, fo. 20; LC5/34, fo. 280.

assuming an independent and paramount importance. Robert Naunton stated that admittance was restricted to servants of the department and to those who were 'well known' – a term obviously open to interpretation at the queen's convenience. Access, when granted to those in favour, could be removed much more easily than formally appointed Privy Chamber staff could be dismissed. Out of favour courtiers could suddenly find the doors of the Privy Chamber, and therefore their route to the queen, closed to them. The well-known incident concerning Simon Bowyer, a Gentleman Usher of the Chamber, illustrates the point.[52] Bowyer was a well-respected court official who had found favour with several members of the Privy Chamber, and stood high in the queen's good will as well. She had ordered him to look into all admissions to the Privy Chamber and to turn away those whose credentials were insufficient. In executing his task he had the misfortune to refuse entry to a client of Robert Dudley, earl of Leicester, thereby incurring the earl's wrath. That the queen supported Bowyer in the resulting conflict made plain that she would allow no-one – not even a chief favourite – to meddle with the granting of the *entrée*. To have done otherwise would have thrown away all the advantages of her rigorous control of the personnel of the Privy Chamber. It also meant, of course, that it was impossible for faction leaders like Leicester to go round about and get indirect control of the Privy Chamber by building up a group of supporters who enjoyed the *entrée*. The right was uncertain and even when accorded too irregular, unreliable and impermanent to serve as a useful political instrument.

In view of all this it is natural to wonder whether the Privy Chamber had any importance at all. Certainly some contemporaries were agnostic, even frank unbelievers. At the beginning of the reign De Peria noted that the queen had resolved not to discuss business with her Ladies;[53] while at the end one of Robert Cecil's correspondents, Sir Robert Cross, recalled 'your speech to me in your chamber at Nonsuch some three years past which was that I depended and was at charge with women to solicit for me and that the queen would give them good words yet they should never effect suit. I have found that to be true advice'.[54] George Boleyn, dean of Litchfield, was equally critical of the value of the intervention of his cousin, Mary (*née* Shelton), lady Scudamore, on behalf of the earl of Shrewsbury and informed the earl

---

52. Sir Robert Naunton, *Fragmenta Regalia*, ed. Edward Arber (1895), p. 17.
53. *CSP Sp.* (*Eliz.*) I (1558–67), p. 21.
54. Hatfield House, Salisbury MS 78, fo. 96.

I am afraid that your lordship is not likely to hear in haste from my cousin Scudamore . . . She is one that is wont to delay more than needs and loseth many a tide for the taking, though she must watch for her tide if she will speed her business . . . But the question will be how to get either my letters or the chapters to her Majesty for my Lord Chamberlain certainly will not deliver it and as far as my cousin Scudamore there is no sure confidence in her. But as her speech is fair and smooth as a reed, so do I beseech your honour to take this as a watchword spoken under *benedicite*. For women be waspish and will do a man more harm when they be angered than good when they be quiet.[55]

On the other hand, Ladies of the Privy Chamber could and did regularly promote the suits of individual courtiers for pardons, licences to travel abroad, deaneries, stewardships of royal lands and so on,[56] and could assist the promotion of larger suits and requests for favour. Dorothy, lady Stafford's letter written to Philip Gawdy, sheriff of Norfolk, in 1576 deals with the typical kind of preferment handled by members of the Privy Chamber. In the letter she 'requested' Gawdy to appoint one Nicholas Farmer 'being one of my lord of Leicester his gentleman' to the post of under-sheriff of Norfolk, assuring him that in making the appointment he would 'bind' Lady Stafford to do the like if occasion were afforded.[57] At this level the exercise of influence by members of the Privy Chamber was readily accepted. However, there was a clear divide between this kind of patronage and the promotion of the major interests of faction groups. Here the Privy Chamber's role was one of supplementary persuasion and there was a strict limit to the queen's tolerance of this kind of pressure. Lady Scudamore, for instance, found the queen obstinate in her refusal first to read and then to make any positive comment about letters from Sir Robert Sidney presented by her while pressing his case to be appointed warden of the Cinque Ports (a post that was to be given yet again to a member of the Cobham family).[58] Elizabeth obviously considered Lady Scudamore's persistence out of order and indicated her displeasure.

But within their limited sphere the Privy Chamber's influence was well worth the having. The Ladies knew this and took advantage of their security and non-alignment to operate a free market economy of favours. For the longer their service, the more entrenched their position and the higher the bargaining power of their stock. Sometimes, as in Lady Stafford's proposed deal with

55. Lambeth Palace Library, Shrewsbury MS 707, fo. 221.
56. Cf. SP38/5, 6; S03/1, fos. 193, 198, 310.
57. BL, Egerton MS 2713, fo. 54.
58. See Maidstone RO, U1475 (Sidney MSS), C12, fo. 75.

Gawdy mentioned above, the currency was a mutual trade-off of one good turn deserving another; sometimes though straightforward cash was involved. A letter from Sir William Cornwallis to Cecil contained the complaint that 'a base merchant's son of Norwich' was to get away without punishment after tangling with his daughter because he had lent 'my Lady Scudamore £500 five years ago, or rather indeed by putting some purse in her pocket, gathered around him friends akin to the knave'. He went on to add that had it been the queen's wish to pardon the offender he would have accepted her decision humbly, but not 'when it is wrought by a base fellow for such a base respect as lending money or giving some £60, or one hundred marks by such a barbarous brazen-faced woman'.[59] Nor was the incident an isolated one as Anthony Bacon's problems with Dorothy, lady Edmunds in 1595 show.[60] Bacon had been offered £100 and a bond of £500 (which would pay out £300 immediately) to secure a pardon for one Robert Boothe from the queen. His agent at court, Anthony Standen, was given the task of finding a suitable promoter with the initial £100 as bait. Bacon had suggested Lady Edmunds as a likely candidate and Standen's letter back listed the problems involved. Dorothy, lady Edmunds had been appointed an Extraordinary Gentlewoman of the Privy Chamber at the queen's accession and had succeeded to a salaried post in the autumn of 1570.[61] By 1595, therefore, she was one of the longest-serving members of the department. Standen reported that Lady Edmunds 'made no difficulty' with the matter, provided she could get the Lord Chamberlain 'who was unfavourably disposed to Boothe' not to cross it. On approaching the Lord Chamberlain she found him 'wilful but for her sake ready to relent' but – and here she reached the bargaining stage – he had advised her that she would be unwise to make the suit if her reward were to be less than £1,000. Standen was well aware of the arguments that were to follow and lamented to Bacon:

Now here comes in the cogging [from 'to cog' or cheat at dice] of this place: she says she must make an express suit thereof to her Majesty and therein plead her ancient and long service for a recompense . . . . And that the manner of the queen is to ask what the suit will be worth, so that naming the £100 which is the sum I offered her, she says the queen will not be moved with it for so small a matter to employ her credit and forces she will not.

59. Hatfield House, Salisbury MS 29, fo. 21.
60. Lambeth Palace Library, Bacon MS 652, fo. 312.
61. LC5/4(3), fo. 105; E351/1795, fo. 30.

Bacon then had a problem. Although Lady Edmund's price was too high, he could not decline her offer to secure the pardon and take his £100 to another member of the Privy Chamber who was willing to accept less for her help. This was because Lady Edmunds was convinced that she already had the 'coin in coffer', and, as Standen confirmed, would 'by her own and friends utterly overthrow it' if they took their business elsewhere. They were in fact cornered and Standen in his summing up of the situation gave a candid opinion on the influence of Privy Chamber Ladies in patronage matters.

This ruffianry of causes I am daily more and more acquainted with and see the manner of dealing which groweth by the queen's straightness to give these women whereby they presume thus to grange and huck causes.[62]

In all this there is little trace of consistency and none of principle. Instead, such patronage was a mere commercial transaction in which faction 'barriers' were crossed and broken with equanimity. And yet the venality, as well as the neutrality, of the Privy Chamber can be exaggerated. For all its fallen state the department remained worth cultivating politically; while for all their prior commitment to the queen the Privy Chamber took sides in the larger battles of the court.

The clearest evidence of definite alignments between an outside patron and members of the Privy Chamber is for Sir William Cecil and a number of the men in the Privy Chamber. Both Heneage and Stanhope advanced from being Extraordinary Gentlemen to high office in the Chamber. By all accounts both were Cecil associates. Heneage early in the reign was in touch with Cecil and Lady Carew of the Privy Chamber to test out how high his favour was at court.[63] Stanhope's relationships with the Cecils, both father and son, was more that of disciple and junior associate. His mother was a distant connection of the Cecils,[64] and probably exploited her relationship to obtain Privy Chamber positions for both John and his younger brother Michael. But more was involved than ties of blood. Cecil and the boys' father, Sir Michael, had been fellow members of the Somerset faction under Edward VI, when Stanhope had been Chief Gentleman of the Privy Chamber during the Protector's ascendancy (above, p. 125). That of course made the family a 'service' one, which gave it a further claim on Privy Chamber office. But whatever his route to the department, from his appointment in the early 1570s

---

62. See note 60.
63. HMC, *A. G. Finch MSS*, pp. 6, 10.
64. Lady Anne Stanhope was first cousin to Lady Mildred Cecil; therefore her sons were Cecil's second cousins by marriage.

John Stanhope made the most of his access to the queen and was a main link in the network of information and promotion maintained by Cecil at court and continued by his son Robert. Stanhope was a skilled practitioner of the arts of courtly prevarication and evasion, and, while at heart very much a Cecil man, he is nevertheless a good example of the fluidity of alignments at court. He kept on good terms with Charles, lord Howard of Effingham and both Sir Thomas Leighton and Sir Robert Sidney (out-and-out Essex men) looked to him for help.[65] Yet when the chips were down as in the Essex–Cecil struggle there was no doubt where his true loyalty lay. Roland White, Sidney's contact at court, was convinced for example that Stanhope was 'too beholding to the party that favours Lord Cobham to do anything for you' in Sidney's desired promotion to the wardenship of the Cinque Ports.[66] And the loyalty had its reward. A little earlier, in December 1595, White had commented that though the queen had promised an Essex man, Sir Henry Unton, the Treasureship of the Chamber, if William Cecil, lord Burleigh and Robert Cecil had their way Stanhope would get it.[67] The Cecils indeed had their way and Stanhope was appointed the following June with a knighthood to follow. If Stanhope's own papers survived a much fuller account of his position would come to light. As it is his correspondence with Cecil, usually noted for its great insight into the queen's domestic routine, indicates that Stanhope was in service often round the clock presenting business to the queen at times when it would have been difficult if not impossible for the Secretary to be present.[68] Stanhope in short is the main example that something resembling the influence of a Privy Chamber Gentleman earlier in the century could be recreated with the right backing.

Similarly from the extant correspondence several of the Grooms of the Privy Chamber can be identified as looking to Cecil for patronage (though there is no parallel evidence for other faction leaders). The Grooms who had a Cecil connection include Thomas Knyvet, Edward Denny, Sir Thomas Gorges and Michael Stanhope (incidentally illustrating again the importance of both the 'service' tradition – Knyvet, Denny, Stanhope – and the Somerset connection – Stanhope and Denny – in recruitment to Elizabeth's Privy

65. Maidstone RO, U1475 (Sidney MSS), C12, fo. 31.
66. Ibid., fos. 72, 75.
67. Ibid., fo. 45.
68. Hatfield, Salisbury MS 38, fo. 18.

Chamber).[69] It would be making too much of their links with Cecil to maintain that they worked together to form an identifiable party within the department; nor is there any indication that such a grouping was even necessary. What is evident, however, is that Cecil had sufficient supporters and friends within the Privy Chamber by the middle of the reign to rest assured that there was no likelihood of the department developing into a force of its own or of its members massing behind a rival interest group. Although there was no need, given the composition of the department, for Cecil to have the Privy Chamber under his absolute control like a latter-day Cromwell, he certainly had more than a good working relationship with its members.

Among the women evidence for a clear-cut Cecilian allegiance is thinner – in part no doubt because of their tendency to a carefully cultivated neutralism. As their letters to Cecil show, most accepted the need for a reliable support network while sensibly believing that it was folly to close off any avenue of worthwhile contact. Nevertheless many did have priorities of attachment – whether as a result of blood ties, or from an aware realization of their own best interests. One such was Frances, lady Cobham who firmly committed her allegiance to the Cecils and no other.[70] In particular there is a very interesting letter from her to Burleigh written in the aftermath of the execution of Mary, Queen of Scots, in which she wishes him back to court and offers her service:

I do beseech your lordship to hasten your coming hither. If you will write I will deliver it. I do desire to be commanded by you. Others here in presence do speak for themselves and do excuse that which is done in putting their hands to the letter as though they knew not what they did nor what was therein contained. I do mean the two lords which are here'.[71]

The Cobham family were Cecil's friends but here their factional allegiance extends to Lady Cobham's use of her position both to keep a direct channel to the queen open to the lord treasurer in his absence and to keep him informed of the activities of his colleagues (the 'two lords', who were probably Leicester and Howard) as they attempt to shift the blame elsewhere for Mary Stuart's execution.

Cecil's chief rival, Robert Dudley, naturally had his supporters in the department too, though they were neither so many nor so

69. Ibid. 57, fo. 60; 30, fos. 35, 37.
70. SP12/200, fo. 20.
71. Ibid.

powerful. Blanche Parry and Dorothy Bradbelte, both of whom had served Elizabeth from the 1540s, were willing to act as informants to his agent at court whilst he was away, briefing him on how best to approach the queen.[72] Dudley's sister, Mary Sidney, was appointed to the Privy Chamber without the fee in 1558[73] and was extremely close to the queen in the first decades of the reign, although her attitude to her brother was ever variable; while John Tamworth, one of the Grooms of the Privy Chamber and Keeper of the Privy Purse up to his death in 1569, was definitely a Dudley man. Gifts from his patron were detailed in his will,[74] and it was Tamworth who was mentioned by the queen in her famous 'deathbed confession' in 1562 as sleeping in Dudley's room. He was to receive an annuity of £500 a year on her death – a remarkable sum.[75] Tamworth was obviously useful and, had the Privy Purse retained its former weight, he would have been really important. Beyond this there is no evidence to indicate that Dudley attempted to construct a group of supporters in the Privy Chamber. On the other hand of course he made the most of his friends. In 1567 for example, De Silva noted that after a temporary decline in his standing at court, Dudley had returned to the queen's favour but, he thought, 'with no other pretensions than to maintain his position which he could easily do, as he has won over the sympathies of the queen's favourites and those who surround her closely. They have been firm and steadfast to him through all the past troubles'.[76]

As well as the two main contenders for power many other great nobles and office holders prudently cultivated Privy Chamber links. For example, Mary, lady Scudamore, Lady Cobham's successor as Mistress of the Robes, acted as the Privy Chamber contact for the earls of Shrewsbury and Rutland,[77] and – in conjunction with Ann Russell, countess of Warwick – for the Sidneys in the second half of the reign.[78] Her activites on behalf of the Shrewsburys are best documented. In 1592 shortly after her husband's knighthood she wrote to the earl: 'I do offer myself, ladyship and all, to be at your service. I have both presented her Majesty with both your humble duties and showed her your letter at which she hath been

72. SP15/13, fos. 7–8.
73. LC2/4(3), fo. 104.
74. PROB11/52, 8 Lyon.
75. *CSP Sp.* (*Eliz.*) I (1558–67), p. 263.
76. Ibid., p. 627.
77. Lambeth Palace Library, Talbot Papers H, fo. 441; M, fo. 7; Lambeth Palace Library, Shrewsbury MS 707, fo. 221; Belvoir Castle, Rutland MS IV, fo. 99.
78. Maidstone RO, U1475 (Sidney MSS), C12, fos. 75, 167.

very merry and very highly contented'.[79] Robert Kidman, the earl's agent at court, was forever trying to catch Lady Scudamore on the earl's behalf. This was easier said than done as Kidman pointed out in October 1593: 'I have been at my Lady Scudamore her chamber four times, and cannot yet speak with her for she hath been always with her Majesty'.[80] But of course the very reason for her elusiveness showed why she was worth waiting for.

So that members of the department had contacts, often close, with the participants in the great game of politics is certain. It remains to be discovered how far – whether through these contacts or otherwise – members of the department found themselves caught up in the game as well. Naturally, in view of the length of the reign, the game changed character over the years. Issues came and went and so did faction groups: the network of contacts and alignments that formed them was not stable but fluid and largely dependent on the short-term interests of the individuals involved. The mobility was highest in the first years of the reign, before the new regime had established itself.

Two issues of the fraught politics of the 1560s touched the Privy Chamber particularly: the queen's marriage and the succession, and the tempestuous beginnings of Dudley's career as Elizabeth's favourite. In the first, members of the Privy Chamber did become involved – albeit ingloriously and with no very clear links with interest groups at court. Their involvement, in view of their closeness to the queen, was more or less inevitable. Still it was dangerous as the queen – determined to preserve her freedom of action – vigorously suppressed any unauthorized meddling by her Ladies. No-one was exempt and in August 1562 Catherine Asteley and Dorothy Bradbelte, both long-serving members of Elizabeth's household before her accession, were put under house arrest for writing to the king of Sweden concerning the queen's marriage.[81] They were restored to their positions the following month. But the warning not to interfere, particularly in writing, without the queen's consent was clear.

Where that consent, even command had been forthcoming, it was a very different matter. An episode involving Mary, lady Sidney shows that members of the Privy Chamber could work with the queen to confuse rival interest groups over her proposed marriages.

79. Lambeth Palace Library, Talbot Papers H, fo. 441.
80. Ibid., fo. 571.
81. BL, Additional MS 48,023, fo. 366 and *CSP Rome*, ed. J. M. Rigg (2 vols, 1916–26) I, pp. 104–5.

Early in the reign Lady Sidney acted as mediator between the queen and the Spanish ambassador, in effect to comfort and reassure him with false promises and delaying tactics, so persuading him to continue with the archduke's suit for the queen's hand. Lady Sidney informed him that he should not mind what the queen said as, 'it is the custom of ladies here not to give their consent in such matters until they are teased into it'. She added that 'if this were not true' he might be sure she would not say such a thing as it might cost her her life and that she was now acting with the queen's consent.[82] As a result of this interplay the queen could make the most of the archduke's suit without compromising herself at all. Another Privy Chamber contact of the Spanish ambassador – again with the queen's knowledge and consent – was Elizabeth Brooke, who became marchioness of Northampton. Her influence in the department was notable until her untimely death of cancer in 1565. Indeed, De Silva described her as 'a person of great understanding, [who] is so much esteemed by the queen that some little friction exists between her and Robert [Dudley]'.[83]

So it was not issues, however sensitive, that were barred to the Privy Chamber; it was independent initiative. That broke their contract of service with the queen. She saw the Privy Chamber as an extension of herself: that they should be seen to be promoting policies contrary to her wishes was as though (in her father's phrase) 'the foot should rise against the head'. The most notorious incident was the fracas surrounding Catherine Grey's clandestine marriage to Edward Seymour, earl of Hertford. Wisely, Elizabeth (like her father with the earl of Devon – above, p. 107) had put Catherine, her possible successor, in the Privy Chamber where it should have been possible to keep a close eye on her.[84] So when Catherine so conspicuously eluded the queen's vigilance, Elizabeth feared the worst: a conspiracy against her known wishes within the Privy Chamber itself. Catherine was ordered to confess 'not only what ladies and gentlewomen of this court were thereto privy, but also what lords and gentlemen; for it doth appear that sundry personages have dealt therein'.[85] In fact, nothing turned up apart from the discovery that poor Elizabeth St Loe – fearful of the queen's wrath – had failed to

---

82. *CSP Sp.* (*Eliz.*) I (1558–67), p. 95.
83. Ibid., p. 381.
84. LC2/4(3), fo. 105 lists her as a Maid of Honour.
85. BL, Harley MS 6286, fos. 32–40, 78–83.

pass on Catherine's hysterical admission of her marriage.[86] This hardly amounted to the 'great practices and purposes' the queen suspected, yet she was implacable. Elizabeth was imprisoned in the Tower for six months; dismissed the Privy Chamber, and after her release left court with a mere £30 from the queen, paid through Kate Asteley.[87]

While the Grey fortunes declined, the rise and levelling out of Lord Robert Dudley's aspirations had their own repercussions on the Privy Chamber. A contemporary account in the Yelverton Manuscripts, anonymous and as yet unpublished, bears testimony to Dudley's influence in the 1560s.[88] The author was not an admirer of Lord Robert's, but allowing for prejudice, his narrative is an impressive indication of Dudley's power, which reached even into the Privy Chamber, to punish his adversaries. The Elizabethan section of the account begins with a note concerning the imprisonment of Drue Drury of the Privy Chamber in September 1559: 'for that it was suspected lest he would have slain the Lord Robert, whom he thought to be uncomely to be so great with the queen'.[89] The evidence concerning the episode indicates that Dudley secured Drury's discharge from his office as Gentleman Usher of the Privy Chamber in September 1559 when he also disappeared from the Privy Chamber payments section of the Cofferer's account.[90] He was not reinstated in his position until 1576 when he also received five years' back pay, 'by letters of the count of Leicester'.[91] Another household account drawn up in 1576 notes Drury as receiving a further twelve and a half years' arrears to the tune of £375.[92] Dudley's wrath had obviously been long-standing. It is possible, considering the earl's later problems with Bowyer, that he did not want someone as unsympathetic to his interests as Drury plainly was holding the position of Gentleman Usher, with its effective veto on admissions to the Privy Chamber. And evidently (unlike Bowyer)

---

86. She was a Gentlewoman of the Privy Chamber, 1558–61 (E351/1795, fos. 12–13). She is often confused with Elizabeth St Loe, wife of Sir William, and the future 'Bess of Hardwick'. But in fact she was unmarried and was probably Sir William's sister.
87. E351/541, fo. 38; J. Bayley, *History and Antiquities of the Tower of London* (2 vols, 1821) Appendix II, p. 52.
88. BL, Additional MS 48,023.
89. Ibid., fos. 352–3.
90. E351/1795, fo. 12.
91. Ibid., fo. 36.
92. BL, Lansdowne MS 21, art. 67, fo. 143.

the protection afforded to Drury by his office was insufficient to shield him when crossing the favourite. Drury was not the only member of the Privy Chamber to suffer as a result of Dudley's displeasure. January 1561 brought another, though more temporary, Privy Chamber casualty when 'Mr Asteley for displeasure of my Lord Robert was committed to his chamber and after put out of the court but after six weeks restored'.[93] John Asteley was at this time the only feed Gentleman of the Privy Chamber,[94] and was married to the Chief Gentlewomen, Catherine Asteley. And it was probably only his wife's favour that saved him from a longer exile.

But all of this, though interesting, is very fragmentary. Nor is there much more evidence available for the calmer years after Norfolk's execution in 1572, when the principal contenders for power seem to have decided that while competition was healthy, full-blown factional disputes were a destructive and time-consuming diversion from the serious business of running the country and lining their pockets. This *modus vivendi* among the leaders chimed nicely with the instinct of everyone else to run with the hare and hunt with the hounds. And it was not until the rise of Essex that the situation changed. His attitude was black and white: you were for him or against him. This he thought was the means to carve his way to power. But in fact in a political world where compromise, merger and flexibility were the order of the day his insistence on firm commitment both strained the workings of the system to breaking point and cut the earl himself off from any possible general basis of support.

Essex's chief rival was Robert Cecil, and both, like William Cecil and Robert Dudley earlier in the reign, had their allies in the Privy Chamber. Paradoxically Cecil, who was almost always at court and so needed the Privy Chamber less, had both a larger following there (inherited from his father) and a better grasp of what use could be made of Privy Chamber personnel. He benefited accordingly. On the other hand, the earl, who was very frequently absent, asked too much of his friends like the countess of Warwick, Lady Leighton and Lady Scudamore. Even with the best will in the world, under the Elizabethan dispensation, the Privy Chamber were not influential enough to do as he hoped and keep up his credit as he blundered from controversy to controversy in Cadiz, Ireland or wherever. And too often the good will was lacking as Essex's behaviour put intol-

93. BL, Additional MS 48,023, fo. 353.
94. E351/1795, fo. 13.

erable strains on the most long-suffering. A vivid insight into all this comes from the correspondence between Lady Leighton and her friend, Edward, lord Zouche.[95] *Née* Elizabeth Knollys, Lady Leighton was Essex's aunt. She had been a feed Gentlewoman of the Privy Chamber since 1566,[96] and was regularly in service up to 1583 despite her marriage to the queen's captain of Guernsey, Sir Thomas Leighton. She was then intermittently absent through ill health but as the 1590s progressed she became increasingly reluctant to attend at court on political grounds as well.[97]

In these circumstances Zouche's main task was to persuade her to take up her position in the Privy Chamber, particularly when she had been summoned to attend. He gave her injunctions not to fear 'any encounters' and impressed upon her that only by making the most of her post could she 'breed strength' in herself and 'perfect affection in her Highness to the working of good to yourself, children and friends'.[98] But whatever her misgivings, Essex's execution plunged her into a deep melancholy from which Zouche sought to lift her when he wrote in April 1601:

Dear Lady, as your grief is witnessed by your letter, I beseech God . . . you may find such recovery as you may return to court that being so comforted by so gracious a princess as you may also be a comfort to her who you see doth sometimes want her servants about her. Which if the unhappy earl had considered he should not have had so great occasion to let such temptations enter into him by such as are more fit to set forward discontented minds than to draw them backward by good advice.[99]

Zouche in the letter reserved full judgment of the causes of Essex's downfall until he could return to court himself and talk 'those which will not write'. But reading between the lines it is clear that both Zouche and Lady Leighton blamed the earl's death on the maliciousness of his enemies and the follies of those who had led him astray.

Yet suspicions voiced privately were as far as Lady Leighton went. She continued to serve in the Privy Chamber for the remainder of the reign and was quite prepared to use Cecil himself as chief mediator to the queen in a suit of her husband's. Her approach was business-like, not emotional. Cecil was asked to evaluate the chances of success and if he thought them good then she together with Lady Walsingham would decide on a suitable gift to

95. BL, Egerton MS 2812.
96. E351/1795, fo. 17.
97. BL, Egerton MS 2812, fos. 11–12, 139.
98. Ibid., fos. 12–13.
99. Ibid., fos. 139–41.

present to the queen to tip the balance decisively in her favour.'[100] But behind the facade of hard-headedness and studied neutrality was surely strain and it is not too fanciful to suspect that the formula covering her grant of a pension under James I 'for long and painful service to the late queen' came near the truth.[101]

Lord Herbert neatly described Sir William Compton, Henry VIII's first Groom of the Stool, as 'more attentive to his profit, than public affairs'.[102] In that he was something of an exception in Henry VIII's Privy Chamber. Under Elizabeth, though, it would be hard to think of an apter characterization of the attitude of almost everybody in the department. Political involvements happened of course, as was inevitable with a group so much at the centre of affairs. But they were often accidental, rarely sustained, and never pursued to the uttermost. Nor frankly were they very important. With patronage it was another matter: the Privy Chamber had a real role here, as Lord Zouche well knew when he urged Lady Leighton 'to live at court where both I and others may reap the benefit'.[103] Even in this, however, they were not major patrons in their own right. Instead they were holders of a metaphorical spanner which, if they were sweetened, could be used to tighten up a suit in progress or, if they were crossed, could be thrown in to seize up the works altogether.

So the Elizabethan Privy Chamber was a household department in the narrowest sense of the term. It was the queen's *familia*, largely staffed by her cousins, and wholly by her chosen and direct dependents. And it was essentially female. The result was a notable neutralization of the department, which turned from the cockpit faction, as it had been under Henry VIII, to the prime barrier against faction, as it had been under Henry VII.

100. Hatfield, Salisbury MS 96, fo. 19; 62, fo. 11.
101. IND 6744 (June 1604).
102. Edward, Lord Herbert of Cherbury, *The Life and Reign of King Henry the Eighth* (1649), p. 8.
103. BL, Egerton MS 2812, fo. 12.

CHAPTER SIX

The revival of the entourage: the Bedchamber of James I, 1603–1625

Neil Cuddy

Elizabeth I died on Thursday, 24 March 1603. On Saturday, after riding non-stop, Robert Carey knelt at James's feet at Holyrood and saluted him as king of England. Told to name his own reward, he asked to be made a Gentleman of the Bedchamber. The revival of the entourage had begun.[1] Within the household, the revival was marked by structural change as the Bedchamber displaced the Privy Chamber as the focus of the monarch's private life; without, there was an even more far-reaching change in the structure of politics and the texture of public affairs. The balance of power swung away, increasingly, from the Privy Council and a bureaucrat-minister towards the Bedchamber and the royal favourite; the 'bureaucratic' agencies of the Secretaryship and the Exchequer retreated before the revived administrative activity of the inner household; and finally, and above all, the Bedchamber became a key issue in James's management of his dual inheritance of Scotland and England. Intended by James to be the flagship of Union, it became instead the symbol of failure, and a prime stumbling-block in the relations between king and parliament.

The argument, therefore, cuts deep. James's decision to rule personally, rather than fit into the pre-existing structure built round the more distant, less urgent monarchical control of a semi-deified Gloriana, has been both misunderstood and consistently caricatured.

---

1. My thanks to the editor and to Dr G. E. Aylmer for their comments and criticisms of earlier drafts of this chapter. F. H. Mares, ed., *The Memoirs of Sir Robert Carey* (Oxford 1972), pp. 63–4. Chamberlain reported that Carey had been sworn Groom of the Stool – uncorroborated and unlikely, unless James was unaware of the significance of the English office: N. E. McLure, ed., *The Letters of John Chamberlain* (2 vols, Philadelphia 1939) I, p. 192.

Rule by a favourite through the Bedchamber was *not* a sign of indolence; it was part of a deliberate policy, conditioned by his previous experience in Scotland.[2] Adapting this experience to English conditions took time and caused many problems and misunderstandings. It is perhaps above all the task of the historian to make more of an effort to understand the court of James I than did most of his English subjects.

Organization: from Privy Chamber to Bedchamber

Many observers regarded the peaceful accession of James I as near-miraculous. In fact, it was a carefully (and secretly) planned political bargain which had been in the making since Essex's death two years before. Mutual political advantage guaranteed Sir Robert Cecil, and the Howard grouping at court with which he had worked and consulted, pre-eminence under James's new regime. James would widen this settlement somewhat by reviving the fortunes of Southampton, leader of what remained of the defeated Essex faction, and by bringing to court Northumberland, regarded as leader of the Catholics. Certain substantive points of policy agreed by the Privy Council late in Elizabeth's reign were foisted onto James, in particular, peace with Spain. James's sobriquet of 'Peacemaker', he recalled later, had not been of his own devising. But in general, the broad adaptation of English factions and policy to the new king was smoothly effected. Much of the purely political bargain had been agreed beforehand, and caused few problems.[3]

But the actual organization of the new regime was another matter. This was what was at stake during the period between the theoretical and the practical transfer of the throne – between Elizabeth's death on 24 March and James's arrival at Theobalds (Cecil's house) to 'take possession' on 3 May. The question revolved around the king's

2. D. H. Willson, *James VI and I* (1956), especially ch. XI: 'A Sylvan Prince', represents the most extreme caricature of James as a moral degenerate. Jenny Wormald, 'James VI and I – Two kings or One?', *History* 68 (1983) offers a suggestive critique of these charges, which she attributes largely to (English) xenophobia. Her exploration of the effects of James's Scottish background on English politics is important; the present essay is an attempt to analyse them systematically as they affected the court.
3. S. Adams, 'Spain or the Netherlands? The Dilemmas of Early Stuart Foreign Policy', in H. Tomlinson, ed., *Before the English Civil War* (1983), p. 93; G. Parry, *The Golden Age Restor'd: The Culture of the Stuart Court, 1603–1642* (Manchester 1981), pp. 16, 21, quoting James's *Meditation upon the Lord's Prayer* (1616).

freedom to retain his trusted Scots advisers and courtiers after his move to England, and whether or not they should be granted English office. Cecil and Henry Howard trod carefully on this issue, sending messengers and meeting the king personally at York. In the process, they destroyed the leaders of two sub-factions of the late Elizabethan court, Sir Walter Raleigh and Sir John Fortescue, by portraying them to the king as extreme exponents of a policy of completely excluding the Scots. There was almost certainly some truth in their portrayal; but there was also hypocrisy. The attitude of Cecil and his allies towards Scotsmen holding English office was decidedly negative: their preferred outcome was that the existing regime should as far as possible continue with the simple substitution of one monarch for another. James naturally had different views. According to rumours at the time, which are amply confirmed by his later actions, he wanted a half and half division with equal numbers of English and Scots holding both formal offices and the more informal court posts. In part this looked to the past – to the king's long ties of trust and affection for his Scottish servants; it also looked to the future – to James's dream of a full and equal Union between the two nations. This explains his readiness to admit so many Englishmen to his Chamber both in Edinburgh, and on the journey south.[4]

But these high hopes came up against hard reality at Theobalds on 3 and 4 May. Then a compromise on the division of both formal and informal offices was reached. This completed the ruin of Raleigh and Fortescue, and with savage irony their offices were given as part of the deal to the very Scots whom they had tried to exclude. On the formal side of government, five Scots were admitted members of the English Privy Council, and two of them given strategic English offices. Sir George Home, lord treasurer of Scotland (later to become earl of Dunbar) became chancellor of the Exchequer, in place of Fortescue; and Edward Bruce, lord Kinloss, was made master of the Rolls in Chancery. The lords treasurer and chancellor

---

4. PRO31/3/35, Beaumont to Henri IV, 1 April and 8 April 1603, and R. C. Munden 'The Defeat of Sir John Fortescue: Court versus Country at the Hustings?' *EHR* 93 (1978), 811–16, especially p. 814 n. For those sworn as Gentlemen of the Chamber between Edinburgh and London see HMC, *Salisbury* XV (1603), 10 (Sir Edward Cecil); ibid. 28 (Eure); ibid. 19 (Cromwell); HMC, *Portland* IX, 129 (Holles). Cf. H. S. Scott, ed., 'The Journal of Sir Roger Wilbraham, 1593–1616', *Camden Society Miscellany X* (1902), p. 55; and I. H. Jeayes, ed., *The Letters of Philip Gawdy* (Roxburghe Club) 1906, pp. 130–1 for their expulsion into the new Privy Chamber.

were thus placed in tandem with Scottish subordinates, so that the key financial and legal departments were subjected to James' 'equal partition' principle.[5] Beyond this, James had similar designs for the secretariat and Privy Council: he had apparently intended to make his Scottish Secretary of State an equal partner with Cecil, and to make his cousin Ludovic, duke of Lennox lord president of the Council (perhaps to compensate for the failure to procure more equal partition of that body). But neither of these rumoured intentions came to anything.[6] Such was the settlement of the formal bureaucracy as it had come down from Elizabeth. For the rest the Elizabethans remained in office – a remarkable degree of continuity by comparison with other early modern successions to the English throne, especially when one considers the king's age and experience. The application of equal Anglo/Scots partition of offices had been partial and limited; given James's appetite for personal control, the formal side of the bargain was disadvantageous.

Partly as a consequence of this, the informal part of the bargain represented a victory for the king: a negative victory, perhaps, but one with important consequences in the future. At Theobalds, the king took his place at the centre of the English court which had come there to meet him. For the moment, he retained the entourage which had served him in Scotland and followed him south, together with its recently admitted complement of Englishmen. Nomenclature was changed: the 'Chalmer' of James VI, staffed with Gentlemen, Varlets and Pages, became the 'Bedchamber' of James I, and the Scots Varlets became 'Grooms'. The new Bedchamber fitted into place at the heart of the basically unchanged outer layers of the late Elizabethan court.[7]

This was an interim solution. A committee of the Privy Council was set up to reach a final settlement, composed equally of English and Scots, and dominated by Home and Cecil. Settlement was accomplished and effected when the king reached his first royal 'standing house' as king of England, the Tower of London, about 11–13 May. Here the Bedchamber was purged of a large number of now politically unimportant Scots and all the Englishmen

5. BL, Additional MS 11,402, fo. 88; *APC* XXXII (1601–04), 497.
6. *CSP Ven.* X (1603–07), 33; PR031/3/35, Beaumont to Villeroy, 7 May 1603.
7. T. M, *The True Narration of the Entertainment of his Royall Majestie . . . from Edinburgh [to] London* (1603), E (rectior F)3; *CSP Ven.* X (1603–07), 25 (5/15 May 1603): 'Three days ago his Majesty began to live with English attendants in the English style at Theobalds. Up to that time he had followed his Scottish custom.' John Gibb, a 'varlet' in 1596 (Scottish RO, E34/47) was 'one of the Bedchamber' by late April 1603 (SP15/35/4).

(including Sir Robert Carey) who had obtained posts on their own initiative: these men, together with new recruits who bought their places, were formed into a new Privy Chamber, half English, half Scots, two stages removed from the king.[8] Those remaining in the Bedchamber were all Scots of personal or political importance to James; agents whom he could trust, companions with whom he was familiar.

James, having compromised over Scotsmen in formal office, won without concessions the battle over his Scots entourage. The politics of the succession produced a new English court where the royal presence was reserved as a matter of course to the custody of Scotsmen; no wonder Cecil was accused of having sold out the English to the Scots.[9] The Bedchamber itself was the most important substantive product of the political settlement of the succession: given these origins, it is unsurprising that it continued to be of central political importance during the reign. But in order to understand this importance, the structural character of the new Bedchamber/Privy Chamber system must be examined, and its practical functioning described; and to establish fully its institutional pedigree, we must briefly look back to the courts of England and Scotland before 1603. The Elizabethan court had to change in some way to take account of the simple fact of James's masculinity; but the way in which it did change, though influenced by accession politics, was powerfully affected by the equally simple fact of his nationality.

The English court that James I inherited has already been fully described above. It depended essentially on the rigorous limitation of the '*entrée*'. Under Henry VIII the crucial frontier had been at the door of the Privy Chamber. On one side lay the semi-public outer chambers; on the other, the Privy Chamber itself and the still more private world of the Privy Lodgings, centring on the royal Bedchamber. Only the Gentlemen of the Privy Chamber had ordinary access to the apartment, while, in theory at least, only the head of the department, the Groom of the Stool, gave attendance in the Privy Lodgings. Under Elizabeth things changed somewhat. Another room, the Withdrawing Chamber, was interposed in the sequence of chambers, between the Privy Chamber and the Privy

---

8. BL, Additional MS 11,402, fo. 88; APC XXXII (1601–04), 497. For the committee's activity, see LS13/168, fos. 45v–50. The influence of the committee on the Bedchamber/Privy Chamber settlement is my inference. For events at the Tower, Jeayes, *Letters of Gawdy*, pp. 130–1. Mares, *Memoirs of Carey*, pp. 65–6.
9. PRO31/3/35. Beaumont to Villeroy 17 May 1603; *CSP Ven.* X (1603–07), 33.

Lodgings; at the same time, and largely because of her sex, the queen's personal life became more private and withdrawn. She spent more time in the Privy Lodgings; while the Privy Chamber, to which access was still jealously limited however, took on a markedly more formal and official character. Her private servants, also women of course, changed character too. They played little part in politics; while the Ladies of the Bedchamber, who divided out the functions of the Groom of the Stool among themselves, enjoyed neither the status, the departmental authority nor the administrative powers of the Henrician officer. In one sense the Elizabethan dispensation represented a weakening of the Privy Chamber; on the other hand, it actually strengthened its ethos, which was the restriction of intimacy between monarch and subject (above, pp. 147–53). As the contemporary Bishop Goodman rightly observed, 'no king . . . in Christendom did observe such state and carried such distance from the subjects as the kings and queens of England'. He also correctly observed that 'there was no such state observed in Scotland'.[10]

The planning of the Scottish palace tells its own story. The sequence of rooms consisted of the Hall or Guard Hall, Presence Chamber and Bedchamber. Beyond lay a Cabinet; then a door leading to the queen's Chamber.[11] The whole suite functioned as the royal lodging: James worked in his Cabinet; slept in his Chamber and dined in his Presence, chatting informally as he did so with the waiters at his table and lookers-on alike. There was thus no separation, as in England, between the public ceremonial of the Tudors' outer chambers and the private world of the Privy Lodgings; and no frontier, like the Privy Chamber, to hold the two apart. Indeed there was very little privacy at all.

Even in the most private room, the Cabinet, two Gentlemen were assigned to keep the doors, and one or two had the routine duty of giving attendance there. Similarly all the staff of the Chamber served directly in what was the king's actual bedroom: twenty-four Gentlemen in 1580 and sixteen in 1601, together with four Varlets and three Pages, all waiting in quarterly shifts.[12] By 1601 this got too much even for James and complaint was made of 'the confused number of persons of all ranks who have the *entrée* in his Majesty's

10. G. Goodman, *The Court of King James I*, ed. J. S. Brewer (2 vols, 1839) I, p. 29.
11. See the plans of Linlithgow and Stirling in Murray Baillie 'Etiquette and the Planning of the State Apartments in Baroque Palaces', *Archaeologia* 101 (1967), 181.
12. *Register of the Privy Council of Scotland* III (1578–85), pp. 316, 322–3: Scottish RO, E34/47 (January 1596); *Register of the Privy Council of Scotland* VI (1599–1604), pp. 207–8 (1601).

Bedchamber'. So access was limited to it and the outer chambers as well. But what is striking to English eyes is the generosity of the limitations: even under the new dispensation the Presence, for example, was to be available to 'noblemen and masters and the lords of his Privy Council' – which is rather as though the English Privy Chamber had been open to the entire peerage and their eldest sons.[13]

The lack of distinction between public and private was reflected in the managerial structure of the Scottish court. Instead of the English duality of the Lord Chamberlain and the Groom of the Stool, who, as head of the Chamber and Privy Chamber respectively, enjoyed separate and often jealously clashing jurisdictions, there was unity, with the one man being both Lord Great Chamberlain and First Gentleman of the Chamber. As the former he was in charge of the staff of the Presence – the Ushers, Cupbearers, Carvers and Sewers, who attended the king as he dined; as the latter he was himself the king's principal body servant. He had the general oversight of the Chamber's staff (and indeed the appointment of them when the king was still a minor); he enjoyed *ex-officio* the right to lodge as close as possible to the king's Chamber, and the first option on sleeping there; and he was in charge of dressing and undressing the king.[14] In England, all these were the tasks and privileges of the Groom of the Stool; the Groom's eponymous functions, however, enjoyed none of the prestige they did in England and were discharged instead by a menial – a 'dichtar' or cleaner – of the Chamber.[15]

Clearly there were important differences between the English and Scottish courts. *Prima facie* it is tempting to attribute the latter's much more casual style to its poverty and smallness; in 1590 its full complement of 180 for both king and queen, above and below stairs, was about one third the size of the English household of an unmarried queen regnant.[16] But the differences cut far deeper and were in fact systemic: the English court was designed for the preservation and manipulation of distance; the Scots for the management of relatively free and open access. Or to put it differently: the English

---

13. Loc.cit. (1601 orders).
14. G. Donaldson, ed., *The Register of the Privy Seal of Scotland* (Edinburgh 1982) VIII (1581–84), pp. 278–9 and 1601 orders cited above. Carey in 1603 was sworn in by Lennox, Lord Great Chamberlain/First Gentleman, and immediately helped undress the king: Mares, *Memoirs of Carey*, p. 64.
15. J. Craig, ed., *Papers relating to the Marriage of James VI and Anne of Denmark* (Bannatyne Club) Edinburgh 1828, Appendices (separately paginated) pp. 19, 24.
16. Ibid. (appendices) pp. 23–9; LC2/4(4), supplemented with reference to G. E. Aylmer, *The King's Servants* (1974), pp. 472–5.

etiquette was English, while the Scottish was French. James's court was 'governed more in the French than in the English fashion', the Englishman Sir Henry Wotton remarked on a visit there in 1601. In terms of palace geography, the parallel is almost exact. The state apartments in the Louvre in 1585, for example, consisted of an *antichambre*, the *chambre royale* or Bedchamber, and a *cabinet* leading to the queen's chamber. The palaces of Falkland and Stirling were built by French masons, and the particularly close coming together of the 'auld alliance' under James V in the early sixteenth century was probably mainly instrumental in bringing about the full transfer of the system. The lack of Privy Lodgings, and consequent free access to the monarch, were also prime characteristics of the French court. The easy-going familiarity of the dinner ritual was equally characteristic. Wotton remarked that 'anyone may enter the king's Presence while he is at dinner, and as he eats he converses with those about him': this struck Wotton as particularly French. The importance of the Captain of the Guard was again typically French. The basic nomenclature and structure of the main court departments tells a similar story; compare the Great Master of Household and his subordinate Masters with the French *Grand Maître* and the *Maîtres d'Hôtel*; the Great Master of the Esquierie with the *Grand Ecuyer*; the Lord Great Chamberlain with the *Grand Chambellan*. The arrival in 1579 of Esmé Stuart, duke of Lennox, James's cousin and favourite, from the court of Henri III explains even closer parallels. He personally set up James's first full adult household in 1580, and invented for himself a uniquely Scottish combination of French offices – Lord Great Chamberlain and First Gentleman of the Chamber. He also gave James an enduring taste for courtly French manners to which, much later in England, Carr and Villiers had to conform.[17]

So James's accession in 1603 brought together not only two kingdoms but two courts whose basic principles were wholly foreign to

17. L. Pearsall Smith, ed., *The Life and Letters of Sir Henry Wotton* (2 vols, Oxford 1966) I, pp. 314–15; L. Batiffol, *Le Louvre sous Henri IV et Louis XIII* (1930), p. 21, plan, pp. 24–5; J. Wormald, *Court, Kirk and Community* (1981), pp. 8, 9, 59. On French familiarity, see P. Champion, *Henry III, Roi de Pologne* (1951), pp. 173–4; *CSP Foreign* XIX (1584–85), 184–5; R. Doucet, *Les Institutions de la France au XVIème siècle* (2 vols, 1948) I, pp. 122–6 corrected by R. J. Knecht, *Francis I* (Cambridge 1982), pp. 89–91. Scottish RO, E34/35 (May 1580) for Scottish structure – 4 Masters of Household, 4 Master Stablers. Of their superiors, no Lord Great Master of the Household seems to have been appointed under James. For Lennox's appointment as 'Great Master of the Esquierie and haill hors' see Scottish RO, PS1/63, fo. 22 (24 November 1591). On keys, *Calendar of Scottish Papers* VI (1581–83), 220–1 (December 1582); C. Loyseau, *Cinq livres du Droit des Offices* (1610), p. 430.

each other. What was the hybrid produced by the grafting together of the two?

The least affected were the outer layers of the court. The Lord Chamberlainship, greatly revived in prestige under the female rule of the later sixteenth century, continued to be the most visibly prestigious court office, particularly since the senior post of Lord Steward remained unfilled till 1616.[18] Similarly with personnel. Elizabeth's stand-in Chamberlain, the earl of Suffolk, and his deputy, Sir John Stanhope, Cecil's nominee as Vice-chamberlain in 1601, held their offices undisturbed till 1614 and 1616 respectively. Suffolk's successor as Lord Chamberlain, his son-in-law Robert Carr, earl of Somerset, represented more of a break with tradition. Not only was he a Scot, he was also *de facto* head of the Bedchamber. The resulting combination of offices broke the rule, fundamental to the English court, of the separation of powers of the heads of the inner and outer Chambers. It was also in the event the exception that proved the rule. The arrangement lasted only eighteen months and both the king and prince of Wales recognized that it would set no precedent since Carr was 'a favourite'.[19]

Less remarkably, a handful of other Scots were also appointed to key Chamber posts at the beginning of the reign, among the Gentlemen Ushers daily waiters, the immediate efficient subordinates of the head officers of the Chamber, and among the Guard. James was obsessive about security; he also took a Scottish rather than an English view of the importance of the Captaincy of the Guard. The result was that the post was given to his great favourite, Sir Thomas Erskine, subsequently Viscount Fenton and earl of Kelly, who combined it with the Groomship of the Stool. Thanks to so well placed a Captain, the Guard did very well and increased in both numbers and pay. The commanders of the other guard, the Gentlemen Pensioners, remained English, but the Pensioners themselves were subject to the principle of equal partition between English and Scots. The change, however, was not effected at a blow

18. The office was formally vacant between Leicester's death (1589) and Lennox's appointment (1616). Charles Howard, earl of Nottingham was appointed temporarily in time of Parliament in 1597, 1601, 1604–10 and 1614 for ceremonial reasons, but exercised no control over the Household (*pace* G. P. V. Akrigg, *Jacobean Pageant* (Cambridge, Mass. 1962), p. 26); LS13/168, fos. 176v ff. shows Lennox's impact after appointment.
19. On Carr's Bedchamber supremacy, see below, pp. 208–14; Mares, *Memoirs of Carey*, pp. 73–4. A second exception was in fact made for Carey in the prince's household, but when Charles became king the division of control was strictly maintained.

but gradually as death and resignation vacated posts. And elsewhere among the teeming personnel of the Chamber not even this gesture was attempted: instead the Elizabethan incumbents remained securely in possession.[20]

James proved equally accommodating – even enthusiastic – about the ceremonial that was the *raison d'être* of these outer layers of the English court. He continued the pompous epiphanies of the Tudor procession to the Chapel Royal, indeed clarifying the rules of precedence and specifying, among much else, that 'both noblemen and others use great distance and respect to our person, as also civility one to another'.[21] He also revived the practice of dining in state in the Presence on special occasions. Different views were taken of this: the Venetian ambassador thought that the king was being 'corrupted' and that if left to himself would retain his 'French familiarity' and rough dining habits; others saw political calculation.[22] Not content with continuation and revival James also innovated: the office of Master of Ceremonies was set up to oversee the increasingly elaborate and contentious etiquette that surrounded the reception of foreign ambassadors; while masques became a more prominent, and expensive, feature of court life. In both areas James was following the dictates of French fashion – to the occasional dismay of his English subjects. In 1607, Chamberlain reports,

The king was very earnest to have [a masque] on Christmas night . . . but the lords told him it was not the fashion; which answer pleased him not one whit, but said 'what do you tell me of the fashion? I will make it a fashion'.[23]

James might put his foot down over a masque, but evidently on the substance of Chamber organization his reign brought no more

20. LS13/168, fo. 49, Sir James Maxwell and Sir John Drummond appointed at York in April 1603, pairing two English with two Scots; LC2/6, fo. 39, three English serving with two Scots in 1625. S. Pegge, *Curialia* (5 parts, 1782–1806). Part III, p. 33 (using Stowe). I owe my information on the Gentlemen Pensioners to Dr William Tighe, who has studied the band under Elizabeth. For continuity of personnel among Gentlemen Ushers, Quarter Waiters, Sewers of the Chamber, Gentlemen Waiters, Grooms and Pages, compare LC2/4(4) (Elizabeth's funeral list) with the entries in LS13/168 passim.
21. BL, Additional MS 34, 324, fo. 215 (1 January 1623), reported in *Letters of Chamberlain* II, p. 470. These orders, including the clause quoted, were closely followed by Charles I in January 1631 (SP16/182/31).
22. *CSP Ven.* X (1603–07), 46 (12 June 1603); *Letters of Chamberlain* I, p. 251 (5 January 1608); see E. K. Chambers, *The Elizabethan Stage* (2 vols, Oxford 1923) I, p. 15 for the revival.
23. Sir John Finet, *Finetti Philoxenis* . . . (1656); Akrigg, *Jacobean Pageant*, ch. 6; Parry, *The Golden Age Restor'd*, pp. 40–2; *Letters of Chamberlain* I, p. 250 (5 January 1608).

than tinkering. This was perhaps only to be expected in view of the Chamber's political insignificance. Robert Naunton, a future Secretary of State, was particularly scathing on this score. In 1605 he got his 'first sight . . . of the Presence Chamber', which he 'observed to be but a mere passage . . ., and little better to improve a man in matters of importance than the road between this and Royston'. At the end of the road to Royston lay James's hunting lodge; on the other side of the 'passage' of the Presence were the Privy Chamber and the Privy Lodgings. These were the goals of Naunton's 'men of any understanding', and these were the subject of radical change.[24]

In 1638 the Gentlemen of the Privy Chamber petitioned Charles I in a body, complaining that 'of all other places in your Majesty's service' theirs was 'most changed and fallen'. The 'change and fall' had taken place in May 1603.

The change was not unheralded, however. By Elizabeth's reign, as we have seen, the original 'institution' of the Henrician Privy Chamber had undergone modification. There was a clear division of its staff into those who were also 'of the Bedchamber' and those who were not; while life in the apartment itself was markedly more formal. But under James these internal subtleties were translated into hard, institutional distinctions. Bedchamber and Privy Chamber were separated, in staff and functions. The former took over the whole of the king's intimate, informal service; the latter was left only with the formal and the ceremonial – and not even very much of that as we shall see. And with this change of character came a change of control as the Privy Chamber and its staff were now subject, without reservation, to the authority of the Lord Chamberlain.[25]

The details can be quickly sketched. In mid-May 1603, as we have briefly seen, the Bedchamber was purged of 'at least twenty Scotch gentlemen' and an unknown number of Englishmen, who had been hastily sworn in the weeks after the accession. Those displaced, together with some new recruits, of both nations, were formed into a new Privy Chamber. This consisted of forty-eight Gentlemen, half English and half Scots, who waited in quarterly shifts of twelve. The number of Gentlemen was cut to thirty-two in July 1610, more English than Scots being displaced to even up the numbers. This was the only change in the initial Privy Chamber establishment during

24. HMC, *Cowper* I, 58 (Robert Naunton to John Coke, 29 October 1605).
25. Above, pp. 176–7. SP14/2/35 (6 July 1603), a draft order for the Privy Chamber, is explicit about the Lord Chamberlain's control.

the reign.[26] The Gentlemen received no fee or other allowance; furthermore they had very little to do.

James seems to have used the Privy Chamber for two main purposes: formal audiences with Secretaries of State and masters of Requests, and the semi-public dining in the Scoto-French fashion which he so much enjoyed. The former offered the Gentlemen, who had the duty of providing 'company' for the king in the apartment, little opportunity of real contact with him; nor was dining much better. Four of the Gentlemen in waiting brought in the dishes, but the actual table service was carried out by the Carvers, Cupbearers and Sewers of the outer Chamber.[27] And it was they who reaped the benefit of James's habit of conducting debates at this 'trial of wits' – so that Cupbearers like George Villiers (later favourite and duke of Buckingham), Carvers like Sir John Digby (later Vice-chamberlain and earl of Bristol) or Sewers like Sir Thomas Overbury (later the favourite's favourite) went on to make spectacularly successful court careers. Meanwhile the Gentlemen got comparatively little by way of either reward or promotion and were reduced, even for their own urgent suits, to snatching at the king's promises made 'instantly before his journey to Royston'.[28] Their translation from the 'efficient' to the 'ornamental' side of the court is also shown by the burgeoning number of supernumeraries: in 1625 there were some fifty Gentlemen Extraordinary, and by 1638 more than 200.[29] The key office of the early Tudor court had become a useful (and cheap) mark of distinction for amenable country gentlemen.

Of the other members of the Privy Chamber staff the Grooms fared even worse, as the Elizabethan incumbents were dismissed and replaced by men of markedly lower family status.[30] The Gentlemen

26. Above, note 8: T. Birch, *The Court and Times of James I*, ed. R. F. Williams (2 vols, 1848) I, p. 130 (Sir Dudley Carleton to Sir Thomas Edmondes, 17 July 1610). In official lists, the 1610 reform was still in force in late 1614 (SP15/40/28, my dating of a list of the Privy Chamber) and 1617 (SP14/90/118, eight Gentlemen in quarter waiting to go on the Scots visit). There is nothing to suggest any further change in numbers before 1625.

27. This simplifies a complex area: cf. BL, Harley MS 589, fo. 197v and SP15/40/28 (dated note 26 above).

28. J. Hacket, *Scrinia Reserata* (1692), p. 38. For Villiers, see below p. 214 ff.; Digby, BL, Harley MS 1857; Additional MS 31,825 for his position as carver in 1610; Overbury, BL Additional MS 15,476 fo. 92v (item 4). HMC, *Salisbury* XIX (1607), 276 (11 October 1607).

29. LC2/6 fos. 37–8: an undifferentiated list headed 'Gentlemen in Ordinary', but clearly including those extraordinary.

30. See Cofferer's Accounts, E351/1796–1821 (payment of their £20 fee); LC5/50 (Great Wardrobe livery warrants). For the Elizabethan Grooms' status, see above p. 156.

Ushers, on the other hand, did rather better. They remained responsible for the apartment's smooth running; they also retained a toehold in the Privy Lodgings, since the essentially informal character of the Bedchamber dictated that no separate Gentlemen Ushers of the Bedchamber were appointed. The result of all this was that the Ushers, who had been the Gentlemen's inferiors, now claimed – successfully – the superiority.[31]

This indignity formed one of the Gentlemen's many complaints in the Petition of 1638. But, as they recognized, their individual grievances were mere symptoms; the general cause about which they could do nothing, was that 'the Constitution of the Court is far changed' from 'the institution of the Privy Chamber in the reign of King Henry the Eighth'. Then, as they correctly asserted, 'the Gentlemen . . . had nearest access to the king's person of all other'. But after the 'change and fall' of May 1603 that 'nearest access', which carried everything else, had been transferred to the Bedchamber.[32]

The new Bedchamber established in 1603 was an amalgam of English and Scottish practice. At first it consisted of four Gentlemen, six Grooms and six Pages. These numbers increased somewhat with time, but never excessively: there were twelve Gentlemen in late 1622 and eleven Grooms by the end of the reign. This pattern of offices was wholly English and followed closely the precedent of the Henrician Privy Chamber. Numbers, save at the bottom end of the department, were also similar, as was the Bedchamber's structure of command. In honorific control was Ludovic Stuart, duke of Lennox and the king's cousin and heir before the birth of Prince Henry. In Scotland he had held the double appointment of Lord Great Chamberlain and First Gentleman of the Chamber; in England he was regarded as First Nobleman of the Bedchamber and was thus styled in the inscription on his tomb in Westminster Abbey, 'cubiculariorum . . . principalium primus'.[33] But, like the Henrician noblemen of the Privy Chamber before him, there is no evidence that Lennox exercised any practical, official supervision over the department.

That task instead devolved on Sir Thomas Erskine (later Viscount Fenton and earl of Kelly), who was Captain of the Guard in Scotland and also in England after 1603. He was appointed to the revived

---

31. BL, Harley MS 589, fo. 197v, espec. item 10.
32. *CSP Dom.* XII (1637–38), 216, January 1638.
33. A transcript of the inscription is in G. Crawfurd *The Lives . . . of the Officers of . . . State in Scotland* (Edinburgh 1726), p. 333.

Henrician office of Groom of the Stool and First Gentleman – now of course of the Bedchamber rather than the Privy Chamber. And not only the name, but the duties and privileges of the office were revived as well: indeed the new Bedchamber Ordinances were almost certainly written round a description of the Henrician Groomship.[34] Thus the Jacobean Groom retained his predecessor's eponymous lavatorial tasks. That is why Erskine wrote to Salisbury in 1610 with the news that 'his Majesty has been a little loose since his coming to Royston, but not in the extremity, and he does not lose his meat, so I hope he is past the worst'. (Given the menial nature of these tasks in Scotland, Erskine's capacity to adapt to English practice can only be admired.) He continued to enjoy the right to lodge closest to the king's chamber, and to sleep there on a pallet at the foot of the royal bed; to put on the king's under-shirt, and to command the Gentleman of the Robes (who put on the king's doublet and outer garments); and to attend the king wherever he went – Erskine was 'in the coach with his Majesty all alone', for example, in 1620.[35]

But undercutting the formal continuity was an important change of substance. In the Eltham Ordinances of 1526 all these duties – like the right of access to the Bedchamber itself – were solely the Groom's. In 1603, in contrast, the Groom had only the first option on performing these services: all of the provisions in the Bedchamber Ordinances explicitly involved the other Gentlemen of the Bedchamber in sharing the first Gentleman's duties, either as a matter of course or by acting as deputy in his absence. This development had been clearly foreshadowed under the Tudors with the appointment of first two, and subsequently four Principal

34. The Groomship was on Cecil's list of offices to be filled in 1603 (HMC, *Salisbury* XV (1603), 25). No copy of the Jacobean Bedchamber ordinances has apparently survived. But Charles II's Bedchamber Ordinances (Nottingham University Library, Portland MS PwV92, especially fos. lv–2v, 9v [my foliation]), reissued by William III (BL, Stowe MS 563)), claim to be based on James I's. Despite the doubts raised during the 1683 dispute between the Lord Chamberlain and the Groom of the Stool (see *CSP Dom.* XXIV (January–June 1683), Index sub 'Charles II . . . dispute respecting right of entry to the Bedchamber of', and below pp. 231–2), the claim is probably to be believed. Used with caution, therefore, the 1661 ordinances can give us important information about Jacobean practice; but of course at all points I have tried to obtain corroboration from contemporary sources.

35. HMC, *Salisbury* XXI (1609–12), 255 (17 October 1610); Nottingham UL, Portland MS PwV92, article 17, article 11, with explicit reference to precedent (and see below pp. 234–5); article 11, article 3, article 19, article 4, article 14; HMC, *Mar and Kelly Supplement*, 104 (23 October 1620). All these duties clearly represent a revival of Henrician practice.

Gentlemen, who exercised conjointly the office of Groom of the Stool. But the influence of the populous intimacy of the king's Scottish Chamber was equally strong. The effect was to make the Jacobean Groom only a first amongst equals, distinguished from his fellows by his dignity rather than by any peculiar duties or especially intimate access to the king.[36]

The administrative powers of the Henrician Groomship were subject to a similar partition. The Jacobean Ordinances still regarded the Groom as *ex officio* Keeper of the Privy Purse, when no special keeper was appointed. In fact such an appointment was invariably made and the Privy Purse was kept by Gentlemen and Grooms of the Bedchamber throughout the reign: first by Sir George Home (Dunbar), who was also Chancellor of the Exchequer until 1606; then by Dunbar's deputy and personal servant Robert Jossie, whom he placed as a Groom of the Bedchamber; then, after Dunbar's death in 1611, by John Murray (later earl of Annandale), first as a Groom of the Bedchamber, then (after his promotion in 1622) as a full Gentleman. With the Privy Purse went control of any stamp of the king's signature. Murray kept this in 1624–25 when the king could not sign due to illness and a hand injury.[37]

Similarly, the Groom shared informal opportunities for procuring the royal signature to warrants with the other Gentlemen and the Grooms of the Bedchamber. Elizabeth's long reign had bestowed a formalized monopoly of performing this task on the Principal Secretaries, the Signet clerks, the masters of Requests and the law officers. These men continued to be of great importance in procuring signatures, but the Bedchamber played from the start a significant role which grew appreciably in numerical terms. The Bedchamber as a whole procured about one-sixth of all known signatures to signet warrants in 1614; by 1624 they were procuring nearly one half. Erskine rarely used his opportunities as head of department to

36. The provision of the 1661 Ordinances (Nottingham UL, Portland MS PwV92, article 8) that the Groom of the Stool 'may wear a gold key in a blue ribbon as a badge of his office', seems to have been a later, Caroline development, connected with Buckingham's status after 1625 as informal head of the Bedchamber (see below, p. 232 note 28).
37. Nottingham UL, Portland MS PwV92, article 14. *CSP Dom.* VIII (1603–10), 9, 626 (Jossie as deputy): LS13/168, fo. 60, appointed Groom of the Robes. His appointment as Groom of the Bedchamber does not figure in the Exchequer or Great Wardrobe records. SP14/57/83, Jossie as 'servant to the . . . earl of Dunbar'. Murray: *CSP Dom.* IX (1611–18), 36 (30 May 1611). Signature Stamp: SP14/169/20, 26, 32 (July 1624). SP39/17, Original king's Bills containing examples of its use, 16–27 March 1625. SP14/173/109 (first use), 28 October 1624.

procure warrants, and then in the main for his own private interest. Others in the Bedchamber were routinely far more active than he, most notably the successive favourites, Carr and Villiers, who successively took over many of the duties of the Secretaries for considerable periods; and the Grooms of the Bedchamber – as a group – who could probably devote more time and attention to this task than could the more eminent Gentlemen. Theoretically, the Bedchamber had no business to be involved in procuring the royal signature; that they were involved was due to their intimate, institutionalized access to the king; that their administrative involvement was ordinarily shared out between them (except when these tasks were briefly monopolized by the favourites) reflected the fact that their intimacy also was shared.[38]

The fate of the Groomship of the Stool was characteristic of the department as a whole. Within an essentially English institutional architecture was fitted a mainly Scottish ethos and style. And in personnel the Bedchamber was wholly Scottish: indeed, until 1617 James's 'English' Bedchamber was a mere continuation of his Scottish Chamber. As we have seen, both the First Nobleman and the Groom of the Stool had also been the chief officers of the king's Chamber in Scotland; while of the four Gentlemen formally admitted in 1603 – solely by oath to the Groom as no reward or fee of any kind went with the position – all had served in Scotland.[39] Sir John Ramsay (a gentleman's second son) had played a major part three years before in the Gowrie conspiracy, allegedly by saving the king's life. Lennox's younger brother, Esmé Stuart, lord Aubigny, owed his position in the Bedchamber to his father's memory and his brother's inability to produce heirs. These men were aged about twenty-five when appointed. The other two were in their early forties, men of political experience. Sir Roger Aston had been one

38. Above, pp. 98–100 G. R. Elton, 'Tudor Government: The Points of Contact. III. The Court.' *Transactions of the Royal Historical Society*, 5th series 26 (1976), 216–17. My analysis of procurements of the royal signature was made from S03/6, S03/7, S03/8 (March 1614–March 1625). See below, pp. 218–19 and cf. the parallel analysis in David Starkey, 'The King's Privy Chamber, 1485–1547' (unpublished Cambridge Ph.D. dissertation), pp. 342–55 on which above, pp. 98–100 are based.

39. Without formal records, establishing the identity of the Gentlemen during James's reign depends on inferring a pattern from scattered references. That four were initially appointed can be inferred from an explicit 1661 reference to precedent (Nottingham UL, Portland MS PwV92, article 11). The only institutional lists which indicate, albeit silently, who the Gentlemen were are those of carts allowed for hunting journeys, in which the Bedchamber appears, unlabelled, as a group: LS13/168, fo. 124 (1607); fo. 239v (July 1622).

of Cecil's most important correspondents in arranging the succession; the illegitimate son of a Cheshire gentry family, he had made his career in Scotland since at least 1580, and while the Scots at that time regarded him as English, twenty years later the English saw Aston as a Scot. In both kingdoms he was the king's Master Huntsman and invariable companion in the field. Sir George Home had been Master of the Wardrobe, lord treasurer and a Gentleman of the Chamber in Scotland, and beyond these offices, 'the only man of all other most inward with the king', as Aston told Cecil in 1600. He has been mentioned as chancellor of the Exchequer and Keeper of the Privy Purse in England; in addition, he was appointed in 1603 Master of the Great Wardrobe and Gentleman of the Robes, continuing the Scottish practice of bestowing Chamber office on the chief Robes officer. As well as these four formal appointees, two other noblemen of the Scots Chamber, Lords Lindores and Sanquhar, seem to have had some rights to attend in the English Bedchamber.[40]

In July 1603 the Gentlemen were increased to six. Sir James Hay, eldest son of a distinguished Scots gentry family, was in his early twenties and, like Ramsay and Aubigny, had recently polished his manners in France. In 1605 he assumed Dunbar's office of Gentleman of the Robes, and eventually passed it on to his brother Robert, appointed a Groom of the Bedchamber in 1611. Sir Philip Herbert, the earl of Pembroke's younger brother (made earl of Montgomery in 1605), was sworn in at the same time; he too was in his early twenties, though without any French education. Exceptionally, before 1615, Herbert was an Englishman.[41] The dual appointment of Hay and Herbert in 1603 appears to have been the beginning of

40. Ramsay: *DNB; CSP Dom.* XII (Addenda, 1580–1625), 442 (18 April 1604), first reference. Aubigny: LS13/168, fo. 312 (Pantry liveries, 1604–05, with Ramsay). Aston: *DNB sub* Sir Thomas (1600–45), possibly Sir Roger's legitimate half-brother; Scottish RO, E34/35 (22 May 1580), fo. 8v, 'Roger Asston an Englishman', first reference. *CSP Dom.* VIII (1603–10), 65 (9 January 1604), an exceptional grant of livery as Gentleman; HMC, *Salisbury* XXI (1609–12), 269 (15 December 1610): James 'would make me a secretary, as well as I am master falconer and master hunter'. Home: *CSP Dom.* VIII (1603–10), 9 (17 May 1603), appointed Keeper of the Privy Purse, first reference as Gentleman. *Calendar of Scottish Papers* XIII, Part 2 (1597–1603), 723 (1 November 1600); HMC, *Salisbury* XV (1603), 375 (as Gentleman of the Robes, replacing the Elizabethan Sir Thomas Gorges.). Lindores and Sanquhar: Scottish RO, E34/47 (Noblemen of the Chamber in 1596), *CSP Ven.* X (1603–07), 119; HMC, *Salisbury* XIX (1607), 193.

41. Mares, *Memoirs of Carey*, p. 66: a dual appointment at the queen's suit soon after her arrival. E351/2807, Account as Gentleman of the Robes beginning December 1605. *CSP Dom.* IX (1611–18), 73, 514 (Robert became Gentleman of the Robes in February 1617). Herbert: see *DNB*, and below, p. 197.

the application to the Bedchamber of the 'equal partition' principle. The application went unrepeated in the Bedchamber, mainly due to the failure to achieve full legislative and parliamentary Union between 1604 and 1607 (below, pp. 202ff.). In the latter year the earl of Dunbar's young Scottish protégé and former page, Robert Carr (later earl of Somerset) was promoted from Groom to Gentleman of the Bedchamber,[42] finally bringing the numbers of Scots to English among the Gentlemen to the proportion of eight to one. This situation did not change until the rise of George Villiers in 1615, who by 1622 had succeeded in bringing in three Englishmen as Gentlemen, and five more as Grooms of the Bedchamber.[43]

The persons and duties of those who held the office of Groom of the Bedchamber tell a similar story of continuity with the Scots Chamber, only disrupted after 1615 by Villiers. All of the Grooms were Scottish until Buckingham had his brother Christopher appointed in 1617. Five out of eight Scots serving in 1604–05 had been either Scottish Varlets or Pages of the Chamber in 1596. The Grooms came from respectable, even eminent gentry families: John Murray was a cousin of the earl of Tullibardine, and Barnard Lindsay a relative of Lord Spynie. The powerful tried to get their younger relatives and followers a place there: first Dunbar (Carr was a Groom from 1604–07), then Carr himself (his nephew William was appointed in late 1614). Sir John Ramsay obtained a place for his brother. The demand for these places had no connection with the official rewards – fees of £20 per annum and livery of similar value, adopted from the inflation-eroded rates for Elizabethan Privy Chamber staff. More important were fees and gratuities. These men played an important role in the management and administration of patronage. Their opportunities stemmed from their close, familiar attendance on the king, and, since their duties were less honourable and more practical than those of the Gentlemen, their attendance was likely to be more necessary and more continuous.[44]

42. *CSP Dom.* VIII (1603–10), 147; BL, Additional MS 15, 476, fo. 92v; *Letters of Chamberlain* I, p. 249 (30 December 1607).
43. *Gentlemen*: Fulke Greville (Lord Brooke), Henry Feilding (earl of Denbigh) and Christopher Villiers (earl of Anglesey). *Grooms*: Christopher Villiers (1617, promoted 1622), Edward Wray (1618, displaced 1622), Edward Clarke (1621?–25), Richard Turpin (1622–25), James Palmer (1622–25), and Arthur Brett (1622, displaced 1623).
44. E351/1796–1821 (Cofferer's accounts, 1603–25), LC5/50 (Great Wardrobe livery warrants, 1603–25); Scottish RO, E34/47 (1596). SP15/35/60 (December 1603) for adoption of Elizabethan Privy Chamber rates. HMC, *Mar and Kelly Supplement*, 127 (making clear that a Privy Chamber place is simply the first move), 178, 189, 194–5 for Kelly's advice on placing a younger relative in the Bedchamber.

The Grooms made the king's bed, kept his linen and 'made him ready' – that is, helped him on with his underwear as a preliminary to the more formal dressing ritual performed by the Groom of the Stool and the Gentlemen. At night, two of them slept on a pallet bed in the Withdrawing Chamber, both in one bed as in Scotland – the Ordinances specify that 'two in one bed' should not be exceeded.[45]

The Pages of the Bedchamber performed more menial duties. They made the pallet bed of the Gentleman who slept in the king's chamber; made the fires, and swept and perfumed the rooms. One of them was responsible for washing the king's sheets.[46] Perhaps because the Pages' place was relatively unimportant, some Englishmen were appointed from the first; again, the equal partition principle was applied. These men were not necessarily as young as their title might imply; John Carse or Kerse, in attendance as Page from 1603 until 1616, had been a dichtar of the Scots Chamber in 1591.[47] Their status could be equivocal: on one hand, the earl of Montgomery managed to have his former barber appointed; on the other, Alexander Foster had the grant of some bailiwicks in Glamorganshire, and when the king and Council wrote to the local sheriff to ensure his support for the grant, they expressed their certainty that he would 'think this gentleman, being so near a servant to his Majesty, one of the Pages of the Bedchamber, as worthy to enjoy the benefit of his Majesty's favour . . . as any other.' But apart from a Page who was promoted Groom, and another who gained a knighthood and the Clerkship of the Great Wardrobe, the position was not usually one which led to greater things. Scots like Carse had originally been menials; and some of the English Pages seem to have been members of the 'gentlemanly profession of serving men', which was developing in this period.[48]

---

45. Nottingham UL, Portland MS PwV92, article 12 (1661, with explicit reference to Jacobean precedent), article 27, and cf. *Register of the Privy Council of Scotland* VI (1599–1604), p. 208.

46. Nottingham UL, Portland MS PwV92, article 15; *CSP Dom.* IX (1611–18), 5 (sheet-washing).

47. By 1605, Richard Greene and Bevis Thelwall (English) served alongside John Kerse and Walter Todderick (Scots). Scottish RO, E34/42 (1591); S03/6, December 1617, grant to Alexander Stephenson, Kerse's replacement.

48. *Letters of Chamberlain* II, p. 79 (4 June 1617); *CSP Dom.* X (1619–23), 64; *APC* XXXVII (1619–21), 212 (30 May 1620). Patrick Maull was promoted from Page (January 1604) to Groom of the Bedchamber (October 1604); *CSP Dom.* VIII (1603–10), 66, 162. On Bevis Thelwall's rise, *Letters of Chamberlain* II, p. 535. Examination of the careers of the Pages points to a connection with the Robes office, and to expertise in matters of clothing.

But if the personnel of the Bedchamber was, with a few exceptions, wholly Scottish, then the rules of *entrée* were entirely English and preserved jealously the traditional limitations on access to the Bedchamber and Privy Lodgings. The Ordinances make it quite clear that

no person of what condition soever do at any time presume or be admitted to come to us into Our Bed-chamber, but such as . . are . . sworn of it, without our special licence, except the Princes of Our Blood.[49]

This effectively excluded on a routine basis the greater and lesser officers of state and the Privy Council from that access to the king which the Bedchamber's own personnel exclusively and routinely enjoyed. The Secretaries of State and lesser officers (masters of Requests, signet clerks, the attorney and solicitor general) had their audiences in either the Privy Chamber, or the Withdrawing Chamber, into which the king would emerge from his Bedchamber to see them; and in this room also, the 'next little Drawing Chamber to our Privy Chamber' – and so the room next before the Bedchamber – the Privy Council was appointed to wait when they came as a body to see the king, 'where they may both confer together, and attend our pleasure to be called into our Inner lodgings when we shall command'.[50] The experience of the lesser formal officers who had to deal with the king vividly conveys a picture of the consequences of these arrangements. On 16 December 1608, Sir Roger Wilbraham, the master of Requests, delivered one of Salisbury's letters to the king. In reporting this to Salisbury, Wilbraham recited some familiar badinage which had then taken place, but after thus conveying an impression of his personal familiarity with and proximity to James, Wilbraham went on to give news of the king's health, and then to reveal the true nature of the relationship: 'in the night [the king's] sleep was hindered by toothache; but this day (though private), yet his Chamber say he dined merrily and is well'.[51] In short, the formal officers did not enjoy free access to the king; instead, they had audiences. This said, it must be remembered that we are dealing with the letter of the Bedchamber regulations. If the king chose to see an individual frequently in his Bedchamber, then of course he would. The realities of politics could trespass on the formalities of court usage. Thus by early May 1603, the French ambassador reported that

---

49. Nottingham UL, Portland MS PwV92, article 17 (fo. 7v, my foliation).
50. BL, Harley MS 589, fo. 197v (Jacobean Privy Chamber Ordinances, ?1610 or later) article 2.
51. HMC, *Salisbury* XX (1608), 281 (17 December 1608).

Cecil 'begins to grow great with the king, staying alone with him shut up in the 'cabinet' for three or four hours together'.[52] Nevertheless, court usage had a way of re-asserting itself; those of political importance had to use the staff of the Bedchamber to procure access, and to remind the king of their existence. By 1608, Salisbury's meetings with the king were formal audiences indeed, and the Bedchamber eventually broke Salisbury, as it was to break other great officers who tried to use it or work through it.[53]

The Bedchamber's exclusivity, firmly grounded in court etiquette, was further reinforced by two personal traits of the king's. First was his love of hunting. In 1607 the Venetian ambassador reflected that his addiction to the sport was so great that 'he throws off all business' and 'is more inclined to live retired with eight or ten of his favourites than openly, as is the custom of the country'.[54] Over the whole reign, James must have spent about half his time either in hunting lodges thirty or forty miles from London – Royston and Newmarket were his favourites – or on progress. When hunting, between the end of the summer progress and Christmas, and then again between Christmas and Easter, he took with him a small household composed of one or two clerks, the Guard, the Privy Chamber, and, above all, the Bedchamber.[55] The hunting lodges themselves were architecturally adapted to suit this rural intimacy. In 1605, the lord treasurer explicitly drew up the new requirement: not 'lodgings of state,' but rather 'lodgings of necessity'. Building collapses at both Royston and Newmarket show what these lodgings consisted of. In 1607 a chimney fell down at Royston, revealing damage in the Bedchamber itself, and the obviously contiguous chambers of the Gentlemen of the Bedchamber: those of Lennox, Fenton, Montgomery and Ramsay were named. Over the next two years new lodgings were build with extra room for the new Gentleman, Carr. New buildings in 1614 after a more serious collapse at Newmarket contained rooms over and under the usual

---

52. PR031/3/35, Beaumont to Villeroy, 17 May 1603.
53. Below, pp. 206ff. For the frequency and formality of Salisbury's meetings with the king in 1608, see L. M. Hill, ed., 'Sir Julius Caesar's Journal of Salisbury's First Two Months and Twenty Days as Lord Treasurer: 1608', *Bulletin of the Institute of Historical Research* 45 (1972), 311–27. The fate of Suffolk and Cranfield mirrors that of Salisbury.
54. *CSP Ven.* X (1603–07), 510, 513; SP14/12/13 (January 1605): James's instructions to the Council when he was 'retired' at the hunt.
55. LS13/168, fo. 124: the party used 43 carts compared with as many as 250 for a summer progress.

sequence of state apartments, solely for 'Noblemen and Gentlemen of the Bedchamb[er]'.[56]

As important, however, as James's fondness for sylvan retreat was his loathness to admit new faces to his inner circle. The king was remarkably faithful to his intimates. In 1603 he did his best for his Scots chamber; while of all the Gentlemen appointed thereafter, Carr was the only one to lose his place. Similarly with the Grooms; despite Carr's fall, his nephew William continued in his place and was still in attendance in 1625. Only Buckingham in the last years of the reign managed to break this conservatism, effectively removing his kinsman Arthur Brett first from attendance and then from his place as Groom of the Bedchamber in 1622–23. (Brett was being hailed as the next favourite; Buckingham made certain that the rumours were exaggerated – below, p. 221.) This loyalty left few places for newcomers; it also meant that James looked long and hard before committing himself. Never, in fact, did James appoint to a place which involved frequent access, however formal, without some previous personal knowledge of the applicant. Applied to the Bedchamber, the king's conservatism meant that such promotion to the department as occurred usually followed a period of approval elsewhere at court, or in a lesser Bedchamber office. Carr's promotion to Gentleman in 1607 followed four years service as a Groom; Villiers served as a Cupbearer in the Privy Chamber for some months before being sworn a Gentleman. Chamberlain grasped the point in 1618 when he noted the 'gross error' of Sir William Monson's backers (who were trying to foist him onto James as a new favourite), in having 'thrust him on so forward before they had procured him some ordinary place of attendance'.[57] Allied to this was a complicated domestic mechanism by which the queen's approval was required before Bedchamber appointments could be made. Archbishop Abbot remembered that

King James had a fashion, that he would never admit any to nearness about himself, but such as the queen should commend unto him . . .; that if the queen afterwards . . . should complain of this Dear One, he might make the answer, 'it is long of yourself, for you were the party that commended him unto me'.

Whether or not Abbot told the full story, between 1603 and the queen's death in 1619 there is positive evidence that three of the four

56. H. M. Colvin, ed., *The History of the King's Works* (6 vols, 1963–82) IV, p. 32; E351/3369; Colvin, op. cit. pp. 175 and 237.
57. *Letters of Chamberlain* II, 151 (27 March 1618).

Gentlemen appointed had first to gain her approval. There is also the rather negative evidence that Carr's nephew was appointed in 1614 'in a needless bravery of the queen', as the king said. Anne clearly had a voice in these appointments, but it could be overruled.[58]

Conservatism in allowing additions to the Bedchamber on the part of the king (and queen) limited markedly scope for purging or packing the department as an instrument of factional strife. Even the Groom of the Stool, the formal head of the department, who actually swore in the new Gentlemen and Grooms, had little part to play in deciding on the appointments themselves. Still less did the great officers of state. Instead the Bedchamber was subject to the king's personal management as he took account of the political and personal pressures on him in furthering his own aims. Buckingham alone had the ability, from about 1619 onwards, and more especially after 1622, to persuade the king to alter the department's membership in his favour, by both allowing him to admit his relatives and dependents, and to suspend and dismiss those who gave him trouble. To others the Bedchamber was a closed elite. The duke of Newcastle, decades later, recalled that 'William earl of Pembroke, that most excellent person, [did] labour as for his life all the reign of King James . . . to be of the Bedchamber and could never obtain it – as also Thomas the great earl of Arundel did labour'. The failure of two of the most powerful of the English nobility was shared by the rest of the political establishment of James's southern kingdom, until the rise of Buckingham rewrote the rules.[59] In thus treating the Bedchamber as his private *familia*, James was following Elizabeth's example; the motives and consequences of his actions were fundamentally different, however.

Politics: from bureaucrat–minister to Bedchamber favourite

Nowhere does the difference show more sharply than in politics. Elizabethan government was unitary. Of the twin power centres of Henrician politics, one – the Privy Chamber – had gone into eclipse.

58. J. Rushworth, ed., *Historical Collections* (4 parts in 7 vols, 1657) I, p. 456. On Hay and Montgomery, above, note 41, I can find no evidence that the queen's approval was involved in Carr's appointment; this may explain her hostility to him. Akrigg, *Letters of James VI and I*, p. 336 (dated to early 1615).
59. 'The Duke of Newcastle on Government' in S. A. Strong, ed., *A Catalogue of Letters . . . at Welbeck* (1903), p. 213.

The result was that 'under Elizabeth ministers had no need to place their creatures in the Royal Bedchamber . . ., Household officers had no special advantages of contact with the Queen, and . . . Council, Household and Monarch revolved within the same orbit'. In this universe the dominant body was the Council, whose powers towards the end were largely concentrated in the person of Robert Cecil, Secretary of State. He controlled both the formal apparatus of state and the more personal machinery of the sign manual and the queen's Coffers.[60] Essex's increasingly desperate manoeuvres only reinforced Cecil's monopoly; James's accession, however, undercut its very foundations. Within weeks Cecil was writing, 'I wish I waited now in [Elizabeth's] Presence Chamber, with ease at my board, and rest in my bed. I am pushed from the shore of comfort, and know not where the winds and the waves of a court will bear me'. Five years later James himself pointed the contrast between the two styles of government when, temporarily absent from London, he mockingly wrote to Cecil and the Council, 'Ye and your fellows there are so proud now, that you have got the guiding again of a feminine court in the old fashion [in fact Queen Anne's 'court' at Greenwich] that I know not how to deal with ye'.[61]

It is important to be clear about the reasons for the change. The near doubling in size of the Privy Council, from fourteen to twenty-six, presented in itself no necessary threat to the late Elizabethan regime. The most significant additions, Henry and Thomas Howard (later earls of Northampton and Suffolk respectively), had already worked in close co-operation with Cecil in arranging James's peaceful accession; and, once on the Council, simply became members of the existing 'inner ring'. The result was business as before. 'My lord', wrote Sir George Home to Cecil in 1604, 'since you are come to a good point with his Majesty, let a secret course be kept with him in his weightiest affairs by you four [i.e., Cecil, Suffolk, Northampton, Worcester] and let his general errands be done by his whole Council'. Salisbury took the same high Eliza-bethan line in his account of the 'State of a Secretary's Place, and the Peril'; as did Bishop Goodman in his later account of the regime of 1603–10: Salisbury and Northampton, abetted by Suffolk, were in control; while the other main councillors 'did only manage their

---

60. P. Williams, 'Court and Polity under Elizabeth I', *Bulletin of the John Rylands Library* 65 (1983), 264; W. T. MacCaffrey, *Queen Elizabeth and the Making of Policy* (Princeton 1981), pp. 432, 437–8. See above, pp. 152–3

61. H. Harington, ed., *Nugae Antiquae* (2 vols, 1804) I, p. 345; J. O. Halliwell, ed., *Letters of the Kings of England* (2 vols, 1848) II, p. 113 (5 August 1608).

great offices and looked no further'. And Salisbury's correspondence bears out the verdict.[62]

What changed, then, was not how the Council was run, but how the chief minister and Council related to the monarch. With the institution of the Bedchamber, even the inner councillors no longer had an automatic claim to the nearest access to the monarch; and even if the *entrée* were granted, it was enjoyed in much greater measure by the Bedchamber's staff. And they – all practised operators in Scots politics and some James's companions since his childhood – were well able to take advantage of the fact. Now, to paraphrase Dr Williams, the Bedchamber did possess special advantages of contact with the king; Bedchamber and Council were now separate entities with, for the most part, separate membership; Council and minister now revolved in a different orbit from the king and Bedchamber.

Such a powerful and independent entity presented an unavoidable challenge to a would-be chief councillor like Cecil. In order to maintain his authority he had either to control the Bedchamber, to place his own agents there, or at least to come to terms with it. James's attitude to his entourage ruled out the first approach but in the second Cecil was remarkably successful to begin with. His greatest coup came in June 1603 when, exploiting his prestige as successful stage manager of the accession, he was able to get two of his men appointed Gentlemen of the Bedchamber. One, Sir James Hay, was a Scot. Formally he was recommended by the French ambassador, but was regarded by Cecil as 'an excellent good instrument to conserve his Majesty's good opinions'. The other was the Englishman, Sir Philip Herbert, soon made earl of Montgomery. He was Cecil's nephew; while his expertise with dogs and horses won the king's particular esteem, and gave him the reputation of being the king's 'favourite'. If he made little personal or political capital from his position, he at least represented an asset to Cecil in keeping the king diverted.[63] Cecil's most active correspondent in the Bedchamber, however, was Sir Roger Aston: the two had been in

---

62. Willson, *James VI and I*, p. 175–6 (where Home is quoted); J. R. Tanner *Constitutional Documents of the Reign of James I* (Cambridge 1930), pp. 124–6; Goodman, *Court of King James I* I, p. 51. Dorset worked through Cecil to the king, as he had no contacts in the Bedchamber – HMC, *Salisbury* XV (1603), 51 (April 1603).

63. Mares, *Memoirs of Carey*, p. 66, and n. 41 above: *Letters of Chamberlain* II, p. 52 (8 February 1617, on French ambassador's role); SP14/13/88 (? April 1605); Edward Hyde, earl of Clarendon, *The History of the Rebellion and Civil Wars in England*, ed. W. D. Macray (6 vols, Oxford 1888) I, p. 74; Goodman, *Court of King James I* I, p. 40.

contact before James's accession, while Cecil may have helped
smooth Aston's successful transfer from the king's Scottish Chamber
to his permanent Bedchamber establishment in England. At all
events, Cecil's brother Burghley referred to him as 'an honest man
to our house and worthy to be made of. He is not like some
of our old mistress's servants about her, that would say much and
do little'.[64]

But that was all. In the long term James would no more tolerate
the packing of his Bedchamber than he would have stood for a
Cecilian purge. The rest of the Bedchamber depended upon the king
alone. Here Cecil could not command, he could only lubricate. And
he did so freely. Lennox, Fenton, Haddington, Aubigny and Dunbar
gained massively by direct patronage from the crown's English
income and land during Cecil's regime: both before 1606–07 – the
'first three years that were as Christmas' – and after, under Salisbury
as lord treasurer. Cecil also cultivated the Grooms of the
Bedchamber: John Murray for one 'always held very great corre-
spondency with the Secretary, and ... got many a thousand pound
by his assignment'. Goodman justified Cecil's behaviour against
Weldon's rabidly xenophobic denunciation in practical terms: 'men
are to associate themselves with whom they have greatest cause to
converse, and of whom they have the greatest use'.[65]

Already, then, it is clear Cecil could not aspire to take the same
high line with the royal entourage of an earlier generation of
ministers like Wolsey and Cromwell. His ground was further weakened by administrative developments, as the revived Bedchamber

64. *Calendar of Scottish Papers* XII, XIII (1595–97, 1597–1603) *passim* (index sub
Aston). HMC, *Salisbury* XV (1603), 31 (4 April 1603).
65. E. R. Foster, ed., *Proceedings in Parliament, 1610* (2 vols, New Haven, 1966) I,
p. 7; Stone, *The Crisis of the Aristocracy*, pp. 470–6, 774–6. Professor Stone's
figures, roughly calculated as they are, dramatically illustrate the Bedchamber's
gains. They show that over the entire period 1558–1641, nine individuals
received 45 per cent of all crown gifts (on Stone's criteria) to the English peerage.
Lennox and Haddington were among them, and received most of their patronage
before 1612. Twenty-nine individuals received 75 per cent of crown gifts,
including Aubigny and Dunbar (who was eligible for only eight years,
1603–11). Fenton fails to appear through his lack of an English peerage, but my
calculations suggest he belongs in the top nine rather than the top twenty-nine.
Cecil also did well for his men: Hay and Montgomery made the top nine. Carr
and Villiers were later to benefit on a similar scale, making six out of Stone's top
nine – the others were Elizabeth's Essex and Leicester, and James's corrupt lord
treasurer Suffolk – and ten of the top twenty-nine who were Gentlemen of
James' Bedchamber. (Along with Fenton, John Murray (appointed Gentleman
in 1622) is omitted from the figures by reason of not holding an English peerage.)
Goodman, *Court of King James I* I, pp. 31, 38, 52.

trespassed on the Secretary's Elizabethan monopoly of the 'private' governmental machine of the sign manual and the royal Coffers. As for the first, the bureaucratic technicalities evolved under Elizabeth made it difficult for the Bedchamber to procure the royal signature directly; instead they appropriated the deputy Cecil had appointed. This was Sir Thomas Lake, a clerk of the Signet to whom James had taken a liking. By 1610 Cecil would have liked very much to get rid of him, but he was immovable, 'being now in possession by the Scotsmen's intercession'.[66] But if the Bedchamber was obliged to act at one remove over signing, in the serious business of patronage broking that preceded the issue of a formal sign manual warrant, they were from the first very active, both for themselves and others. 'Such as were beggars were left to the ordinary masters of Requests', ruefully reflected Sir Roger Wilbraham, one of the latter; while 'suits of bounty or grace were preferred by most of his Chamber'.[67]

This sort of initiative in patronage went far beyond anything practised by the Elizabethan Privy Chamber, and was unwelcome to Cecil both politically and, more and more, financially. He could of course have stopped grants through his control of the signet (and the privy seal before 1608). But he was too practised a politician to risk shutting the stable door after each individual horse had bolted. Instead he looked to a bureaucratic solution. From May 1603 a committee of six of the Privy Council was to meet weekly to examine all grants (particularly those involving land and reversion to office), and only those they countersigned were to be submitted to the king for his signature. The machinery was further tightened up when, after becoming lord treasurer in 1608, Cecil issued the 'Book of Bounty'. This laid down strict ground rules for grants, and once again was particularly stringent about alienations of crown land. But still the floodgates of patronage remained open: the Council themselves had recognized that saying 'no' was 'a sour office', not willingly done, but the main problem was James and his entourage. In October 1608 James called on the Council to bear

---

66. Goodman, *Court of King James I* I, pp. 175–6. S03/4, S03/5 (Register of King's Bills, 1608–14) shows Lake procuring the overwhelming bulk of warrants, where earlier (1603–04) there had been more alternation with other signet clerks such as Windebanke. Lake never achieved full rights of Bedchamber access, but dispatched business in frequent, semi-formal audiences, especially on hunting journeys. HMC, *Salisbury* XXI (1609–12), 216 (30 April 1610). Nevertheless, he could exhibit a sort of fellow-worker camaraderie with the Bedchamber proper, however exalted their rank. He referred to 'my brother of Dunbar' in 1607 (HMC, *Salisbury* XIX (1607), 207 (5 August 1607).

67. 'Journal of Sir Roger Wilbraham', *Camden Society Miscellany X*, p. 57.

witness to his adherence to the 'Book of Bounty'; one month later, he granted a forfeiture on customs to Patrick Ramsay, brother of John, viscount Haddington, a Gentleman of the Bedchamber. The grant clearly fell within the restricted categories, yet Lake, when asked directly by James whether it were allowable, could only prevaricate. Haddington had told James that the grant had been cleared with Salisbury, and the minister seems to have capitulated. The 'Book' proclaimed that James would 'not suffer any . . . advantage to be taken by one man's nearness more than another'; cases like Haddington's, which could be multiplied, put such pieties into perspective.[68] It was not that the 'Book' was 'honoured only in the breach'; rather, by limiting patronage it heightened competition and thereby put a yet greater premium on the Bedchamber's strategic position.[69]

Control of the king's Coffers and the Privy Purse also slipped from the once firm grasp of the Secretary and the lord treasurer. Immediately the scale of the Privy Purse changed: from a turnover of £2,500 a year under Elizabeth to a total of £23,000 for the first two years of James. Exchequer subordination remained for the time being, however. The Keeper declared his account in the Exchequer; and the Exchequer also supplied most of his income by regular warrants. Probably the fact that the Keeper, Dunbar, was also chancellor of the Exchequer had something to do with this; certainly his resignation from the Exchequer in 1606 coincided with a major change. In 1605 the Privy Purse ceased abruptly to render accounts in the Exchequer, and Exchequer funding also began to tail off: only £11,600 was paid between 1605 and 1611 and scarcely anything thereafter. In the absence of accounts it is impossible to be sure of what revenue sources were used instead, but everything points to casual windfalls, like the £1,200 from the sale of an export licence noted in the 1603–05 account. Partly this was a matter of mere necessity, since an increasingly bankrupt Exchequer was unable to

---

68. HMC, *Salisbury* XV (1603), 99–101 (22 May 1603) – cf. SP14/1/106, fuller guidelines which envisage the involvement of the Bedchamber. First sitting was on 30 May 1603 (BL, Additional MS 11,402, fo. 89). The 'Book of Bounty' as printed in 1611 is summarized in W. Notestein, F. H. Relf and H. Simpson, eds, *Commons Debates 1621* (7 vols, New Haven 1935) VII, pp. 491 ff. BL, Additional MS 11,402, fo. 103 (16 July 1605); SP14/37/23 (Lake to Salisbury, 21 October 1608); SP14/37/91 (Lake to Salisbury, 24 November 1608); SP14/37/96 (Lake to Salisbury, 27 November 1608). SP14/37/74, 1608 draft of the Book of Bounty, which gives the full preamble.

69. Cf. M. Prestwich, *Cranfield: Politics and Profits under the Early Stuarts* (Oxford 1966), pp. 32–3.

supply even the king's own wants. But it may also point to the development of a two-tier 'system' of finance, as an Exchequer in chronic deficit was left to fend off the king's creditors as best it might; while the windfall revenues, from projects, sales of office and titles and the like, which became increasingly important after 1610, were fed directly into the king's Coffers. And certainly the expenditure side of the Privy Purse suggests some such change. Under Elizabeth it had been dominated by the queen's modest personal expenses on the one hand, and small fixed charges for such items as lute strings and the seasonal decoration of the Privy Lodgings on the other. In 1608 over £1,000 of such recurrent charges were hived off to the Treasurer of the Chamber – the usual paymaster of the Household-above-stairs. Instead the account was dominated by new categories, like gifts and rewards to 'persons as well English and Scots as strangers', which had already totalled £18,000 in 1603–05. James's Privy Purse, in short, was as new as the Bedchamber that administered it: from its Elizabethan position as a small, domestic spending department entirely subordinate to the Exchequer, the Privy Purse had become by 1610 a largely independent king's treasury, possibly with a significant role as revenue department, certainly disposing of large sums, not for lute strings, but for the king's 'important services and urgent affairs'.[70]

Despite these structural changes, Cecil remained in effective control of the routine administration, and his voice continued to be decisive on issues of policy. Particularly so with foreign policy. Between 1603 and 1612 foreign affairs provoked little domestic tension; peace with Spain, resolved in Council before the accession, was swiftly concluded after it, and Cecil thereafter steered England along a middle course of mediation between France and Spain. Day-to-day policy consisted of changes of emphasis in this centre position, and in this Cecil predominated until his death because, as the Spanish Ambassador observed 'this king makes his decisions with Salisbury only, without his Council'. The Bedchamber seems to have had some, mainly negative effect on Cecil's conduct of foreign

---

70. G. E. Aylmer 'Studies in the Institutions and Personnel of English Central Administration 1625–1642', (unpublished Oxford D.Phil. dissertation, 1954), p. 162; E351/2792 (Privy Purse account, 1 May 1603–30 April 1605). Exchequer warrants to the Privy Purse in *CSP Dom.* VIII (1603–10), 356, 386, 399, 559, 580, 604, 626, 628, 652; IX (1611–18), 3, 12. On the Exchequer's plight see E. Lodge, *Life of Sir Julius Caesar* (1827), pp. 25–30. LC5/81–3 for the 1608 expenditure change (and LC5/115/18 for confirmation in 1614). D. Thomas, 'Financial and Administrative Developments' in Tomlinson, *Before the English Civil War*, p. 105 for the deficit and cf. *CSP Dom.* VIII (1603–10), 628.

policy but made little difference to the understanding on this point between king and minister. Control of the foreign dispatches in fact was the element of the Secretary's official power least trenched on by the Bedchamber while Cecil lived.[71]

Structural change in Cecil's position had the greater effect on his conduct of domestic policy. The domestic scene, unlike the foreign, was dominated by two great issues – the Union and finance – and the settlement of these questions was in turn conditioned by the constant presence, actual or potential, of a parliament unprecedented in length of sittings, overall duration and frequency of calling since that of 1529–36. To contemporaries the 1604–10 parliament was the original 'long parliament', and it was so because of repeated attempts and repeated failures to settle the Stuart dynasty on these key issues: in 1604, stalemate on the Union, failed attempts to bargain away wardship and purveyance and a climb-down over asking for subsidies; in 1605–06 the enforced deferral of Union legislation, and another failure to bargain purveyance for supply (while with two subsidies agreed on, a third passed the house only by a single vote); in 1606–07 the complete collapse of Union legislation; and in 1610, failure to secure supply either by bargain or by more than one traditional subsidy, while even raising the issue of Union provoked 'interruption and whistling'.[72]

Two things are clear in this. First, whatever the 'revisionists' may argue, there *was* opposition. The opposition, moreover, was sustained and principled; it almost always commanded a majority in the Commons and latterly in the Lords as well, and it was focused explicitly on the two key issues of government policy: Union, which lay closest to the king's heart, and fiscal reform, which was his chief minister Cecil's principal concern.[73] Second, and more directly to the

---

71. S. Adams, 'Spain or the Netherlands?' in Tomlinson, *Before the English Civil War*, pp. 93–5; A. J. Loomie, 'Sir Robert Cecil and the Spanish Embassy', *Bulletin of the Institute of Historical Research* 42 (1969), 46, 53.

72. J. E. Neale, *The Elizabethan House of Commons* (1949), 368; Foster, *Proceedings in Parliament, 1610* I, p. xi; W. Notestein, *The House of Commons 1604–10* (New Haven 1971), pp. 180–1, 208 and Ch. III; Foster, *Proceedings in Parliament, 1610* II, pp. 4–5.

73. This is not the place to rehearse the positions for and against 'revisionism', evolved following the publication of Conrad Russell's seminal article 'Parliamentary History in Perspective, 1603–29', *History* 61 (1976), 1–27. But for the argument sketched here, cf. R. C. Munden, 'James I and "the Growth of Mutual Distrust": King, Commons and Reform, 1603–1604' in K. Sharpe, ed., *Faction and Parliament: Essays on Early Stuart History* (Oxford 1978), p. 71; *Ambassades de Monsieur de la Boderie en Angleterre, 1606–1611* (5 vols, 1750) II, pp. 199–200 (2 May 1607).

point here, the Bedchamber settlement played a crucial role in triggering and sustaining this opposition. The settlement itself, which consigned the Bedchamber wholly to the Scots, was (as we have seen) James's initial riposte to the failure of the English political establishment to embrace Union wholeheartedly; and thereafter the king's exclusively Scottish inner entourage became a prime sticking-point in relations with parliament, especially where supply was concerned.

The issue, on the other hand, was as sensitive as it was important: thus it only emerged fully into the light of day (however much it was in people's minds) at moments of real crisis. The first such came at the height of the naturalization debate in February 1607. On the 13th, Sir Christopher Piggott denounced Scots in general and Scottish courtiers in particular as proud, beggarly, quarrelsome and untrustworthy. This was going too far. Three days later the House itself sent Piggott to the Tower; while on the day following that (the 17th) Bacon made the official reply to his slanders. Apart from 'some persons of quality about his Majesty's person here at court', Bacon claimed, the number of Scots families resident in England was 'extremely small'. It was a characteristically subtle performance. But it in no way answered the real charge that these 'some persons' enjoyed a wholly disproportionate share of both political power and royal patronage. These unsatisfied doubts surfaced constantly in the debates on supply.[74]

The first occasion came in March 1606, when after two subsidies and fifteenths had been granted for 'love,' further supply was being debated. One Mr Gawyn spoke to the effect that 'whereas it is moved we should fill the king's coffers, it would be likewise understood whether they will be filled for if the bottoms be out then can they not be filled'. Nor could John Hoskins accept that 'subjects ought not to examine how [supply] is spent', since 'a supply may easily be spent, so may a re-supply, . . . and whatsoever we give, we cannot give that [which] may suffice'. In the event, a motion for further supply passed the house by a single vote. Salisbury was pleased with the result, and was apparently 'popular' in parliament that summer; but the forebodings of the Commons were apparently being fulfilled. In the same breath as he retailed Salisbury's felicity, a news-letter writer noted the grants of land and viscountcies to Ramsay and Erskine of the Bedchamber and commented, 'the king's

74. J. Spedding, ed., *The letters and life of Sir Francis Bacon* (7 vols, 1861–74) III, pp. 306–7, 311. For the Bedchamber's share of patronage, see above, note 65.

land, inclosed to all other, is only open to them'.[75]

Names might be named in a news-letter; in parliament, however, they had spoken in code. The code was to be broken, as we have seen, in the next session of 1607 on the issue of Union; and it was again, with still more dramatic effect, in the fourth and fifth sessions of the parliament in 1610. At the beginning of the fourth session in February, Thomas Wentworth asked 'to what purpose to draw a silver stream into the royal cistern if it shall daily run out thence by private cocks'; while in the fifth session, Sir Nathaniel Bacon observed that 'the wants of the King and the Kingdom are two distinct things', and Samuel Lewkenor, who had voted for additional supply in 1606, had now instead come to approve of the example of the Emperor Antoninus, who remedied his wants 'by discharging an unnecessary train of such as lived idle in his court'.[76] This was coming pretty near home. At the end of November John Hoskins went further. 'The royal cistern,' he proclaimed, 'had a leak, which till it were stopped, all our consultation to bring money into it were of little use'. He had said as much in 1606; now he came within a hair's breadth of belling the cat. 'This fault could not be personal but national', he explained. And having acquitted the Irish, Dutch and English from blame, he left his listeners to their own verdict about the Scots. One week later a newsletter reported the current rumour that the Commons would give subsidies freely if it did not believe that the king's largesse *to his Scots* would cause a 'continual and remediless leak'.[77]

The king's immediate reaction to Hoskins's speech, and fear of rumours of worse to come, show just how inflammable the issue was. Two days after Hoskins's speech, the king was reported as viewing it, and others, as 'so scandalous . . . that some of them reach very near to the point of treason'; and he spoke of 'taunts and disgraces as have been uttered of him and *those that appertain to him* [my italics]'. A week after James still 'discoursed long to show in

75. D. H. Willson, ed., *The Parliamentary Diary of Robert Bowyer* (Minneapolis 1931), pp. 77–8 (12 March 1606): E. Sawyer, ed., *Memorials of Affairs of State . . . from the original papers of Sir Ralph Winwood* (3 vols, 1725) II, p. 226.

76. S. R. Gardiner, ed., *Parliamentary Debates in 1610* (Camden Society, 1st series, 81) 1862, p. 11; Foster, *Proceedings in Parliament, 1610* II, pp. 336, 403 (16 November 1610); compare Notestein, *Commons 1604–10*, 185 on Lewkenor in 1606.

77. Foster, *Proceedings in Parliament, 1610* II, p. 344 (23 November 1610); Sawyer, *Winwood Memorials* III, 326 (John More to Winwood, 1 December 1610). And cf. G. L. Harriss, 'Medieval Doctrines in the Debates on Supply, 1610–29' in Sharpe, *Faction and Parliament*, especially p. 85.

what degree of treason they were that should seek to remove servants from a Prince'. Three days later, James, still indignant, addressed the issue directly:

> If whenever the tenor of bounty is touched, the Scots must ever be tacitly understood, I will be forced to disabuse the world in that point, and publish the truth that the English have tasted as much and more of my liberality than [*sic*] the Scots have done.

James's reply in 1610 was as disingenuous as Bacon's in 1607 and equally failed to quell doubts.[78] The most explicit statement of these was also prepared for the 1610 Parliament. It took the form of a 'grievance', to be presented to parliament by Sir John Holles, a former Gentleman of James's Privy Chamber.[79] To the king's need for supply, the 'grievance' proposed a dual response: 'from our purse' and 'from our counsel', to remove the cause which had put the king in need; here Holles echoes the earlier and later imagery of men seeking to fill a leaky cistern. Holles's value lies in his unequivocal identification of the problem: 'the Court is the cause of all,' and especially because, surrounding James

> the Scottish monopolize his princely person, standing like mountains betwixt the beams of his grace and us; and, though it becomes us not to appoint particulars about him, yet we most humbly beseech his Majesty his Bedchamber may be shared as well to those of our nation as to them, that this seven years brand of jealousy [and] distrust may at last be removed . . . and that the same Chamber may have the same brotherly partition which all the other inferior forms of the court, the Presence and Privy Chamber have.

He went on to identify a 'twofold unequal distribution of benefits' stemming from this monopoly. The Bedchamber themselves got the richest patronage pickings, ordinary and extraordinary, including fines and escheats. Second, 'by the grace of their place all favours and honours directly or indirectly pass through their hands; for not only do they possess the royal presence, they be warm within, while the best of ours starve without'. Holles concludes that national equality in the Bedchamber – 'that they should not seem to be the children of the family and we the servants' – would both promote

---

78. SP14/58/35 (Lake to Salisbury, 25 November 1610); HMC, *Salisbury* XXI (1609–12), 263 (Lake to Salisbury, 3 December 1610); ibid. p. 265 (James to Salisbury, 6 December 1610). For James's disingenousness, see above, note 65; and see also the almost punitive cash grants to the Bedchamber which followed the failure of 1610 (*CSP Dom.* IX (1611–18), 5 (1 January 1611), HMC, *Downshire* III, 20).
79. Printed in HMC, *Portland* IX, 113.

Anglo-Scottish amity, and remove the cause of financial necessity. If these thoughts were ever put to the Commons committee for grievances, they went no further.[80] Silence on the issue prevailed, and the events which followed when the silence was broken indicate powerful reasons for its having been kept.

By 1610 all this conspired to put a question mark over the continuance of Salisbury's ministry. He had failed to deliver in parliament – not least because of the problems caused by the Bedchamber; at the same time the Bedchamber, now substantially beyond his control, offered both an alternative (and more effective) route to the king, and possibly even the power-base for a new sort of regime. Salisbury, in short, could be saved only by a conspicuous parliamentary success. Hence the Great Contract, which aimed to heal, once and for all, the running sore of James's finances by bargaining away the royal rights to wardship and purveyance in return for a fixed annual income from parliament.

Traditional accounts of the abortive Contract have focused on opposition in Parliament; in fact Cecil had at least as much of a problem with the king.[81] To overcome it, he relied extensively on his allies in the Bedchamber, the earl of Montgomery and Sir Roger Aston. Aston was particularly active. A week after the deal was formalized in late July he wrote an enthusiastic account: 'the little beagle hath run a true and perfect scent, which brought the rest of the great hounds to a perfect tune which was before by their voice much divided'. Four Councillors – Cecil, Northampton, Suffolk and Worcester – had eventually combined to put the figure of £200,000 to the king, to which he finally agreed; they returned, put the figure to the Commons, and upon their agreement, Aston, also a member of the House, 'presently went to his Majesty to let him understand [it] was done'.[82]

But Aston's was not, of course, the only voice about the king. Six weeks earlier, on 10 June, an observer wrote that the king could, if he wished, settle the difficulties surrounding the Contract. 'Yet is he so distracted with variety of opinion, from a number about him, especially Scots, that though he would, he cannot resolve that

80. Foster, *Proceedings in Parliament, 1610* II, p. 359.
81. A. G. R. Smith, 'Crown, Parliament and Finance: The Great Contract of 1610' in P. Clark, A. G. R. Smith, N. R. N. Tyacke, eds, *The English Commonwealth 1547–1640: Essays in Politics and Society presented to Joel Hurstfield*, (Leicester 1979), pp. 111–27.
82. SP14/56/42 (Aston to unidentified, 24 July 1610). And cf. SP14/58/35 (25 November 1610, Lake to Salisbury).

he desires, which is the cause that, as often as he can, he absents himself the town'.[83] Most powerful of the Scottish voices was probably that of Sir George Home, earl of Dunbar. Goodman makes Dunbar the bearer of a message to the king from a 'great peer of the realm, lying upon his deathbed'. The burden of the advice was that James should have nothing to do with the Contract: first, because it involved the diminution of the prerogative, for which (and for wardship in particular) the subject obeyed the king more than for any other laws; and second, because in any case the subject was bound to supply the king without contract or bargain. In fact, since Dunbar was the only great peer near to death in 1610, he was probably the author of the advice as well as the messenger.[84] And it was from Dunbar's stable too that came the weightiest written argument against the Contract. This was written by Sir Julius Caesar, Home's successor as chancellor of the Exchequer in 1606. Central to Caesar's argument is the injury which the Contract would do to the 'imperial prerogatives and flowers of [the] Crown', which chimes not only with Dunbar's mysterious message but also with the earl's known general stance: 'no man', it was observed, 'was so tender of the king's prerogative'.[85] Indeed, Dunbar's movement between Scotland and the court may be the chief key to James's shift from grudging acquiescence in the Contract (while Dunbar was absent) to outright rejection (when he returned).[86]

Against such powerful and well placed opponents Cecil was forced, perhaps, to call on some strange allies. In the last stages of the Contract debate, in July 1610, the French and Venetian ambassadors, as well as Carleton, had all reported attacks on the Scots; now, just before the summer recess, a rumour was current that the supply element of the Contract would be appropriated by parliamentary treasurers to ensure that it went to pay off the debt, and not into the 'bottomless pockets' of the Scots courtiers. The source of the rumour may well have been Cecil himself. In the sessions of 1606–10 a group of oppositionist MPs had formed. They were 'patriots' in

83. HMC, *Downshire* II, 490 (Samuel Calvert to William Trumbull, 10 June 1610).
84. Goodman, *Court of King James I* I, pp. 40–1; cf. J. Hurstfield *The Queen's Wards* (1958), p. 322, neither confirming nor denying the story. G. E. C[ockayne], *The Complete Peerage* (13 vols in 14, 1910–40) *passim*, for peers dying in late 1610–early 1611. Dunbar held the English barony of Home of Berwick.
85. Gardiner, *Parliamentary Debates in 1610*, Appendix D, p. 167. A. G. R. Smith, art, cit. n. 74 to p. 124. Goodman, *Court of King James I* I, p. 21.
86. M. Lee, *Government by Pen: Scotland under James VI and I* (Illinois 1980), p. 99; SP14/57/60 (Dunbar to Sir Robert Carr, 19 September 1610, dated at Alnwick); A. G. R. Smith, art. cit, p. 123.

their resistance to Union; and 'commonwealth-men' in their rejection of supply, unless 'your Majesty's expense growth by Commonwealth'. A key member of the group was Sir Henry Neville, spokesman and friend of the earl of Southampton. In late July 1610 Neville and his associates had a meeting with Cecil in Hyde Park. The ostensible subject was impositions; but there are signs that Cecil also gave them broad hints that the destination of any new funds to be raised by the Contract would be closely watched.[87]

But if Cecil could strike a deal with the 'patriots', Dunbar and the Bedchamber could play a stronger card still: the king. James had never been happy with the scheme; in the summer recess he turned against it decisively. That ditched Salisbury. At the beginning of the year Cecil himself had reflected ruefully, it is reported, 'it fareth not with me now as it did in the queen's time: she heard but few, and of them I may say myself the chief; the king heareth many, yea of all kinds'.[88] By the winter his fallen state was obvious to all. And as he fell, so a new political structure emerged.

Its form became clear at the beginning of 1611. Meanwhile Dunbar, chief architect of the attack on Cecil, had died. James 'bewailed him tenderly, and spent the whole day of his death in bed'. In place of Dunbar stepped the favourite, Robert Carr. He had been first Dunbar's protégé, then his collaborator, and now he emerged as his political heir. 'It would seem that he is to dispose of everything', the Venetian ambassador wrote in April, which 'is displeasing to the English; all the same everybody is endeavouring to secure his favour and goodwill'. Over patronage that was clearly true; but otherwise Carr's initial role was not to act as a power in his own right, but rather as James's broker between the two main English political groupings that fought for Cecil's inheritance.[89] One of these was the Howards, led by the earls of Northampton and Suffolk; the other was the ex-Essexians, who now looked to the earl of Southampton. At the moment the main issue between the two (apart from personalities) was finance: Northampton, the great deviser of projects, was willing to try anything rather than risk another parliament; the Southampton group, on the other hand, were committed

87. Foster, *Proceedings in Parliament, 1610* II, p. 295, n. 3; C. Roberts and O. Duncan, 'The Parliamentary Undertaking of 1614', *EHR* 93 (1978), 484; Foster, *Proceedings* I, p. 158; II, p. 278.
88. J. Cumming, ed., 'Henry Yelverton's Narrative of what passed on his being restored to the king's favour in 1609', *Archaeologia* 15 (1806), 51.
89. *CSP Ven.* XII (1610–13), 116, 135. Cf. L. L. Peck, *Northampton: Patronage and Policy at the Court of James I* (1982), p. 30.

to a parliamentary solution. Both groups had their route to the favourite: Northampton dealt directly and officially with him as a councillor; whereas Southampton, distrusted by James both personally and politically, operated instead at twice remove and used his favourite and 'dear Damon', Sir Henry Neville, to negotiate with Carr's 'bedfellow, minion and inward councillor', Sir Thomas Overbury.[90]

Cecil's continued clinging to life and the increasingly empty shell of office spared the king and favourite from any pressing need to choose between the two groupings. But Cecil's death in May 1612 both increased the pressure for choice and created a third grouping of bereaved ex-Cecilians, headed by the earl of Pembroke and his brother, and Cecil's sometime agent in the Bedchamber, Montgomery. James's first response to Cecil's death, however, was simultaneously to secure a breathing space and to increase the prestige and field of action of his favourite. Neither of Cecil's great offices was filled: instead the Treasury was put into commission; while the Secretaryship was resumed by the king himself. In theory James was his own Secretary; in practice most of the office's important functions were devolved onto Carr, by this time a privy councillor and Viscount Rochester. At the end of July 1612 he received custody of the signet, temporarily kept by Lake; and at about this time, ambassadors' correspondence began to be addressed to him. He also acted as personal secretary in writing the king's overseas correspondence, apparently with the help of Overbury. Carr did not, however, as contemporaries remarked, possess the whole of the Secretary's powers. Sir Thomas Lake kept the job of presenting signet bills for the king's signature, as he had done under Salisbury; while much of the domestic side of the Secretaryship seems to have devolved onto the earl of Northampton, lord privy seal. The latter took over the ordering of Privy Council business and assumed the direction of the Treasury Commission, set up in the absence of a lord treasurer.[91]

---

90. 'Wilbraham's Journal', *Camden Society Misc. X*, p. 116; Peck, *Northampton*, p. 31.
91. HMC, *Mar and Kelly Supplement*, 40 (11 June 1612); SP14/70/20 (? July 1612) Lord Sheffield to Carr, written 'knowing yo[ur] lo[rdshi]p w[i]th the king doth ma[n]age for foreign affairs of the kingdo[m]'; *Letters of Chamberlain* I, p. 372 (23 July 1612). P. R. Seddon 'Robert Carr, earl of Somerset', *Renaissance and Modern Studies* 14 (1970), 56. S03/5 for Lake's continued dominance of procurements, and Seddon, art. cit., p. 59. Overbury's aid can be inferred from Fenton's comments on his removal from court. HMC, *Mar and Kelly Supplement*, 51 (20 May 1613 – 'I think his Majesty will let the world see that for a time Rochester can make his Majesty's dispatches without the help of Overbury').

This *ad hoc* arrangement proved both durable and practical. Indeed, until early 1614, Carr and Northampton worked as an administrative partnership, as Professor Peck has recently documented.[92] From Northampton's point of view, it became a securer basis for action than any arrangement which Salisbury had constructed with the Bedchamber, simply because Carr was more powerful there than any of Salisbury's agents had been. Northampton revelled in the comparison:

Were I so happy as . . . to meet with my lord of Rochester upon these hills [Greenwich] I should hold myself more happy than the little lord [Cecil] that was so desirous as he said at Bath to spend his whole life without separation from your Welsh Earl [Montgomery].[93]

But if circumstances forced Carr into a close working relationship with the Howards, his ties with the Southampton group remained if anything still closer. Within days of Cecil's death Southampton and his associate Lord Sheffield were meeting in Carr's chamber to discuss their admission to the Privy Council and Neville's appointment as Secretary. Until late 1612 this seems to have been Carr's (and Overbury's) favoured solution; then subsequently, when Neville's previous oppositionist record had clearly ruled him out of court, they transferred their backing to Southampton's other candidate, Ralph Winwood. But to begin with Winwood fared no better than Neville, for James had set his face firmly against the Southampton group.[94]

This division between king and favourite was an embarrassment; it was also leading to a disturbing erosion of Carr's standing. 'He has been so long', as Fenton noted, 'in settling himself to one of the parties that now he cannot do it without some peril to himself'. The solution was to cut Carr off from Southampton and then cement an alliance between Carr and the Howards. The obstacle to both was Overbury. So James arranged for his removal. In late April 1613 he was offered an embassy, which it was known he would refuse, and then imprisoned in the Tower for contempt. Five months later in September 1613 he was murdered. 'Deprived of [his] best instrument', Southampton spent the summer abroad; while the Howards pressed home their advantage by clearing the way for the marriage of Carr with Suffolk's daughter, Frances Howard. Overbury's

92. Peck, *Northampton*, especially pp. 84–89.
93. SP14/70/21 (Northampton to Rochester, 1 August 1612).
94. *Letters of Chamberlain* I, pp. 352 (27 May 1612), 358–9 (17 June 1612): despite James's forcefully expressed opposition, Carr and Overbury persisted for months with Neville as a candidate for Secretary.

murder was one step towards this; Frances's divorce from the earl of Essex (heir to the leadership of the Southampton group) the other. Both accomplished, the marriage was settled by December 1613.[95]

This fixed the Carr/Howard axis as the dominant power at court: instead of balance, as before, Carr, Northampton and Suffolk dominated Bedchamber, administration, the wider court and the day-to-day proceedings of the Council; while the Southampton group proper enjoyed little influence in the latter two, and virtually none in the former. The decision to call a parliament early in 1614 changed this. Parliament inevitably tilted the balance towards the Privy Council in arranging a programme; while by now its very summons was itself a major issue. In these circumstances the ordinary alignment of power at court was disrupted as a Scottish king, Bedchamber and favourite distanced themselves from the deliberations of the English Council on how to conduct an English parliament.

The result was a bewildering series of changes of front. First, Neville's 'undertaking' to manage parliament was floated again. This time its principal backers on the Council were the politically supple Pembroke and, of all people, Suffolk. He and his son-in-law Carr were only 'dissembling', however; more genuine was Carr's continued support for Neville and Winwood in the struggle for the Secretaryship, though once again Suffolk's backing for Neville was a finesse. On the other hand, Northampton was left out in the cold about the manoeuvrings of his family allies over the 'undertaking', and remained implacably opposed to it. He also ran his own candidates for the Secretaryship: first Sir Charles Cornwallis, then the 'insider' Sir Thomas Lake. The Secretaryship was settled just a week before parliament opened with the appointment of Winwood as a compromise candidate: at once close to Carr and Southampton, yet untainted by the now abandoned 'undertaking'. He succeeded, however, only to a rump of the office: Carr retained both the signet and the foreign correspondence, and Lake the procuring of the sign manual to bills. In fact, Winwood was mere assistant to Carr, 'as Secretary Herbert to Robert Cecil'.[96]

---

95. The fullest account is B. White, *A Cast of Ravens* (1965); see also Akrigg, *Jacobean Pageant*, Ch. XVI; HMC, *Mar and Kelly Supplement*, 52; Birch, *Court and Times of James I* I, p. 248 (24 June 1613, Lorkin to Puckering); A. L. Rowse, *Shakespeare's Southampton* (1965), p. 216.

96. T. L. Moir, *The Addled Parliament of 1614* (Oxford 1958), pp. 68–9; Peck, *Northampton*, pp. 207–8, 210. On Suffolk and Neville, Seddon, art. cit., pp. 62–3. On Cornwallis see Birch, *Court and Times of James I* I, p. 248, and on Lake see *Letters of Chamberlain* I, pp. 480, 481 (14 and 27 October 1613). For Winwood, see Seddon, art. cit., p. 64, and *Letters of Chamberlain* I, p. 554.

This was a weak foundation from which to present a programme to parliament. But worse than a 'Secondary' as government spokesman in the Commons were the divisions and cross-purposes within the 'government' itself. Looking back, Bacon attributed the failure of the parliament to the 'distraction [which] had entered into the king's house and Council and amongst his great men'. These distractions 'addled' the assembly almost before it began, but it was finally killed off by the same issue which had also brought the last parliament to an abrupt end: English resentment at James's exclusively Scottish Bedchamber. John Hoskins had joined in the earlier attack; this time he went much further: he insisted that King James's Scots should undergo the same fate as King Canute's Danes when that other foreigner became king of England, and be sent home; otherwise he invoked the threat of a Sicilian Vespers.[97]

The speech, there is little doubt, was a deliberate wrecking tactic, and was planted, most likely by Northampton, through his client Cornwallis. But the electrifying effectiveness of the plant depended on the real sensitivity and importance of the issue. As against the 'revisionist' position, Dr Hirst has already argued for the continuity of principled opposition to impositions from 1610 to 1614. The same, it is now clear, goes for the Scots Bedchamber. Indeed contemporaries paired the two issues and were uncertain which should have priority: when Sir Roger Wilbraham came to account for the Commons' refusal to grant subsidies in 1610, he put 'the facility for favourites to spend the king's treasure' before 'the impositions on merchandise, which [are] unlimited'; while in 1614 Cornwallis 'heard continually in London and out of the country what dissonant voices and distracted conceits were of grievances intended to be preferred as well concerning impositions, as the great number of Scots that are said to reside in this kingdom'.[98]

The parliament dissolved, politics became once more court politics. And here the tendency to monopoly, already marked by 1613, became fully apparent. Salisbury's spoils were still unsettled; while Northampton's offices of lord privy seal and lord warden of the Cinque Ports were also on the market following his death in June 1614. All were now bestowed on Suffolk and his son-in-law Carr:

97. Spedding, *Letters and life of Bacon* V, p. 182 (Advice on calling another Parliament, 1615); Moir, *Addled Parliament*, p. 138.
98. Peck's discussion of this (*Northampton*, pp. 205–10) fails to remove Northampton from the position of prime suspect as the instigator of the plant. D. Hirst, 'The Place of Principle', *Past and Present* 92 (1981), especially pp. 83, 86–7, 89; *idem*, 'Parliament, Law and War in the 1620s', *Historical Journal* 23 (1980), 457–8. 'Journal of Sir Roger Wilbraham', *Camden Soc. Misc.* X, p. 105; SP14/77/43.

Suffolk was appointed treasurer; while Carr took over the Lord Chamberlainship (vacated by Suffolk) as well as the keepership of the Privy Seal and the exercise of the lord wardenship. Since he was already a Gentleman of the Bedchamber and held the lion's share of the Secretaryship with the custody of the signet, the favourite had become Lord High Everything Else – as James himself was to observe in his comprehensive survey of Carr's regime:

Do not all court graces and place come through your office as Chamberlain, and rewards through your father-in-law's that is treasurer? Do not you two, as it were, hedge in all the court with a manner of necessity to depend upon you? And have you not besides your own infinite privacy with me, together with the main offices you possess [i.e. Secretary, lord privy seal, lord warden], your nephew [William Carr, appointed November 1614, a Groom] in my Bedchamber, besides another far more active than he in court practices [probably Henry Gibb, Groom, appointed July 1613] ? And have you not one of your newest kinsmen [Sir Robert Carr, later earl of Ancrum] who loves not to be idle in my son's Bedchamber?[99]

It is striking how highly Bedchamber appointments figure in the king's scale of priorities, as they certainly did in his favourite's. Since 1613, Carr had been emulating Dunbar in placing his dependents as Grooms of the Bedchamber; while over his fellow Gentlemen he exercised a *de facto* supremacy. Fenton, the Groom of the Stool, was ill and absentee, while even the royal duke, Lennox, was reduced to an unseemly scramble for precedence with the favourite.[100]

Such a concentration of public and private office was unprecedented, save perhaps for Cromwell in 1539–40. But whereas Cromwell had deployed his power to devastating effect, the Carr/Suffolk regime was characterized precisely by a lack of policy initiative. The intractability of parliament (as he saw it) had driven James to be a *fainéant* king; what better therefore than a nonentity as minister?

But politics – and particularly court politics – was not only about policy; it was also about place. And here Carr's monopoly aroused an opposition that was as vociferous as it was self-interested. The variety of motives was anatomized by Sir John Holles with *ex parte* disdain: Pembroke disappointed since at least 1612 of a promised major court office, Southampton since 1611 of a Councillorship, Lake of an office to lend weight to his access to the king and place

99. See above, p. 181, for Carr as Lord Chamberlain. Birch, *Court and Times of James I* I, p. 337 (21 July 1614) on the Privy Seal, and below, pp. 215–16; Akrigg, *Letters of King James VI and I*, p. 340.
100. *Letters of Chamberlain* I, pp. 609, 625–6 (Gibb); Birch, *Court and Times of James I* I, p. 257 (Carr of Ancrum). HMC, *Mar and Kelly Supplement*, 55, 56, 59, 60. Ibid., p. 53 on Lennox.

on the Council, Fenton of a suit to licence wool, Arundel of Northampton's legacy. To all of these frustrations there seemed one answer: the promotion of a new favourite.[101]

George Villiers was sworn a Cupbearer – a Privy Chamber position – in November 1614. His backers are traditionally supposed to have been Pembroke and Lake; Montgomery probably pressed home the suit, while Carr's resistance at least blocked Villiers's immediate appointment to the Bedchamber. That came, however, in April 1615. It was apparently the result of a carefully planned strategy, master-minded (according to his own account) by George Abbot, archbishop of Canterbury. Queen Anne was won over, and it was arranged that she should beg of the king first to knight the young man and then appoint him a Gentleman of the Bedchamber. The *dénouement* came in the queen's Bedchamber, with Villiers carefully positioned in an adjoining room. Etiquette, however, excluded both Villiers's backers and Carr himself as Lord Chamberlain. Instead, in accordance with the strict letter of the regulations, James was attended only by Fenton, Groom of the Stool.[102] Fenton, indeed, back in regular attendance after his absence the previous year, may well have been the key figure in the plot, whose outcome he forecast to his cousin: 'I think it may so fall out that ere it be long your lordship [will] hear that I shall accompany one a fellow servant in the Bedchamber more than now we have'.[103] Not only did Fenton command the technical instruments of access to the king and the right to swear in new members of the department, he also had both an unparalleled knowledge of James and a resolute determination to remain his man: that March, he had noted, Carr and Suffolk were displeased with him, but, he protested, they had no reason 'except that I will be subject to none but to his Majesty and only run his way'.[104]

To run the king's way in 1614 meant to run with Villiers. James

---

101. P. R. Seddon, ed., *The Letters of John Holles, 1587–1637*, Vol. I (Thoroton Society Record Series, XXXI) 1975, p. 74 (18 July 1615). On Pembroke's promise of office: SP14/71/6 (8 October 1612); *Letters of Chamberlain I*, p. 542 (30 June 1614); Birch, *Court and Times of James I* I, p. 336 (21 July 1614).

102. J. O. Halliwell, ed., *The Autobiography and Correpondence of Sir Simonds D'Ewes* (2 vols, 1845) I, p. 86 for Pembroke's role. For Lake, D. Lloyd, *The Statesmen and Favourites of England since the Reformation* (1665), pp. 552, 614. *Letters of Chamberlain* I. p. 559 (24 November 1614) for Carr's blocking of Villiers by placing his nephew in the Bedchamber. Rushworth, *Historical Collections* I, pp. 456–7 (Abbot's account).

103. HMC, *Mar and Kelly Supplement*, 59 (2 March 1615), 60 (19 April 1615). *OED* sub 'Accompany', I, 1.

104. Ibid., p. 59 (27 March 1615).

– there can be little doubt – was in love with the young man. But he had been similarly smitten before and was to be again with no such repercussions as in 1614–15. The difference was this time that James's head pulled in the same direction as his heart and suggested good reasons for Villiers's promotion: his connections with Pembroke and Southampton would counterbalance Somerset's now exclusive ties with the Howards; while having two favourites, an English and a Scottish, would be better than having just one. For it is clear from the first that Villiers was intended to be not merely a personal toy, but a favourite like Carr. He would be a royal patronage broker and a personal secretarial *aide*; entirely dependent on the king, he would be above the war of faction, which he would both balance and distance from the king. Court ceremony quickly made the message plain. Two knights of the Garter were created in May 1615: Fenton and Knollys. In the procession Knollys had a train of Howards; Fenton, one of Villiers's backers and their followers, who 'did him the honour to wear his feathers, which were black and white; as the other's were ash colour and yellow'. But Villiers himself was not among them; instead he watched the procession with the king from Somerset House: an observer, not a participant.[105]

On the other hand, of course, Villiers had been put forward by a faction and his rise was soon followed by Carr's fall. Information implicating Carr in Overbury's murder came to Secretary Winwood's hands in the summer of 1615; by October 1615 Carr was destroyed. There followed a distribution of his extraordinary concentration of offices. Lord Zouche, an associate of the anti-Carr coalition, was made lord warden of the Cinque Ports; while Pembroke, the coalition's weightiest member, became Lord Chamberlain. Winwood's share of the spoils was the substance, as well as the name, of the Secretary's office: in July, the French correspondence was transferred from Carr to Winwood, and in October the signet itself, which Carr had held since Salisbury's death, was put in his hands as well. With the signet, 'the badge of a principal Secretary', Winwood emerged as full-blown Secretary of State; in contrast, Lake, made Secretary in January 1616 for turning against his erstwhile Howard allies, cautiously insisted on the style 'Secretary to the king's Majesty'. The privy seal, similarly held by Carr since Northampton's death, was first given temporarily to John Murray, Groom of the Bedchamber and Keeper of the Privy Purse, and then bestowed formally on the earl of Worcester in January

105. *Letters of Chamberlain* I, pp. 597, 599 and Seddon, *Letters of Holles* I, p. 68.

1616. Worcester was practically a sinecurist, and many of the seal's surviving administrative functions were discharged by one of its clerks, John Packer, who was Villiers's secretary.[106]

Indeed, Worcester's appointment as Privy Seal was a mere *quid pro quo* for the earl's agreeing to surrender his existing office of Master of the Horse to the new favourite. James had long been dissatisfied with Worcester, whom he had inherited from the previous reign, and in 1612 had intended to appoint 'one who did continually attend upon his person', Carr. But as so often Carr proved unable to clinch the deal. Villiers, in sharp contrast, did. The result was a unique control of access: as favourite Villiers ruled the Privy Lodgings; as Master of the Horse he was in immediate attendance on the king wherever he went outside the palace: in his coach, in his barge, or in the hunt.[107]

Thus securely planted in both favour and office Villiers could translate his role of arbiter, already prefigured in the 1615 Garter procession, from pageant to reality. Quickly he moved to distance himself from his erstwhile backers. Late in 1616 there were problems between him and Montgomery; and already in August Fenton, who for more than a year had referred to Villiers as his 'son', reported that he had 'lost much affection of his particular friends and generally of all men'.[108] This cooling-off coincided with Villiers's (and James's) moderation of the attack on Carr and the Howards. The attack, orchestrated by Sir Edward Coke as chief justice, had broadened from the principals to their followers in the Bedchamber, Privy Chamber and the prince's household. Now the purge was halted and in June Coke – the Fouquier-Tinville of the affair – deprived of office.[109] More positive steps were also taken to preserve the balance:

106. Akrigg, *Jacobean Pageant*, Ch. XVI. *Letters of Chamberlain* I, p. 605 (13 July 1615), p. 611 (August); *CSP Dom.* IX (1611–18), 316, (*c.* 17 October 1615); Seddon, *Letters of Holles* I, p. 74; HMC, *Cowper* I, 91. SP14/83/13 (9 November 1615); SP14/84/26 (?12 December 1615); R. Lockyer, *Buckingham: The Life and Political Career of George Villiers, First Duke of Buckingham 1592–1628* (1981), pp. 25–6; Aylmer, *The King's Servants.* p. 15.
107. SP14/71/6 (8 October 1612); Nottingham UL, Portland MS PwV92 (1661 ordinances) articles 4, 14; Lockyer, *Buckingham*, pp. 25–6, concentrates on Villiers's achievements in horse-breeding.
108. *Letters of Chamberlain* II, p. 41 (7 December 1616): Hay incurred Villiers's displeasure for acting as Coke's intermediary: Birch, *Court and Times of James I* I, p. 447 (12 December 1616): HMC, *Mar and Kelly Supplement*, 65 (12 August 1616).
109. Between October 1615 and April 1616, at least twelve appointees and followers in the Bedchamber, Privy Chamber and prince's household were suspended, arrested and questioned. See Coke's treatment of John Lepton (SP14/86/31, 49: 2 and 8 February 1616). In the event, all but three survived the reign in office and Gibb, Stewart and Carr became Buckingham's clients.

the earl of Arundel, head of the house of Howard, though on bad terms with most of his relations, was made a privy councillor; while Sir John Digby, the chief negotiator for a Spanish match, was appointed Vice-chamberlain and deputy to Pembroke, the Lord Chamberlain and chief opponent of the Spanish connection.[110]

As this last extraordinary pairing suggests, the range of opinion and factional allegiance contained within the Council and outer court during these years was astonishingly wide. A king and favourite above faction were able to deal with all factions. And all factions were willing to deal with them because James's political style changed. In the early years his commitment and energy had broadcast his views to all and sundry. But time and disappointment had worn James down into negativism and listlessness. This meant that though his views – on finance, prerogative, foreign policy – remained as fixed, if not more fixed than ever, the fact could easily be overlooked. A man who wishes to do nothing can easily seem like a man who will do anything. So every shade of opinion thought, and bid accordingly for its place in the sun.[111]

But the balance achieved was dynamic rather than static. Before 1615 no political figure of importance had fallen since those implicated in the mysterious 'plots' of 1603–05, Raleigh and Northumberland. After 1615, however, snakes and ladders became a fact of official life. By 1619, Chamberlain remarked wryly that it was possible to hold a Council meeting in the Tower, since so many great officers had been sent there; while by 1624, he was able to list 'four lord treasurers living at once, four Lord Chamberlains, four Secretaries, three masters of the Wards, two keepers or chancellors', and so on. And at the centre, as the fulcrum round which the swirl of faction turned, was Villiers, created successively earl (1617), marquess (1618) and finally duke (1623) of Buckingham. Each fall of a politician from grace involved the attempt, by an individual or faction, to unseat Buckingham. Each attempt failed and left Buckingham stronger than before, until, by 1622, he had turned from the king's *alter ego* into the formulator (with Prince Charles) of distinctive policies of his own.[112]

110. K. Sharpe, 'The Earl of Arundel, His Circle and the Opposition to the Duke of Buckingham, 1618–28' in Sharpe, *Faction and Parliament*, pp. 211–12. Digby's appointment, promotion and personal gains puzzled the court; they came directly from the king. *Letters of Chamberlain* I, pp. 619–20 (6 April 1616). Stone, *Crisis of the Aristocracy*, p. 475: Digby (earl of Bristol) was one of the few outside James's Bedchamber to make Stone's top twenty-nine (above, note 65).
111. Cf. Russell 'Parliamentary History in Perspective', pp. 19–20; *idem, Parliaments and English Politics 1621–29*, (Oxford 1979) pp. 8–25.
112. *Letters of Chamberlain* II, pp. 274, 592 (20 November 1619, 18 December 1624).

In part Buckingham's invulnerability was due simply to the king's unshakeable trust in him. But Buckingham also moved to consolidate his own power base, by taking a uniquely firm hold over both the personnel of the Bedchamber and its bureaucratic machinery.

Buckingham has rarely figured in the pages of history as a bureaucrat. Yet the record shows him to have devoted a minute, painstaking, personal attention to the machinery of patronage that was unique amongst Jacobean politicians. Central to this machinery was the sign manual. The complex realities that underlay the Secretary's formal control of the royal signature in the earlier years of the reign have already been anatomized. Under Buckingham the gap between theory and practice if anything widened. Even with the formal reconstitution of the Secretary's office in Winwood's hands in 1615 the Bedchamber continued to procure a high proportion of warrants: about a quarter in October 1616 and 1617, and rising sharply to 40 and even 50 per cent from 1618 on. And Buckingham was most active of all. Once again 1618 is the axis year. Secretary Winwood died in 1617, while Secretary Lake was progressively deprived of the functions of office in the winter of 1618–19. Thereafter Buckingham, assisted from 1619 by his own secretary John Packer, was almost always more active in procuring the sign manual than either one or both of the new Secretaries, Naunton or Calvert. Particular circumstances could take things further and turn Buckingham's dominance into a near monopoly: in the last session of the parliament of 1621, Buckingham and Packer procured fifty-three warrants to Secretary Calvert's seven; and in the months before the Madrid journey of 1623, eighty-four to forty-eight. At times like these Buckingham was clearly the real Secretary. Only indeed with Conway's appointment as Secretary in 1623 was the favourite content to leave the Secretary's duties to the Secretary.[113]

In this there is a sharp contrast with Cecil, who, though Secretary, had left the procuring of bills to a deputy. The contrast

---

113. This analysis is based on figures derived from the records of king's Bills (and who procured the king's signature to them) S03/6, S03/7. The share of the Bedchamber (and the agent for Irish business, first a Privy Chamber Groom, then a dependent of Buckingham's; together with John Packer his secretary) in percentages of total warrants whose procurers are known, runs:

1614	19%	1619	44%
1615	17%	1620	43%
1616	27%	1621	45%
1617	23%	1622	48%
1618	42%	1623	31%
		1624	50%

highlights the different bases of their power. Cecil ruled as a councillor and great officer; Buckingham as a Bedchamber favourite and
patronage broker. And he could use his command of the machinery
of patronage to bring even officers as powerful as the attorney
general under his control. Henry Yelverton, for instance, got the
attorneyship independently of Buckingham's patronage in 1617, but
he was forced retrospectively to acknowledge his dependence by
giving his warrant of appointment to the favourite to get it signed.[114]

Buckingham was also active, though not as decisively, in the
private finances. Here the key figure remained John Murray, Groom
of the Bedchamber and Keeper of the Privy Purse from 1611 to 1625.
He continued to draw, as he had done since 1610 at least, most of
his income from cash windfalls that bypassed the Exchequer: in July
1614, for instance, he received £5,400 in admission fines for new
serjeants-at-law and five years later £6,000 'for the king's use' from
the City for the confirmation of London's charters. These recorded
payments are only the tip of the iceberg since, as his discharge states,
his 'particular disbursements are not convenient to be publicly made
known'. But alongside Murray figure other members of the
Bedchamber, in particular Hay, Master of the Great Wardrobe, and
Buckingham himself. They too received broad general discharges,
without formal submission of accounts, but only on 'private satisfaction . . . given to his Majesty'. In both cases the revenue from
peerage sales, which increased sharply after 1615, was probably the
prime source. Such sales certainly financed Hay's French and European embassies of 1616 and 1619; while most of the rest went to
Buckingham. Generally it is supposed that the money was used only
to line his own pocket; but what we now know of his private
finances makes it more likely that Buckingham was acting rather as
a private royal treasurer supplying the king's purposes (which of

---

For July to December 1622:

	Calvert	Buckingham and Packer
July	13	16
August	8	13
September	13	15
October	4	19
November	2	4
December	8	17

Conway, appointed January 1623, took over the lion's share. During March
1623–March 1624 (inclusive) Conway procured 149 warrants; Calvert 59; Buckingham (and Packer, who last procured in January 1624) 10.
114. Lockyer, *Buckingham*, pp. 40–1.

course included costly support of the favourite's state). Chamberlain indeed made the distinction explicitly, remarking that the traffic in peerages was 'less to be misliked if it [the cash] came to the king's Coffers'.[115]

Buckingham's control of much of the private administration was a formidable instrument of power, as his treatment of Yelverton shows. Equally important, however, was his iron grasp on the personnel of the Bedchamber. What Carr achieved late and partially was his swiftly and near absolutely. Numbers alone tell much of the story. In 1614 there were seven Gentlemen (six Scots, one English) and ten Grooms (all Scots); by 1625, in contrast, there were twelve Gentlemen (seven Scots, five English) and eleven Grooms (eight Scots, three English). The changes in the department's size and national balance were due largely to Buckingham's packing the department with relatives and dependents (beginning with his brother Christopher in March 1617 and his 'innermost friend', Edward Wray in July 1618) on the one hand, and his coming to terms with two of the remaining independent powers in the Bedchamber on the other. One of these was the new Scottish favourite, the marquess of Hamilton, appointed in March 1620 'without the privity . . . of the marquess of Buckingham'; the other was John Murray, who, as James's health failed in 1624, was to add the custody of the stamp of the sign manual to his Keepership of the Privy Purse, thus largely reconstituting the administrative side of the Henrician Groomship of the Stool. The favourite reached accommodation with these men in the Bedchamber settlement of 1622. Murray, still only a Groom, was made a Gentleman of the Bedchamber, along with Buckingham's brother Christopher and his brother-in-law Viscount Feilding. At the same time a three-way marriage alliance between Hamilton's and Murray's sons and Feilding's daughters sealed the bargain. Left out in the cold by this were the long-serving Scots in the Bedchamber, headed by Lennox, and his brother Aubigny (now earl of March), and Fenton, the Groom of the Stool and by now earl of Kelly. Kelly riposted first by moving closer to his fellow-countrymen and second by floating

---

115. I have counted only thirteen surviving warrants to supply the Privy Purse from the Exchequer, 1611–25: CSP Dom. IX–XI (1611–25); S03/6, S03/7. *Letters of Chamberlain* I, p. 548 (21 July 1614); S03/6, July 1619 – from City of London. *Foedera* XVIII, 733 (13 July 1626); Stone, *Crisis of the Aristocracy*, pp. 104–15, S03/6, December 1618 (Buckingham's discharge). S03/6 March 1619 (for Hay's 1616 Embassy); S03/7 April 1621 (£14,000 for the 1619 embassy); Lockyer, *Buckingham*, pp. 61–2, 120–1, 211–13. *Letters of Chamberlain* I, p. 601 (15 June 1615); APC XXXVI (1618–19), 277–8.

schemes to resign the Groomship. These schemes came to nothing, however, since the incumbent and the favourite could never agree on a candidate. Instead Kelly remained in office to the end of the reign as an occasionally effective thorn in Buckingham's side.[116]

Such pin-pricks aside, however, the 1622 settlement gave Buckingham a near-absolute control of the Bedchamber, as the appointment and dismissal within a few months of his kinsman Arthur Brett made clear.[117] The settlement was thus the culmination of Buckingham's whole previous approach to the department; it was also the foundation of his new commitment (in association with Prince Charles) to a forward foreign policy. Events abroad, in particular the fall of Heidelberg and the Lower Palatinate in September 1622, were making James's wait-and-see diplomacy increasingly implausible, but the king clung resolutely to his prejudices. So he had to be by-passed. The altered pace of marriage negotiations with Spain (which had spun out happily for years in the hands of Digby, wholly James's man) was achieved by sending a new agent to Madrid. This was Endymion Porter, at once a Groom of the Bedchamber to Charles and a confidential agent of Buckingham's, to whom, according to the Venetian ambassador, he served as 'gateway to all favours'. Porter was dispatched in late 1622; at the same time in September 1622 there is the first clear evidence that an *entrée* list was being used to limit attendance on the king. Kelly reported that the king had gone to visit Buckingham at his house of New Hall, 'only the prince with him and his Bedchamber, all others debarred, both court and Council, but those of the Bedchamber that were in the list'. A few months later, at Christmas 1622, the usual proclamation sending home the nobility and gentry to keep hospitality in their counties was enforced with unusual rigour, and Whitehall was so deserted that all the Gentleman Pensioners and Gentlemen of the

---

116. Above, notes 43, 44. *Letters of Chamberlain* II, pp. 52 (Christopher Villiers), 161 (5 May 1618, Wray), 297 (20 March 1620, Hamilton). For Murray, see above, note 37; *Letters of Chamberlain* II, pp. 441–2 (22 June 1622); LS13/168, fo. 239v (20 July 1622), allocation of carts to 3 new Gentlemen. Kelly's reaction: HMC, *Mar and Kelly Supplement*, 123–5 (4 July 1622), 125–7 (17 July 1622). M. Lee, *Government by Pen*, pp. 212–13 on Hamilton's strength in Scots politics after mid-1622. On Erskine's attempted resignation: HMC, *Mar and Kelly Supplement*, 124, 130, 148; more rumours in December 1623 (*Letters of Chamberlain* II, p. 535, referring to the Groomship, not the Captaincy of the Guard, relinquished by Erskine in 1617), with Anglesey or Sir Henry Rich as his replacement; and again in August 1624 (SP14/171/49), with Denbigh as replacement. Cf. Lockyer, *Buckingham*, p. 116 on these changes.

117. *Letters of Chamberlain* II, pp. 441–2, 571; SP14/170/2, 44I; Lockyer, *Buckingham*, pp. 121–2, 201–2.

Privy Chamber were ordered to attend. The Venetian ambassador regarded this as a strategy to make the court more manageable.[118]

In these manoeuvres prince and favourite were working as one. Buckingham from the beginning had cultivated the prince almost as carefully as the king: he had put his brother in Charles's Bedchamber as early as 1616; two years later their friendship was plain and from 1620 Buckingham used one of his agents in the prince's Bedchamber as patronage secretary to what by then may have been a joint operation.[119] Charles's public political role developed a little later. He sat in informally on Privy Council meetings in early 1621, but was not formally sworn a councillor until March 1622. Thereafter he took a leading, often indeed a dominant, part in the Council's discussions. But it is important to be clear about the nature of his authority. He was not setting himself up, like a Hanoverian Prince of Wales, as the reversionary interest in opposition to the court. Rather he exercised power through the court. He was the ally of one great power there, Buckingham; and he was himself the other. Always the Ordinances had provided for the access and attendance of royal princes in the Bedchamber, with rights of far greater intimacy than ordinary Gentlemen. And Charles exercised these rights to the full: in fact he became, with Buckingham, joint head of his father's Bedchamber.[120]

And this was crucial to the new policies pursued by prince and favourite. For it was in the Bedchamber that James, still for all his withdrawal the final arbiter of policy, took the decisions, which were then presented to the Council as *faits accomplis*. This situation, and the prince's role in it, is visible as early as 1619. Secretary Calvert

---

118. S. Adams, 'Spain or the Netherlands?' in Tomlinson, *Before the English Civil War*, especially p. 97. Lockyer, *Buckingham*, pp. 128–35. LC2/5 (Queen Anne's funeral, 1619: Porter as Groom of Charles's Privy Chamber; his appointment to the prince's Bedchamber probably occurred in 1621). *CSP Ven.* XVII (1621–23), 439. HMC, *Mar and Kelly Supplement*, 136 (25 September 1622: written just after the receipt of the news of the loss of Heidelberg). *Letters of Chamberlain* II, p. 468 (21 December 1622); *CSP Ven.* XVII (1621–23), 530 (23 December 1622).

119. Sir John Villiers, later Viscount Purbeck, appointed Gentleman of the Robes and Groom of the Bedchamber to Charles: *Letters of Chamberlain* II, pp. 32–3 (9 November 1616), Lockyer, *Buckingham*, p. 38; ibid., p. 34 for the onset of Charles and Buckingham's friendship. *Letters of Chamberlain II*, p. 279 (1 January 1620) asserts that Purbeck was acting as Buckingham's patronage secretary. For Porter's role in 1622, see above, note 118.

120. *APC* XXXVII (1619–21), 352–3; SP14/128/97I (26 March 1622): *Letters of Chamberlain* II, p. 457 (12 October 1622). Nottingham UL, Portland MS PwV92 (1661 Ordinances) article 17, and above p. 192).

informed Hay, who had departed on his major European embassy in an attempt to settle the Bohemian crisis, that the important letter he had left behind as lost had been located: 'the prince seeking for other papers this morning in his Majesty's Bedchamber found that very letter in one of the windows behind a cushion, which you thought you had put up in your pocket'. Also in the Bedchamber, Charles's resolution to go with Buckingham to Madrid in early 1623 was argued out with the king; and there the ensuing dispatches were read by James alone. When, therefore, it transpired that the whole correspondence had been seen by the Spanish ambassador in London, Charles could only lament to his father 'that you are betrayed in your Bedchamber'.[121]

And the risk of such 'betrayal' only grew for Charles and Buckingham after the Spanish fiasco. They turned to open breach with Spain and they pursued this aim by giving parliament its head to ride roughshod over the king's doubts. Both the policy and the methods used crossed James's deepest instincts; they also alienated the two surviving great powers of the Bedchamber who had been excluded from Buckingham's settlement of 1622: Lennox and Kelly. They disapproved of the thrust of the new policies as such; and they were further encouraged in their opposition by their awareness of James's own distaste. Buckingham countered by tightening his hold on king and prince, but that only soured relations still further. In January 1624 it was remarked that Lennox and Buckingham were at odds, and that most of the 'great ones' were backing Lennox, because 'it seems the duke of Buckingham engrosses the prince's favour so far as to exclude all other both from the father and the son . . . he [Buckingham] stirs not from the king, but keeps close about him, to cut off all access'. It was thus a great stroke of luck for Buckingham that Lennox died on the day that the 1624 Parliament was to be opened. Even so, Kelly acting alone was able to provoke a real crisis in Buckingham's favour in mid-1624. Exploiting his right as Groom of the Stool to appoint audiences and to admit ambassadors to the Bedchamber, he arranged a series of meetings between James and the Spanish ambassadors in April. The ambassadors accused Buckingham to the king of 'affecting popularity,' and of planning forcibly to retire James to a country house in order to allow the prince to govern. These charges were credible enough to persuade

---

121. BL, Egerton MS 2592, fo. 39 (Calvert to Hay, 4 May 1619). See Clarendon's description of the arguments about the Spanish trip in Clarendon, *History of the Rebellion* I, pp. 13–14, 21. Halliwell *Letters of the kings of England* I, pp. 184, 190, 226.

James to order an interrogation of all the councillors on oath. Only Buckingham's illness during May seems to have saved him in James's eyes – by late May the king was refusing to admit the Spanish ambassador again for fear of killing Buckingham with grief. The prince's continued support was also crucial in dissuading Buckingham's opponents from exploiting the opportunity to push the attack home.[122]

But the crisis surmounted, Buckingham and Charles were unstoppable. One victim of their power was Lionel Cranfield, broken in the 1624 parliament for his opposition to the breach with Spain (as well as his attempts as lord treasurer to control expenditure). James had clearly parted reluctantly with his servant; while the old Scots in the Bedchamber, Kelly and Haddington (now earl of Holderness), had offered Cranfield consistent support – getting, for example, Cranfield's petition for mitigation into James's (apparently willing) hands by taking 'advantage of the prince and Buckingham turning about'. But to no real avail. To rehabilitate Cranfield would have meant an impossible break with both his heir and his favourite.[123]

Another casualty was the Privy Council. With the treaties broken, military preparations on foot, and negotiations for a French marriage and alliance in train, Buckingham and Charles could afford once more to reduce the scope of their consultations. By December 1624, indeed, the Privy Council was so far excluded from matters of foreign policy that it had to ask the reason for the bonfires burning all over London. The fires had been lit to celebrate the successful outcome of the negotiations for a French marriage. At the formal ceremony, only the king, prince, Buckingham and Secretary Conway were present, and it was of them, together with the actual negotiators of the marriage, Hay and Henry Rich, viscount Kensington, that Abbot was thinking when he remarked, allegedly, that there were now two Councils in England of which 'that of Newmarket was the higher'.[124]

122. Russell, *Parliaments and English Politics*, Ch. III; R. E. Ruigh *The Parliament of 1624* (Cambridge, Mass. 1971), especially Ch. I. *Letters of Chamberlain* II, p. 542 (31 January 1624): he died 16 February. Nottingham UL, Portland MS PwV92 (1661 Ordinances), article 10. Lockyer, *Buckingham*, pp. 192–5.
123. Ruigh, *Parliament of 1624*, Ch. VI. For Cranfield's attempts at expenditure control as lord treasurer 1621–24 see J. F. Larkin and P. L. Hughes, eds, *Stuart Royal Proclamations* (2 vols, Oxford 1973) I pp. 524–5; *CSP Dom.* X (1619–23), 453, 458 (7, 13 October 1622); Prestwich, *Cranfield*, pp. 359–64, 464 n. 1. HMC *Fourth Report*, 288 (11 May 1624, Kelly to Middlesex; 10 January 1625, Nicholas Herman to Middlesex). *Letters of Chamberlain* II, p. 562, 5 June 1624.
124. Lockyer, *Buckingham*, pp. 209, 216: cf. Adams, art. cit., p. 97.

But the real victim was James himself. Towards the end his attitude to the favourite was one of resignation, and by October 1624 Chamberlain was unsure how welcome Buckingham and the prince were in visiting the king at Royston.[125] The Bedchamber, which had begun as the instrument by which James both protected and proclaimed his independence, had become his prison.

---

125. *Letters of Chamberlain* II, p. 584 (23 October 1624): Cf. Clarendon, *History of the Rebellion* I, p. 13.

CHAPTER SEVEN
The image of virtue: the court and household of Charles I, 1625–1642

Kevin Sharpe

The government of seventeenth-century England was personal monarchy. The king was the centre of patronage and power. A change in the person (and personality) of the king fundamentally affected the course of politics. The continuity of institutions and offices, even of personnel, should not lead us to underestimate the power of the king's person. In the seventeenth century the succession of a new monarch was still the fundamental change in the political climate – the event which decided who would grow in the sun of royal favour and who would wither in the cold of obscurity.

At first sight the succession of King Charles in 1625 brought no major change. It was a peaceful and undisputed succession – the first succession of an adult male who was direct heir to the throne since the succession of Henry VIII in 1509.[1] The new king too was already a familiar figure in the world of affairs. Since 1623 he had played a major role in domestic and foreign policy in alliance with his father's favourite, George Villiers, duke of Buckingham.[2] Buckingham's own career adds to the impression of continuity. For Buckingham managed with great political agility the feat rarely performed by favourites: surviving the death of one sovereign to entrench himself more firmly in the affections (though not the embraces) of another. Charles I succeeded too to the throne of a kingdom at war since 1625 – a war which, spanning the two reigns, tempts some historians to underplay the importance of the succession.

To those at court, however, things quite rapidly looked different.

---

1. For a suggestion concerning the importance of this, see K. Sharpe, 'Personal Monarchy' in Lesley Smith, ed., *The Making of Britain: the Age of Expansion* (1986).
2. R. Ruigh, *The Parliament of 1624* (Cambridge, Mass. 1971).

Charles I was in many respects a complete contrast to his father: where James was informal to the point of familiarity, at times unkempt and (by English standards) undignified, a lover of debate and wit even descending to vulgarity and irreverence, Charles I was stiff, proud and prudish.[3] His manner and morals owed little to the bawdy camaraderie of the Scottish court in which James I had learned his kingcraft. It was the grave ceremonial of Spanish court etiquette which appealed to Charles's disposition.[4] As with any other head of a household, Charles I's manners and morals were soon reflected in his domestic arrangements, that is to say in the organization of the court. But the king's domestic world was also the world of politics. At a time when access and proximity to the king's person were the goals of political ambition, and access was determined by the arrangement of the royal household, a change of personal style could re-arrange the patterns of court politics.

The king's person was not the only force for change in 1625. Charles I came to the throne betrothed to a princess who was Catholic and French. Since the death of Queen Anne of Denmark in 1619, the politics of influence had been played in two courts: that of James I and (certainly from 1621) that of Prince Charles himself. From 1625 there were also two courts, but the game was to be very different. For now the second court was that of a youthful queen who was (by treaty) to be attended by French, by Catholics and, of course, by women. For those outside the area of the king's entourage and favour the politics of reversionary interest fostered by an ageing king and an adult, politically active prince gave way to the politics of influence upon a young and hence impressionable foreign queen.

Though the personality and domestic circumstances of Charles I brought immediate changes, the succession did not see a complete turnover of personnel. For a time this was in doubt. Almost on the day of James I's death, the Venetian ambassador reported debate among courtiers concerning 'whether the household of the dead king or that of the prince shall be the household of the present king'.[5] It was after all a real problem, one which had not arisen for over a century. Charles had his own servants to reward. But he had to

---

3. J. Wormald, 'James VI and I: two kings or one?' *History* 68 (1983), 187–209. There is no really satisfactory biography of Charles I. See R. Ollard, *The Image of the King* (1979); P. Gregg, *Charles I* (1981); C. Carlton, *Charles I: the personal monarch* (1983).

4. For an example that Charles experienced, see the account of the ceremony to mark the departure of the prince of Wales from the Spanish court, BL, Additional MS 30,629.

5. Pesaro to Doge and Senate, 25 April 1625, *CSP Ven.* XIX (1625–26), 21.

satisfy the officers of his father's household (whose tenure terminated with James I's death) who now petitioned for confirmation of their places – among them many Scots.[6] It seems that the eventual settlement was a compromise: Charles settled his own household 'for the most part with his then own servants', but retained James I's officers, either in their posts or as supernumeraries, until their death. This compromise inevitably resulted, for a time, in superfluity of officials, additional expense and some odd arrangements like that by which two Master Cooks (the one to James, the other to Prince Charles) shared the post and the diet assigned to the place at court.[7] It meant too that only gradually, with death or retirement, did the officers of the royal household reflect Charles's personal choice.

Change in the style of the court was more immediately effected. The Venetian ambassador reported a new regime within days of Charles I's succession:

The king observes a rule of great decorum. The nobles do not enter his apartments in confusion as heretofore, but each rank has its appointed place and he has declared that he desires the rules and maxims of the late Queen Elizabeth . . . The king has also drawn up rules for himself, dividing the day from his very early rising, for prayers, exercises, audiences, business, eating and sleeping. It is said that he will set apart a day for public audience and he does not wish anyone to be introduced to him unless sent for.[8]

These preferences and rules enacting them spread rapidly throughout the court. Sir John Finet, Master of Ceremonies, discovered that on escorting an ambassador from the Council Chamber to the king, he was halted at the door of the Privy Chamber by a Gentleman Usher, 'all further passages being begun then to be debarred to all but Privy Councillors and Bedchamber men'.[9] A servant of the Spanish envoy was ordered to leave the Privy Gallery.[10] When he set off on his first

---

6. Petition of George Kirke, *CSP Dom.* I (1625–26), 16; 'His Majesty does not wish to exclude his father's old servants or abandon his own'. (*CSP Ven.* XIX (1625–26), 21) and cf. reports of the English ambassador, 2 May: 'The king is trying to keep the Scots satisfied and has confirmed many in their charges, almost in greater numbers than the English' (ibid., pp. 26–7).

7. Petition of Thomas Smith, 31 July 1633, *CSP Dom.* VI (1633–34), 157. LS13/30 contains an order that 'Supernumerary officers and servants of Household to our late royal father King James are to be our servants and to have these allowances ensuing during their lives and then to cease'. Compare the list with LC2/6, a list of officers of the household of James I; Order for payment to some Grooms of the Bedchamber to James I, now supernumeraries, *CSP Dom.* I (1625), 564; *Foedera* XVIII, 225.

8. *CSP Ven.* XIX (1625–26), 21.

9. LC5/1, fo. 94; *Finetti Philoxenis: Some Choice Observations of Sir John Finett Knight and Master of Ceremonies to the two last Kings* (1656), 145.

10. LC5/1, fo. 94v.

summer progress to meet his queen at Dover, Charles issued a proclamation for the better order of his household, forbidding 'unnecessary pestering' of the court, or the resort thither of those not listed as required for the king's service.[11] While the commissioners appointed for the regulation of the household discussed,[12] the tone of the new court was already set: a tone of order, formality and decorum. We must now turn to describe the organization of and orders for the Caroline household and court and then to the political consequences of the changes in domestic arrangements.

Orders and organization

The king's principal residence was the sprawling Tudor palace of Whitehall – a building of perhaps two thousand or more rooms, with additional closets, garrets and kitchens.[13] The palace was divided into two geographically separate as well as administratively distinct sections – the king's and queen's sides – because, given the distance of the queen's palace at Greenwich, Whitehall served as the London home for both monarchs. On both sides were lodgings for the household servants of the king and queen. The number of rooms assigned to each office reflected the duties and status of the place held. We know, for example, that in Charles II's reign the Lord Chamberlain occupied forty rooms, the Controller nineteen and the Master of the Horse twenty.[14] Since these last were described as 'once the duke's' and since the duke of Buckingham had been Master of the Horse, we may assume that the distribution of suites had not changed very much.[15]

Certainly little had changed in the structure of the building since the reign of Henry VIII. Even the furnishings and fabrics of the state rooms dated back to the early Tudors. As soon as he succeeded to the throne, Charles formulated plans to rebuild the palace with expedition. As early as February 1626, the month of the king's coronation, John Burgh, writing from court, expected that Whitehall

11. *Foedera* XVIII, 78–80.
12. Pesaro to Doge and Senate, 2 May 1625, *CSP Ven.* XIX (1625–26), 26–7.
13. I take my calculation from 'A Survey or Ground Plot of His Majesty's Palace of Whitehall' (BL, Lansdowne MS 736). This manscript is believed to be *temp*. Charles II, but references to lodgings held by courtiers of Charles I confirm the impression that little of the fabric had been changed in the interim.
14. BL, Lansdowne MS 736, fo. 5v.
15. Ibid., fo. 5.

would be rebuilt 'with much beauty and state and that suddenly'.[16] Through lack of money Whitehall was not rebuilt. Few physical changes were effected. As late as 1639, Abraham Van der Dort, the keeper of the king's pictures, referred (somewhat derogatorily) to the 'old fashioned rusty iron tongs' and old furniture of the royal Chair Room.[17] Charles I then came to Whitehall like a vigorous new manager to an unwieldy, chaotic and decaying hotel. Perfect order and beauty demanded reconstruction along more rational, classical ordered lines (such as those proposed by Inigo Jones).[18] But if reconstruction remained a dream, then the best possible order must be established within the limitations of the old fabric. The palace of Whitehall, like our unwieldy hotel, contained large state rooms and intimate corners, (below, p. 245) grand halls and stairways and little known back passages and entrances. It housed a permanent staff of many hundreds, all vying for promotion and favour, for legitimate perquisite and illicit backhander. It also lodged a fluctuating horde of visitors, on public and private business, with *their* households and servants. It was this anarchy of rooms and persons which Charles early determined to organize, and which he fashioned gradually into what Sir Philip Warwick boasted was 'the most regular and splendid court in Christendom'.[19] The means by which he did so were orders for regulation and reform and measures of retrenchment.

Before we describe the various orders for the government of the several branches of the household, we shall need to pause to consider the evidence from which our picture will be drawn. Few of the books of orders which were issued have survived and none of those that I have used is authentically dated precisely. British Library Stowe MS 561, a collection of orders for the king's, queen's and royal family's households is listed as 'temp. Charles I' with no

16. John Burgh to Viscount Scudamore, 24 February 1625/6, C115/N4/8606: Chancery Masters Exhibits, duchess of Norfolk deeds. Scholars have not appreciated the richness of this cache of newsletters for early seventeenth-century history. I am preparing a short report on the papers.

17. BL, Additional MS 10,112, fo. 17: 'An Index or Catalogue of all such implements and other things in the . . . Chair Room'. 'This Catalogue was drawn up by Van der Dort himself' (ibid., fo. 1).

18. E. Shepphard, *The Old Royal Palace of Whitehall* (1902) prints an engraving of Charles I's projected palace. On the projected palace, see J. Harris, S. Orgel and R. Strong, *The King's Arcadia: Inigo Jones and the Stuart Court* (1973), p. 147. They suggest (p. 170) that we may discern an expression of Jones's vision of a new classical palace in the masque *Albion's Triumph*. See S. Orgel and R. Strong, eds, *Inigo Jones: The Theatre of the Stuart Court* (2 vols, Berkeley and London 1973) II, pp. 454–78.

19. Sir Philip Warwick, *Memoirs of the Reign of King Charles I* (1701), p. 113.

further information.[20] The fullest account is provided by a parchment book of household regulations in the Lord Chamberlain's department at the Public Record Office (LC5/180). This is signed, in the king's hand, 'Charles I' but the date inscribed at the top, '1630' is in a later hand.[21] There are, however, reasons for believing that it is correct. For in March 1629 a memorial concerning attendance on the king and queen, found among the papers of Secretary Sir John Coke, established principles which underlay the orders in LC5/180.[22] Moreover excerpts from the orders relating to behaviour in the Privy Chamber and royal Chapel, dated 1631, are among the manuscripts of the earl of Bridgewater and in the State Papers Domestic.[23] These all, then, suggest a date between 1629 and 1631, as do other references to the settling of the king's household in the sixth year of his reign.[24] The parchment book may be used with confidence.

No book of orders has survived for the Caroline Bedchamber. We do, however, have a book of orders issued in 1689 for the Bedchamber of William III which announces that the orders are 'in the same form as they were established in the reigns of our royal uncle and grandfather of ever blessed memory'.[25] There is no reason to doubt the statement: William III's orders may well have been a direct repetition of Caroline ordinances.[26] But as disputes during Charles II's reign clearly illustrate, such orders were open to controversy and interpretation in practice.[27] Most obviously the distribution of authority and relationships between the Lord Chamberlain and the Groom of the Stool (Chief Gentleman of the Bedchamber) depended upon the personalities and status of those who held the posts. And for all his theoretically independent sphere of jurisdiction,

20. 'Orders for the king's family Temp. Car I', BL, Stowe MS 561. Fo. 18 is headed 'Orders signed by the King's and Queen's Majesty, Nov. 1631'.
21. 'Household Regulations 1630', LC5/180. The MS also contains marginal notes by Charles I (e.g. p. 18).
22. HMC, *Cowper MSS* I, 382.
23. Huntington Library, San Marino California, Hastings MS Miscellaneous Box I, 'Orders for correct Behaviour on entering the Royal Chapel and Privy Chamber'; *CSP Dom*. IV (1629–31), 478: Orders dated 9 January 1631.
24. LS13/169, p. 299.
25. 'A book Containing His Majesty's Orders for the Government of the Bedchamber and the Private Lodgings. . .', BL, Stowe MS 563, dated 1689, and see above p. 186 note 34. Quotation from fo. 2.
26. 'It appears they have ever been most exact and particular in their care. . .', ibid., fo. 2.
27. An account of 'Points in dispute between the Ld. Chamberlain and the Groom of the Stool May 1683', and 'The Lords' opinion in the difference . . . 15 June 1683', manuscript lately in the private possession of Hugh Murray Baillie. I am grateful to David Starkey for copies of this MS.

Sir James Fullerton, Groom of the Stool to Charles I, could not have claimed equality with William, earl of Pembroke, who as Lord Chamberlain and a courtier of massive political weight probably effectively governed the Bedchamber for all that it lay beyond his technical jurisdiction.[28] Our evidence then may be used, but it must be used with caution. And, as we sketch the orders for the government of the royal household, the Hall, the Presence, the Privy Chamber and the Bedchamber, we should never forget that there may have been other such interpretations and adjustments in practice.

The parchment book of orders signed by the king himself, like the Eltham Ordinances on which it is modelled, contains regulations concerning the government of the court from the outer precincts to the Privy Chamber.[29] The Knight Marshal and Porters at the Gate were ordered to scrutinize carefully those entering the precincts of the court and none was to enter but those enrolled upon a list kept at the Gate. The porters were to have 'special regard that no ragged boys nor unseemly persons be suffered to make a stay in any of the courts'. Royal servants were reminded, in language that was to become typical of Charles I's style, that their own domestics should be 'comely and seemly persons, well apparelled' and mannered. If any was 'noised to be a profane person or outrageous rioter or ribald, a notorious drunkard, swearer, railer or quarreller', he was to be ousted from his place and banished the court. A renewed emphasis upon decorum and order was the hallmark of the Caroline ordinances. On Sundays and offering days, it was decreed, the Lord Chamberlain was to dine in the Great Chamber and all with tables at court were to attend. The Gentlemen Ushers who waited at meals were ordered to remain after dinner 'for some reasonable time that so strangers and men of quality that shall have occasion to resort to our court may not find it empty'. When the king dined in the Presence, only peers, bishops and privy councillors were permitted to tread on the carpet surrounding his table. The Gentlemen Ushers

---

28. This was certainly the claim of the Lord Chamberlain in 1683. The suggestion that in Charles I's reign Pembroke governed the Bedchamber (which was technically beyond his jurisdiction) is supported by the Wilton Van Dyck of the earl which shows him, as was claimed in 1683, wearing the triple keys to the bedchamber, (Christopher Brown, *Van Dyck* (Oxford 1982), p. 201; below, pp. 244, 253). I am grateful to David Starkey for advice on this problem and for the observation that the Pembroke portrait shows the keys on a blue ribbon knotted to his belt beneath the sash. Of course the authority of the Groom of the Stole may well have revived when the earl of Holland held the place.

29. LC5/180, *passim*.

were ordered to see that none pressed too close to the king in his presence, or to the cloth of state in his absence. And they were themselves reminded to keep the reverence and distance which it was the duty of their office to safeguard.

At the time of the Eltham Ordinances of Henry VIII's reign, the Presence Chamber had marked the formal divide between the king's public rooms and the Privy Lodgings. Throughout the sixteenth century it had been a door which had separated two distinct worlds – in reality as well as in name. But by 1625, the Privy Chamber had declined in importance and altered in function with the creation of the Bedchamber by James I.[30] Charles I's orders for the regulation of the household themselves acknowledge the change and the somewhat redundant nature of the Privy Chamber now that its staff no longer performed body service for the king: 'for our Privy Chamber though we find it much changed from the ancient institution both in the number of gentlemen and their service, nevertheless we are pleased to continue a fit number'.[31] Charles seems to have wished to re-assert the geographical (and psychological and political) significance of the Privy Chamber as the first step inside the Privy Lodgings. The Privy Chamber was closed to all but noblemen, councillors and those sworn of it. None was to enter booted or spurred.[32] Most interestingly, in houses where there was only one chamber which served as a Presence Chamber and Privy Chamber, the king insisted upon the maintenance of a distinction: 'the said chamber shall be avoided and become the Privy Chamber after warning given to cover the table there for our meals and also at other times when our pleasure shall be to have the same private'.[33] And for all that the Gentlemen of the Privy Chamber no longer lived in intimacy with the king by reason of their duties, Charles I, the Venetian envoy reported, 'every morning shows himself in the Privy Chamber in the presence of all the lords and officials of that apartment. He detains some in conversation and salutes the others and leaves them all happy and devoted'.[34] Other evidence suggests that whilst they had declined from their earlier importance, Gentlemen

30. See Neil Cuddy's account, above, pp. 183 ff.
31. LC5/180, p. 21. A copy of these orders in the hand of Sir John Coke is to be found in the State Papers, with the duties of the Privy Chamber clearly specified, see N. Carlisle, *An Enquiry into the Place and Quality of the Gentlemen of his Majesty's Most Honourable Privy Chamber* (1829), pp. 109–16; *CSP Dom.* XII (1637–38), 216.
32. LC5/180, pp. 22–3.
33. Ibid., p. 24.
34. *CSP Ven.* XIX (1625–26), 26–7.

of the Privy Chamber enjoyed access to the king and the favours which stemmed from it (below, pp. 249ff.)

The Privy Chamber, however, was no longer the innermost sanctum. Gentlemen of the Privy Chamber were barred admission to the Privy Lodgings beyond, and even peers and bishops who were permitted to enter the outer Withdrawing Room (next to the Privy Chamber) were denied further passage.[35] Here too the parchment book of orders for the regulation of the household concludes – with injunctions that they be read twice yearly and be distributed to the various offices at court.[36] Significantly the book prescribes no rules for the government of the Bedchamber. In this, the nature of the archive reflects the new situation. The orders we have examined are concerned with household departments within the jurisdiction of the Lord Chamberlain. The Privy Chamber, once a separate common-wealth ruled by an independent head, has now fallen beneath his sway. Outside the Lord Chamberlain's authority, however, lies the Bedchamber, now performing the personal body service once the duty of the Privy Chamber; and here now we find an independent governor of familiar name – the Groom of the Stool.

It is during James I's reign that the Groom of the Stool emerges as First Gentleman of the (new) Bedchamber, with sole responsibility for admitting and supervising the officers of that chamber – 'excepting only at public ceremonies' when they observed the dictates of the Lord Chamberlain 'as the other noblemen usually do'.[37] Through all the changes consequent upon minor and female rule, the Groom of the Stool re-emerges in his former place of intimacy. In the reign of Charles I the orders suggest that he helps to dress the king in the mornings; he rides (along with the Master of the Horse) in the king's coach; he attends as cupbearer when the king dines in the Bedchamber or privately with the queen, and he performs, in general, 'all other offices and services of honour about our person'.[38] These evidently included the functions from which the officer derived his name, for it was specifically ordered that 'none of our Bedchamber whatsoever are to follow us into our secret or privy room when we go to ease ourself, but only our Groom of the Stool'.[39] As the symbol of his office, he wore 'a gold key in a blue ribbon'. This was a treble key to the Bedchamber which also

35. LC5/180, p. 22.
36. Ibid., pp. 29–30.
37. Cf. Cuddy, above, pp. 186ff., 214; BL Stowe MS 563, fos. 3–3v.
38. Ibid., fo. 5v.
39. Ibid., fos. 14v–15.

opened 'every door of all our gardens, galleries and privy lodgings', and all the rooms in the various royal palaces.[40] Under his surveillance, Gentlemen of the Bedchamber waited on the king and slept by turns, either in the same room or in the Withdrawing Room, on a pallet (or put-you-up bed). Six grooms of the Bedchamber, waiting by rota, saw that linen and other necessaries were provided; Pages, waiting beyond the doors, were brought in to make fires and beds. Leave to enter the Bedchamber could be granted only by the Groom of the Stool. His physical proximity to the king's person was not only implicit in his duties; it was recognized in his perquisites. For by virtue of his service, the Groom of the Stool enjoyed the rights of the leftovers after the king's repast – doubtless substantial 'scraps' from a diet of twenty-eight dishes.[41] He had also the right to the spoils of the king's goods, furniture and utensils on the death of the monarch.[42] It is clear that in moving from the now more ceremonial Privy Chamber into the Bedchamber, the Groom of the Stool had retained his personal services and proximity to the king.

When we step back and survey the ordinances, it would appear that the household of Charles I differed little from that of his immediate predecessors. There was nothing very novel about the orders promulgated. The parchment book of orders dated 1630 at most points echoes the Eltham Ordinances and the practices of Henry VIII. Throughout the 1630s, the various commissions appointed to investigate the household grounded their recommendations on Tudor precedents.[43] As the Reverend Garrard informed Wentworth in 1638, 'They look back to Henry the Seventh, Henry the Eighth and Queen Elizabeth's time'.[44] But we should not assume that what was grounded in precedent effected no alteration. Indeed by their very harking back to the days of Henry VIII, by the conscious renovation of rules and customs lost during the intervening years of a minor, two women and a Scot, the orders indicated a shift in the style, behaviour and character of the court. After

---

40. Ibid., fos. 7v–8; but cf. note 28 above.
41. Ibid., fos. 6v–7. 'A Declaration of the particular fare of the king's Majesty on a flesh day', LS13/30, shows the king's diet to be 28 dishes at dinner.
42. BL, Stowe MS 563, fo. 18.
43. E.g. BL, Stowe MS 561; BL, Harley MS 7623, fo. 16, an order to Newcastle to enquire into the number of servants allowed in the prince's household, 'having regard therein to such ancient records as shall specify the same'. The Lords Commissioners for the Household in 1637 took the Eltham Ordinances as the yardstick by which to determine the diet of the Groom of the Stool (PC2/44, fo. 244, 15 March 1637).
44. Rev. Garrard to Sir Thomas Wentworth, 16 December 1637, W. Knowler, ed., *The Earl of Strafford's Letters and Dispatches* (2 vols, 1739) II, p. 140.

the bawdy decadence of James I's reign, Charles sought to establish a well-regulated court as a shrine of virtue and decorum. Perusing the orders, we are struck by the repeated emphases on the moral *gravitas* expected of courtiers and the solemnity and ceremonial of court life. Any servant found 'so vicious and unmannerly that he be unfit to live in virtuous and civil company' was to be banished; passage to the king was not to be permitted via backstairs or privy galleries: rather 'all accesses generally shall be made through the rooms of state that thereby the honour of our court may be upheld'.[45] Elaborate rules prescribed a hierarchy of status 'limiting persons to places suitable to their qualities':[46] seats in the royal Chapel, places in the royal barge were reserved for those listed as entitled to them. None, Clarendon tells us, presumed to be seen 'in a place where he had no pretence to be'.[47]

Renewed emphasis on rules and forms was not the only change. The succession of the new monarch was also marked by a campaign of reform and retrenchment. Charles, we must not forget, inherited a war and a near impossible financial problem.[48] In the first year of his reign the Exchequer virtually stopped the payment of wages to household officers. By 1628 they in their turn were threatening to suspend the performance of their duties.[49] To add to the burden, the newly formed household was very large: as we have seen Charles retained many of his father's servants (probably hundreds) as supernumeraries; he had also to provide for a queen, both in addition to the thousand or more who constituted the regular household.[50] As well as superfluous officers, there were the endemic diseases of corruption and waste.

Early attempts were made to check these cancers. The records were studied and the number of places in each department was specified; none was to be admitted into any vacancy until the household was reduced.[51] Courtiers reported in 1629 that the horde of attend-

45. LC5/180.
46. Sir Philip Warwick, *Memoirs*, p. 67.
47. E. Hyde, earl of Clarendon, *The History of the Rebellion*, ed. W. D. Macray (6 vols, Oxford 1888) IV, p. 490.
48. The preamble to the Eltham Ordinances makes it clear that war was the impetus behind them, but cf. above, p. 105.
49. See, for example, APC XL (1625–26), 14, 221, 441; cf. ibid., 37–8; F. C. Dietz, *English Public Finance, 1554–1641* (1932), pp. 223, 228; APC XLIII (1627–28), 501.
50. G. Huxley, *Endymion Porter: The Life of a Courtier* (1959), p. 126.
51. LS13/30, though the order adds 'except upon special occasion His Majesty shall think fit to increase the same'.

ants was to be pared to the parsimonious level of Elizabeth's reign.[52] Courtiers and royal officials were forbidden to retain an excessive number of servants – presumably because these, along with their masters, fed at the king's expense.[53] Economies were ordered in all departments, in matters large and small: the Groom of the Stool was advised to purchase at the cheapest price rather than to take provisions automatically from the Great Wardrobe;[54] the number of carts assigned to each department on progresses was regulated and listed;[55] utensils of pewter, iron and wood were to be repaired rather than discarded;[56] and, amusingly, dogs were banned from household servants' chambers because they consumed food which might otherwise have gone to the poor.[57] On 5 May 1627, the Lord Chamberlain revived the ancient order of eating meat on trenchers made of bread in order to eliminate waste and provide scraps for the poor.[58] After 1634, the household expenses of visiting ambassadors were no longer defrayed beyond their first audience.[59]

Corruption was perhaps the biggest problem, not least because those responsible for its eradication were often those most guilty of peculation. Here in his own household Charles I adopted the methods which he was to apply to the government of the realm: the elaboration of detailed rules, the demands for regular reports, and the repeated hectoring enquiry, all of which reduced the scope and perhaps blunted the nerve for fraud.[60] The Clerk Controller was held personally responsible for seeing that provisions ordered were both received and serviceable.[61] Meat delivered was to be weighed daily, the weights entered in the books of the Counting House and the figures tallied monthly.[62] All officers were made accountable for

---

52. Sir George Gresley to Sir Thomas Puckering, 15 November 1629, T. Birch, ed., *The Court and Times of Charles I* (2 vols, 1848) II, p. 36; in 1637 attempts were still being made to secure the same economy, HMC, *De Lisle and Dudley MSS* VI, 139.
53. SP16/386/97; cf. Knowler, *Strafford Letters* II, pp. 140–1.
54. BL, Stowe MS 563, fo. 16v.
55. LS13/30; LS13/169, p. 196.
56. BL, Harley MS 7623, fo. 17v (prince's household).
57. Ibid., fo. 15v.
58. Order of 27 May 1627, LS13/169. For the effects of these attempts to reduce the costs of diet, see G. E. Aylmer, 'Studies in the Institutions and Personnel of English Central Administration, 1625–1642' (unpublished Oxford D.Phil. dissertation, 1954). I am grateful to Gerald Aylmer for permission to cite this thesis and for his generous advice.
59. Order of 22 August 1634, LS13/169, p. 243.
60. I shall be developing this argument in my study of the personal rule of Charles I.
61. BL, Harley MS 7623, fo. 18.
62. Ibid., fos. 18–18v.

arrears arising in their own departments. On 9 February 1627, for example, arrears in the Buttery, Pantry and Cellar were charged at the end of each month to those waiting during that period.[63] In 1628 the wages of all those in arrears were detained and when the sum held was inadequate to meet the deficit the relevant officers were summoned and discharged of their places.[64]

The most effective weapon in the war against corruption was an insistence upon efficient accounts. Accounting systems were evidently slack enough to allow many to purloin provisions without any risk of detection other than the occasional scrutiny of the Porter at the Gate. Some action was taken: in November 1628 it was ordered that arrears should be reckoned within fourteen days of the end of the month.[65] But deficient accounting remained. Auditors investigating the Board of Greencloth, as part of the commission for reform of the household in 1638, discovered serious deficiences in the accounting of receipts and expenditure.[66] Blanks in the records and vague statements which made it impossible to attribute responsibility had very likely covered a multitude of sins. But for all the defects discovered, the arrears appear to have been greatest for the first two years of the reign 'at which time the household was un-settled and many occasions of waste and losses'.[67]

The attempt at reform was never more than a heavily qualified success;[68] arrears and losses, pilfering and peculation continued. The records reveal many instances of royal household property missing or found in private hands.[69] But this in itself is evidence, perhaps, that crimes were investigated and detected, even if they were not always solved. Whatever the verdict of historians, contemporaries felt the sharp edge of reform. Indeed requests like that of the Treasury commissioners in 1635 for a certificate of all fees and annuities paid 'together with a medium of all the receipts and the

63. Order of 9 February 1627, LS13/169.
64. Order of 17 November 1628, LS13/169.
65. Ibid.
66. There is a full and detailed report on the deficiencies of accounting methods in LS13/169, pp. 313 ff. The commissioners recommended major changes. See, for example, p. 342.
67. LS13/169, pp. 34–5.
68. G. E. Aylmer, 'Attempts at Administrative Reform, 1625–40', *EHR* 72 (1957), 229–59.
69. See, for example, a list of losses of plate from the royal scullery between September 1634 and April 1640, LS13/169, PC 2/42, pp. 106, 235 and BL, Harley MS 7623, fo. 15v. One dish was reported 'lost between the kitchen and the waiters' chamber at Whitehall'!

payments in your said office, cast up for the five years last past' must have chilled dishonest hearts.[70]

The limitations to reform lay often within the very nature of the court itself. Henry Lawton, Keeper of the king's Closet and hence a man close to the king, evidently stole a pair of candlesticks. Not only was he pardoned, he was given the candlesticks as a New Year's gift![71] More generally, retrenchment was always compromised by the king's overriding concern with maintaining the honour and majesty of the court. The St George's day feast, for instance, was to be provided with all that was necessary and honourable 'and not with niggardliness nor yet with prodigality and waste, but in such a mean way as it may be seen and known to be most to the king's honour'.[72] The mean is of course a matter of interpretation. But Sir Thomas Herbert scarcely veiled his criticism of flamboyant extravagance when he reported to Lord Scudamore that at Newmarket many men were less well shod and fed than the gallants' horses.[73]

For if the accession of Charles I brought a new morality, a new formality and an impetus to reform and order, the new reign was most marked by another concern – a renewed emphasis upon ceremony and ritual. Emphasis upon the ritual associated with the person of the king and the office of monarchy not only pervades the regulations for the government of the court; it often provides the subject of ambassadors' and courtiers' correspondence. If the English as a race, then as now, were naturally inclined to formality, it was the king himself who fostered and insisted upon it. Charles, unlike his father but like Elizabeth, maintained the board of state in the Presence Chamber.[74] When he dined there, elaborate ceremony was prescribed. The Cupbearers and Carvers were ordered

Before they give their attendance upon the king's person to wash their hands; the while they are with the Gentlemen Ushers in washing, every man in the chamber is to be uncovered; after the Gentleman Usher is to call for a bowl of sack . . . and to drink to one of the gentlemen that have washed. After the Carver hath his towel upon his shoulder, he and the Gentleman Usher goeth together in the Presence Chamber where they make three *congés* at three several parts of the Chamber and so come to the board.[75]

The ceremony of the king's retreat in the evening was similarly

---

70. LS13/169, p. 256.
71. 'New Years Gifts given by the King's Majesty. . .' BL, Harley Roll T2. The candlesticks were 'pardoned by his Majesty to Henry Lawton'.
72. BL, Sloane MS 1494, fo. 45.
73. Sir Thomas Herbert to Viscount Scudamore, 2 March 1632, C115/N3/8548.
74. LS13/169, p. 221. Cf. HMC, *Denbigh MSS* V, 8.
75. BL, Stowe MS 561, fo. 4v.

marked by a ritual which underlined the physical move from public
to private rooms and the personal transmogrification from public
office to individual person. At the command of the king, the
Gentleman Usher called for torches at eight or nine o'clock; a Groom
bearing the torch lights the way for the Yeoman Usher of the night
watch who leads the party to the Pantry for refreshments. Thence
they proceed to the Great Chamber where they surrender governance of the household to the Squires of the Body, until eight
o'clock the following morning.[76]

This concern with ceremony in the daily round of court life
becomes an obsession on public occasions, such as the receipt of
ambassadors or festive days. Finet, we recall, commented early upon
the new formality in receiving ambassadors.[77] The Reverend Joseph
Mede noted in 1629 that envoys were now novelly entertained by
great officers, not at the king's table.[78] Though he evidently spoke
the language well, Charles addressed the envoy from France, for
form's sake, not in French, but in English through an interpreter.[79]
The duties of the Gentlemen Ushers concerning the reception of
visitors,[80] the assigning of rooms and the conducting of envoys to
audience were carefully delineated.[81] All were attended with due
state, not least because on important public occasions the nobility
were warned to attend at court.[82] The Venetian ambassador was
clearly somewhat surprised (as well as flattered) to find that in 1626
he was accorded the honour of attendance by a privy councillor and
knight of the Garter;[83] in 1637 it was the earl of Arundel and duke
of Lennox, the premier peers of England and Scotland, who escorted
an ambassador to his coach.[84] Especial care was taken over public
processions. When the king went to Chapel, the Lord Chamberlain
informed the Gentlemen Ushers what ambassadors would resort to
court 'and then the Gentlemen Ushers shall send warning to all the

76. Ibid., fos. 6–7; cf. 'The order of All-Night as described by Ferdinando Masham
    Esquire of the Body to K. Charles I and K. Charles II', in Samuel Pegge, *Curialia
    or an Historical Account of Some Branches of the Royal Household* (1782), pp. 19–23.
77. Above p. 228 and also Finet's observation that the ambassador of the United
    Provinces was no longer after 1628 admitted by the backstairs, *Finetti Philoxenis*,
    pp. 200–1.
78. Mead to Sir Martin Stuteville, 25 July 1629, Birch, ed., *Court and Times of
    Charles I* II, p. 24.
79. Ibid., II, p. 25.
80. BL, Stowe MS 561, fos. 5v–6.
81. On Easter day, for example, BL Sloane MS 1494, fo. 34.
82. Ibid., fos. 9, 21, 34.
83. Contarini to Doge and Senate, 4 September 1626, *CSP Ven.* XIX (1625–26),
    524–5.
84. Sir J. Finet to Scudamore, 17 April 1637, C115/N8/8804.

noblemen wheresoever they be in town . . .'.[85] When the nobility attended 'the Lord Chamberlain is to appoint the greatest estate [i.e. rank] at the time being present to accompany . . . the said ambassador till they come to the Closet'.[86] Meanwhile those in procession to Chapel were ordered to progress in orderly ranks 'and not break them with pretences of speaking one with another', 'that being one of the most eminent and frequent occasions whereby men's ranks in precedence are distinguished and discerned'.[87] The service in the Chapel repeated the elaborate ceremony of the household and undoubtedly the king's personal inclination to ritual was one of the major influences for liturgical changes.[88]

At the time of offering, a Groom of the Chamber was sent for the king's donation – a noble (i.e. 6s. 8d.). This was delivered to a Gentleman Usher who in turn handed the coin to the most eminent nobleman present, 'who shall kiss it and deliver it to the king immediately before the offering when the king is set on his knees . . .' After the king had kissed the chalice, he received the noble from the nobleman kneeling on his right and offered it to the cleric officiating.[89] If ritual was the court's religion, the religion of the court was undoubtedly ritualized.

Religion and ritual combined in the most spectacular public occasion in Caroline England – the feast of St George. The ceremony associated with the order had declined since the death of Henry VIII. Elias Ashmole, the historian of the Garter, recalled, however, that 'in the beginning of King Charles I's reign . . . the gallantry of attendants began to increase and augment'.[90] Those attending the knights companions were conspicuous in greater numbers and for the enhanced richness of their habit.[91] Behind the renewed interest lay Charles I's own passionate concern for the Order of the Garter, and the due proprieties of its regulations and ceremonies.[92] The Garter exemplified the courtly culture of chivalry and piety, manliness and chastity.[93] Charles, one of his Bedchamber men tells us,

85. BL, Sloane MS 1494, fo. 9.
86. Ibid., fo. 9.
87. LC5/180, p. 16.
88. I shall be arguing in a study of the personal rule of Charles I that Charles rather than Laud was the prime initiator of the liturgical changes of the 1630s.
89. BL, Sloane MS 1494, fo. 10.
90. Elias Ashmole, *The History of The Most Noble Order of the Garter* (1715), p. 438.
91. Ibid., pp. 85, 317–18.
92. For Charles's proposals for 'the most complete and absolute Reformation' of the order, Ashmole, *History of the Garter*, pp. 148–9.
93. The Van Dyck portraits of Caroline courtiers, like those of Charles himself, show the Garter prominently displayed. See R. Strong, *Charles I on Horseback* (1972).

never failed to wear the George.[94] In 1629 he revived the custom, long lapsed, of the sovereign's proceeding in person to Windsor on the eve of St George's day.[95] He commissioned for the walls of the Banqueting House a magnificent canvas depicting the procession – though only Van Dyck's sketch for the painting was completed.[96] It is, however, sufficient to convey something of the majesty of the day – which was a public occasion of the sort in which the early Stuarts rarely showed an interest. In 1635 the earls of Danby and Moreton 'disposed themselves for their more commodious passage and the people's view'.[97] For the ceremony of the investiture of Prince Charles in 1638, the king designed a public cavalcade from Somerset House in the Strand to the gates of Windsor Castle.[98] The Garter procession was clearly the public vaunting of the order, dignity and spirituality of the new royal court.

These then, for all the superficial continuity, were the changes apparent at court: retrenchment and reform, a return to original rules and their enforcement and a renewed emphasis upon ritual and ceremony. Together they led Lucy Hutchinson to observe that 'the face of the court was much changed in the king'.[99] What was the significance for the court of these changes?

Charles I's court undoubtedly placed greater emphasis on the awful majesty of the king's presence. Custom and ritual, most notably the touching for the king's evil, had traditionally endowed the king's body with semi-divine qualities.[100] The new orders for the court reinforced this. Throughout stress is laid on the preservation of distance from the king's person, and rooms and objects immediately associated with the king's person. Gentlemen Ushers were ordered 'to see that no man of whatsoever degree he be of be so hardy to come to the king's chair, nor stand under the cloth of state

94. Sir T. Herbert, *Memoirs of the Last Two Years of the Reign of King Charles I by Sr. Tho. Herbert, Groom of the Chamber to his Majesty* (1813), p. 146. Charles intended that his body should be laid in the Tomb House of the chapel at Windsor, Ashmole, *History of the Garter*, p. 85.
95. Ashmole, *History of the Garter*, p. 444.
96. C. Brown, *Van Dyck*, plate 190. Sir Robert Crane, the Chancellor of the Order of the Garter, had three drawings by Van Dyck, probably relating to this, BL, Egerton MS 1636, fo. 89.
97. Ashmole, *History of the Garter*, p. 318. For a full description of an elaborate Caroline procession see BL, Sloane MS 1494, fos. 40–60.
98. Ashmole, *History of the Garter*, p. 319; LC5/193: 'Earls and Lords to attend the King's Majesty at St. George's Feast 1638. . .'
99. L. Hutchinson, *Memoirs of the Life of Colonel Hutchinson*, ed. C. H. Firth (1906), p. 69.
100. See M. Bloch, *The Royal Touch: Sacred Monarchy and Scrofula in England and France* (1973).

. . . nor to lean upon the king's bed, nor to approach the cupboard where the king's cushion is laid, nor to stand upon his carpet'.[101] By extension, however, the mystical power of the king's person was evidently believed to rub off on objects and persons in contact with it. We recall that the Groom of the Stool inherited the personal objects of a deceased monarch (above p. 235). More graphically, it was ordered that that part of the towel which had been in contact with the king when he washed, the Gentleman Usher should raise above his head as he walked.[102] It was an emblem of the reverence due to the king, and a badge too of the special place held by his servant. These ideas were influential. It is not only the ignorant and superstitious, flocking to be cured of the king's evil, who bear testimony to the power of the king's person. Within their more sophisticated world courtiers themselves believed that the cramp rings given by the monarch to his servants (on Good Friday) had the capacity 'as it hath been often proved' to cure fits.[103] For the king's servants, living with their sovereign as the apostles with Christ, the image of divine monarchy became reality. Bishop Wren captured their world nicely when he turned to the king at grace and prayed 'Give us this day our daily bread'.[104]

If more emphasis were placed on the mystical person of the king, fewer than ever enjoyed access to his presence. Charles I was not, it must be said, as isolated in Whitehall as some historians have maintained. He did, at least until 1637, undertake annual progresses – to Oxford and Woodstock, to Newmarket and the New Forest, even to Huntingdonshire and Lincolnshire.[105] But apart from the journey to Scotland in 1633, in the course of which the king dined with the earl of Newcastle at Bolsover, with the earl of Exeter at Worksop, with Lord Willoughby en route to Grantham and enjoyed other 'great entertainments',[106] the progresses were confined to the south of England, to a circuit bounded by royal parks and residences.[107] Nor were they public displays in the style of earlier

101. BL, Stowe MS 561, fo. 5.
102. BL, Sloane MS 1494, fos. 12–12v.
103. Ibid., fos. 30v–31. I am grateful to David Starkey for a discussion of this subject.
104. BL, Harley MS 4931, fo. 8.
105. I have followed the royal progresses through the *Calendar of State Papers Domestic* 1625 to 1640.
106. The Privy Council at Berwick to the Privy Council in London, 11 June 1633, *CSP Dom.* VI (1633–34), 94.
107. D. Townshend, *The Life and Letters of Mr. Endymion Porter: Sometime Gentleman of the Bedchamber to King Charles the First* (1897), p. 116; G. Huxley, *Endymion Porter*, p. 226; L. Aikin, *Memoirs of the Court of King Charles I* (2 vols, 1833) I, pp. 345–6.

progresses: Charles did not, like Elizabeth, end his summer progress by a ceremonial procession through the City to Whitehall.[108] When Sir Thomas Herbert on progress in the spring of 1632 reported that 'the season and company conspiring together make Newmarket the theatre of our world', he referred not to the world of the county populace, nor even that of the minor county gentry, but to the confined world of the court.[109]

Even within the court, the renewed emphasis on formality, distance and privacy limited access to the king to a select few. James I's easy familiarity was succeeded by Charles I's near obsession with privacy.[110] Charles literally retreated behind closed doors. In 1626, to check the 'too much liberty given for the making and dispensing of the keys of his Majesty's privy lodgings', Charles ordered new treble locks to replace the old double locks.[111] A decade later a royal proclamation was issued further to prevent 'the freedom of access that sundry persons do take unto themselves into his Majesty's houses, gardens and parks by undue procurement of keys'. Only those in places of especial trust were issued keys, and Mr Boreman, the royal locksmith, engraved on each key the name of the person for whom it was made. The keys were then delivered to the Gentlemen Ushers.[112]

Few passed beyond the locked doors. Whilst the regular household of the king numbered in excess of a thousand, very few of these had direct contact with the monarch. A list of the names of the servants in the Privy Chamber in 1629 reveals four Gentlemen Ushers, eight Grooms, five Cupbearers, five Carvers, four Sewers and six Esquires of the Body.[113] The staff of the Bedchamber was smaller still. And apart from domestic servants, few were permitted to enter the Privy Lodgings. None below the degree of baron was allowed within the Privy Chamber,[114] and tighter still were the rules governing the Bedchamber. Only the Gentlemen themselves and the Princes of the Blood could come and go freely. The royal physicians,

108. Aikin, *Memoirs* I, p. 345.
109. T. Herbert to Viscount Scudamore, 2 March 1632, C115/N3/8548.
110. J. Wormald, 'King James VI and I'.
111. Warrant to Mr Boreman, LC3/31, p. 3.
112. Order of 26 March 1636, *Foedera* XX, 122; Order of Council, 1 January 1637, PC 2/47, p. 105. Significantly the warrants for the making and issue of the keys came from the Lord Chamberlain, cf. note 28 above.
113. SP16/154/76. We do not have complete lists for the reign of Charles I; cf. for 1625, SP16/2/118; for 1647, Bodley, Tanner MS 317.
114. LC5/180, p. 22.

apothecaries and barbers were allowed in at specific times to discharge their functions; while the head officers of the household, the Lord Steward and the Lord Chamberlain, the rest of the Privy Council, and a handful of others who appeared on the Groom of the Stool's *entrée* list could also enter the apartment after leave had been asked and granted.[115] All others of quality waited upon the king in the Withdrawing Room where the Secretaries of State and Masters of Requests also had their audiences.[116] Most household officers dined with the Lord Chamberlain in the Great Chamber. Only the Gentlemen of the Bedchamber 'and those whom it shall please the king to appoint' supped with the monarch and partook of his own diet in the intimacy of his privy quarters.[117]

Here, for all the formality beyond, a more familiar world unfolds. This reflects not only human nature – the king's needs for informal communication, even for confidants – but also the geography and architecture of the palace. The stately grandeur of the Great Chamber and Presence gave way to the more domestic proportions of the Privy Lodgings. These, for all their majesty, may have been more confined than historians have believed. In 1633 for example a quarrel over precedence arose between Sir Maurice Drummond and the earl of Carlisle because the two met 'in a narrow passage next to the Bedchamber where two can hardly pass one by the other'. It is revealing too that whilst he could make no claim by his rank, Drummond must have presumed that his post of Gentleman Usher entitled him to vie for the precedency.[118]

Certainly the glimpses which the evidence allows shows the king living on close terms with his servants within the Bedchamber. Philip Warwick's *Memoirs* contain the intimate insights of a Gentleman of the Bedchamber whose 'near attendance,' as the preface explains, provided details of the king's manners and conversation, personal habits and private devotions.[119] During the last two years of his reign, under the strain of war and defeat, Charles confided principally in Sir Thomas Herbert who attended in his Bedchamber. Herbert literally knew his king as one might a flatmate: he noted the king's regular habits, his donning the George and

---

115. BL, Stowe MS 563, fos 14–14v.
116. Ibid. fo. 15.
117. BL, Sloane MS 1494, fo. 15; LC5/180.
118. See the Privy Council investigation of 25 March 1633, PC2/42, fo. 529.
119. P. Warwick, *Memoirs*, preface, and *passim*; cf. K. Digby, *Private Memoirs of Sir Kenelm Digby, Gentleman of the Bedchamber to King Charles I* (1827).

Garter first thing in the morning and winding of his watch before bed; more interestingly he records discussions with the king of his dreams.[120]

The new emphasis on orders, rules and ritual underlined the proximity and authority enjoyed by those who waited personally on the king. When they handed over their keys at the service of all-night, the Gentlemen Ushers daily waiters surrendered their power and the care of the king's person to the Esquires of the Body whose jurisdiction was total, overriding all rank.[121] One recalled

In the time of war, upon all occasions that required, I went into the Bedchamber and awaked his Majesty and delivered all letters and messages to his Majesty and many times by his Majesty's command, I returned answers to the letters and delivered orders. And I remember that coming to the king's Bedchamber door, which was bolted on the inside, the late earl of Bristol then being in waiting and lying there, he unbolted the door upon my knocking and asked me what news? I told him I had a letter for the king. The earl then demanded the letter of me which I told him I could deliver to none but the king himself, upon which the king said, 'the Esquire is in the right; for he ought not to deliver any letter or message to any but myself, he being at this time the chief officer of my house'.[122]

Examples such as these then remind us graphically of the intimacy and authority with the king that men holding no major functional office could enjoy. They suggest too that the Eltham Ordinances described a reality when they enjoined that Gentlemen of the Privy Chamber should come to know their king so well that they could tell his wants or moods by his countenance.[123]

Intimacy with the king was not confined to the Bedchamber. David Starkey has argued for the proximity which ensued (indeed the institutions of intimacy which emanated) from Henry VIII's pleasure of jousting with his courtiers.[124] Certainly we should not forget Charles I's relaxations and pastimes or those with whom he participated in games and sports. Charles, like his father, had a passion for hunting;[125] he enjoyed tennis and bowls – it was he who

120. T. Herbert, *Memoirs of the Two Last Years*, pp. 145, 146, 184.
121. BL, Stowe MS 561, fos. 6–7; Pegge, *Curialia*, p. 16.
122. Ibid., pp. 22–3.
123. Eltham Ordinances, Ch. 64 (*HO*, 156), Carlisle, *Gentlemen of the Privy Chamber*, p. 37.
124. D. Starkey, 'From Feud to Faction: English politics *c.* 1450–1550', *History Today* 32 (1982), 16–22.
125. The French ambassador frequently complained of difficulty in obtaining audience because Charles was hunting, e.g., PRO31/3/66, fo. 139, 'leurs chasses . . . qui est leur plus grand divertissement' and PRO31/3/68, fo. 120.

added a bowling green to the Privy Gardens at Whitehall[126] – billiards and a game of chess.[127] Just as important, he loved to gamble on his skills.[128] These were relaxed moments when ceremony was dropped: sports and wagers are the encounters of equals who have suspended social rank for the trial of force, expertise or wits. Charles not only dined and played bowls with Richard Shute at Barking Hall, he evidently peppered his conversations with the indiscretions which only unguarded relaxation indulges. Samuel Pegge relates one episode which is at least indicative, if not (without substantiation) reliable. 'Ah Shute', the king allegedly said, 'how much happier than I art thou in this blessed retirement from the cares of a crown'.[129] On occasions such as these, the king went attended by only a few select gentlemen – perhaps those who shared his interests – or, when hunting, the equerries and stable attendants who served him. Probably it was on such an occasion that a mere footman sold Charles a ring.[130] What we know for certain is that in and out of Whitehall a few men, men not always of the highest rank or most elevated office, enjoyed by their place access to and the trust of their king. If Clarendon is to be believed, Charles recognized the importance of these relationships: he 'saw and observed men long before he received them'.[131] Those who attended upon his person owed their places to the king's personal choice.

The importance which Charles attached to access and proximity can be clearly seen in the case of the queen's court. Charles, after all, was a young adult male; the new queen an impressionable teenager away from her mother and country for the first time. The king devoted great attention to the appointments of those who were to serve his wife.[132] Orders issued by Charles for the government of the queen's household, like those promulgated for the regulation of his own, were concerned with the maintenance of distance and with the control of access to the queen's Privy and Bedchambers.[133] In

126. Warrant to pay Thomas Hooker, keeper of the tennis court at St. James's, money the king had lost to him at play, *CSP Dom.* I (1625–26), 577; Shepphard, *The Old Palace of Whitehall*, pp. 84–5.
127. A payment for billiard staves for the king is listed in BL, Additional MS 32,476, fo. 32; Herbert, *Memoirs of Last Two Years*, p. 17.
128. *CSP Dom.* In (1625–26), 577.
129. S. Pegge, *Curialia Miscellanea: or Anecdotes of Old Times*, (1818), pp. 317–18.
130. LC3/31, p. 27: warrant for payment.
131. N. Carlisle, *Gentlemen of the Privy Chamber*, p. 116.
132. The transcripts of French ambassadorial correspondence are dominated by this subject, e.g., PRO31/3/66–8. Cf. *CSP Ven.* XIV (1624–26), 198, 457, 495, 607.
133. BL, Stowe MS 561, fos. 12 ff.

part this reflects the king's personal taste and desire for privacy with his wife. But the ordering of the queen's household was also at the centre of domestic politics and international diplomacy. For the first two years of his reign relations with France were dominated by the question of the queen's servants. The purge of the French from the English court in 1626 lay behind the breach and the war. Even after the peace of 1629 the debates continued. Successive French ambassadors manoeuvred to exact the terms of the original marriage treaty, to place a French bishop, doctor and chief Woman of the Maids as confidants to the queen. Charles I persistently denied their requests.[134] There can be little better evidence that domestic proximity meant influence. Within days of the expulsion of the French, Charles appointed four Protestant ladies to the queen's Bedchamber; Buckingham, anxious to secure his position in the new political circumstances, obtained one post for his mother.[135] The French ambassador, meanwhile, jockeyed to bring the countess of Carlisle into disfavour with the queen, largely because her husband was believed to be powerful and pro-Spanish.[136] The politics of Bedchamber appointments was the politics of access and influence. When policies depended upon personalities, the politics of access was the determinant of power.

Politics

It is at this point that we must examine more carefully the importance of the domestic arrangements for court politics. Several questions present themselves: what were the fruits of access? How influential were the king's (and queen's) domestic servants? What part did the Privy Chamber and Bedchamber play in the factional struggles to place men or dictate policies? And more generally what was the importance of the household and court in the history of the reign of Charles I?

For many men the *raison d'être* of attendance at court was the quest for place or favour. It was a hazardous world where none who might be a rival could be trusted as a friend. As William Murray put it, 'the court is like the earth, naturally cold, and reflects no more

---

134. PR031/3/66–72 *passim*.
135. Pesaro to Doge and Senate, 31 July 1625, *CSP Ven.* XIX (1625–26), 129.
136. Soranzo to Doge and Senate, 11 January 1630, *CSP Ven.* XXII (1629–32), 264.

affection than the sunshine of their master's favour beats upon it'.[137] It was the king alone who could fulfil or frustrate ambition. In the receiving of suits, as in all else, Charles insisted on order and formality. Philip Warwick recalled that 'in suits or discourses of business he would give way to none abruptly to enter into them, but looked that the greatest persons in affairs of this nature address to him by his proper ministers'.[138] The Master of Requests himself was obliged to wait for audience in the Withdrawing Chamber.[139] In the race for favour then, the Gentlemen of the Bedchamber and Privy Chamber, those who depended upon no intermediaries, were undoubtedly the front runners. When we peruse lists of their names, we see that most of them received some grant or pension and many enjoyed a multiplicity of favours. Thomas Carey of the Bedchamber was granted in 1628 the profits of royal manors in Wiltshire and Somerset;[140] the same year William Murray received £800 worth of timber from the Forest of Dean.[141] George Kirke, Groom of the Bedchamber, was pardoned his offence of building houses on the Spring Garden wall and even granted that part of the wall on which he had built them.[142] Later, with his fellow servant Sir Robert Killigrew, he entered the infamous and profitable undertaking to drain the Great Level in Lincolnshire.[143] Posts within the Bedchamber led often and rapidly to profitable office: George Kirke became Gentleman of the Robes and keeper of the register in Chancery,[144] Sir James Levingstone, one of the auditors of the court of Wards,[145] Sir William Balfour, lord lieutenant of the Tower.[146] The most spectacular success story, of course, was Endymion Porter. A confidant of Charles as prince of Wales, he held no major formal office but that of Gentleman of the Bedchamber. But Porter was showered with grants and favours: royal lands, the customs on French wines, the farm of the wines at Chester, the surveyorship of the Petty Customs of the Port of London, the profits of the manufacture of white writing paper, and more.[147] By 1628, Porter's

137. William Murray to Sir Henry Vane, 18 December 1631, *CSP Dom.* V (1631–33), 205.
138. Warwick, *Memoirs*, 66.
139. LC5/180; BL, Stowe MS 563, fo. 22.
140. *CSP Dom.* II (1627–28), 573; *Foedera* XVIII, 95.
141. *CSP Dom.* II (1627–28), 269.
142. Dockets of Letters Patent, 1634–40, BL, Harley MS 1012, fo. 42.
143. Ibid., fos. 49v, 63, 68v; *CSP Dom.* XIII (1638–39), 558.
144. *Foedera* XIX, 37; *CSP Dom.* IV (1629–31), 553.
145. BL, Harley MS 1012, fo. 34v.
146. *CSP Dom.* IV (1629–31), 362.
147. Huxley, *Endymion Porter*, pp. 214–17, 219–20.

gross income was estimated at £3,000 a year, a sum which surpassed the wealth of some in the House of Lords. In 1631, he established a landed seat by purchasing – evidently on favourable terms – Hartwell Park, Northamptonshire from the king.[148] If few scaled Porter's peaks, all Charles's Bedchamber servants ascended with ease a mountain of patronage on which most scrambled for a toehold.

The king's personal servants not only advanced themselves, they promoted suits for others. Orders for the government of the Bedchamber suggest that the Groom of the Stool 'and in his absence some one of the Gentlemen or Grooms of our Bedchamber' were those 'to whom we are pleased to give leave to move us as they shall see cause . . .'.[149] In 1628, for example; Thomas Carey of the Bedchamber successfully procured a pardon for his kinsman, Ferdinand Carey;[150] William Murray obtained for his son a scholar's place at Winchester College.[151] Several suitors wrote to Endymion Porter to request that he use his influence with the king on their behalf.[152] More significantly, even members of Buckingham's family worked through Porter in advancing their suits to the king.[153] Examples abound of the influence exercised by the Bedchamber in securing favours and grants for themselves, their families and their friends.

Nor was this the limit of their influence or activities. Even when they held no other official position, Gentlemen of the Privy Chamber and Bedchamber were often engaged on missions of a sensitive nature as personal appointees of the crown. The Eltham Ordinances had specified Gentlemen of the Privy Chamber should possess the linguistic qualifications which would enable them to act as occasional ambassadors, and this remained one of their important, if occasional, duties.[154] The king's privy servants attended ambassadors, and conducted them to their audience: in 1638 they were sent to meet Mary de'Medici, the queen mother, at Harwich.[155] Porter, of course, was sent on a variety of missions in which his skills of connoisseurship and diplomacy were both called upon. Charles I also revived the responsibilities of his domestic servants for the guard of his person. In 1628, in addition to the Gentlemen Pensioners and the Esquires of the Body, 'his Majesty doth expect that the Gentlemen

---

148. *CSP Dom.* IV (1629–31), 265; ibid. VI (1633–34), 331.
149. BL, Stowe MS 563, fo. 13v.
150. *CSP Dom.* II (1627–28), 224.
151. Ibid., p. 167.
152. To take one year, see ibid., pp. 237, 521, 566, 567.
153. Huxley, *Endymion Porter*, p. 195.
154. Carlisle, *Gentlemen of the Privy Chamber*, p. 26.
155. Ibid., p. 107.

The image of virtue

of the Privy Chamber . . . restore the practice and exercise of horsemanship'.[156] In 1633, on the progress to Scotland, the king was accompanied by a special regiment of horse consisting of servants from the Presence and Privy Chambers.[157] The performance of these duties could be the first rung on the ladder to high office: Lord Hunsdon, Lord Chamberlain to Elizabeth, explained to James VI that the Gentlemen Pensioners were no mere ornament to the monarchy, but 'a nursery to breed up deputies of Ireland and ambassadors into foreign parts'.[158] Occasionally we may catch glimpses of the king's domestic servants in overtly political roles: Lord Newburgh told Secretary Coke that in the summer of 1638 it was Patrick Maule, a Bedchamber Scot, and the marquis of Hamilton with whom Charles most discussed Scottish affairs.[159] Ten years earlier in 1628, when many tried to persuade the earl of Carlisle to hurry back to court, it was Thomas Carey whom lord treasurer Weston sent to invite the earl into a 'strict friendship'.[160] The very informality and sensitivity of such roles makes it unlikely that many instances survive in the records. But the evidence we have is sufficient to suggest that they were played often.

Clearly contemporaries believed this to be the case – even those who were the greatest figures on the Council and in the conduct of business. All too often we write history around the personalities of the men who held the great offices of state. Contemporaries saw things otherwise. Philip Warwick judiciously phrased what he knew from experience: 'everywhere, much more in court, the numerous or lesser sort of attendants can obstruct, create jealousies, spread ill reports and do harm'.[161] During the 1630s Sir Thomas Wentworth suffered constant anxieties about his position and reputation because his distance deprived him of access to the king: 'a man's presence', he knew well, 'moves much'.[162] Even those ministers seemingly well entrenched at home sought to place agents close to the king within the intimate confines of the Bedchamber. Archbishop William Laud, despite all the manifestations of Charles's favour, manoeuvred to

156. Order of Council, 18 January 1628, APC XLIII (1627–28), 240.
157. Carlisle, Gentlemen of the Privy Chamber, p. 117. A special guard of Privy Chambermen was mentioned in 1639, CSP Dom. XIII (1638–39), 378; C115/N3/8854.
158. Pegge, Curialia (1782), pp. 57–8.
159. D. Coke, The Last Elizabethan: Sir John Coke, 1563–1644, (1937), p. 254.
160. CSP Dom. III (1628–29), 412.
161. P. Warwick, Memoirs, p. 116. Cf. the competition for a place in the Bedchamber on the death of Thomas Carey, Strafford Letters I, p. 242. Pory reported that Newcastle paid £2000 to be sworn of the Bedchamber, Birch, Court and Times of Charles I II, p. 187.
162. Strafford Letters, II, p. 410.

have his friend William Juxon, dean of Worcester, sworn Clerk of the Closet 'that I might have one that I could trust near his Majesty, if I grow weak or infirm'.[163] Laud's biographer, Peter Heylyn, adds that Laud promoted Francis Windebank to clerk of the Signet for the same reason – that so he might have 'the king's ear on one side and the Clerk of the Closet on the other'.[164] We cannot know how many such alliances were forged between the Privy Lodgings and the king's ministers. But when access was not the preserve of high office and the personal whim of the monarch could make or break a career, ministers had to look to their subordinates as well as to their equals.

Despite all we have said, however, there are no strong reasons for believing that the Bedchamber or Privy Chamber were hotbeds of factional politics in the reign of Charles I. There is no evidence for Charles's reign that politics was controlled by ministers creating a following in the Bedchamber, as the earl of Salisbury had done; nor did any figure rise from the king's intimate service to the highest place of power and influence as had first Sir Robert Carr, earl of Somerset and, second, George Villiers, duke of Buckingham.[165] Here what dictated the change appears to have been the succession of Charles I in 1625. For, somewhat surprisingly, the evidence suggests that, for all that he remained firmly in the king's confidence, Buckingham never gained control of the Bedchamber. In 1625 the new monarch had others to satisfy and many candidates for his favour, as well as the duke. We have seen that Charles swore in former members of his household as prince and retained James I's former domestics – some of them Buckingham's enemies. The Venetian ambassador also reports that Charles was anxious to secure the goodwill of the Scots and 'has confirmed many in their charges almost in greater numbers than the English'.[166] The list of domestic servants bears both statements out: the recurring names suggest continuity of families and personnel and a high proportion of Scots. Buckingham's exact position in the new Bedchamber remains something of an enigma. The duke, we know, was by Charles's side when news came of James I's death. The new king ordered that apartments be provided for Villiers next to his own.[167] Conway

163. The 'Diary' of William Laud, 10 July 1632, in W. Scott and J. Bliss, eds. *The Works of . . . William Laud* (7 vols in 9, Oxford 1847–60) III, p. 216.
164. P. Heylyn, *Cyprianus Anglicus* (1668), p. 214.
165. Cuddy, above pp. 208ff.
166. *CSP Ven.* XIX (1625–26), 26–7.
167. Ibid., p. 3.

reports that Buckingham was the first to be sworn Gentleman of the Bedchamber, but here the problem starts.[168] For on 18 April 1625, dispatching the same news, Pesaro, the Venetian envoy, added that the duke had been made First Gentleman of the Bedchamber (presumably Groom of the Stool), 'receiving the golden keys and the pass everywhere, whereby he can have access to the king at all hours, even though shut in by triple keys, a confidence he enjoyed with the deceased'.[169] A week later, however, Pesaro, correcting his earlier report, informed the Doge that fuller enquiry had not borne this out: 'the duke did not take the oath as First Gentleman of the Bedchamber as I wrote, but was only received by his Majesty therein and so were the little duke of Lennox and the marquis of Hamilton'.[170] It is not clear what happened, but it seems likely that Pesaro had picked up a current rumour which had not materialized as fact. In the end Buckingham was made Master of the Horse, while the post of Groom of the Stool and First Gentleman of the Bedchamber went to Sir James Fullerton, former Gentleman of the Bedchamber and Master of the Wards and Liveries to Charles as Prince of Wales.[171]

This may have been significant, and deliberate policy. Though Buckingham clearly continued and even added to his strength as first minister, it was his personal relationship with the king rather than any control of the Bedchamber on which his power and influence rested. Later events show that it was a special relationship which was not repeated. It may be that from the beginning Charles determined to allow no one dominance of the Bedchamber: indeed the early arrangements for his household suggest attempts to heal faction, and incorporate a wide range of men and opinions. It was to Buckingham's house that Charles took the earl of Pembroke whom he then appointed to the junta for foreign affairs;[172] it was the young duke of Lennox who was sworn of the Bedchamber with Buck-

---

168. Conway to Dudley Carleton, 31 March 1625, Birch, *Court and Times of Charles I* I, p. 4.
169. Pesaro to Doge and Senate, 18 April 1625, *CSP Ven.* XIX (1625–26), 11.
170. Ibid., p. 21.
171. G. Aylmer, *The King's Servants: the Civil Service of Charles I, 1625–42* (1974), p. 317. Fullerton had been Groom of the Stool to Charles as prince of Wales. It may be that he was not Chief Gentleman of the Bedchamber and that in 1625, as in 1536, the two posts were separated – though there is no evidence for this. Buckingham clearly remained the king's intimate but with Fullerton as Groom, Pembroke, the Lord Chamberlain, appears to have wielded influence even in the Bedchamber. Above, p. 232 and note 28.
172. R. Lockyer, *Buckingham: the Life and Political Career of George Villiers, first Duke of Buckingham, 1592–1628* (1981), p. 235.

ingham. The king's Privy Lodgings were never the preserve of the Villiers clan, their progeny or their policies.

Certainly after Buckingham's death the Bedchamber did not emerge as the key to factional politics. But this negative conclusion is not insignificant. The privacy behind which the king enshrined himself, the new formalities governing access at court, distanced Charles from his ministers, and separated too those who governed from those who held places of intimacy near the king. On the one hand, none from the Bedchamber rose to high office; on the other, many who governed in his name were in only infrequent personal contact with the king. This may have been deliberate policy: the separation of favour and proximity from functional office and the business of government. But whether or not it was so intended, the consequences were equally important. For free from the jockeyings of faction, within the privy quarters in which he spent much of his time, Charles was more able to exercise independent judgment on matters of policy. This independence, a determination to hear all sides of a question, was noted by the Venetian ambassador at the beginning of the reign; it remained a feature of the king's character in his handling of conciliar business.[173] Privacy too enabled the king to work uninterrupted, and whilst he never rose to the standards of bureaucratic diligence set by Philip II of Spain, Charles, by recent English precedents, was a monarch who worked – studying advice, perusing and annotating papers.[174] We know that when he thought and wrote, he liked to be alone.[175] And when the king was alone it was his own mind which was most at work.

The separation of personal service from government business, and the privacy and independence of the king influenced the political course of the reign. Charles, for the most part, remained above faction. Especially after the death of Buckingham, a wide variety of views on domestic and foreign affairs was expressed at court. And whilst on certain matters the king listened on some occasions to particular men – Weston on questions of finance, or Laud on religion – the evidence suggests that men were chosen to reflect rather than

173. *CSP Ven.* XIX (1625–26) 26–7; K. Sharpe, 'The Personal Rule of Charles I' in H. C. Tomlinson, ed., *Before the English Civil War* (1983), pp. 53–78.
174. This has been specifically denied by C. Carlton, *Charles I. The Personal Monarch* (1983). Both Warwick and Herbert, however, claim that Charles read his papers. The best evidence that he studied letters carefully comes from his emendations to Sir John Coke's drafts, Coke MSS, Melbourne Hall, Derbyshire. I am grateful to Lord Lothian and Derbyshire Record Office for permission to use this important collection.
175. Herbert, *Memoirs of the Last Two Years*, p. 62.

to determine the personal views of the king. None emerged as the king's confidant on all aspects of business: Clarendon and Sir Philip Warwick agreed that Charles limited 'persons to places suitable to their qualities', retaining what Secretary Dorchester called the 'total directory' in his own hands.[176] Charles was never really close to those like Weston and Laud whose views he most respected;[177] by contrast he seldom agreed with Holland and Hamilton who were among the principal recipients of his favour (below, p. 256).

This may in turn have contributed to a reign of greater stability. Under James I factional rivalries had risen to such a level that they had overflowed into parliament and the localities, thrown up and swept away ministers and flooded the Council Chamber and the House of Lords. Rivalries of course persisted into the new reign. But after the death of Buckingham, newswriters commented frequently on the peace prevailing at court: James Howell told Wentworth in the spring of 1635 that 'All things pass calmly at court and no factions fomented';[178] the countess of Devonshire described a 'great calm'.[179] For all the satirical contempt which he expressed for 'Lady Mora' in his correspondence with Wentworth, Laud was obliged to live in peace with Weston and Cottington, and was rebuked by Charles when he tried to make political capital out of a minor incident.[180] The very longevity of Charles I's ministers bears testimony to the muted tone of factional rivalries. Weston died as the longest serving lord treasurer since Salisbury – a remarkable feat during a period of retrenchment; no minister during the 1630s lost his place as the consequence of factional warfare. Indeed Charles was quick to discourage and suppress attempts to unseat his ministers and followed as his policy the rule which he delivered to Wentworth: 'the marks of my favour that stop malicious tongues are neither places nor titles, but the little welcome I give to accusers and the willing ear I give to my servants'.[181] Wentworth grasped the point. When, in 1638, he advised Newcastle concerning conduct at court he urged him not to trust to factions nor 'to seek to strengthen or

176. Warwick, *Memoirs*, 66; above, p. 236; Dorchester to earl of Carlisle, ·30 September 1628, *CSP Dom.* III (1628–9), 339.
177. Weston failed to get a place for his son at court, *Strafford Letters* II, p. 389; Laud remained paranoid about his position with the king, pp. 251–2.
178. Howell to Wentworth, 5 March 1635, *Strafford Letters* II, 377.
179. HMC, *Portland MSS* II, 126.
180. S. Gardiner, *History of England from the Accession of James I to the Outbreak of the Civil War, 1603–42* (10 vols, 1883–84) VIII, pp. 87–8.
181. Charles I to Wentworth, 3 September 1636, *Strafford Letters* II, p. 32.

value yourself with [the king] by any other means than those of his own continued grace'.[182]

A balance of factions and a king who, exercising his own judgment, remained above the strife of faction was not pleasing to all. Those for whom personal favour was subordinate to the exercise of power, those for whom the advancement of personnel was linked with the promotion of particular policies were often discontented. It is both interesting and illuminating that the best example of discontent, of the frustration of favour without power, comes from within the Bedchamber itself. Henry Rich, earl of Holland, undoubtedly enjoyed the king's (as well as the queen's) personal favour. Appointed, for a time, Master of the Horse, the recipient of several grants and gifts, Holland was reputed, in 1629, a, perhaps *the* court favourite. By 1636 he was chief justice of the Forests and Groom of the Stool. But for all the favours he enjoyed, on matters of religion and foreign affairs, Holland never got his way. He remained puritan and pro-French. For these reasons, in addition to normal rivalries, he was hostile to both Weston and Laud and twice tried to embarrass the lord treasurer, on the second occasion with some measure of success. Yet Holland failed to unseat his enemies and to advance his policies.[183] He is the paradigm of the court in which personal favour was not the same as political power.

In order to wield greater sway, Holland, along with others, pursued another avenue of influence: the court of Henrietta Maria.[184] For in the queen's court Holland wielded influence as well as enjoyed favour. In Henrietta Maria's household, affection for persons and support for policies were more closely intertwined. That is not to say that the queen's court was a monolith committed to one cause, or dominated by one faction. Among the queen's domestics and followers were her court ladies, and her minions (such as Wat Montagu and Thomas Jermyn) many of whom were Catholic, and a third group described by Professor Smuts as the queen's 'puritan followers'. These last may not be as puritan as Smuts (and the ambassadors upon whose evidence he relies) believes, but they were clearly a group distinct from and even antagonistic to the queen's

182. Wentworth to Newcastle, 1 June 1638, ibid. II, p. 174.
183. *Strafford Letters* II, p. 225; HMC. *Buccleuch-Whitehall* III, 346; *DNB*; B. Donagan 'A Courtier's Progress: Greed and Consistency in the Life of the Earl of Holland', *Historical Journal* 19 (1976), 317–53; Gardiner, *History of England* VII, p. 218.
184. R. M. Smuts, 'The Puritan Followers of Henrietta Maria in the 1630s', *EHR* 93 (1978), 26–45.

Catholic entourage. What assembled them as a group within the queen's household was their commitment to a French alliance – as the arm of military intervention for the restoration of the Palatinate. Under Henrietta Maria's patronage and protection they attempted two goals: to overthrow those sympathetic to Spain or committed to peace and to use the queen in order to persuade the king to their policy.[185] It is indicative of the nature of Caroline court politics that on both counts they failed.

Charles remained hostile to attempts to proselytize or to mount palace coups which stemmed from the queen's household. Courtiers were banned from the queen's Chapel and the king scarce concealed his anger at conversions to Rome fostered by the queen's confessors.[186] Similarly, Holland's attempt, backed by the queen, to unseat Weston by an affray with his son resulted for a time in the earl's disgrace and the queen's embarrassed retreat. Throughout the 1630s, the Catholic *dévots* and the 'puritan followers' manoeuvring from within the queen's court remained an irritant to the king. But there is no evidence that by means of such machinations they came near to achieving their aims.

Indeed Charles I's relationship with his wife exemplifies his domestic arrangements. After Buckingham's death, Charles, as Thomas Carey reported, 'wholly made over all his affections to his wife'.[187] But it would seem that the queen exercised little influence or power.[188] Whatever her natural inclination, there were many who by interest pressed her to do so. Charles, however, remained determined and the influence wielded by the queen and her followers was limited to intrigues played behind the scenes. Until the years of crisis and war, when his trusted ministers were off the stage, Charles maintained even in his relations with his wife the separation of favour from influence which had characterized the style of his court.

Court and kingdom

It is time for us now to reflect on a broader question still: what may we learn from the institutional organization and politics of the court

185. Ibid.
186. J. Flower to Scudamore, 13 March 1630, C115/M31/8124. Garrard to Wentworth, 15 March 1636, *Strafford Letters* II, p. 524.
187. *CSP Dom.* III (1628–29), 393; cf. ibid., p. 412.
188. The French ambassadors frequently complained of her powerlessness.

about Charles I as king or about his aims and values for the government of the country? It was, of course, a contemporary truism that subjects followed the examples set by sovereigns. John Owen versed it nicely in one of his popular epigrams, published in 1628.

All subjects in their manners follow kings
What they do, bids; forbearing forbids things
A king's behaviour sways his subjects lives
As the first mover all the fixt stars drives.[89]

Charles I clearly attached great importance to the belief. As he set a personal example of order, comeliness and sobriety at court, so, in turn, the court, reflecting his virtues, would become the model for the country. The orders of 1630 for the regulation of the household made the wider purpose clear: 'to establish government and order in our court which from thence may spread with more order through all parts of our kingdoms'.[190] Sir Edward Moundesford writing to Framlingham Gawdy recognized the broader significance of changes at court. 'There is', he opined, 'a general reformation in hand for court and country'.[191]

The point is reinforced by a study of the culture of the court. Paintings, plays and masques were not an empty show for the self-enhancement of the king's majesty. Charles I personified the belief, shared by advanced connoisseurs such as Inigo Jones and the earl of Arundel, that art and architecture performed an essentially moral function, that art might elevate men to what they might become. This is an important subject which awaits full investigation. It is perhaps significant that in the privy galleries we find a predominance of paintings on religious subjects, suitable objects perhaps for the private meditations of a king who, exercising his power by divine authority, owed account to God. In the state rooms at St James's, by contrast, hung the famous Van Dyck of Charles I and his riding master, placed at the end of a series of portraits of the emperors of Rome.[192] Its effect, as Sir Oliver Millar argued, 'must have been most spectacular, as if Charles were riding out through the arch to join the Roman emperors of Titian and Guilio Romano'.[193]

The masque was the fullest expression of the belief that culture might inculcate values to be emulated – by courtiers and ultimately those beyond. To take the best example, the theme of Thomas

189. John Owen, *Certain Epigrams* (1628), p. 31.
190. LC5/180, p. l.
191. 8 November 1631, HMC, *Gawdy*, 136.
192. BL, Additional MS 10,112, Van der Dort's Catalogue.
193. M. Whinney and O. Millar, *English Art, 1625–1714* (1957), p. 72.

Carew's *Coelum Britannicum* was reform at court and throughout the realm.[194] The masque opens with a panegyric on the monarch whose exemplary life has 'transfused a jealous heat of imitation through your virtuous court'. The power of example, we are told, has spread outside the court even to the gods and the stars whose claims to virtue are upheld now only in so far as they reflect the standards of the king's shining example, the quintessence of virtue. Over the king's Chamber door, behind which (in contrast to former profligate days) he lived in perfect love and harmony with the queen, is inscribed 'Carlo Maria', an emblem of the essence of all pure love, the model for all. With immorality banished, with love and union exemplified by the king and queen at court, it could not be but that their example would be followed in the country: 'there is no doubt of a universal obedience where the law giver himself in his own person observes his decrees so punctually'. *Coelum Britannicum* is all the more interesting to us because its author Thomas Carew was a Sewer in ordinary to Charles I, a Gentleman of the Privy Chamber and in high favour with the king. Something of a profligate himself, he evidently framed his masque in accordance with the king's tastes and values – and possibly under royal direction.[195]

If the court were to be the model for the reform of the country, the attempts to order the household, establish hierarchy and deference, remove abuses, cut waste, preserve honour and establish authority in the proper hands takes on a broader significance. For much suggests that the qualities which he sought at court, the fundamental conservatism which underlay them, the new vigour and intricate rules which were the methods by which he hoped to establish them, were those which he urged in the government of the country. The country, as we know, fell long short of the 'universal obedience', which in Carew's masque followed the king's example. Even at court, the perfect world was never established. Peculation continued; rivalries were thinly veiled. The king's favourite poet probably died of syphilis; his court painter, Van Dyck, kept a mistress.[196] At court as in the country, for all the reforms, the evils lurked in corners or underground. As Robert Reade ironically told Windebank in 1640: 'We keep all our virginities at court still, *at least we lose them not avowedly*'.[197] In the Caroline court itself lay the

194. T. Carew, *Coelum Britannicum* (performed 18 February 1634), ed. Orgel and Strong, *Theatre of the Stuart Court* II, pp. 567–80.
195. R. Dunlap, ed., *The Poems of Thomas Carew*, (Oxford 1949), introduction.
196. BL, Egerton MS 1636, fo. 2.
197. Robert Reade to Tho. Windebank, 23 January 1640, *CSP Dom.* XV (1639–40), 364.

achievements and the limitations of Caroline government.

Study of the court and household has led us to reflect on the king's intentions for the government of the country. For in a personal monarchy, the changes made by a monarch in his own household are intimate revelations of his person, and the king was the government. This was perhaps never so true again after the reign of Charles I. After 1660 Charles II received a public revenue for the duties of public office; feudal revenues were abolished; ministers needed to account to parliament as well as the king; the emergence of parties linked royal favour to the capacity to wield influence; boards and departments removed the business of government yet further from the royal household. In 1688 ideas concerning the separation of the king's person from his office (first aired in 1642) were translated into action. The court lived on as an important focus of politics. Under Charles I it had been *the* focus of politics, the centre of personal monarchy.

Index